IPSE – Identités Politiques Sociétés Espaces (ed.)
Doing Identity in Luxembourg

Scientific Advisory Board
Wilhelm Amann, Sonja Kmec, Sophie Neuenkirch, Agnes Prüm, Rachel Reckinger, Christian Schulz, Christian Wille

Authors
Wilhelm Amann, Christel Baltes-Löhr, Viviane Bourg, Marion Colas-Blaise, Paul Dell, Fernand Fehlen, Paul Di Felice, Sylvie Freyermuth, Peter Gilles, Georg Mein, Sonja Kmec, Fabienne Lentz, Agnes Prüm, Gian Maria Tore, Sebastian Reddeker, Rachel Reckinger, Christian Schulz, Sebastian Seela, Heinz Sieburg, Melanie Wagner, Christian Wille

IPSE – Identités Politiques Sociétés Espaces (ed.)
Doing Identity in Luxembourg
Subjective Appropriations – Institutional Attributions –
Socio-Cultural Milieus

[transcript]

Bibliographic information published by the Deutsche Nationalbibliothek
The Deutsche Nationalbibliothek lists this publication in the Deutsche Nationalbibliografie; detailed bibliographic data are available in the Internet at http://dnb.d-nb.de

© 2011 transcript Verlag, Bielefeld

All rights reserved. No part of this book may be reprinted or reproduced or utilized in any form or by any electronic, mechanical, or other means, now known or hereafter invented, including photocopying and recording, or in any information storage or retrieval system, without permission in writing from the publisher.

Coverlayout: Kordula Röckenhaus, Bielefeld
English translation: Marion Gretscher, Eva Nossem, Dietmar Zehl
Editing & proofreading: Matthias Müller, müller translations (in collaboration with Steven Jefferson, Aardvark Translations)
Typesetting: Jörg Burkhard, Bielefeld
Imprint: Majuskel Medienproduktion GmbH, Wetzlar
ISBN 978-3-8376-1667-5

Global distribution outside Germany, Austria and Switzerland:

Transaction Publishers
New Brunswick (U.S.A.) and London (U.K.)

Transaction Publishers   Tel.: (732) 445-2280
Rutgers University   Fax: (732) 445-3138
35 Berrue Circle   for orders (U.S. only):
Piscataway, NJ 08854   toll free 888-999-6778

Content

1. **Preface | 7**
   RACHEL RECKINGER, CHRISTIAN SCHULZ, CHRISTIAN WILLE

2. **Researching Identity Constructions | 11**
   RACHEL RECKINGER, CHRISTIAN WILLE
   2.1 A theoretical-conceptional approach to identities | 11
   2.2 Methodology and Interdisciplinary Collaboration | 24
   2.3 References | 35

3. **Socio-Cultural Milieus in Luxembourg | 39**
   WILHELM AMANN, FERNAND FEHLEN, GEORG MEIN
   3.1 Changing Social Structures. From the vertically orientated concept of stratification to the horizontally diversified milieu landscape | 39
   3.2 Profiles of Socio-Cultural Milieus in Luxemburg | 50
   3.3 Final remark | 62
   3.3 References | 62

4. **Languages and Identities | 65**
   PETER GILLES, SEBASTIAN SEELA, HEINZ SIEBURG, MELANIE WAGNER
   4.1 Introduction: Germanic/Romance Diglossia | 65
   4.2 Key Survey Results Concerning the Linguistic Situation | 68
   4.3 Controversies in Readers' Letters concerning the Linguistic Situation | 81
   4.4 'Linguistic Landscape': Public Signage and Multilingualism | 93
   4.5 Conclusion: Linguistic Polynomia as an Opportunity | 103
   4.6 References | 104

5. **Spaces and Identities | 107**
   MARION COLAS-BLAISE, SYLVIE FREYERMUTH, SONJA KMEC,
   GIAN MARIA TORE, CHRISTIAN SCHULZ
   5.1 Introduction: Geographic Discourses and Tourism Practice | 107
   5.2 Between Seduction and Reality: Luxembourg City and its Discourses | 110
   5.3 Representing and Revaluating the City: the Geo-Graphy and Visual Identity of Luxembourg City | 120

5.4 Between National Unity and Regional Individualism 'Sways the Heart of Luxembourg' | 125
5.5 The Image of Luxembourg as a 'Melting Pot' | 133
5.6 The "Greater Region" – Spatial Constructions between Desire and Reality | 144
5.7 Conclusion: Spatial Identities – Multiple Readings? | 155
5.8 References | 158

6. **Images and Identities** | 165
   WILHELM AMANN, VIVIANE BOURG, PAUL DELL, FABIENNE LENTZ, PAUL DI FELICE, SEBASTIAN REDDEKER
   6.1 Images of Nations as 'Interdiscourses'. Preliminary Theoretical Reflections on the Relation of 'Images and Identities': The Case of Luxembourg | 165
   6.2 Symbolisms in the Media-Based Perceptions of Self and Others of Luxembourg | 168
   6.3 The Superjhemp Saga – an Ideal Projection Screen | 179
   6.4 Collective Symbols and (New) Identity Options in Luxembourg's Advertising | 190
   6.5 Decontextualising and Deconstructing Representations of Identity: an Analysis of the Works of Seven Photographers | 202
   6.6 The Representation of Italian Immigrants in the Exhibition Catalogue *Retour de Babel* | 216
   6.7 Conclusions: National Identities in a Post-national Age? | 225
   6.8 References | 226

7. **Everyday Cultures and Identities** | 233
   CHRISTEL BALTES-LÖHR, AGNES PRÜM, RACHEL RECKINGER, CHRISTIAN WILLE
   7.1 Introduction: On the Reciprocal Relevance of Everyday Cultures and Identity Constructions | 233
   7.2 Permanent Performances: Gender in Motion | 238
   7.3 'Good' Food. Oscillation between Political Concept and Individual Everyday Practice | 255
   7.4 Cross-Border Workers as Familiar Strangers | 271
   7.5 Conclusions: Identities and Ambivalences of Everyday Cultures | 283
   7.6 References | 285

8. **Identity Constructions in Luxembourg** | 291
   RACHEL RECKINGER, CHRISTIAN SCHULZ, CHRISTIAN WILLE

Authors | 295

1. Preface

RACHEL RECKINGER, CHRISTIAN SCHULZ, CHRISTIAN WILLE

So what exactly is it that typifies the Luxembourgers? This is the question we were faced with again and again over the past years whenever there were reports about the work on this book. Apparently the enterprise to research socio-cultural identities has created expectations that we cannot but disappoint. For the aim of this book is not to specify what makes up the supposedly 'typical' Luxembourgers, but rather to investigate identity structures at various levels of social life. More specifically, this involves examining processes of appropriation or attribution performed by the subjects themselves as well as by public institutions. Such processes, of which researchers frequently only manage to catch a snapshot glimpse, were revealed in different sectors of society within the context of Luxembourg society. Hence, it was not so much Luxembourg with its particular conditions and features that provided the starting point for the following chapters, but rather the question as to what kinds of socio-cultural identities can be found there and how they are articulated. Adopting this perspective makes all the more sense if one considers the diversity created by labour migration, the multilingual context or the international interdependency and therefore the pluralisation of identity options within Luxembourg society.

This book is the outcome of a three-year research project entitled: "IDENT – Socio-Cultural Identities and Identity Policies in Luxembourg". The idea for the IDENT project emerged in 2006 while establishing a research unit (Unité de Recherche) named "IPSE – Identités, Politiques, Sociétés, Espaces" (UR IPSE) within the faculty of Language and Literature, Humanities, Arts and Education of the University of Luxembourg. The acronym "IPSE" already points to the research unit's orientation: it primarily addresses the field of identity constructions and examines these from different topical perspectives and with interdisciplinary approaches. The IDENT project, besides other activities of the newly established research unit, provided an excellent framework to prove the efficacy of the UR IPSE.

For instance, over 20 researchers from twelve different disciplines[1] were involved in this major project whose added value – as will be shown – lies in the topical and methodological diversity of approaches to the research subject. During the three-year work on the project crossdisciplinary – by no means always uncomplicated – learning processes were initiated which are reflected in the contributions of this book. Essential for this was the curiosity, openness and above all the courage of the researchers involved to also enter unfamiliar territory and assert themselves there. The interdisciplinary collaboration has not only broadened the researchers' outlook but has, equally important, also contributed to the supportive character of the IDENT project. For instance, the numerous thematic teams and internal workshops which convened and took place regularly and were always result-oriented provided a framework within which the colleagues became increasingly better acquainted on a professional as well as a personal level. This also promoted the cooperation in other contexts of day-to-day research work and strengthened the self-image of the IPSE research unit. This brief glimpse into the genesis and the workings of the IDENT project will help the readers to classify the contributions of this book, which in terms of academic discipline follow what appears to be (as yet) unconventional methodological-conceptual paths. For the more than 20 authors who come from at least four different national university systems it is precisely this that constitutes the specific merit of their collaboration, which they intend to refine and develop further in other projects of this kind.

The results of the identity research presented here relate to the following subject areas: Languages, Spaces, Perceptions of Self and Others as well as Everyday Cultures. They are preceded, in chapter 2, by a detailed explanation of the IDENT project architecture in conceptual, methodological and research-practical terms, which serves as a guideline for the chapters that follow. Chapter 3 centres on a discussion of socio-cultural milieus, applied for the first time to the context of Luxembourg society and elaborated with the help of illustrative profiles the authors will subsequently refer to. In chapter 4, language-related identities in different socio-cultural environments and their public forms of expression are examined, as well as the public debate about languages in the print media. Based on a constructivist approach, chapter 5 profiles the 'Luxembourg region', tracing the various contours conferred on it on various levels by the tourist discourse, and contrasts it with the spatial identity structures of Luxembourg's resident population. In Chapter 6, the subsequent investigation of visual and linguistic images or perceptions is carried out within an interdiscursive-theoretical framework revealing mechanisms of identity structure in the areas of industry, culture and migration. Finally, in chapter 7, consumer and gender identities as well as alterity relations are examined from the angle of everyday cultures, on the basis of a praxeological culture concept.

---

1 | Essentially, these are: English Studies, Gender Studies, Geography and Spatial Planning, German Studies, History, Intercultural Communication, Luxembourgish Studies, Media Studies, French Studies, Sociology and Visual Arts.

Chapter 8 comprises a final survey of the research results that draws conclusions on processes of identity formation in Luxembourg and in the dynamic field of attributed and appropriated identities.

Special thanks are due to all those without whom the IDENT project would not have been possible or who have helped support and assist it. This includes all those inhabitants of Luxembourg who took part in our quantitative and qualitative surveys and those persons who provided us with advice and practical support during the different project phases, especially: Ralf Bläser, Pascale Fack, Daniel Gardemin, Jean-Marie Klinkenberg, Charles Margue, Antonella Di Pasquale, Jürgen Pohl, Michael Vester and many others who are not mentioned by name. For their generous support of this enterprise, we would like to thank the University of Luxembourg, respresented by its Vice-President for Research, Luciënne Blessing, as well as the Dean of the Faculty of Language and Literature, Humanities, Arts and Education, Michel Margue. Last but not least, we would like to thank our publisher for the professional cooperation and also our translators who have rendered a multilingual[2] manuscript containing the ideosyncrasies of different academic fields and university traditions into a French, German and English version.

---

2 | The participating researchers were free to write their contributions in the language of their choice.

2. Researching Identity Constructions

Rachel Reckinger, Christian Wille

2.1 A theoretical-conceptional approach to identities

Identities in Luxembourg

This book is about identities in Luxembourg. The choice of the plural form already indicates that it has not been our aim to define once and for all a 'national identity' or to establish what makes up a 'typical Luxembourger'. Instead, our focus has been on the processes of identity formation and their modes of expression empirically accessible to the researchers at different levels. So why choose 'Luxembourg' as the investigative context for examining identities? Or in other words: What makes Luxembourg interesting for studying identity construction? To approach this question we first have to clarify the process of de-traditionalisation and its effects on identities and subsequently consider some specific features of Luxembourgish society.

In the research community the concept of identity is interpreted in a variety of different ways. As will be shown later, these can be classified by different criteria, which already brings us to a characteristic feature of the 'identity question': the attempt to produce order(s). Such attempts to create some kind of order use categories either attributed or rejected by themselves or by others that characterise very specific (group) affiliations. These can refer to, among many other things, regions, nations, occupations, family, gender, and aesthetic styles by the means of which the identity options circulating at different levels are 'processed'. However, such processing has become more complex due to ever increasing differentiation, individualisation and pluralisation of societies. These keywords sum up the process of de-traditionalisation, which challenges what are perceived to be the traditional parameters of identity. In effect, this means a relativisation of what is considered normal or taken for granted through an augmentation of identity options, resulting from the global circulation of commodities, images, symbols, ideas, and life styles.

Due to the fragmentation and mixing of 'homelands', traditions and systems of meaning that provide a sense of purpose, frequently designated with the term 'Postmodernism', the notion of stable and coherent identities or orders is no longer tenable. Rather, identities are understood as something established through personal performance or as construction tasks – in terms of *Doing Identity* – which Eickelpasch and Rademacher (2004) as well as Keupp et al. (1997; 2006) associate with the concept of "*Identitätsarbeit*"[1].

Identitäten gleichen in einer zerrissenen Welt der Spätmoderne nicht fertigen Behausungen mit einem dauerhaften Fundament und einem schützenden Sinn-Dach, sondern permanenten, lebenslangen Baustellen, auf denen die [...] Individuen ohne festgelegten Bauplan und unter Verwendung vorhandener Bausätze und Sinnangebote sich (bis auf weiteres) eine Unterkunft schaffen. Je nach situativem und biografischem Erfordernis sind An- und Umbauarbeiten fällig[2] (Eickelpasch/Rademacher 2004: 14).

The contributions in this book take up this notion, based on the thesis that Luxembourg offers almost a laboratory setting for the investigation of processes of identity construction under de-traditionalised conditions. This touches on the pluralisation of identity options within Luxembourg society created by the manifold interdependent relationships that have evolved on a social, cultural, political and economic level, already apparent at least since 1900. For it was indeed at the end of the 19th century, with progressive industrialisation, that the first Italian and German immigrants came to Luxembourg, which had previously been an exclusively agrarian society, so that at that time already about 60 percent of the steel workers in the south of the country were made up of foreigners. Further waves of immigration – in particular from Italy – followed during the growth periods of the 1920s and after the Second World War. The great demand for labour in the industrial sector prompted many Italian workers to have their families join them in the 1950s. The 1970s saw the first influx of Portuguese immigrants who, to this day, make up the largest share of the resident foreign population, and during this time the Italians progressively moved up the social ladder (Willems/Milmeister 2008; figures 2008).

While as early as 1970 one fifth of Luxembourg's population were resident foreigners and, with the crisis of 1973, the problems associated with immigration

---

1 | Personal translation: "Identity work".

2 | Personal translation: "In the fragmented world of postmodernism identities do not resemble completed dwellings with a firm foundation and a sheltering roof of meaning, but rather permanent, lifelong building sites on which the [...] individuals erect – without a specific building plan and making use of any available construction kits and choices that offer sense and meaning – a (temporary) domicile for themselves. Situational and personal needs might necessitate further extension and rebuilding works" (Eickelpasch/Rademacher 2004: 14).

increasingly came into focus, the cross-border workers from the neighbouring regions of Saarland and Rhineland-Palatinate, Lorraine and Wallonia entered the picture. Until the early 1980s, their proportion of the workforce was still less than ten percent; in the course of the rapid development of the service industry that followed the heyday of the iron and steel industry their numbers grew explosively in the 1980s: in 1990 cross-border workers already constituted twenty percent of the workforce; in 2009, 147,000 Germans, French and Belgians made up almost half of the workforce in the Grand Duchy.

In addition to classical immigration and cross-border worker employment, the Grand Duchy has for some years also seen a strong increase of highly-skilled personnel. In general they tend to hold executive positions, either sent abroad by their companies or coming to the Grand Duchy as 'international corporate nomads'. This highly mobile group, which includes managers of international companies as well as EU officials, is recruited for the most part from European countries. At the most important location of Luxembourg's EU institutions, the Kirchberg plateau in downtown Luxembourg, developed during the 1960s, and at other locations in the south and centre of the town, for example, 11,000 people work for the EU administration (Chilla 2009). A large number of highly qualified personnel are also employed in the commercial sector, particularly in the financial industry: in 2008, four fifths of the executive workforce of the *Banque Centrale de Luxembourg*, for example, were foreign residents (Fehlen/Pigeron-Piroth 2009: 6). Already in the 1970s, the financial sector superseded the iron and steel industry that had dominated until then and has, at least since the 1980s, influenced also other industries. Thus, the service industry in the Grand Duchy saw an impressive boom and the society, which had already transformed from an agrarian to an industrial one, underwent in a short time a virtually unprecedented and radical process of change towards becoming a tertiary economy.

Today, the presence of highly qualified personnel from across the world, including the EU officials, has perceptible effects in Luxembourg. They lend an international character to the country, in particular the capital, which is by far more cosmopolitan than other European towns of comparable size. Furthermore, English is becoming increasingly significant alongside the usual languages French, German and Luxembourgish, particularly in the international financial sector and in developing expatriates communities (Fehlen/Pigeron-Piroth 2009: 6). As a consequence, what the region now has to offer in terms of cultural activities is very varied and multicultural, even if the major event "Luxembourg and Greater Region – European Capital of Culture 2007" succeeded only partially in elevating the Grand Duchy above its 'avant-garde provincialism'. In addition, the city management of the city of Luxembourg is making efforts to integrate the famous UNESCO world heritage into the daily life of the inhabitants and to enhance the awareness for it among tourists visiting the region; the country's museums and new decentralised cultural facilities are providing an environment for the growth of a critical intellectual mass. The Minette region in the south of the country is currently undergoing substantial changes thanks to cultural upgrading, the establishment of service enterprises and the forthcoming relocation of the university of Luxembourg to the site of the former brownfield of Esch-Belval, which will see an architectural marriage of tradition and modernism. The rural regions in the north, the west and the east of the country are also implementing future-oriented development strategies via self-confident funding bodies and civil participation. In short: Luxembourg is undergoing profound transformations while at the same time there has been little change in the distribution of political power, which reflects another specific feature of the Grand Duchy.

As an outlook to the following chapters, this *tour d'horizon* already indicates that Luxembourg is a place that generates multiple and continuously changing identity options. Besides other distinct features of Luxembourg society, three particularly salient ones are the pluralism created by labour migration, the multilingual context, and international interdependencies in nearly all aspects of society. On account of Luxembourg's history, geographic location and limited size, all these features already have an inherent transnational dimension. Thus, Luxembourgish society can be seen as an almost exemplary case of a 'region' within 'transnational landscapes' ('scapes'[3]) where traditional classification categories apply less and less. With this in mind, the following section of this introduction will focus on the concept of identity work or *Doing Identity* described above, in order to emphasize the fleeting and constructional nature of identities that is the point of departure of this study.

Putting Identities in a Theoretical Framework

The issue of 'identity' has for quite some time received a great deal of attention – both as a question of everyday life and as a subject of research. Even though the questions "Who am I (have I become)?/Who am I not (have I not become)?" and "Who are we (have we become)?/Who are we not (have we not become)?" (see Abels 2006; Straub/Renn 2002), which are inseparably connected, constitute an ontological constant of human reflexivity and have been documented in written evidence at least since antiquity (Keupp et al. 2006), they have attained a new significance in postmodern times. As Rosa notes: "*Identität [stellt] eine anthropologische Notwendigkeit dar und keine Erscheinung der Moderne [...]. Subjekte beziehen ihre Handlungsfähigkeit zu allen Zeiten und in allen Kulturen aus ihrem Sinn dafür, wer sie sind. Allerdings wird dieser Sinn in der Neuzeit in besonderem Maße*

---

3 | Under the concept of 'scapes', Appadurai sums up intermeshed and changeable 'landscapes' in order to describe social, cultural or economic figurations that crystallise in the course of globalisation. He draws a distinction between ethnoscapes, financescapes, mediascapes and ideoscapes (see Appadurai 1998).

*fraglich [...]"*⁴ (Rosa 2007: 50). This advanced detraditionalisation, differentiation and individualisation of social structures in Western capitalism (Straub/Renn 2002) has led to a hightened level of self-design in all aspects of life, whose ambivalent responsibility lies increasingly with the individual (see Ahbe 1997; Bauman 1999). This personal responsibility means at the same time more freedom of choice and more room for questioning, since such individually designed lifestyles hold the possibility of success as well as failure. In other words: Circumstances such as these imply a continuing and never completed *"Identitätsarbeit"*⁵ (Keupp et al. 2006; Straus/Höfer 1997) while always having to be seen as a *"riskante Chance"*⁶ (Keupp et al. 2006; Eickelpasch/Rademacher 2004).

Despite this pluralisation of possibilities of identity construction, their scope is limited by the quantity and quality of social interactions as well as economic and everyday-cultural resources – and therefore by structural capitals of social inequality (Bourdieu 1992; 1972) –, by which identity constitutes itself through mechanisms of *"Sich Erkennen, Erkannt- und Anerkanntwerden"*⁷ (Greverus 1995: 219)⁸. Therefore identity constructions contain a twofold ambivalence: due to eroding dependencies on predefined paths there is, on the one hand, a *compulsion to make a choice*, which still holds the possibility of either success or failure, and, on the other hand, there is the *freedom of choice* which still is socio-culturally moulded. Richard Sennett sums up this ambivalent condition in a humorous way: *"In der Moderne übernehmen die Menschen die Verantwortung für ihr Leben, weil sie den Eindruck haben, es hängt von ihnen ab"*⁹ (1996: 48).

From the 1950s and in particular from the 1980s onwards, 'identity' – as *"das je spezifische Selbst- und Weltverhältnis sozialer Subjekte"*¹⁰ (Rosa 2007: 47) –, became a central subject of research in the social and cultural sciences. The academic

---

4 | Personal translation: "Identity constitutes an anthropological need and is not just a phenomenon of the modern age [...]. Subjects draw their capacity to act at all times and in all cultures from their sense of who they are. In modern times, however, this sense has become increasingly precarious [...]".
5 | Personal translation: "Identity work".
6 | Personal translation: "Risky opportunity".
7 | Personal translation: "Recognising oneself, being recognised and appreciated".
8 | Identity constructions that are understood in this way relate to the "postmodern foil and therefore to processes of performance, repetition, subversion, recognition, being rooted, as a constant shift between potentialities and facticities, between differences and similarities, between variances and continua, embedded in power and knowledge structures". (Baltes-Löhr 2006: 64) To clarify this mobile complexity, she writes metaphorically: "The pattern originates while weaving" (idem: 37).
9 | Personal translation: "In the modern age, people accept responsibility for their life because they are under the impression that it depends on them".
10 | Personal translation: "The social subject's unique relationship with her/himself and the world".

canon makes a conceptual distinction between personal and collective identity (see Luckmann 2007); that is to say, on the one hand, *"die Art und Weise, wie sich der Einzelne als Individuum verstehen soll"*[11] – in developmental-psychological[12] as well as historico-socio-cultural terms – and on the other hand, *"die Form des Selbstverstehens, in dem sich der Einzelne als Teil eines Kollektivs definiert"*[13] (Reckwitz 2001: 21). This collective may be structural (e.g. gender, age, state of health, etc.), social (e.g., family, networks, milieu affiliation, employment, educational level etc.), everyday-cultural (e.g., intimacy, normative standards, values and preferences, consumption style and lifestyle, community of values such as religious communities or civic, political or leisure associations etc.), national, ethnic, etc. In everyday life, however, these spheres of experience, separated here for the sake of clarity, are closely intertwined:

L'un des paradoxes de l'identité personnelle est précisément de s'exprimer par l'appartenance à des groupes et donc par le croisement d'identités collectives (je suis un homme, libraire, père de famille, militant politique, amateur d'opéra, d'origine italienne, etc.)[14] (Halpern 2009: 13).

Nevertheless, we regard the notion of the collective within the identity discourse less as something determined by group affiliation – in a metaphor that expands stepwise and ranges, both in linear and disjointed form, from the individual via groups defined by interaction and affinity all the way to large-sized social-cultural groupings[15] – but rather by the permanent reference to moral concepts and norms, resources and stocks of knowledge shaped by society and that guide every individual action. Depending on the subject of analysis, this individual action can be initiated by individuals or by groups. The crucial point here is, in our view, a consistent empirical registering of the *"Wir-Schicht"*[16] (Elias 1986) in every single action, which can be regarded as an identity project – without the agents necessarily being aware of this. In this we follow traditions of research which centre primarily, on a theoretical level, on *"die Balance zwischen individuellen Ansprüchen und*

---

11 | Personal translation: "The way a person should recognise himself or herself as an individual".

12 | We will discount the developmental-psychological perspective here, since it transcends the scope of the interdisciplinarity practised by us.

13 | Personal translation: "The structure of the specific self-understanding in which the individual defines her/himself as part of a greater whole or a collective".

14 | Personal translation: "One of the paradoxes of personal identity is precisely that it expresses itself via group affiliations and therefore by mixing collective identities (I am a man, a bookseller, a father, politically active, an opera lover, of Italian origin, etc.)".

15 | Halpern 2009 or Ruano-Borbolan 1998 are an example for this approach.

16 | Personal translation: "We-layer".

sozialen Erwartungen"[17] (Abels 2006: 254; see Krappmann 2005) and do not limit themselves to the functional (multiple) affiliations (Goffman 2003; Lahire 1998) that have multiplied in postmodern times.

It is precisely in this point where our view on collective identity differs from discourses emerging from everyday life or often used to ideological-political ends, which frequently employ standardising and reifying arguments. The notion of 'identity' – particularly when used in the singular – is emotionally charged and employed in statements that tend to be rather simplistic, for instance when there is talk that a "village identity" should be protected, a "national identity" seems threatened, or when an "European identity" is evoked. 'Identity', according to this view, refers to a presumed sense of community of a group whose members are homogenised; they are denied individual possibilities of development and alternative loyalties are suppressed. They are seen not so much as individuals in their own right that share a certain commonality than as a quantitative alibi for cooptations in the name of the group. Above all however, this kind of discourse tends to refer to a supposedly naturalised essence (see Weinreich/Saunderson 2003; Reckwitz 2001), which has not been empirically verified and effectively serves as a basis for a further abstract and generalising treatment of the issue.

This social circumstance has spawned a certain scientific mistrust towards the concept of collective identity (see Kmec 2007; Kaufmann 2004; Brubaker 2001; Giesen 1999; Bayart 1996), which was held to incorporate an inherent "*Tendenz zum Fundamentalismus und zur Gewalt*"[18] (Niethammer 2000: 625). Although one could take the view that collective identities do not exist *per se* (since they form no physical entities capable of language and action), their social and cultural performativity is nevertheless real (see Meyran 2008), since they are, precisely because of their "*Nebulosität bestens für eine ideologische Diktion geeignet*"[19] (Straub 2004: 293) and, therefore, still worthy of research. This is why Niethammer re-commends "*dass wir, anstatt irgendeine kollektive Identität zu beschwören, ‚wir' sagen*"[20] because "*Wir-Aussagen [...] vor allem in ihrer Subjektivität leichter erkennbar und dadurch diskutabel sind*"[21], i.e. they lend themselves less easily to the "*Totalisierung einer speziellen Gruppe*"[22] (2000: 628-629). Bayart suggests speaking of identitary strategies (see 1996) instead of an 'independent' identity, MacClancy prefers "modes of identification" (2004: 64), which stress the subject-centred, relational, active

---

17 | Personal translation: "The balance between individual demands and social expectations".
18 | Personal translation: "Tendency towards fundamentalism and violence".
19 | Personal translation: "Nebulousness ideal for ideologically tainted discourses".
20 | Personal translation: "That, instead of invoking a collective identity, we say 'we'".
21 | Personal translation: "The subjectivity of we-statements [...] is easier to identify, making them discussable".
22 | Personal translation: "Totalisation of a specific group".

and motivated aspect of identities, as well as their fragmented and pluralistic processuality. Straub specifies:

> Unter einer kollektiven oder Wir-Identität verstehen wir das Bild, das eine Gruppe von sich aufbaut und mit dem sich deren Mitglieder identifizieren. Kollektive Identität ist eine Frage der Identifikation seitens der beteiligten Individuen. Es gibt sie nicht 'an sich', sondern immer nur in dem Maße, wie sich bestimmte Individuen zu ihr bekennen. [...] Nach der nahe gelegten Auffassung sind kollektive Identitäten Konstrukte, die nichts anderes bezeichnen, als eine näher zu spezifizierende Gemeinsamkeit im praktischen Selbst- und Weltverhältnis sowie im Selbst- und Weltverständnis Einzelner[23] (2004: 299).

Rosa sums it up as follows: Although building blocks of personal identity refer to the collective, *"trägt jede Einheitsunterstellung [...] einen potentiell ideologischen und normierenden Charakter. [...] Individuen und Gruppen sind daher stets zu einer dialogischen (und konflikthaften) Klärung kollektiver Identität gezwungen"*[24] (2007: 51-52).

For the reasons mentioned above we have decided not to choose collective identity as a direct subject of research but to focus instead – more modestly, yet empirically justified – on so-called 'identities'[25]. In doing so, we have investigated the interactions and discrepancies between institutionally 'attributed' and everyday 'appropriated' identities – regardless of whether these were collectively (in whatever constellation) or individually based. This neutral and plural wording aims to emphasise that, in our view, the constructivist and non-essentialistic *conceptual approach* to the issue of identity is more significant than focussing on the reference units within this field. Moreover, the perspective we have chosen offers fertile ground for the analysis of personal as well as collective 'identity patterns' which we see as reference points on a dynamic spectrum – with its transitions and transgressions. The concept of 'identity pattern' suggests that specific structures of

---

23 | Personal translation: "By a collective or we-identity, we understand the image which a given group builds of itself and with which its members identify. Collective identity is a question of identification on the part of the individuals involved. It does not exist 'in itself' but only to the extent that specific individuals profess their affiliation. [...] According to this concept, collective identities are constructs that merely denote a shared communality, to be specified in greater detail, in terms of an individual's practical relationship with and image of her/himself and the world around".

24 | Personal translation: "every assumption of unity [...] has a potentially ideological and standardising quality. Hence, [...] both individuals and groups are always forced into a dialogue-based (and conflict-charged) clarification of collective identity".

25 | We are dealing here not with 'national identity', but with 'identities in Luxembourg', not with 'cultural identity' but with the coexistence (in terms of interactions and representations) of everyday identity patterns of people of different origin and different orientations in Luxembourg.

identities may be revealed empirically; however, there are several of these and they can be shaped with a certain amount of freedom of action in personal effort but in interaction with *meaningful others* – just the opposite of an innate 'identity' that one 'would carry inside oneself for good' (see Avanza/Laferté 2005; Brubaker 2001). A similar metaphor to the one of 'identity patterns' is that of 'patchwork identity'. It is meant to convey that

[dass von] einzelnen Personen eine hohe Eigenleistung bei diesem Prozess der konstruktiven Selbstverortung zu erbringen ist. Sie müssen Erfahrungsfragmente in einen für sie sinnhaften Zusammenhang bringen. Diese individuelle Verknüpfungsarbeit nennen wir 'Identitätsarbeit', und wir haben ihre Typik mit der Metapher vom 'Patchwork' auszudrücken versucht[26] (Keupp et al. 2006: 9-10).

We proceed empirically by basing our analysis on the responses of individuals who we either interview personally or by means of a questionnaire, directing our interest on how they design, negotiate and represent their identities, in the sense of a *"subjektiver Konstruktionsprozess [...], in dem Individuen eine Passung von innerer und äußerer Welt suchen"*[27] (Keupp et al. 2006: 7). In actively claiming such identity patterns for themselves, individuals who are geared to the care of the self, find orientation in the midst of a complex role system (see Abels 2006). However, since social circumstances as well as individual thought, action and perception patterns (see Bourdieu 1980) can be synchronically and diachronically subject to change – even if not arbitrarily so[28] – the resulting identities can, at best, only be "temporary" (Keupp et al. 2006: 276; see Rosa 2007), "transitory", "processual" (Straub 2004; Straub/Renn 2002), "precarious" or "fundamentally incomplete" (Straub 2004: 280). Self-evaluations and assessments by others too, in identifying various degrees of success or failure, are flexible, historically, socially and culturally alterable, i.e. contingent (see Straus/Höfer 1997). They can be considered as lifelong "projects" or "aspirations", continuously redesigned during interactions – as a *snapshot of an*

---

26 | Personal translation: "Individuals are obliged to make a significant personal effort during this process of constructive self-placement. They need to put fragments of experiences into a context that makes sense to them. We call this individual joining work 'identity work', and we have attempted to express its typicality with the 'patchwork' metaphor".
27 | Personal translation: "Subjective process of construction [...] in which individuals seek to harmonise the internal and external worlds".
28 | Straub calls this phenomenon, very appropriately, a "structurally anchored mobility" (in 2004: 281). Social conditions and individual aspirations and resources appear to be undergoing change; this change is relative since it still perpetuates social injustice. Whith the overall social structure moving towards liberalisation and culturalisation of everyday life, individuals may subjectively perceive change, yet the socio-cultural milieu affiliations remain much the same (see Vester et al. in 2001) and "predetermine a certain range of possibilities for the development of identities" (Straus/Höfer 1997: 218).

ongoing process of "technologies of the self" (Foucault 1994; 1984). Even though the identity work is based on "*Selbstdistanzierung durch Selbstreflexion und Selbstkritik*"[29] (Straub 2004: 282; see Giddens 1991; Bauman 1999), it does not require the subjects' constant attention. For

> Subjekte arbeiten (indem sie handeln) permanent an ihrer Identität. Deren Basis(akte) bestehen aus situativen Selbstthematisierungen, die unser Denken und Handeln kontinuierlich begleiten[30] (Straus/Höfer 1997: 273).

Therefore, the *"[individuelle] Antworten auf die (praktische) Identitätsfrage [müssen] nicht unbedingt explizit artikuliert werden"*[31] (although this is often the case in the narrative and discursive mode); they can also be "dem Handeln [auch] implizit [sein] bzw. handelnd zum Ausdruck gebracht werden"[32] (Straub 2004: 280).

However, regardless to what degree this self-reference is reflected, it is a "*Sinnfrage*"[33] (Reckwitz 2001: 22) which in everyday life takes the social and cultural form of a striving for continuity and coherence, "*angesichts der Vielfalt lebensweltlicher Selbsterfahrungen und der Abnahme gesellschaftlich verfasster Kohärenzmodelle*"[34] (Straus/Höfer 1997: 270).

This claim need not necessarily be free of contradiction; it is rather a matter of finding a meaningful balance between synchronous coherence and flexibility on the one hand and diachronous continuity and change on the other (Rosa 2007: 48). The dynamism of this "*stimmig[e] aber kontingent[e]*"[35] (Straub 2004: 287) structure corresponds more to the concept of *selfhood* (or ipseity, from Latin *ipse*, self), than to that of *equality* (or identity, from Latin *idem*, equal, identical). Ricoeur (1990) makes reference to this dual meaning of the concept of identity, *idem* and *ipse*, in order to point out that the latter dimension puts more emphasis on change and subjectivity while implying the link to alterity.

We subscribe to this approach to identity and identities on the basis of ipseity, because we feel it clearly indicates our wish to avoid the latent danger inherent to contemporary identity theories as outlined by Reckwitz. He distinguishes between 'classical' concepts (1940s to 1970s) – which were "*universalistisch und*

---

29 | Personal translation: "Self-dissociation through self-reflection and self-criticism".
30 | Personal translation: "By acting, subjects are permanently at work on their identities Their basic acts comprise situative self-thematisations that continuously accompany our thoughts and activities" (Straus/Höfer 1997: 273).
31 | Personal translation: "[Individual] answers to the (practical) question of identity [...] need not necessarily be articulated explicitly"
32 | Personal translation: "Implicitly implied in the action or expressed through action".
33 | Personal translation: "Question of meaning".
34 | Personal translation: "In view of the diversity of experiences of self-awareness in everyday life and a progressive paucity of coherence models provided by society".
35 | Personal translation: "Consistent but contingent".

kompetenztheoretisch orientiert und auf das Problem des Verhältnisses zwischen Individuum und sozialen Zwängen sowie das Problem der temporalen Konstanz zentriert"[36] – and models from the 1970s onwards, which were rather *"hermeneutisch und historisch orientiert sowie auf das Problem des kontingenten Selbstverstehens bezogen"*[37] (2001: 25). According to Reckwitz, these current theories run a dual risk of overinterpretation: on the one hand, due to the *"Dramatisierung der Stabilität von Differenzen"*[38], which suggests a certain culturalistic essentialism; on the other hand, due to the *"Dramatisierung der permanenten Veränderbarkeit von Identitäten"*[39], i.e. the *"Bild eines hyperflexiblen, seine Identitäten austauschenden Subjekts [...], das den Boden der Alltagspraktiken zu verlassen scheint"*[40] (2001: 34-35). The reference to ipseity serves as a reminder that the identities we have investigated carry the respective differences *inherently* as a complement (see Rosa 2007) and that they have been empirically ascertained in terms of their social embeddedness and milieu affiliation.

To sum up, we have, in order to stress the relational nature of identity patterns, directed our attention to the intricate interplay between the different forms of internal self-understanding and self-relationship and external influences, or, in other words, on the interplay between *bottom up* "identifications with" and *top down* "identifications of" (Hark 1999). The circulating identity projects and options – analysed here in the form of representations and negotiations – are intrinsically dialogical and political. There is a negotiation of *"Machtkämpfe um die Bedeutung, Stellung und den Wert von Lebensformen, Eigenschaften, Tätigkeiten und Verhaltensweisen"*[41] (Rosa 2007: 52). Identities are formed for the most part in linguistic and everyday-cultural negotiations as well as in spatial representations and in the confrontation between images of self and others, which is why these thematic areas are empirically elaborated in this book and interlinked with the cross-cutting theme of socio-cultural milieus (Vester et al. 2001). Our primary focus of interest here are the active processes currently in progress, involving the different forms of identity work of the conscious self – in other words *Doing Identity*.

---

36 | Personal translation: "Which had a universalistic and competence-theoretical orientation and centred on the problem of the relationship between the individual and social constraints as well as on the problem of temporal constancy".
37 | Personal translation: "Hermeneutically and historically oriented as well as relating to the problem of contingent self-understanding".
38 | Personal translation: "Dramatisation of the stability of differences".
39 | Personal translation. "Dramatisation of the permanent changeability of identities".
40 | Personal translation: "Image of a hyper-flexible subject permanently changing its identities [...], which seems to depart from everyday practices".
41 | Personal translation: "Power struggles over the meaning, status and value of lifestyles, characteristics, activities and behaviours".

Analytical Categories and Research Design

In order to apply it in our interdisciplinary project, we have operationalised the identity concept as defined within the general theoretical framework presented above. For this, we have adopted two different perspectives that are only separable for analytical purposes and that give rise to a third perspective, which seems crucial for statements about current and possibly also future social developments. This involves, on the one hand, the concept of attributed and appropriated identities and on the other, their interdependency. With the aid of the concept of *attributed identities*, the attributions and structural mechanisms of the so-called 'desirable identities' are examined as to how they manifest themselves in the discourses in politics and the media. This means that the research interest here focuses on identity-related attribution processes *via* vectors in different areas of society. By contrast, the concept of *appropriated identities* refers to the identity patterns articulated in social practice. Of particular interest here are the so-called 'lived identities' of the Luxembourg resident population in different socio-cultural milieus which – according to our initial thesis – relate transversely to milieu-specific dispositions. Finally, by making a contrastive comparison of attributed and appropriated identities according to the respective thematic fields under investigation, it is possible to indicate the interplay and possibly also the divergences between both analytical categories, which should be seen as an approach to social practice in terms of a *structure-agency link* (see Giddens 1997) in the field of identity construction.

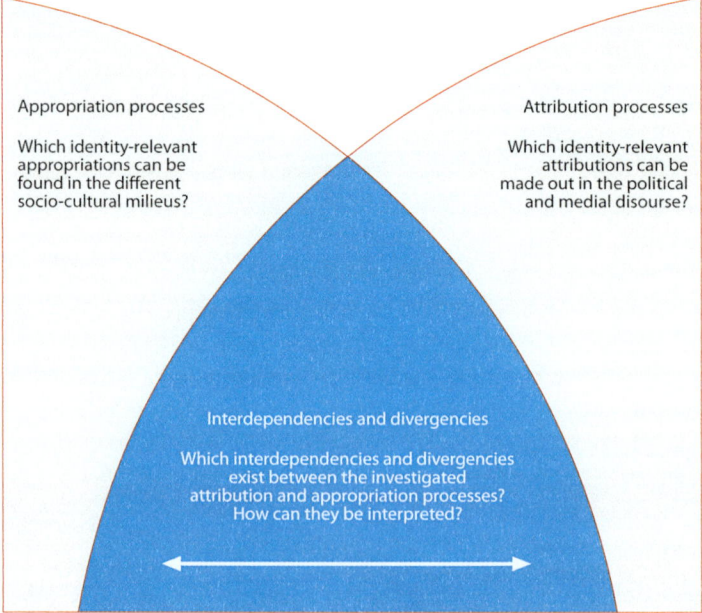

Figure 1: Heuristics of processes of identity construction.

On the basis of the analytical foundation of the identity concept and against the background of the disciplines represented in the IPSE research unit, five main thematic areas have emerged that have structured the project.

- *Socio-cultural Milieus in Luxembourg (chap. 3)*: For a differentiated and transversal examination of appropriated identities, we first of all empirically identified socio-cultural milieus in Luxembourg society. The category of milieus describes people with their typical attitudes and life orientations and incorporates these into social groups with accordingly similar value orientations, life goals and lifestyles. The pioneering work of identifying milieus follows the social milieu approach proposed by Pierre Bourdieu, further developed by Michael Vester (see Vester et al. 2001) and adapted in the framework of the IDENT project, taking into account the plural conditions in Luxembourg. The identified socio-cultural milieus – and the appropriated identities reflected in them – are an integrating element of the IDENT project, as becomes clear by the continuous reference to milieu classification by the authors of the thematic areas below.
- *Languages and Identities (chap. 4)*: Another thematic area centres on linguistic identities in multilingual Luxembourg. We have first looked at aspects of contact between languages as well as the experience of multilingualism, which – differentiated in terms of sociocultural milieus – provides insights into language-related identities. Appropriated identities are also examined in connection with the question of which conflict lines and positions characterise the social debate surrounding multilingualism. Finally, we have investigated in which way 'lived' or 'desired' linguistic identities are articulated in the public space.
- *Spaces and Identities (chap. 5)*: This focus area is concerned with spatial identities, the central point of interest here being the attributed identities and their representations in the tourism discourse. Observations extracted from communication media ranging from the local to the inter-regional level are contrasted with the notions of space and spatial practices of Luxembourg residents, whereby we were able to elucidate the discrepancies between attributed and appropriated identities on different levels of scale.
- *Images and Identities (chap. 6)*: This thematic area involves linguistically and visually created images of self and others in regard to 'Luxembourg', as found in specialised and popular media. It explores the question which conclusions can be drawn from the statements made as well as from the genesis of the viewed images, in respect to identity-related appropriation and attribution processes. The work carried out in this area of our project places particular emphasis on the analytical nature of the conceptual categories which (may) converge in the process of reception of the investigated media.
- *Everyday Cultures and Identities (chap. 7)*: This thematic area focuses on appropriated and attributed identities in the everyday – yet politically and economically moulded – contexts of gender, consumerism and alterity. Of special interest here are the identities observed in various socio-cultural milieus

in regard to their ambivalent appropriation in the practice of everyday culture, where 'resolved contradictions' but also overlaps emerge.

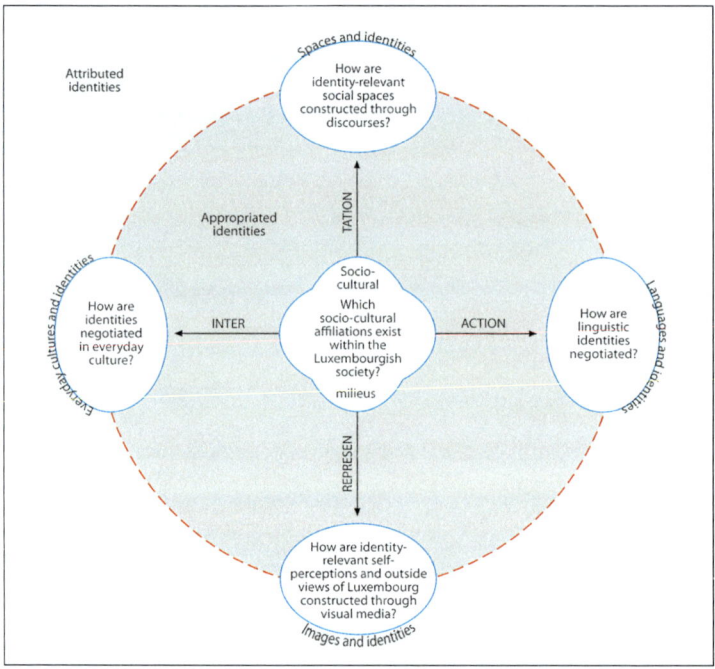

Figure 2: Thematic areas and their conceptual framework.

Defining the position the project occupies within the scientific discussion about identity and identities and the elaboration of analytical categories has, during the three years of research, proven indispensable for establishing a common basis for interdisciplinary collaboration. In the following paragraphs, we will explain the methods used in analysing the subjects of investigation in the thematic areas described above and subsequently present some points relating to research practice in terms of our scientific interdisciplinary collaboration.

2.2 Methodology and Interdisciplinary Collaboration

Based on the thematic-conceptual framework outlined above, we will, in the following, explain the methods employed and provide insights into the structure and implementation of the project stages that were jointly worked on, in particular those of the empirical survey. To begin with, we wish to give an overview of the topics examined in the thematic areas.

- *Socio-cultural milieus*: The identification of socio-cultural milieus within Luxembourg's residential population for the examination of appropriated identities was based on the analysis of quantitative statistical data that were gathered within the framework of the IDENT project.
- *Languages and Identities*: For the investigation of identities regarding contact between and experience with languages, we first used quantitative statistical data from the present study; in addition, we evaluated by means of text-analytical methods letters to editors in the relevant print media of Luxembourg as to the positions represented in them. Finally, public signs in Luxembourg were subjected to a quantitative analysis to reveal appropriated and attributed linguistic identities.
- *Images and Identities*: Images of self and others as attribution or appropriation of identities were identified in both popular and specialised media such as newspapers, comics, exhibition catalogues, print advertisements or photographs and subsequently discussed. Here we applied for the most part content-analytical procedures which were supplemented by quantitative statistical data from the present study.
- *Spaces and Identities*: In this thematic area, the attribution of spatial identities was deconstructed in a discourse-analytical approach using tourist pamphlets, topographic maps, travel guides and journalistic publications. They were contrasted with appropriated spatial identities of Luxembourg's resident population, which were identified on the basis of the data of our own quantitative and qualitative survey.
- *Everyday Cultures and Identities*: The identities of everyday practice involving the appropriation or attribution of gender constructions, views concerning 'good' food and experiences with cross-border workers are based on the data of our own quantitative and qualitative surveys and on corresponding content analyses in which we also evaluated official pamphlets and legal texts.

The presentation of the topics investigated in the individual thematic areas indicates a broad range of 'subjects of analysis'. This diversity was managed by employing similarly varied methodological instruments and an approach based on the division of labour, which has become possible only thanks to the experience and the broad methodological competence of the disciplines represented in the IPSE research unit. The applied methodological procedures can be summarised under the project modules "quantitative survey", "qualitative interviews" and "content analyses".

Quantitative Survey

A crucial part of the IDENT project was the quantitative representative survey of Luxembourg's resident population. It aimed to achieve two goals: On the one hand, to identify socio-cultural milieus of Luxembourg society and the identity patterns to be found there; on the other, to elaborate specific questions from the thematic areas (languages, images of self and others, spaces and everyday cultures) under the aspect of identity construction. Accordingly, the questionnaire jointly developed by us is subdivided into different thematic areas[42], which were operationalised by using open, half-open and closed questions. The multilingualism in the Grand Duchy of Luxembourg made it necessary to create a Luxembourgish, German, French, English and Portuguese version of the questionnaire (just like the interview guideline presented below). However, the survey results could only be put into relation to each other if it was guaranteed, by means of the interview tools, that the treated topics and/or key concepts retained the same meaning – what is referred to in the methodological debate as "functional equivalence" (see Braun 2006). This touches on the multi-layered and socio-culturally anchored range of meaning of lexical elements, which raises the question, when it comes to the translation of interviewing tools, as to what extent, or whether at all, the target language can provide equivalent wording that excludes semantic shifts[43]. This involves both the level of denotation, as in the case of educational qualifications, and that of the connotation, when using, for example, socially charged concepts (see Lüsebrink 2005: 47). One way of conducting an equivalence check is to create a back-translation, entailing the transfer of a questionnaire or interview guideline from the target language back into the source language by unbiased translators, in order to then be able to exclude semantic shifts by comparing the resulting text with the source version of the respective interviewing tool. In addition, there are discursive procedures, where the translations of interviewing tools are discussed with persons sensitised to functional equivalence or with native speakers. Since we had persons with these qualifications at our disposal, as well as bilingual and sometimes even trilingual native speakers, we chose for the IDENT project the discursive procedure of equivalence check, which was applied in several joint and structured sessions.

The composition of the random sample was carried out by the leading polling institute in Luxembourg, which was also responsible for conducting the quantitative survey. Between October 2008 and February 2009 a total of 1,579 people of age 16 and above as well as resident in the Grand Duchy of Luxembourg were interviewed. Two thirds of the interviews were conducted via Internet (*computer-assisted web interview*), the remaining third by telephone (*computer-assisted telephone interview*), in order to be able to reach both persons with media competence and those with more traditional media usage. The random sample was weighted according to the variables of age, gender, region, nationality and employment (status) and is

---

42 | See section 3.2 for a detailed treatment.

43 | One should mention that due to subjective reception mechanisms even in a monolingual investigation context the interviewees rarely reconstruct meanings in absolutely identical ways.

representative for the inhabitants of Luxembourg. The gathered data were evaluated *via* the processes of descriptive and multivariate[44] statistics[45].

Qualitative Interviews

On the basis of the quantitative representative survey outlined above, additional interviews were conducted in spring 2009 with those residents of Luxembourg who had agreed to this in the quantitative survey. The decision to carry out a large-scale qualitative survey was motivated by the desire to be able to make statements on subjective attributions and interpretations of meaning that a quantitative procedure would have been unable to capture. Consequently, the project partners decided to jointly conduct focussed interviews. This is an open to partly-standardised procedure which is supported by an interview guideline and aims for in-depth re-presentation (*Repräsentanz*[46], see below) instead of representativity (*Repräsentativität*) (Lamnek 2005).

Due to the significant academic interest attached to the interview survey, we developed three thematic interview guidelines ("everyday cultures", "images of self and others", "languages and spaces") in which concisely worded questions and conversation-generating impulses were noted down. The thematic teams, which had developed the individual questions, were asked to state in point form the background or the aim of the respective question. This approach enabled the interviewers – who had become familiar with the questions in the course of their joint work on the project, but had not necessarily internalised the strategic thrust of all of them – to prepare individually for the interviews, which were shared out among the members of our research team. Hence, the detailed interview guidelines were edited down to point form by the researchers, which in turn allowed for a flexible and in most part open interview procedure. Two meetings were organised to promote the dialogue between the authors of the questions and the interviewers, who were not necessarily identical.

It was not the aim of the interview survey to determine specific frequencies of phenomena, but rather to arrive at a detailed understanding of social phenomena, i.e. to examine the nature of their in-depth representation (*Repräsentanz*). In other

---

44 | See section 3.2 for a detailed presentation.
45 | The complete data collection including the questionnaire can be inspected at the Luxembourg University library.
46 | The contrast between *Repräsentanz* and *Repräsentativität* is not easily translatable into English from its German sociological origin: *Repräsentanz* signifies the specifically qualitative form of scientific insight, i.e. the multi-facetted "representing something", "being vivid, eloquent, meaningful", that is to say, an in-depth understanding of selected case examples, with the aim to embrace the widest possible spectrum of meanings of a given phenomenon. It is opposed to quantitative methods that give priority to a larger, comparable, abstracting yet more superficial representativity (*Repräsentativität*).

words, our interest was not so much focussed on a random sample in order to be able to form conclusions about a general population, as on examining concrete and varied cases in order to record a phenomenon in the most multi-faceted manner possible. When it came to sampling, this approach required "[...] eine Entscheidung gegen den Zufall und eine theoretisch-systematische Auswahl [der zu Befragenden]"[47] (Lamnek 2005: 186). Lamnek is here referring to the deliberate procedures of qualitative random sample implementation, which include, among others, the advance specification of the sample structure (Weischer 2007: 207-209). Central criteria of the deliberate random sample configuration were gender, age and nationality, designed to illustrate the plurality of the Luxembourg population. This has been achieved to a large extent with the interview random sample that comprised 75 people.

	Topic: Every Day Cultures	Topic: Images of Self and Others	Topic: Languages and Spaces	Total	Luxembourg Population (2007)*	Deviation from Parent Population
Random sample (N)	n=27	n=26	n=22	N=75	476,200	Percentage
	(a)	(b)	(c)	(d)	(e)	(d-e)
Gender						
Men	50.0	48.1	40.9	46.7	49.5	-2.8
Women	50.0	51.9	59.1	53.3	50.5	2.8
Age group						
15-29	23.1	11.1	13.6	16.0	22.6	-6.6
30-44	30.8	44.4	27.3	34.7	29.8	4.9
45-59	26.9	25.9	31.8	28.0	24.7	3.3
60+	19.2	18.5	27.3	21.3	22.8	-1.5
Nationality						
Luxembourgers	61.5	55.6	63.6	60.0	59	1.0
Resident foreigners	38.5	44.4	36.4	40.0	41	-1.0
Of these						
French	10.0	8.3	12.5	10.0	12.7	-2.7
Portuguese	40.0	33.3	25.0	33.3	37	-3.7
Germans	10.0	8.3	0.0	6.7	5.7	1.0
Belgians	10.0	8.3	12.5	10.0	8.3	1.7
Italians	10.0	8.3	12.5	10.0	9.6	0.4
British/Dutch	0.0	8.3	0.0	3.3	4.4	-1.1
Other	20.0	25.0	37.5	26.7	8.3	18.4

Table 1: Random samples of the qualitative surveys by socio-demographical characteristics (Source: Own study; * Statec 2007).

---

47 | Personal translation: "[...] A decision against chance and a theoretical-systematic selection [of the persons to be interviewed]".

The interviews were conducted by the members of the research team, according to language preferences, time availability and thematic interest, so that each participant in the project had around five people to interview. A central objective was the interdisciplinary distribution of the interviewers who therefore worked with guidelines that had been developed by another thematic team. The interviews took place by prior arrangement in the homes of the interviewees, in their familiar surroundings and often in the early or late hours of the day. The conversation that lasted between one and one and a half hours, was directed, following the interview guideline, towards a specific topic with its various aspects and the interviewees were given the possibility to express themselves freely, however within certain thematic boundaries. In this way, it was possible to obtain the interviewees' interpretations and reactions in a relatively open manner and make room for aspects not anticipated by the researchers. The digitally recorded interview data were processed using transcription into standard language (Mayring 2007: 91), since the focus of the interviews was on thematic content. This approach, which involves, among other things, the minimal correction of errors in syntax and editing the flow of words, aims at enhancing the readability of the spoken language. The task of transcribing the interviews in Luxembourgish, German, French, English and Portuguese was entrusted to student assistants.

The final interview transcripts were then evaluated by computer, using deductive-selective encoding and/or inductive-free encoding. As a first step, the transcripts were systematised by the project participants following a jointly adopted codification pattern with predefined codes and subcodes (*coarse coding*). This pattern was elaborated during several joint "codification meetings", during which the direct exchange between the project participants was both possible and essential. During the subsequent inductive-free encoding, performed by those colleagues specialised in the respective thematic fields, aspects were brought into focus that had hitherto not been taken into account but had come up during the interview, by using key quotes and memo functions inherent to the software (*fine coding*); situative descriptions of the interaction, written down by the interviewers after every conversation, were also added by memo function. This made it possible to further differentiate the code structure in terms of the so-called fine coding. The texts prepared in this way were evaluated by synoptic analysis (Kelle 2007: 491-493), which in respect to methodology is part of the phenomenological analysis developed by Mayring (Mayring 2002: 107-108) and in technical respect one of the simple retrieval techniques. Its aim is to identify and clarify differences, similarities and relationships between the subjective structures of meaning, through the variation or the process of comparison, as described by Glaser and Strauss (Glaser/Strauss 2005: 107-122) already in the 1970s, in order to penetrate to the *"[den] Wesenskern der Phänomene"*[48] (Mayring 2002: 108). For this purpose, text segments of one or several codes were compiled in a list (*text retrieval*), which then permitted us to

---

48 | Personal translation: "Essential core of phenomena".

compare and interpret differences and similarities. To ensure a smooth handling of the described procedure of computer-assisted analysis of qualitative data, we organised a number of training sessions and internal workshops, which were conducted both by the project participants and by invited experts.

In addition to the large-scale qualitative survey, experts from specific areas of society were interviewed by some of our researchers. In these qualitative expert interviews, however, it was not so much the experts that were the subject of analysis, that is to say not *"[…] die Person mit ihren Orientierungen und Einstellungen im Kontext des individuellen oder kollektiven Lebenszusammenhangs"*[49] (Meuser/Nagel 2005: 72-74). Rather, the experts' function here was to inform about institutional or organizational contexts (Weischer 2007: 281). The goal of the interviews was therefore to identify specific stocks of knowledge the experts in question had acquired in their professional field and that provided insights into concrete areas of investigation. An expert was considered anyone who carries responsibility for specific forms of problem solution in a given field of investigation or who has privileged access to information about social actors. The expert interviews were prepared, conducted and evaluated by those project participants whose particular research interest connected with the interviewees' fields of expertise. They included the areas of administration, culture and economics.

Content Analyses

Apart from the quantitative and qualitative surveys outlined above, we also applied, in view of the considerable variety of investigated items, methods that can be summarised under the concept of content analysis. These involve, based on a broad approach to the text, text-analytical procedures comprising discourse-analytical methods and semiotic techniques. The methods used will be explained more fully in the respective sections.

As indicated earlier, investigating the various thematic areas necessitated a variety of methodical procedures leading to an abundance of empirical data. The project participants representing the different disciplines judiciously intertwined the available qualitative and quantitative data according to thematic orientations. On the one hand, in combining quantitative and qualitative methods and corresponding data, we wanted to ensure the validity of the investigation results, and on the other, it was our goal to supplement the perspectives on the subjects of investigation, by bringing together the different aspects of a phenomenon to form a complete and composite picture (Kelle/Erzberger 2007: 302-304). We were able to implement this procedure, referred to as "triangulation" (see Denzin/Lincoln 2005) in the methodological debate, in numerous team meetings and internal workshops.

---

49 | Personal translation: "[…] The person with her/his orientations and attitudes in the context of individual or collective everyday life contexts".

Interdisciplinary Collaboration

The contributions in this book are not a compilation of single research projects, but the result of a three-year long, intensive collaboration between scientists from various disciplines. In the following, we would like to present a brief overview of what this interdisciplinary collaboration entails and how the IDENT project is organised. It was carried out between 2007 and 2010 under the direction of Christian Schulz, who was closely supported by a steering committee consisting of other project members. In addition to this strategic level, an IDENT coordination office was established in which Rachel Reckinger and Christian Wille coordinated the operative tasks and prepared strategic decisions. The research work was carried out by the IDENT project group, which included representatives from the fields of English Studies, Gender Studies, Geography and Spatial Planning, German Studies, History, Intercultural Communication, Luxembourgish Studies, Media Sciences, French Studies, Sociology and Visual Arts. The level of the operative tasks, that is to say the organisational forms and the implementation of the research projects which will be considered in greater detail below. They can be subdivided into three core stages: Preparatory stage (2007-2008), empirical stage (2008-2009) and final stage (2009-2010).

In the course of the project, a variety of collective working methods of interdisciplinary collaboration were used, which include thematic teams, internal workshops, round-table discussions and international conferences.

Thematic teams: In order to enable an intensive exchange between the project partners, we formed different thematic teams, one set with a permanent and thematic orientation, and another set with a temporary and methodological one. The thematic teams maintained over the entire duration of the project each focussed on one of the thematic areas outlined above. The thematic teams, which convened every two to three weeks, depending on the particular phase of the project, were staffed with five or six researchers from the following disciplines:

TT Socio-cultural milieus	TT Languages	TT Images of Self and Others	TT Spaces	TT Everyday Cultures
Sociology, German Studies	German Studies, Luxembourgish Studies	Visual Arts, German Studies, History, Media Sciences	French Studies, History, Geography and Spatial Planning	Gender Studies, English Studies, Sociology, Intercultural Communication

Table 2: Thematic teams.

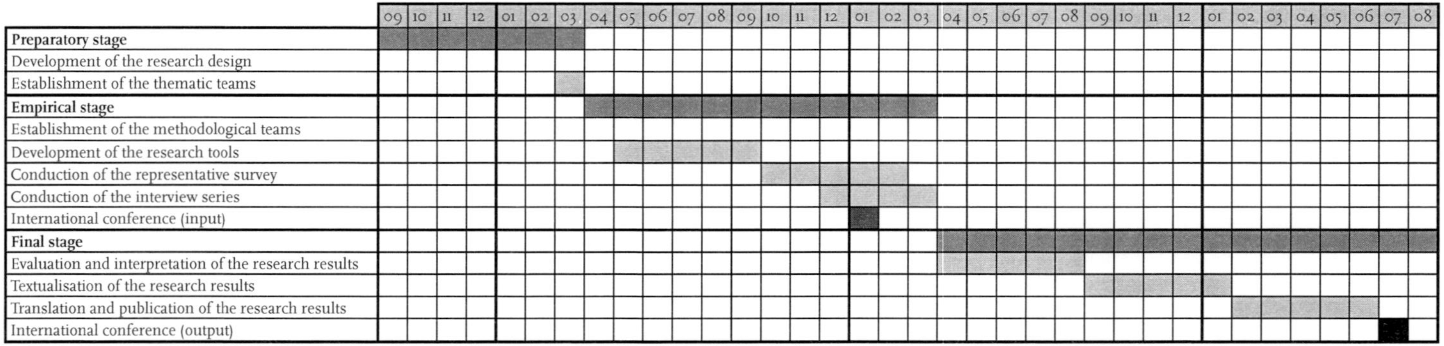

	09	10	11	12	01	02	03	04	05	06	07	08	09	10	11	12	01	02	03	04	05	06	07	08	09	10	11	12	01	02	03	04	05	06	07	08
Preparatory stage																																				
Development of the research design					■	■	■																													
Establishment of the thematic teams							■	■																												
Empirical stage																																				
Establishment of the methodological teams								■	■	■	■	■	■	■	■	■	■	■	■																	
Development of the research tools												■	■	■																						
Conduction of the representative survey																	■	■	■																	
Conduction of the interview series																			■																	
International conference (input)																																				
Final stage																																				
Evaluation and interpretation of the research results																				■	■	■	■	■	■	■	■	■								
Textualisation of the research results																									■	■										
Translation and publication of the research results																													■	■	■	■	■	■		
International conference (output)																																			■	

Figure 3: Main project stages 2007-2010.

The tasks of the thematic teams consisted, depending on the project stage, in developing a common theoretical-conceptual framework and research design, gathering and processing empirical data, jointly interpreting the research results and writing a chapter for this book. The research within the thematic teams was conducted around different case examples, which were elaborated and discussed in the perspective of a common research question. The thematic teams were assisted and supervised in their activities by the project coordinators, one of the challenges being to synchronise these five thematic teams, each with its specific features, in a conceptual and methodological way, according to the requirements of the main project stages.

Other teams, formed only during certain stages of the project, had a methodological mandate. It was their task to develop the multilingual research instruments in close collaboration with the thematic teams. Accordingly, the multidisciplinary methodological teams "Questionnaire" and "Interview" collected and integrated the questions compiled by the thematic teams, checking the wording and processing them for the quantitative and qualitative research instruments. They were also responsible for the pretests, which, for the "Interview" team, included organising two trainings on interview techniques using role plays, as well as one training on computer-aided interview processing for interpretative work.

Internal workshops: In order to avoid a fragmentation of the IDENT project group as a result of scientists working in different thematic teams, we also organised a series of internal project workshops. All project participants assembled every four to eight weeks in plenary sessions where different issues were discussed, depending on the particular project stage. While in the project preparation stage, the workshops mainly served to share information about the various disciplines' specific features and to reach, to some degree, a common and cross-disciplinary understanding of certain concepts, the internal workshops were also indispensable for jointly working out the project architecture. Particularly during the empirical stage, the plenary sessions were an important instrument for communicating about organisational problems of complex survey procedures. The internal workshops conducted by the project coordinators were used particularly towards the end of the project to share and link information on the results presented by the thematic teams. Due to the limited time available in the workshops, we organised an additional 2-day symposium to allow sufficient room for interpreting the research results in a comprehensive exchange of information, embracing all thematic teams and disciplines involved in the project.

Round-table discussions: In addition to the regular workshops, we set up a series of round-table discussions designed to give participants the opportunity to meet with external experts in a relaxed atmosphere. In particular during the stage of project preparation, consultation with experts, who had already worked on similar problems, proved very helpful for the development of the common theoretical-conceptual framework, the project architecture and the research instruments that were finally used. We would especially like to thank the following for their support: Michael Vester and Daniel Gardemin (Hannover University), Jean-Marie Klinkenberg (University of Liège) and Jürgen Pohl (Bonn University).

International conferences: The international conferences organised in the course of the project provided a further platform for sharing information with experienced scientists in the area of identity research. These events were strategically integrated into the project, so that we can distinguish between an 'input conference' (2009) and an 'output conference' (2010). The conference organised in 2009, with the title "IDENT – Socio-Cultural Identities: Interaction and Representation", invited selected lecturers to give their critical appraisal of the approach and the concept of the IDENT project, besides providing an overview of their own work. For the resulting suggestions which were subsequently incorporated into the project, we would like to extend our sincere thanks to Brigitta Busch (Vienna University), Thomas Dörfler (University of Bayreuth), Britta Kalscheuer (University of Frankfurt/M.), Claudia Lenz (Center for Studies of Holocaust and Religious Minorities, Oslo), Albert Lévy (Université Paris VIII), Lydia Martens (Keele University), Rolf Parr (Bielefeld University), Albert Raasch (University of the Saarland), Klaus Sachs-Hombach (University of Applied Sciences, Chemnitz) and Jürgen Straub (Ruhr-University Bochum). The 2010 conference with the title "Doing Identity in Luxembourg: Subjective Appropriations – Institutional Attributions – Socio-Cultural Milieus" had been organised to present the research results both to a professional audience and the interested public and to invite critical discussion.

Besides these forms of interdisciplinary collaboration, we, as coordinators of the project, would like to mention some experiences that were made in the course of the project. One of them is that in other projects of similar scale, sufficient room should be given to those processes that promote exchange and convergence between different disciplines. This means showing patience and also allowing for a certain amount of confusion and 'talking at cross purposes'; intervening with empathy in communication processes and negotiating or 'translating' these in a results-oriented manner. Frequently, it is only the use of different words that stops people from realising that they are talking about the same thing. What really helps here is to take a broad, analytical look at professional contents and engage with the researchers with understanding and empathy for their particular personality. At the University of Luxembourg, with a staff that comes from various European countries as well as from overseas, it takes an additional effort to integrate the diversity of languages and the different experiences of university socialisation into day-to-day academic life. This requires intercultural skills as well as disposable time, which ultimately, however, serves to enrich and enhance the experience of interdisciplinary teamwork.

2.3 References

Abels, Heinz. 2006. Identität. Über die Entstehung des Gedankens, dass der Mensch ein Individuum ist, den nicht leicht zu verwirklichenden Anspruch auf Individualität und die Tatsache, dass Identität in Zeiten der Individualisierung von der Hand in den Mund lebt. Wiesbaden: VS Verlag für Sozialwissenschaften.

Ahbe, Thomas. 1997. Ressourcen – Transformationen – Identität. In Identitätsarbeit heute. Klasssische und aktuelle Perspektiven der Identitätsforschung, ed. Heiner Keupp/Renate Höfer, 207-26. Frankfurt/M.: Suhrkamp.

Appadurai, Arjun. 1998. Globale ethnische Räume. In Perspektiven der Weltgesellschaft, ed. Ulrich Beck, 11-40. Frankfurt/M.: Suhrkamp.

Avanza, Martina and Gilles Laferté. 2005. Dépasser la 'construction des identités'? Identification, image sociale, appartenance. Genèses. Sciences sociales et histoire, no. 61: 134-52.

Baltes-Löhr, Christel. 2006. Migration und Identität. Portugiesische Frauen in Luxemburg. Frankfurt/M. & London: IKO-Verlag für Interkulturelle Kommunikation.

Bayart, Jean-François. 1996. L'illusion identitaire. Paris: Fayard.

Bhaba, Homi. 1994. The location of culture. London: Routledge.

Bauman, Zygmut. 1999. Unbehagen in der Postmoderne. Hamburg: Hamburger Edition.

Bourdieu, Pierre. 1992. Die verborgenen Mechanismen der Macht. Hamburg: Vsa.

Bourdieu, Pierre. 1980. Le sens pratique. Paris: Editions de Minuit.

Bourdieu, Pierre. 1972. Esquisse d'une théorie de la pratique. Précédé de trois études d'ethnologie kabyle. Paris: Le Seuil.

Braun, Michael. 2006. Funktionale Äquivalenz in interkulturell vergleichenden Umfragen: Mythos und Realität. Mannheim: ZUMA.

Brubaker, Rogers. 2001. Au-delà de l'"identité". Actes de la recherche en sciences sociales, no. 139: 66-85.

Chilla, Tobias. 2009. Europa in Luxemburg: Die EU-Institutionen. In Der Luxemburg Atlas du Luxembourg, ed. Patrick Bousch, Tobias Chilla, Philippe Gerber et al., 16-17. Köln: Emons.

Denzin, Norman K. and Yvonna S. Lincoln, ed. 2005. The SAGE handbook of qualitative research. London: SAGE.

Eickelpasch, Rolf and Claudia Rademacher. 2004. Identität. Bielfeld: Transcript.

Elias, Norbert. 1986. Figuration. In Grundbegriffe der Soziologie, ed. Bernhard Schäfer, 88-91. Opladen: Leske + Budrich.

Fehlen, Fernand and Isabelle Pigeron-Piroth. 2009. Mondialisation du travail et pluralité des marchés du travail: L'exemple du Luxembourg. Transcript of the discussion contribution for 12è Journées de Sociologie du Travail, 25 et 26 juin 2009, GREE, Université de Nancy.

Foucault, Michel. 1994. Technologies of the self. In The essential Foucault. Selections from the Essential Works of Foucault 1954-1984, ed. Paul Rabinow and Nicolas Rose, 145-69. New York & London: The New Press.

Foucault, Michel. 1984. *Histoire de la sexualité*. Tome 3: Le souci de soi. Paris: Gallimard.

Giddens, Anthony. 1997. Die Konstitution der Gesellschaft. Frankfurt/M./New York: Campus.

Giddens, Anthony. 1991. Modernity and Self-Identity. Cambridge: Polity.

Giesen, Bernhard. 1999. Identität und Versachlichung. Unterschiedliche Theorieperspektiven auf kollektive Identität. In Identität und Moderne, ed. Herbert Willems and Alois Hahn, 389-403. Frankfurt/M.: Suhrkamp.

Glaser, Barney G. and Anselm L. Strauss. 2005. Grounded Theory. Strategien qualitativer Forschung. Bern: Huber.

Goffman, Erving. 2003. Wir alle spielen Theater. Munich: Piper.

Greverus, Ina-Maria. 1995. Die Anderen und Ich. Darmstadt: Wissenschaftliche Buchgesellschaft.

Halpern, Catherine. 2009. Identité(s). L'individu, le groupe, la société. Paris: Editions Sciences Humaines.

Hark, Sabine. 1999. Deviante Subjekte. Die paradoxe Politik der Identität. Opladen: Leske + Budrich.

Kaufmann, Jean-Claude. 2004. L'invention de soi. Une théorie de l'identité. Paris: Armand Colin.

Kelle, Udo. 2007. Computergestützte Analyse qualitativer Daten. In Qualitative Forschung. Ein Handbuch, ed. Uwe Flick, Ernst von Kardoff and Ines Steinke, 486-502. Hamburg: Rowohlt.

Kelle, Udo and Christian Erzberger. 2007: Qualitative und quantitative Methoden: kein Gegensatz. In Qualitative Forschung. Ein Handbuch, ed. Uwe Flick, Ernst von Kardoff and Ines Steinke, 299-309. Hamburg: Rowohlt.

Keupp, Heiner and Renate Höfer, ed. 1997. Identitätsarbeit heute. Klassische und aktuelle Perspektiven der Identitätsforschung. Frankfurt/M.: Suhrkamp.

Keupp, Heiner, Thomas Ahbe, Thomas, Wolfgang Gmür, Renate Höfer, Beate Mitzscherlich Beate, Wolfgang Kraus, and Florian Straus. 2006 Identitätskonstruktionen. Das Patchwork der Identitäten in der Spätmoderne. Reinbek bei Hamburg: Rowohlt

Kmec, Sonja. 2007. Von Identitäten und Identifikationen. Forum für Politik, Gesellschaft und Kultur in Luxemburg 271: Lëtzebuerg?, Luxembourg, 39-41.

Krappmann, Lothar. 2005. Soziologische Dimensionen der Identität. Strukturelle Bedingungen für die Teilnahme an Interaktionsprozessen. Stuttgart: Klett-Cotta.

Lahire, Bernhard. 1998. L'homme pluriel. Les ressorts de l'action. Paris: Nathan.

Lamnek, Siegfried. 2005. Qualitative Sozialforschung. Lehrbuch. Weinheim: Beltz.

Luckmann, Thomas. 2007. Lebenswelt, Identität und Gesellschaft. Konstanz, UVK Verlagsgesellschaft.

Lüsebrink, Hans-Jürgen. 2005. Interkulturelle Kommunikation. Interaktion, Fremdwahrnehmung, Kulturtransfer. Weimar: Metzler.

MacClancy, Jeremy. 2004. Food, Identity, Identification. In Researching food habits. Methods and problems, ed. Helen MacBeth and Jeremy MacClancy, 63-73. Oxford & New York: Berghahn Books.

Mayring, Philipp. 2002. Einführung in die qualitative Sozialforschung. Weinheim: Beltz.

Meuser, Michael and Ulrike Nagel 2005. ExpertInneninterviews – vielfach erprobt, wenig bedacht. Ein Beitrag zur qualitativen Methodendiskussion. In Das Experteninterview. Theorie, Methode, Anwendung, ed. Alexander Bogner, Beate Littig and Wolfgang Menz, 71-93.Wiesbaden: VS Verlag.

Meyran, Régis. 2008. Le mythe de l'identité nationale. Paris: Berg International.

Niethammer, Lutz. 2000. Kollektive Identität. Heinliche Quellen einer unheimlichen Konjunktur. Reinbek bei Hamburg: Rowohlt.

Ricoeur, Paul. 1990. Soi-même comme un autre. Paris: Le Seuil.

Rosa, Hartmut. 2007. Identität. In Handbuch interkulturelle Kommunikation und Kompetenz. Grundbegriffe – Theorien – Anwendungsfelder, ed. Jürgen Straub and Arne Weidemann. Stuttgart: J. B. Metzler.

Ruano-Borbolan, Jean-Claude. 1998. L'identité. L'individu, le groupe, la société. Auxerre: Sciences Humaines.

Sennett, Richard. 1996. Etwas ist faul in der Stadt. Die Zeit N°5 (26th January): 47-48.

Statec. 2007. Luxemburg in Zahlen. Luxemburg.

Straub, Jürgen. 2004. Identität. In Handbuch der Kulturwissenschaften. Grundlagen und Schlüsselbegriffe, ed. Friedrich Jaeger and Burkhard Liebsch. Stuttgart: J. B. Metzler.

Straub, Jürgen and Joachim Renn, ed. 2002. Transitorische Identität. Der Prozesscharakter des modernen Selbst. Frankfurt/M.: Campus.

Straub, Jürgen. 1998. Personale und kollektive Identität. In Identitäten, ed. Aleida Assmann and Heidrun Friese. Frankfurt/M.: Suhrkamp.

Straus, Florian and Renate Höfer. 1997. Entwicklungslinien alltäglicher Identitätsarbeit In Identitätsarbeit heute. Klasssische und aktuelle Perspektiven der Identitätsforschung, ed. Heiner Keupp and Renate Höfer, 270-307. Frankfurt/M.: Suhrkamp.

Vester, Michael, Peter Von Oertzen, Heiko Geiling, Thomas Hermann and Dagmar Müller. 2001. Soziale Milieus im gesellschaftlichen Strukturwandel. Zwischen Integration und Ausgrenzung. Frankfurt/M.: Suhrkamp.

Weinreich, Peter and Wendy Saunderson, ed. 2003. Analysing Identities. Cross-Cultural, Societal and Clinical Contexts. London: Routledge.

Weischer, Christoph. 2007, 207-209 Sozialforschung. Weinheim: Beltz.

Willems, Helmut and Paul Milmeister. 2008. Migration und Integration. In Das politische System Luxemburg. Eine Einführung, ed. Wolfgang H. Lorig and Mario Hirsch, 62-92. Wiesbaden: VS Verlag.

Zahlen, Paul. 2008. Arbeitsmarktpolitik. In Das politische System Luxemburg. Eine Einführung, ed. Wolfgang H. Lorig and Mario Hirsch, 253-285. Wiesbaden: VS Verlag.

3. Socio-Cultural Milieus in Luxembourg

WILHELM AMANN, FERNAND FEHLEN, GEORG MEIN

3.1 CHANGING SOCIAL STRUCTURES. FROM THE VERTICALLY ORIENTATED CONCEPT OF STRATIFICATION TO THE HORIZONTALLY DIVERSIFIED MILIEU LANDSCAPE

When describing the social structure of modern societies, social research has for a long time drawn on the model of social stratification developed in the 1930s by Theodor Geiger. This concept of stratification primarily aims at classifying the overall population according to specific (economic and social) indicators in such a way that groupings with similar social positions and the attendant typical subcultures and prospects emerge (see Geißler 2002: 117). As opposed to the well-known dictum of Karl Marx, this theory does not make the deterministic assumption that social being determines consciousness, hence that external circumstances translate into concrete behaviour. It does, however, investigate empirically in which areas and to what degree internal and external structures connect. Here, economic indicators such as income, wealth, and occupation come into play as well as social indicators like educational status, social prestige, and group affiliation. These groups can then be arranged into a vertically stratified composite picture of social structure.

However, due to their primarily 'vertical' differentiation, stratification models are largely oblivious to 'horizontal' inequalities resulting, for instance, from gender- and generation-specific disparities or local and regional differences. It was, in particular, the model of 'social milieus' developed in the 1980s by the Sinus Institute of market and electoral research that has consistently and methodically also incorporated the horizontal level of social structure in its approach. While strata analysts first subdivide the population according to objectively similar living conditions in order to subsequently examine which mentalities, attitudes, behaviour patterns and prospects are typically linked with these different living circumstances, the milieu approach groups individuals first according to differences in their social values, aesthetics of everyday life, typical forms of lived experience and lifestyles and then asks which social strata provide these milieus. This model then subsumes individuals in a specific social milieu who are similar in their outlook on life and lifestyle and who, therefore, demonstrate such external living circumstances and internal attitudes as to allow them to develop a common lifestyle. In other words, milieus emphasise the subjective side of society.

Readjusting the theoretical perspective on social reality in this way makes sense, because in view of the radical changes of the socio-cultural environment, many theorists agree in their assessment that the dramatic improvement of the standard of living over the last decades has led to a sweeping change in the basic value system of the population. Since the 1960s, this change has triggered a process of radical individualisation and diversification of situations and lifestyles, which seems to largely confirm Helmut Schelsky's theory of the levelled-out middle-class society. For Schelsky, the social structure is essentially highly mobile with collective up and down movements in social rankings eventually leading to a levelling of social classes and strata. This, he states, finally leads to *"einer sozialen Nivellierung in einer verhältnismäßig einheitlichen Gesellschaftsschicht, die ebenso wenig proletarisch wie bürgerlich ist, d.h. durch den Verlust der Klassenspannung und sozialen Hierarchie gekennzeichnet wird"*[1] (Schelsky 1979: 327).

While the corporate society of the old Europe as well as the competitive one of the bourgeois era, which subscribed to the performance and competition principle, still largely shared the common feature that, for the majority of its members, the main purpose in life consisted in securing one's livelihood, society in present-day Europe differs very clearly, precisely in this point, from the earlier stages of its evolution. In the 1970s, Ulrich Beck published an article *"Jenseits von Klasse und Schicht"*, which describes very clearly that, although there are still certain gaps between social strata, society as a whole has climbed upward on the ladder of affluence. Rising prosperity and mass consumption have led to an increasing standardization of living conditions. Now, in fashioning one's life world one is no longer driven by need or lack, indeed, exactly the opposite is the case. The lack of lack creates the challenge to fill the resulting free time with content and meaning.

This homogenisation of living circumstances leads, on the one hand, to veritable identity and orientation crises; on the other, it leads to a dissolution of the subcultures typical for a given stratum. This socio-economic change, in turn, causes a huge surge towards individualisation because scopes of action increase radically as a result of the discontinuation of traditional ties. The resulting pluralisation of lifestyles leads, in contrast, to a decoupling of external living circumstances, so that the notion of stratum or class affiliation is increasingly fading away from everyday consciousness. Ulrich Beck's programmatic thesis entitled *"Risikogesellschaft"* and the proposition of "capitalism without classes" put forward in it sums up this point succinctly:

---

1 | Personal translation: "A social levelling forming a relatively uniform social stratum which is no more labour class than it is bourgeois, i.e. which is marked by the loss of class tension and social hierarchy".

> Wir leben trotz fortbestehender und neu entstehender Ungleichheiten heute in der Bundesrepublik bereits in Verhältnissen jenseits der Klassengesellschaft, in denen das Bild der Klassengesellschaft nur noch mangels einer besseren Alternative am Leben erhalten wird. [...] In der Konsequenz werden subkulturelle Klassenidentitäten und -bindungen ausgedünnt oder aufgelöst. Gleichzeitig wird ein Prozess der Individualisierung und Divrsifizierung von Lebenslagen und Lebensstilen in Gang gesetzt, der da Hierarchiemodell sozialer Klassen und Schichten unterläuft und in seinem Wirklichkeitsgehalt in Frage stellt[2] (Beck 1986: 121).

Today, inequalities are increasingly perceived on a horizontal level where new allocation criteria are diversifying living circumstances: gender, age, religion, family background, generation affiliation among much else. Traditional social frameworks are becoming less and less important, and cultural cohesive forces are in the process of dissolving. Society seems fragmented into the most diverse milieus, which, due to their opposing lifestyles, seem to coexist side by side rather than with each other.

Little wonder then that, ever since Jürgen Habermas labelled Germany's social structure in the middle of the 1980s as a *"Neue Unübersichtlichkeit"*[3] (Habermas 1985), a totally new approach to classifying and analysing social-structural variety has unfurled in the field of sociology with the rise of the analysis of social milieus and lifestyle groups. As opposed to the traditional strata or position models, these cultural-sociological research approaches take as a starting point a detailed description of the social values, attitudes, behaviour, patterns of interaction and educational resources of social individuals.

Due to the diversity of preferences in terms of aesthetics of everyday life, the composite milieus and lifestyles formed from the different cultural patterns show themselves to be extremely heterogeneous. In particular the milieu analyses presented by Gerhard Schulze, in a sense exemplary for a certain approach of lifestyle research, emphasise the socio-psychological triggers for processes of group formation and identity constructions, while less importance is attached to the objective social positions. Many sociologists consequently hold the view that present-day Western European society can no longer be referred to as a 'stratified' society because it represents a form of community building that is no longer bound to classical vertical strata. The milieu, which has become a core element of this

---

2 | Personal translation: "Even though old inequalities continue to survive and new ones form, today, in the Federal Republic, we are already living in conditions that are beyond a class society, where the image of class society is only preserved for lack of a better alternative. [...] As a consequence, subcultural class identities and class ties are either diluted or dissolved. At the same time, a process of individualisation and diversification of life circumstances and styles is set in motion that undercuts the hierarchical model of social class and stratification and questions its reality content".

3 | Personal translation: "New Complexity".

newly-formed social community, also performs, as a kind of mould for present day efforts to establish individuality, significant integrative functions (see Meyer 2001: 258).

Milieus are made up of groups of individuals that distinguish themselves from other groups by their specific outlook on life and the world as well as by an elevated degree of intra-group communication. They are also always the result of collective social typecasting that determines the way other people are socially perceived, classified and selected for interaction. Partners we relate to in everyday life are chosen on the basis of similarity whereby selection and socialisation effects overlap. The resulting milieus that continue to be reproduced and further differentiated establish mentalities and patterns of cultural orientation. It is therefore possible, by applying the concept of milieu as a heuristic tool as it were, to assign to every milieu specific attributes profiles, mentalities and cultural orientations of its members.

Milieus in the 'Experience Society'. Gerhard Schulze's Approach

Even though authorities such as God, Nature, History and Reason that have traditionally given meaning and orientation to our lives have clearly lost ground in modern society, intuition, against better philosophical knowledge, continues to stubbornly cling to the notion of a pre-ordained order. Admittedly, this state can also be appreciated as a form of new autonomy, which is, however, continuously threatened by collapse due to an overload of the demands for reflection. This is so because a decreased obligation for orientation is accompanied by the awareness that identity concepts are fragile constructions. Reality, which is marked by ever more hectically fluctuating signals, forces the individual to make constant orientation efforts in order to provide the necessary self-assurance of her or his own position. Meanwhile, however, we have reached a stage in history where holding on to illusions of security is out of all proportion to the economic and psychological costs that need to be incurred to maintaining them. However, when external orientation mechanisms become obsolete, these need to be produced internally. There is a change in thinking, from the outside inwards, towards a "*Verschiebung des Brennpunkts der Zieldefinition*"[4] (Schulze 1994: 108). In his relevant study, entitled "*Die Erlebnisgesellschaft*"[5] Gerhard Schulze elaborates:

Außenorientierte Lebensauffassungen zielen primär auf eine Wirklichkeit ab, die sich der Mensch außerhalb seiner selbst vorstellt, innengerichtete Lebensauffassungen verweisen auf das Subjekt[6] (Schulze 2000: 37).

---

4 | Personal translation: "Shift in the focus of the definition of objectives and goals".
5 | Personal translation: "The Experience Society".
6 | Personal translation: "Externally orientated attitudes towards life primarily aim for a reality that man imagines outside his own self, while internally oriented attitudes refer to the subject".

But in what way does a shift to a primarily internally oriented attitude towards life actually provide orientation and what are the conditions for this change to take place? Orientation can essentially be regarded as a movement of repetition, which connects subjective processes with extra-subjective events in a similar fashion. Situations become controllable by the fact that basic patterns, once recognised, can be applied. Orientation thus appears as a form of subjective attribution of meaning in situative contexts, which requires less effort the less variable the situations and contexts are. Schulze clarifies the shift to a primarily internally oriented outlook on life by introducing the notion of the sphere of products. In the social environment products appear under the aspect of consumption, in the sciences under the aspect of the development of theories and in business organisations under the aspect of corporate survival. (Clearly, what we are basically dealing with here are materialist categories: In an ingenious inversion via the product category the reification of the world of commodities is no longer seen as a context of delusion but rather as a reference point for orientation[7]). The fact that products, as a common and comprehensive theme of quite disparate systems of thought, hold such an attraction is due to their incentive for orientation which they provide in a particularly high degree as a material focus for socially organised thinking because they incorporate a merging of both objective and subjective elements. While they are the result of action, and in this sense an expression of subjectivity, they also have a material quality that allows them to be used as a reference point for inter-subjective discourses and collective orientation efforts (see Schulze 1994: 100). By their common orientation towards the product sphere, the different systems of thought themselves interlock like cogs of a clockwork and mutually stabilise each other. The sequences of historical events can in this way be interpreted as a comprehensive context of the history of products, consumption, technology and science, within which, in spite of everything being in constant change and flux, nobody becomes disorientated because transformation takes place in an orderly manner.

One main reason that this clockwork model no longer works is the increase in the amount of the products themselves. For, precariously, in a reality that has formed according to a linear time model, the history of the products too requires a teleological orientation; it has to be able to be conceived as a history of progress. Progress, in this sense, can be both quantitative and qualitative, bearing in mind that, when it comes to actual consumer goods, the potential for innovation is often rapidly exhausted. In other words, when needs are fulfilled, the self-evidence of definitions of usefulness is gradually lost. This generates a problem, at first glance totally absurd, which consists in 'constructing' purposes for products. The world of products has, however, meanwhile evolved to such a degree that barely any niches remain for new definitions of usefulness.

---

7 | An idea that has already been formulated by Hannah Arendt: "Fabrication, the work of homo faber, as he builds the world, consists in reification" (Arendt 1997: 165).

Die Produktentwickler sind aus der ursprünglichen anthropologischen Bodenhaftung entlassen und müssen ihre Konstruktionen ins Vakuum der Unbestimmtheit hineinbauen; man braucht keine Praktiker mehr, sondern Phantasten[8] (Schulze 1994: 104).

For the consumer this means that decisions for one product or another are not made at the level of primary usefulness, which is assumed as a given. Consequently, traditional index categories coupled to the product sphere like usefulness, quality and wealth, lose their orientational function.

It is precisely at this point where the shift from an externally oriented outlook on life to an internally oriented one comes into play. If the usefulness of an object, which can be protected by means of possession (external orientation), is no longer the issue, the focus shifts to the experience the object triggers in the consumer (internal orientation). This is how Schulze arrives at his definition of internal orientation as an experience orientation, establishing the succinct formula: *"Das Projekt des schönen Lebens ist das Projekt, etwas zu erleben"*[9] (Schulze 2000: 38). In view of a vast and unmanageable supply of experience options this project requires constant and consistent navigation. In a way, man becomes the manager of his own subjectivity, by instrumentalising situations for experience purposes and systematising them by means of a rationality of experience (Schulze 2000: 40). This has led to the emergence of a new basic pattern in the relationship between subject and situation since situations are no longer addressed in the mode of an essential lack (money, property, education etc.) which provides orientation and would set natural limits to the scope for action. Hence, the externally oriented categories of usefulness, quality and wealth were applied to an internally oriented reference framework, with 'having' being replaced by 'being'. In other words, what we are dealing with here is a consistent *"Ästhetisierung des Alltagslebens"*[10].

The problem here is that any kind of experience can only be appreciated after prior reflection. *"Reflexion ist der Versuch des Subjekts, seiner selbst habhaft zu werden"*[11] (Schulze 2000: 45). This act of successful self-reflection, however, can only be manipulated to a certain extent, which means that progress of experience is by no means guaranteed in the long term.

Wir können nicht unbegrenzt gewünschte Formen des Seins anhäufen. In reicher Zahl hält die soziale Wirklichkeit Beispiele sowohl für den Versuch der Erlebnisvermehrung als auch

---

8 | Personal translation: "The product developers have been relieved from their anthropological adhesion and are now obliged to build their constructions into the vacuum of indeterminacy; what is needed now are not practicians but utopists".

9 | Personal translation: "The project of a beautiful life is the project of experiencing something".

10 | Personal translation: "Aesthetisation of everyday life".

11 | Personal translation: "Reflection is the subject's attempt to gain possession of her/himself".

für das Scheitern dieses Versuchs bereit: zwischen Dutzenden von Programmen springende Telekonsumenten; angestrengte Urlauber in ununterbrochener Erlebnisarbeit; Trends zur Verkürzung und zeitlichen Überlagerung von Erlebnisepisoden; Museumsbesucher, die vor lauter Bildern nichts mehr sehen; Schränke voller unbenutzter Kleider und Schuhe, Regale voller ungelesener Bücher; wechselnde Partnerschaften mit wenig Tiefe; gutes Essen in Menge mit wenig Genuß; pausenlose Musik, ohne daß man noch mehr wahrnehmen würde als ein Geräusch[12] (Schulze 1994: 116).

To believe that *wealth* of experience can be increased by the *quantity* of experience is a fallacy. Exactly the opposite is the case. Experiences develop only in processes of reflection. However, for these to be able to take place, an extremely scarce resource is required: Time! If the systematic aesthetisation of everyday life has to be conceived as a surfeit of medially produced and designed space, then this is contrasted by a lack of available time. This is due to the fact that time is no longer a bearer of meaning for the present. It can only be comprehended under the aspect of limitation or restriction which restrictively stands in the way of an ever more greedily progressing accumulation of experiences. The logical consequence of a multiplication of experiences is ultimately an insufficient reflection of the individual experiences that therefore can no longer unfold their true wealth and depth. Driven by the longing for a wealth of experience, the experience opportunities are multiplied at an ever faster and frantic rate. The goal is to achieve an increase of being by an increase of having. It is precisely this tendency that leads to a poverty of experience. The failure of the project of experiencing life as a series of happy episodes will necessarily lead to insecurity and disappointment, a finding shared by many perceptive observers of the modern age. From a philosophical point of view one could draw the paradoxical conclusion that we are feeling so bad because we are doing far too well. Indeed, in times of material hardship, perhaps even in life-threatening conditions, goals, perspectives and fulfilment all come naturally. In such circumstances people seem to have at their disposal an ingrained integrative element that provides identity, which results from the gap between unmet needs and the objective life situation. In today's affluent society, however, it is next to impossible to formulate an urgent need arising from a situation of hardship and distress. For despite all sense of crisis life in our society is ultimately taken for

---

12 | Personal translation: "We cannot indefinitely accumulate desired forms of being. Social reality provides ample examples of attempts to multiply experiences as well as of failures of such attempts: television consumers surfing between dozens of different channels; holiday-makers stressed-out by nonstop experience activities; trends towards the shortening and temporal overlapping of experience episodes; museum visitors rendered incapable of seeing anything by the multitude of images around them; cupboards full of unused clothes and shoes, shelves heaped with unread books; changing partnerships with little depth; good food consumed in great quantities with little enjoyment; constant music which is perceived as little more than mere noise".

granted, so it is now a matter of "*es so zu verbringen, dass man das Gefühl hat, es lohne sich*"[13] (see Schulze 2000: 60-61). Orientation towards experience is therefore not the desire to *have* something but rather to *be* someone.

Designing permanent and stable projects for the self and one's place in life is, however, rather problematic, because the continuously rising flood of objects, sensory stimuli and stimulating situations impedes a stable allocation of signs and meanings. Against this background social milieus can be understood as stabilising mechanisms since they provide virtually standardised allocation patterns of signs and meanings. At the same time, such allocation patterns have a distinguishing potential, so that social distinction is no longer primarily negotiated on the classical vertical level of society, but above all on the horizontal level to the neighbouring milieus.

Pierre Bourdieu's Social Space Concept

A major point of criticism against the thesis of the dissolution of classical vertical strata is that the change in the structures of social inequality should not be mistaken for their disappearance. The pluralism of the milieus merely conceals the fact, these critics maintain, that these can still be arranged from the bottom up and thus according to class. Even horizontal differentiation is said to leave enough latitude for exclusion mechanisms, which have meanwhile turned into a permanent precarisation of working and living conditions for significant segments of the population, and for some of them have even led to marginalisation. This is precisely in line with the view of Geißler who criticises the 'culturalisation' of classical situations of inequality by means of a primarily lifestyle-oriented social research approach: "*Die Kritik an sozialen Ungerechtigkeiten weicht der Freude über die bunte Vielfalt*"[14] (Geißler 1996: 323). Indeed, particularly in the area of empirical educational research (notably the PISA studies have impressively confirmed this for many European countries) there is still evidence of a class-specific unequal distribution of educational opportunities, despite the established diversity. The key question here is therefore: How can the explanatory power of lifestyle and milieu research be linked with the findings of class and stratification theory and these, in turn, with metatheoretical ideas on the direction of social change?

Exemplary for this approach is Pierre Bourdieu's model of social space that he developed in his pioneering study entitled *La distinction: Critique sociale du jugement* (Bourdieu 1979)[15]. While maintaining the notion of the continued existence of

---

13 | Personal translation: "Spending it in such a way that one has the feeling it is worthwhile".

14 | Personal translation: "Criticism of social injustices yields to the *delight over colourful diversity*".

15 | The study was first published in German as: Die feinen Unterschiede. Kritik der gesellschaftlichen Urteilskraft, Frankfurt/M. 1982.

'objective' class structures, Bourdieu also postulates a systematic connection between class affiliation – together with the concomitant access to economic, cultural and social resources – and the different symbolic manners in which people lead their lives (lifestyles). In this way, his concept of social space not only connects social positions or strata with different cultural practices, but also reveals the discrete classes and class fractions concealed behind these practices. In this manner, cultural practices can be connected as elements of different lifestyles with customary socio-structural analysis categories: Concrete living conditions, also specifically determinable by class, are interpreted as constituents of habitus types, which in turn comprise open or latent patterns of thinking, perception, evaluation and action. With the concept of 'habitus' Bourdieu tries to grasp the totality of the psychological dispositions of people or groups, i.e. their orientations, attitudes and patterns of perception, thought and judgement. Bourdieu writes:

Wer den Habitus einer Person kennt, der spürt oder weiß intuitiv, welches Verhalten dieser Person verwehrt ist. Mit anderen Worten: Der Habitus ist ein System von Grenzen [...]. Deshalb sind für ihn bestimmte Dinge einfach undenkbar, unmöglich; es gibt Sachen, die ihn aufbringen oder schockieren. Aber innerhalb dieser Grenzen ist er durchaus erfinderisch, sind seine Reaktionen keineswegs immer schon im Voraus bekannt[16] (Bourdieu 1992a: 33).

Habitus, therefore, permits or limits cultural practices which are detectable with a set of lifestyle elements: Views and preferences concerning art, music, literature, painting, sport, food, interior design etc. In this way, cultural practices, although products of human action, develop a certain intrinsic logic and manifest themselves in society as elements that create structure. In other words, the general homogenisation of living conditions may open up wide scopes of action for playing with the relationship of being and seeming and for aiming at improving one's position in the social space via lifestyle *stagings*; however, in particular Bourdieu's theory of capital makes clear that every symbolically produced 'simulation' of social conditions is ultimately limited, by the available objective resources.

The question to be asked here would be how the demarcation lines form at vertical as well as horizontal levels and thus determine the topology of social space. Here the different forms of capital which come into play in the respective fields act as construction principles: "*Kapital – in seiner objektivierten Form als materielles Eigentum wie in seiner inkorporierten Form zum Beispiel als kulturelles Kapital [...] stellt*

---

16 | Personal translation: "If one knows the habitus of a person, one senses or knows intuitively to which type of behaviour this particular person does not have access. In other words: Habitus is a system of borders [...]. Therefore, certain things are simply inconceivable for them, are impossible; there are things that upset or shock them. But within these borders, they can be very inventive and their reactions are by no means always predictable".

Verfügungsmacht im Rahmen eines Feldes dar"[17] (Bourdieu 1995: 10). Capital can only unfold this power because not only is it structured differently – as economic, social and cultural capital – but it is also extremely unequally distributed (see Bourdieu 1992b). The overall picture is that of a symbolic system which organises itself according to the logic of differences. These differences are perceived as distinction in terms of differentiation, i.e. the distinction characterising the lifestyle of a class results from its differential relationship with the lifestyles of the other classes. However, distinction in itself does not inevitably imply the deliberate striving for distinction, rather, every act of consumption or, in more general terms, every action is *"sichtbar, gleichviel ob sie vollzogen wurde, um gesehen zu werden, oder nicht"*[18] (Bourdieu 1995: 21).

If one puts the different positions which are defined by the overall volume and the specific profile of capital in relation to each other, numerous agglomerations and cluster formations stand out. Even though these clusters refer to related modes of action, perception and evaluation and indicate a high degree of congruence with the respective lifestyle, they cannot be seen as evidence for actually existing social classes. For while it is true that there is an antagonism between dominating and dominated groups in social power struggles, social classes merely exist in a virtual mode as it were. Bourdieu's model depicts the hierarchically structured social space as the image of a vibrating social organism which is characterised by the endeavour to accumulate capital, the struggle for the power to define and the striving for influence on the exchange rates of the different types of capital – and offers no manner of consolatory framework. Rather, what is generated here is a differentiated spectrum of social affiliations oriented towards the individual types of capital. Using layers corresponding to different social positions or spaces as an analytical tool, it is possible to chart the horizontal and vertical plurality of different social strata and also reconstruct them with the aid of socio-structural data like education, occupation etc. This permits to register, in the space of milieus, practices and objects of symbolic lifestyle which in turn can be assigned to specific social positions.

Michael Vester's Approach

Bourdieu's social space model was adapted in particular by Michael Vester for the Federal Republic of Germany. He considered milieu-specific lifestyles and individualisation tendencies not as something totally new but rather as a

---

[17] | Personal translation: "Capital – in its objective form as material possession as well as in its incorporated form such as cultural capital [...] constitutes power within the scope of a given field".

[18] | Personal translation: "Visible, regardless of whether it was carried out *to be seen*, or not".

reconversion or *"als einen relativen Umbau der Mentalitäten und Milieus"*[19] (Vester et al. 2001: 145). The starting point here too is the assumption of a multidimensional social space which basically constitutes an extension of the older social milieus which either move up or down in the course of their development. Vester's primary concern is the analysis of the 'direction of modification' of current paths of development of social milieus that are commonly paraphrased with the terms tertiarisation, knowledge-based society, postmaterialism or value shift. His basic thesis here is that, while tendencies towards individualisation and diversification of life circumstances undoubtedly exist, these tendencies have not led to an overall dissolution of the structural characteristics of the 'old' class society, but rather to a vertical and horizontal pluralisation. Following Bourdieu's concept of social space and habitus visible therein, Vester first of all analyses identities of large social groups against this background. According to this approach, people continue to develop their group identities along four vertical affiliation profiles, each with its specific forms of habitus, which in turn consist of different 'stratified' horizontal environments. Each of the three levels, however, also displays a horizontal differentiation by the degree of modernisation. Here, specific behavioural standards are anchored in the milieus of large social groups, which refer to specific orientation patterns and mentalities.

Conclusion

Regarding the identification of signs of everyday aesthetics, Schulze's and Vester's milieu analyses in particular demonstrate clear correlations. Both acknowledge, for instance, that while the actual manner of living does occur along the outlined patterns, this is not necessarily a result of the respective life situation and its limitations but to an increasing degree of individual decision-making processes: it is a matter of personal choice with whom one wishes to interact and who should be a model for orientation. In this sense, milieus are made up of groups of individuals which differentiate themselves from others by their specific outlook on life and the world as well as by increased intra-group communication. And they always also originate from collective social classification by which others are socially perceived, classified and selected for interactions. Partners for interaction in everyday life are selected by similarity patterns, whereby selection and socialisation effects overlap.

While Schulze's "experience society" focuses more on psycho-physically motivated orientation patterns than on cultural preferences, Vester's model offers the advantage of also revealing the migration movements within and between the different milieus (and therefore also being able to predict to a limited extent where members of a milieu are striving to). On the one hand, Vester's approach conforms to a requirement going back to Geiger (1932) to combine the systemic and structural level with the level of social positions and mentalities by means of

---

19 | Personal translation: "As a *relative* remodeling of mentalities and milieus".

social-structural analyses. On the other hand, the model is flexible enough to be able to react to possible closures or (class) divisions, thereby enabling a follow-up to the discussions about newly increasing inequalities and (new) forms of social exclusion. In his studies, Vester also and above all takes into account those aspects of socialisation that relate to politics and power.

In this way, Vester's approach not only takes into account the horizontal diversification of life situations and lifestyles but, in addition, is also heuristically able to bring contemporary inequality and social structures into focus. It is for this reason that we have decided to base the following milieu description of Luxembourg's social structure on this approach.

3.2 Profiles of Socio-Cultural Milieus in Luxemburg

The IDENT Survey

The model for the Luxembourg project is a study conducted under the direction of the social scientist Michael Vester et al. in the Federal Republic of Germany, with the title *Soziale Milieus im gesellschaftlichen Strukturwandel. Zwischen Integration und Ausgrenzung*. It was first published in 1993 and is meanwhile considered a 'classic' of empirical social research of recent years. However, we did not base our work on this original version of the study, but on a comprehensively revised, expanded and updated one (see Vester et al. 2001). In Vester's study – as was already shown in detail in Section 3.1 – a new empirical-theoretical concept was applied which takes into account the rapid pressure for change in modern societies. This concept was put to the test by applying it to German society, so that the study can itself be interpreted as a 'snapshot' of conditions in Germany. The method of analysis, which is based on a close connection of structural change and mentality change, can in principal also be applied to other 'Western' societies.

Michael Vester assisted the project members in an advisory capacity in their task of transferring, re-editing and adapting the fundamentals and results of this study for the particular situation in Luxembourg. Daniel Gardemin, member of the working group "Interdisciplinary Social Structure Research" (agis) of the University of Hannover, carried out the statistical evaluations.

The original questionnaire (Vester et al. 2001: 222-243 and 546-557), which was condensed and partially adapted (see box 1) for the specific conditions in Luxembourg, formed the starting point of our empirical survey.

77 individual statements allowed us to map four different levels of daily life and socio-political orientations:

- Basic attitudes to different aspects of everyday life (habitus, mentality types);
- Social cohesion and styles of association;
- Basic attitudes to the social and political order as well as customs of association;
- Political participation and political styles.

Habitus (Mentality types) (31 Questions)
Factor 1: Rebellious or idealistic hedonism
Factor 2: Realistic hedonism
Factor 3: Underdog frustration
Factor 4: Authoritarian performance ideology
Factor 5: Modern performance optimism
Factor 6: Cultural-pessimistic critique of progress
Factor 7: Sophisticated self-fulfilment
Factor 8: Pseudo-conformism
Factor 9: Consumer hedonism
Factor 10: Convenient arrangement

Social cohesion and styles of association (10 questions)
Factor 1: Orientation towards emotional experience
Factor 2: Conventional reserved centering on family
Factor 3: Sophisticated, externally oriented communication

Basic attitudes towards free time and styles of association (20 questions)
Factor 1: Peer Group
Factor 2: Political public
Factor 3: Cultural public
Factor 4: Individual leisure activities

Political participation and political styles (16 questions)
Factor 1: Island syndrome
Factor 2: Performance ideology
Factor 3: Political disappointment
Factor 4: Employee orientation
Factor 5: Political involvement

Box 1: Synopsis of the milieu questionnaire.

The second part of the survey describes the objective social positions. For this, we queried the usual socio-demographic variables such as household and family status, gender, age, place of residence and religion, sources of livelihood and monthly net income. In addition, there were questions about the highest educational attainment, present or last practiced profession, nature of professional activity, union membership and voting behaviour. Social environment and social development are described by indicators relating to the social status of the parents and the partner (occupation, educational attainment).

Taking into consideration the special multicultural and multilingual circumstances of Luxembourg, further questions were added to the original set of questions, concerning nationality (or nationalities), migration history and linguistic competence.

This milieu study, in the strict sense of the word, was supplemented by further topical areas, in order to cover and statistically record specific partial aspects that will be outlined in greater detail in chapters 4-7: Gender questions, consumer habits, perception of space and borders as well as linguistic-political questions (see box 2).

Consumer habits (31 questions)
Eating and drinking
Shopping
Advertising
Campaign "Healthy eating"

Gender aspects (24 questions)
Gender roles

Language use in Luxembourg (12 questions)

Perception of regions and neighbouring countries (12 questions)

Miscellaneous (9 questions)
Living together
Cross-border workers
Visions for the future etc.

Box 2: Supplementary thematic areas of the quantitative survey.

1,579 people of 16 years and older were interviewed in the period between October 2008 and February 2009 by a Luxembourg polling institute[20]. The random survey is representative for the resident population of Luxembourg and was weighted by age, gender, region, nationality and participation in professional life (as a dichotomous variable).

---

20 | Two thirds of the interviews were carried out via Internet (computer-assisted web interview) and one third by telephone (computer-assisted telephone interview).

The Milieu Study

With a multivariate discriminant analysis, it is possible to constitute different sociocultural milieus[21]. The milieu map in illustration 1 shows the spatial arrangement of nine milieus and their positioning in a two-dimensional space: the vertical axis corresponds to a rising degree of social power, while the horizontal axis shows a differentiation of economic hierarchisation to express the pluralisation of class society.

While milieus in Vester et al. (2001: 48-54) are shown as bold-framed rectangles, we preferred to represent them as partially overlapping coloured clouds with diffuse borders in order to emphasise that milieu affiliation cannot be conclusively determined in individual cases.

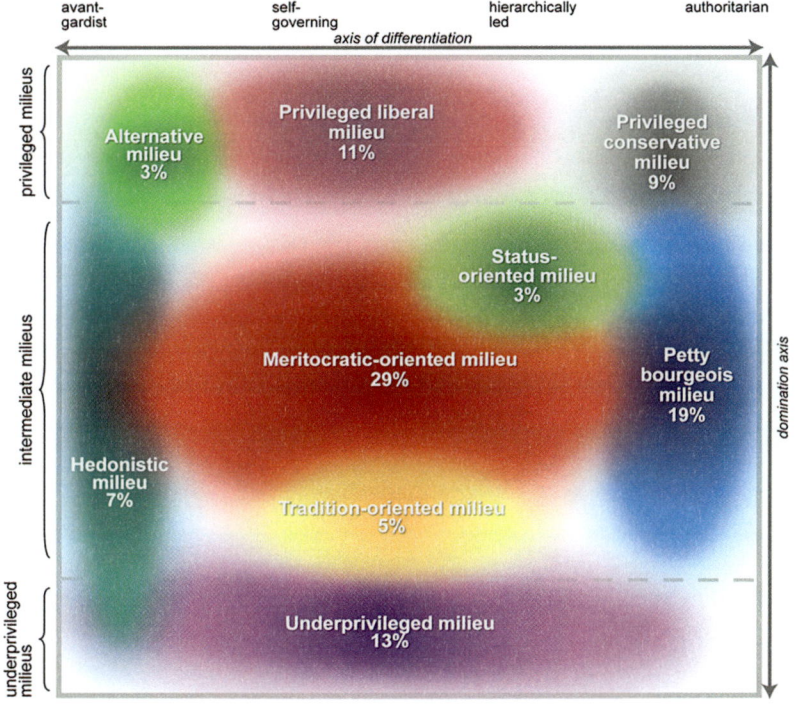

Figure 1: Socio-cultural milieus in Luxembourg (socio-spatial differentiation), Concept: IDENT with the collaboration of Marie-Line Glaesener.

---

21 | "The discriminant analysis is a multivariate procedure for analysing group differences" (Backhaus et al. 2008: 156). It is one of several kinds of classification procedures and makes it possible to assign objects with similar features to one class (see Backhaus et al. 2008: 155-228). For details about this method and also for the cartography of milieus see Vester et al. (2001).

The expansion of the clouds does not correspond to the proportion of the population assigned to them but to the social-spatial dispersion of positions of the individuals that can be respectively assigned to them. The percentages expressing the relative size of the milieus are roughly outlined in Fig. 2.

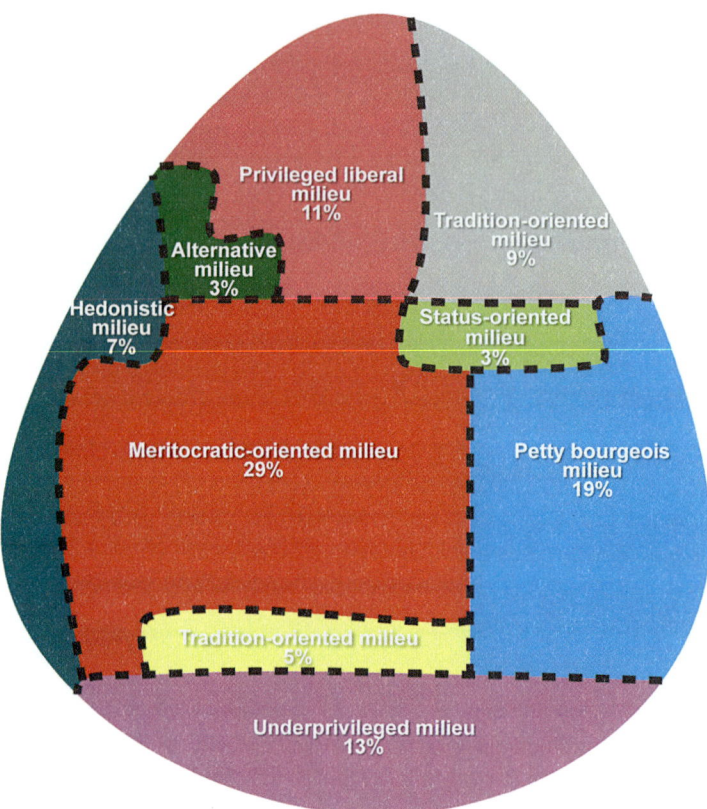

Figure 2: Socio-cultural milieus in Luxembourg (proportion in %), Concept: IDENT with the collaboration of Marie-Line Glaesener.

Milieu Profiles

The following nine milieu sketches, based on Vester's typology (Vester 2001: 503-525), respectively outline the social position, the lifestyle, and the political style of the respective milieu on the basis of a total of 31 statements on different aspects of everyday life (see box 1 above). In these descriptions, the respective significant divergences (e.g. 'strongly under-represented', 'strongly over-represented') from the average values of all milieus are particularly emphasised.

Meritocratic-oriented Milieu (29 %)

Social position: Nearly one third of Luxembourg's resident population belongs to this large milieu, which is also broadly distributed in spatial terms and, in a certain sense, represents the 'centre' of society. It is, therefore, no surprise that we find here a broad distribution of income, with the lower as well as the upper income brackets being somewhat under-represented. 40 % of executive employees belong to this milieu. Here, we also find an especially high percentage of students. 17 % are pensioners. The level of educational attainment basically corresponds to the average profile, only the proportion of persons who indicate *"diplôme de fin d'études secondaires"*[22] as the highest obtained educational certificate is greater.

Lifestyle: In this milieu, modern performance optimism plays an even more dominant role than in the status-oriented milieu. There is considerable confidence in one's own efficiency and the same efforts are also expected from others. The degree of identification with one's occupation is very high and this is also the place where self-fulfilment primarily takes place, while the family does not serve as a personal space for retreat. There is a willingness to reward oneself with material acquisitions because one feels one has earned it, real estate, however, is not a predominant concern. One is in agreement with the state and open to social progress. Critical social commitment is not considered to be necessary and there is no particular appreciation for cultural capital. There is apparently no need to emphasise middle-class virtues, since the accompanying deontological ethics seem to have been internalised naturally.

Political style: In this milieu, the ecological party only has half the approval ratings it enjoys in the overall population, while DP and LSAP are doing better here[23].

Petty bourgeois Milieu (19 %)

Social position: Together with the privileged conservative milieu, the petty bourgeois milieu represents the milieu of the older generation. Even though the average age is lower by six years than in the privileged conservative milieu, both differ from the seven others, which are on average substantially younger. 24 % of the members of the petty bourgeois milieu are pensioners. In no other milieu do the gender affiliations differ as strongly as here: the female proportion amounts to 60 %. In this milieu, one finds a wide distribution of income, which corresponds more or less to the average of all milieus. However, a considerable number of interviewees did not provide information on their income. All levels of educational attainment

---

22 | A secondary school degree roughly equivalent to the English A-Levels.
23 | Luxembourg political parties and their political orientation: ADR: Alternativ Demokratesch Reformpartei (right-wing populist); CSV: Chrëschtlech Sozial Vollekspartei (Christian Democratic); DP: Demokratesch Partei (liberal); Déi Gréng (ecological, green); Déi Lénk (socialist, left-wing); KPL: Kommunistesch Partei Lëtzebuerg (communist); LSAP: Lëtzebuerger Sozialistesch Arbechterpartei (social democrat).

are represented, advanced levels, however, less and lower levels to a higher degree than in the total random sample. The petty bourgeois milieu is represented above average in the south of the country and least in the capital.

Lifestyle: In the petty bourgeois milieu, a distinctive mentality of fulfilment of duties prevails, which can be understood as an expression of a willingness to adapt to existing circumstances. Important here for the inner cohesion of the milieu seem to be such factors as the traditional role allocation within the family as well as Christian values, both of which go hand in hand with the rejection of a modern lifestyle. The rejection of hedonistic ideas indicates an abstention from self-fulfilment (in contrast, for instance, to the underprivileged milieu) in favour of the assimilation into a given social (job) hierarchy. In this context, the acquisition of cultural capital seems to be regarded as something of little value, there is no interest for art and culture. The powerful inclination to ensure material security causes the deferment of personal, spontaneous needs. This also includes the willingness to forgo enjoyment of life in favour of property ownership. A conformist attitude towards government and the state is the rule. Generally, it is considered more important to take one's place in society than to seek advancement by personal achievement. Fears of social decline seem, for the moment, allayed. An indication of a certain degree of confidence here is the fact that the working day is experienced without any marked tendency for frustration.

Political style: CSV voters are represented above average in this milieu, although not as much as in the privileged conservative milieu. DP voters are also less numerous here, while the Greens achieve good results. The main difference to the privileged conservative milieu, however, is the stronger position of the socialist party.

Underprivileged Milieu (13 %)

Social position: With 60 % the underprivileged milieu is the milieu with the highest percentage of foreigners, of which the Portuguese make up more than half. Nearly 40 % of the unskilled workers and 30 % of the skilled workers are found in this milieu. Office employees, of which at least one fifth are found in this milieu, are also over-represented here. In the underprivileged milieu, which is a little younger than the average, the 20 to 45-year-olds are especially strongly represented. There are 13 % pensioners. The level of income is accordingly low. In the underprivileged milieu, the level of formal educational is the lowest of all the milieus: nearly three times more people than for the overall random sample state elementary school as the highest educational attainment. As is the case with the tradition-oriented milieu, the underprivileged milieu is most prominent in the north of the country.

Lifestyle: As in the tradition-oriented milieu, a sense of frustration at the workplace constitutes a kind of general mood in the underprivileged milieu. One feels strongly bound into the working hierarchy. Work ethics continue to be held in high regard. In general, one has abandoned any prospects for professional advancement yet one still participates in the authoritarian performance ideology by clearly disassociating oneself from those 'below'. Self-fulfilment tends to takes place during free time, with the family still offering a certain degree of support, although there is apparently no longer any willingness to give one's all for them. The explicit commitment to hedonism is a typical feature. The ethics of modesty still prevailing in the petty bourgeois and the tradition-oriented milieu have been abandoned. Security thinking or the readiness for short-term restraint in favour of long-term commitments, such as for property ownership, is absent. By contrast, there is a distinct willingness for spontaneous consumption, which apparently also induces discontent about one's own material situation. A certain ideational counterbalance is provided by a clearly sceptical attitude towards technical progress as well as the high esteem held for political and social commitment. This is undoubtedly also a reflection of the high level of unionisation recorded in this milieu.

Political style: If one considers only the Luxembourgers, the underprivileged milieu is the milieu of political disaffection. One third of the survey responders declined to answer the question on party preference.

Privileged Liberal Milieu (11 %)

Social position: Even though the distribution of income covers the entire range of the spectrum, the upper middle and top income brackets are particularly well represented, so that the average income of this milieu takes third place behind the two wealthiest milieus, the status-oriented and the privileged conservative milieu. Teachers are twice as numerous in this milieu than in the overall population and executive employees are also over-proportionally represented. As in the petty bourgeois and in the tradition-oriented milieu, the share of women is exceptionally prominent here, and with 58.1 % is the second highest of all milieus. The level of formal education is very high. Here, in comparison to all other milieus, one finds the lowest number of instances where elementary school is given as the only educational attainment. In contrast to the privileged conservative milieu, which also has high educational attainment levels, polytechnic degrees are more numerous here than university degrees. Like the privileged conservative milieu, the privileged liberal milieu is to be found less frequently in the south of the country.

Lifestyle: The privileged liberal milieu draws its self-confidence from a strong achievement motivation and high work ethics. However, neither manifest themselves in an achievement ideology, since apparently there is no corresponding sense of mission directed towards society. In this respect, but also in the rejection of traditional bourgeois virtues, the privileged liberal milieu delineates itself from more conservatively oriented milieus (privileged conservative, petty bourgeois and underprivileged milieu) and displays similarities with the new employees (status-oriented milieu). The concentration on one's own efficiency has a level-headed, realistic quality to it, disruptions in one's professional life are regarded as a likely possibility. One prefers to keep one's distance to the state, while the family forms a protective private space, and here the traditional gender role allocation is explicitly considered outdated. With a secure material base, there is little proclivity towards consumption. Notable is the pronounced affinity and dedication to culture and art, as is the readiness to enlarge one's cultural capital, a feature otherwise found only in the privileged conservative and alternative milieus.

Political style: In this milieu, the Greens receive two-and-a-half times as many votes than average. The CSV is significantly under-represented.

Privileged Conservative Milieu (9 %)

Social position: Persons belonging to the privileged conservative milieu are consistently older than the overall population, with an average age of 10 years above that of the population as a whole. 39 % of people in this milieu are retired, while in the overall population it is 19 %. 42 % of the privileged conservative milieu are older than 60 and considering only the Luxembourgers belonging to this milieu, the figure stands at a remarkable 57 %. In terms of average salary, the privileged conservative milieu takes first place among all the milieus. Particularly strongly represented are the income brackets above € 9,000. It is followed closely by the status-oriented milieu as well as the privileged liberal milieu, and together they form an income peak ranking far above all other milieus. The privileged conservative milieu has the highest number of university graduates. It is particularly frequent in the centre of the country, more precisely in the capital, whereas it is represented below average in the south of the country.

Lifestyle: In the privileged conservative milieu, restraint and avoidance of excessive self-expression manifests itself indirectly in the consistent, firm rejection of the different forms of hedonism (ideational as well as actual). The marked personal willingness to perform is an expression of an attitude of inner fulfilment of duties, professional success is based on a pronounced work ethic which seems to generate a quasi natural self-confidence. The basis for this is the orientation towards long-established structures, although the traditional role allocation within the family, indeed the family as a protected space, is not (or no longer) particularly emphasised (which might be due to the large number of retirees). The privileged conservative milieu is sympathetic to technical progress and expressly regards itself as a pillar of the state. Social representability is considered important, prestige is relevant. Self-fulfilment is achieved via one's work, but primarily in the upper cultural sector, the latter forming a counterweight to the allure of material consumerism, which is considered superficial. Material security seems to be taken for granted, even though there is a sense that it also needs to be preserved and increased, as the distinct readiness to forgo certain amenities for the sake of property possession clearly shows.

Political style: This milieu may well and truly be called conservative. Here, the CSV has almost twice as many voters as in the population as a whole. There is also a slight over-representation of the ADR. It is surprising that the liberals, at least when it comes to main party preference, are in the minority. Nevertheless, the LSAP enjoys even less support in this milieu.

Hedonistic Milieu (7 %)

Social position: The hedonistic milieu is a young milieu with a high percentage of 30-year-olds and an even higher one of 20-year-olds, with an income which lies only slightly above average. Corresponding to this age structure, the proportion of retirees is only 14 %. The civil service is well represented, however, mainly by middle level civil servants. The members of the hedonistic milieu correspond to a large extent to the average educational profile. University graduates are less strongly represented but there is a higher than average share of "diplôme de fin d'études secondaires" graduates[24]. Of all the milieus, the hedonistic milieu is spatially least represented in the north of the country. The proportion of single households, as well as that of childless couples, is highest in this milieu. Even though the legally regulated civil partnership (PACS, i.e. pacte civil de solidarité) still constitutes a marginal problem (1.5 % for all interviewees), civil partnerships are more than twice as frequent in this milieu.

Lifestyle: The appreciation for material as well as ideational hedonism, and therefore also self-fulfilment via leisure activities and consumption has a secure economic base in this milieu which is not further questioned. Thus, the readiness to engage in spontaneous consumption does not go hand in hand, as it does in other milieus, with a discontent concerning financial possibilities, which points to a sophisticated milieu of origin. Work is a means to an end, professional success is considered unimportant, critical involvement in social issues is rejected, elitist culture is not an essential factor. The clear dismissal of Christian values could be aimed directly against these ideational values that unify the privileged conservative milieu and petty bourgeois milieu from which the generation of the hedonistic milieu seems to have originated. The tendency to identify with attitudes expressing frustration can probably be explained with the impending confrontation with possible performance demands (conflicts with the parental generation). The most remarkable feature is perhaps that in the hedonistic milieu one generally presents oneself as supportive of the state. Here, it seems, basic attitudes of the milieu of origin are reproduced and shared primarily as a result of materialistic rationale. The advantages of state support are presumably also taken into account here, in order to be able to maintain the existing lifestyle for as long as possible.

Political style: There is a slightly higher proportion of LSAP voters, CSV and the Greens are slightly under-represented.

Tradition-oriented Milieu (5 %)

Social position: In this milieu, with its many blue-collar workers and low-ranking employees, salary levels are low. But there is no reticence about admitting this, maybe also because one lives in clear-cut conditions of wage-dependency. Thus, there is hardly any evidence of miniscule wages here, since there seem to be no part-time jobs or precarious working conditions. This is the milieu with the highest

---

24 | A secondary school degree roughly equivalent to the English A-Levels.

percentage of persons on disability pensions and unemployment benefits. Retirees amount to 17 %. With 57.9 %, the proportion of women is particularly high in the tradition-oriented milieu. As in the petty bourgeois milieu, the whole range of educational attainment levels is represented here, the higher degrees, however, less and the lower ones more frequently than in the overall random sample. In terms of spatial distribution, the tradition-oriented milieu is more predominant in the north of the country.

Lifestyle: In contrast to the petty bourgeois milieu, the tradition-oriented milieu is characterised by a clearly more pessimistic basic attitude. Material security is assigned a high value, consumption decisions are made according to the available possibilities and there is a sense of discontent with one's own situation. Frustration levels in working life are high. One feels exploited, hemmed in by rigid hierarchies, and there is little to no prospect of being able to secure the future by one's own efforts. This assessment of one's personal situation comes with a rejection of technical progress, the concerns about the future found within this milieu are considered as a reflection of society's general development. Disappointment leads people to take a reserved stance towards the state, no value is attached to social prestige. Participation in cultural life is considered pointless. As in the petty bourgeois milieu, bourgeois virtues continue to be valued and the traditional role allocation within the family is still very pronounced. But contrary to the petty bourgeois milieu, Christian values no longer constitute a common ground to be particularly emphasised.

Political style: This milieu is a veritable ADR stronghold. The sympathies for this party are at the expense of the CSV for which voting preference in this milieu is slashed almost by half compared to the average, while the LSAP obtains a proportion marginally above its overall result. However, the number of survey responders who were undecided or declined to furnish information is especially high.

Status-oriented Milieu (3 %)

Social position: Solely in terms of income average, the status-oriented milieu takes second place among all milieus discussed here, preceded only by the privileged conservative milieu. In both of them 8 % of interviewees, by no means an insubstantial figure, indicated a monthly salary of more than € 10,000. Together with the privileged liberal milieu, these two milieus form a group at the top, leaving the other milieus far behind. The status-oriented milieu has the lowest proportion of foreigners (only 17 %) and is the youngest milieu, in which the under 20-year-olds (14 % compared with 7 % overall), therefore also the students, are especially well represented. In contrast to the petty bourgeois milieu, the milieu with the highest percentage of women, the share of males is highest in the status-oriented milieu, with 61.5 %. 12 % are retired (total 19 %). In the status-oriented milieu, public service employees, in particular teachers, are considerably over-represented. There is also a significant number of employees in executive positions. The most frequent educational qualification is the polytechnic degree.

Lifestyle: As in the neighbouring meritocratic-oriented milieu, confidence in one's own achievement potential is very pronounced in this milieu. In the status-oriented milieu, one is willing to engage in continued professional development and to take on responsible tasks. This is, however, no longer associated with an authoritarian achievement ideology and there is a marked tendency towards individualism. Self-fulfilment in the professional field is not pursued doggedly. The approach to duty ethics is a relaxed one. Financial worries are not an issue in this milieu. In the final analysis, the private life takes precedence. Here, traditional family values are considered outdated, and from the similarly clear disassociation from Christian values one can deduce an enlightened attitude towards unconventional ways of life. Optimism about personal achievement is accompanied by a generally optimistic stance towards technical progress, there is, however, a tendency to maintain a critical distance to the state. There is no particular interest or affinity for art and culture, and no willingness to participate in any concrete social commitment. Altogether, compared to the meritocratic-oriented milieu, the status-oriented milieu is more self-confident and more independent of general developments, as well as more realistic and level-headed in the professional field.

Political style: In the status-oriented milieu, one tends to vote for the Greens and LSAP, CSV is particularly under-represented.

Alternative Milieu (3 %)

Social position: Most representatives of the alternative milieu are in working age, and there is exactly the same proportion of women and men. Incomes lie below average. The absence of high income brackets points to a lacking willingness to provide pertinent information (compulsion for anti-materialistic attitudes). The fact that about 30 %, almost as many as in the petty bourgeois milieu, decline to reveal their income, might also be associated with a lack of continuous income. The alternative milieu is an exceptionally educated milieu, in which university graduates and polytechnic graduates are well represented and where practically nobody has only an elementary school level. This milieu is especially predominant in the direct environs of the capital.

Lifestyle: Although the guiding value in this milieu is clearly the criticism of the belief in technological progress, there is no longer the direct association with the possible destruction of livelihood resources. This indication for a dwindling sense of mission (for instance in issues of environmental policy) is confirmed by a shift from self-fulfilment through political and social commitment to self-fulfilment in the field of art and culture. Remarkable in this milieu is the presence of an attitude that is distinctly supportive of the state, as is the case in the hedonistic milieu. Apparently one has come to terms with the prevailing conditions, provided there is sufficient leeway for one's own post-materialistic lifestyle beyond the authoritarian achievement ideology, traditional gender roles and the constraints of work hierarchy. The strong disposition to drop out of society might, in this sense, be little more than lip service or a reminiscence of the milieu's roots in the opposition movement.

Political style: Greens and DP voters are substantially over-represented, CSV strongly under-represented. There is practically no support for ADR and LSAP.

3.3 Final remark

The set of milieus described above provides the general heuristic framework for the following chapters of this publication which elaborate individual aspects on the basis of the milieu analysis. The milieu cartography of Luxembourg's social structure should therefore be read as complementary to the qualitative approaches presented in this volume.

The authors would like to emphasise that the results presented here are *one* possible model for describing the social reality in Luxembourg. In this sense, they should not be mistaken for reality, rather, with a view to the complexity of the social structure in Luxembourg, they constitute an initial, tentative avenue that needs to be developed and consolidated by further in-depth analyses. Moreover, the data gathered so far contain a wealth of additional information still awaiting evaluation.

Finally, readers of this publication should bear in mind that the percentages presented here, and this applies for the results of every sample survey, are by principle always impaired by inaccuracy and consequently should be considered in relative terms only.

3.4 References

Arendt, Hannah. 1997. Vita activa oder Vom tätigen Leben. Munich: Piper.
Backhaus, Klaus et al. 2008. Multivariate Analysemethoden. Eine anwendungsorientierte Einführung. Berlin: Springer.
Beck, Ulrich. 1986. Risikogesellschaft. Auf dem Weg in eine andere Moderne. Frankfurt/M.: Suhrkamp.
Bourdieu, Pierre. 1979. La distinction. Critique sociale du jugement. Paris: Minuit. (published in German in 1982 under the title: Die feinen Unterschiede. Kritik der gesellschaftlichen Urteilskraft. Frankfurt/M.: Suhrkamp.
Bourdieu, Pierre. 1992a. Die feinen Unterschiede. In Bourdieu, Die verborgenen Mechanismen der Macht. Schriften zur Politik & Kultur I, ed. Margareta Steinbrücke, 31-48. Hamburg: VSA-Verlag.
Bourdieu, Pierre. 1992b. Ökonomisches Kapital, kulturelles Kapital, soziales Kapital. In Bourdieu, Die verborgenen Mechanismen der Macht. Schriften zur Politik & Kultur I, ed. Margareta Steinbrücke, 49-79. Hamburg: VSA-Verlag.
Bourdieu, Pierre. 1995. Sozialer Raum und 'Klassen'. Leçon sur la leçon. 2 Vorlesungen. Frankfurt/M.: Suhrkamp.

Geißler, Rainer. 1996. Kein Abschied von Klasse und Schicht. Ideologische Gefahren der deutschen Sozialstrukturanalyse. In Kölner Zeitschrift für Soziologie und Sozialpsychologie 48: 319-338.

Geißler, Rainer. 2002. Die Sozialstruktur Deutschlands. Die gesellschaftliche Entwicklung vor und nach der Vereinigung. Bonn: Westdeutscher Verlag.

Habermas, Jürgen. 1985. Die Neue Unübersichtlichkeit. Frankfurt/M.: Suhrkamp.

Meyer, Thomas. 2001. Das Konzept der Lebensstile in der Sozialstrukturforschung – eine kritische Bilanz. In Soziale Welt 52: 255-272.

Schelsky, Helmut. 1979. Auf der Suche nach Wirklichkeit. Munich: Goldmann.

Schulze, Gerhard. 1994. Gehen ohne Grund. Eine Skizze zur Kulturgeschichte des Denkens. In Philosophische Ansichten der Kultur der Moderne, ed. Andreas Kuhlmann, 79-130. Frankfurt/M.: Fischer.

Schulze, Gerhard. 2000. Die Erlebnisgesellschaft. Kultursoziologie der Gegenwart. Frankfurt/M.: Campus.

Vester, Michael et al. 2001. Soziale Milieus im gesellschaftlichen Strukturwandel. Zwischen Integration und Ausgrenzung. Frankfurt/M.: Suhrkamp.

4. Languages and Identities

PETER GILLES, SEBASTIAN SEELA, HEINZ SIEBURG, MELANIE WAGNER

4.1 INTRODUCTION: GERMANIC/ROMANCE DIGLOSSIA

In Luxembourg, the phenomenon of multilingualism is an aspect of the historically evolved social reality. Since the Middle Ages, Luxembourg's location within the overlapping Germanic and Romance zones of contact and mediation has been reflected in a diglossic situation, characterized by the coexistence of German, or its regional variants, and French. The circumstances of Luxembourg's multilingualism have changed fundamentally several times over the centuries, as a result of various territorial affiliations and shifts. A series of French, Dutch and German takeover attempts were also mirrored in various efforts to enforce linguistic hegemony. These were opposed by the determination of Luxemburg's population not to be absorbed by any one side, thereby preserving the basis of their national sovereignty and identity.

As of the 19th century at the latest, Luxembourgish emerged with increasing vigour as an independent and in the minds of the inhabitants of Luxembourg, their own language with a distinct function in creating identity whereby the close linguistic-genealogical relationship with German ('*lëtzebuerger Däitsch*') was initally stressed. Luxembourgish is based on the West-Moselle-Franconian dialect, which has, however, evolved into a language in its own right, covering nearly all linguistic domains. It has its own standardised orthography and since the Language Act of 1984, it also serves as an official national language of Luxembourg.

Luxembourgish is flanked by the two other official languages included in the Language Act of 1984, namely French and German, so that there is, in effect, a triglossic situation. French is cast in a privileged role being the only recognised language of law (see Gilles/Moulin 2003 on the Language Act). One central objective of this, primarily political, revaluation was to increase the sociolinguistic status of Luxembourgish in relation to French and German (Naglo 2007). Thus far however, this promotion to the status of national language has resulted in very few practical consequences, whether in terms of further standardisation or respecting an increased usage within the educational system, in which it serves merely as an auxiliary language during lessons (Gilles 1999: 9; Kraemer 1993). In fact the language was established politically and legally, as a symbol and expression of national Luxembourgish identity.

Even though the virtues of such legally sanctioned multilingualism are immediately apparent, particularly in light of EU developments and the stated requirement for multilingualism, it does, on the other hand, present the inhabitants of Luxembourg with quite specific challenges, for instance in the field of education.

The situation is further complicated by the fact that, as a country of immigration, Luxembourg is also home to large population groups with further (mother) tongues such as Italian, and, currently to a yet greater extent, Portuguese and in the wake of the redevelopment of the country as an administrative and banking centre, English. In addition, there are the various languages of the former Yugoslavia.

Questions of language, therefore, are of fundamental importance to the social structure of the Grand Duchy, in particular because they must be regarded as important aspects of the identity for the inhabitants of Luxembourg. As such, questions into the country's recent linguistic situation not only suggested themselves as subject matter for the present study, they were in fact a mandatory requirement.

It should not be overlooked that the importance of languages is by no means limited to communication content transfer. Such a mono-functional view fails to recognise the relevance of language as a basic social symbol to which multi-layered social values, over and above its communicative power, are attributed (see Mattheier 1991). At the same time, questions of prestige and stigma demand as much consideration as those relating to self-assertion or even heteronomy. Therefore questions of language are invariably also socio-political questions and, in this respect, they can be just as explosive as controversial. They can be laden with any number of different emotions and value assignments whereby often enough the language is named whereas its speakers are meant.

In Luxembourg too the varying linguistic discourses often reflect deeply rooted emotional states and states of mind, which can manifest themselves in various levels of concern, apprehension or feelings of being under threat, or, expressed offensively, in demarcation, push-back and validity claims. Aspects of identity, whether attributed or appropriated, can almost always be identified as a frame of reference factor.

This is borne out by the case study involving an analysis of letters to editors, undertaken within the framework of the present investigation. As a showcase, these demonstrate that the coexistence of the languages of Luxembourg does not always proceed without conflict. Not least because Luxembourg is an extremely dynamic country, both economically and demographically, the ratio of its national languages – which also depends upon the number and nationality of new citizens and cross-border commuters – is always dependent to some extent on partially candid, partly covert negotiation processes that can certainly evince moments of linguistic competition.

To anticipate a central result, one emergent constant is the Luxembourgers' pronounced loyalty to Luxembourgish, which rather than being just the prescribed national language, has, particularly in recent decades, developed into a major factor in terms of identification and integration. Because of its relatively limited communicative reach – a function of the low number of speakers – Luxembourgish is considered by many speakers as potentially endangered and therefore all the more worthy of support. Not infrequently, as a result, defensive reflexes can come to the fore in respect of the two flanking national languages, French and German, whereby the former is often felt to be too dominant in everyday linguistic practice while the latter, at least in the minds of parts of the older generation, is tainted by the stigma of being the language of occupation.

However, one would present a distorted picture were one to place too much emphasis on the aspect of conflict. For on the other hand, in spite of all the difficulties – this is also apparent from the results of the investigation – the substantial added value of multilingualism should not be overlooked. Multilingualism is not only a prerequisite for the country's prospering economy, towards which foreign workers from different countries of origin have made a substantial contribution, but rather multilingualism, in particular French and German language competence, enables Luxembourgers to access an unobstructed zone of communication of a dimension unavailable to other European countries. As the analysis of the data shows, this is also something of which the Luxembourgers are very conscious. The case study on public signage (Section 4.4) presents a vivid impression of the vibrant and dynamic relationships between Luxembourg's languages. This shows graphically how multilingualism manifests itself in written form.

It should be pointed out again that the question of the connection between language and identity is of particular relevance. It is a commonplace that identities are shaped, validated and modified in the form of linguistic constructs. However, the question as to the nature and manner in which these processes of identity formation develop, turns out to be an extremely complicated research task. In terms of 'national identity' – which should be seen not as a monolithic concept, but rather as a complex cluster of identity negotiation processes[1] which are, in addition, weighted and evaluated differently within society – the existence and acceptance of a national language is crucial (see Joseph 2004). It is still not yet possible to determine conclusively to what extent Luxembourgish had already been established as a broad-based language in the 19th century. However, since the first half of the 20th century at the latest, it can be assumed that Luxembourgish had attained national-symbolic importance for the population as a whole (Gilles/Moulin 2003; Moulin 2006). This development probably reached its zenith with the passing of the Language Act in 1984.

---

1 | See also Section 6.2.

The multi-faceted complex of national identity is, however, by no means exclusively rooted in the Luxembourgish language, multilingualism per se also plays a role, at least for a part of today's population. By contrast with territorial multilingualism, as it exists in Belgium or Switzerland, the idea that multilingualism is self-evidently relevant to everyday life at a profound level is gaining ground in Luxembourg, much more so than was still the case right up into the 1970s. Among younger age groups in particular, this social multilingualism, in which a non-competitive relationship of all the languages concerned is fostered, has become a key element of identity formation.

Of course, in addition, the differentiation between *appropriated* and *attributed* identities is relevant for all aspects of language. For instance, an exemplary competence in the three national languages (or four, if one also includes English, which is playing an increasingly important part) is one of the *attributed* identities, expressed, for instance, in official statements about the structure of society or language lessons in schools. *Appropriated* identity, however, can deviate from this ideal. The resulting tensions between appropriated and attributed identity will become evident in the following analysis of public signage, because linguistic practice on official signs differs substantially from that used on private, non-institutional signs.

This chapter is structured as follows: In Section 4.2, the key results of a representative, quantitative survey are introduced, in which, *inter alia*, the pre-eminent position of Luxembourgish is confirmed. Section 4.3 is devoted to public discourse concerning the linguistic situation, on the basis of a sample analysis of letters to editors, whereby it emerges that the public discourse oscillates between a well-balanced multilingual *status quo* and a forced, occasionally militant emphasising of the relevance of and support for Luxembourgish (at the expense of other languages). And finally, in the third part (Section 4.4), there follows an analysis of multilingualism as manifested on public signage (so-called 'linguistic landscape').

4.2 KEY SURVEY RESULTS CONCERNING THE LINGUISTIC SITUATION

In the following, we will evaluate the results of the representative, quantitative survey, in as far as these questions relate to the linguistic situation in Luxembourg. The aim is to document the *status quo* in respect to some central issues[2]. The presented results can also be understood as an indication of *appropriated* identities where they imply linguistic value judgments. Indirectly, reference is made to

---

2 | See in this context the representative research conducted by Fernand Fehlen: *Une enquête sur un marché linguistique multilingue en profonde mutation. Luxemburgs Sprachenmarkt im Wandel.* Luxemburg 2009.

attributed identities, wherever it is a matter of gathering required language skills and governmental control measures.

First of all, one should bear in mind that all the collected linguistic data are of a subjective nature and therefore come with all the imponderabilities that accompany this type of data.

The collected data comprised primarily data on self-assessment as well as attitudes which we assumed, on the basis of experience and research, would be relevant to the description of the research subject. On the one hand, these included questions that reveal a linguistic ranking order according to different criteria (*competence, usefulness, sympathy* etc.), and on the other also those that, on the basis of approval ratings for certain items ("I have several mother tongues" etc.) allowed us to draw conclusions concerning the linguistic attitudes of Luxembourg's resident population. In addition, questions were asked about the orientation towards neighbouring countries. Arguably, here too one can make inferences about the subjects' linguistic preferences.

The number of languages used in Luxembourg goes far beyond the three "official" ones, named as such in Luxembourg's Language Act of 1984: Luxembourgish, French and German. The study takes this into account by also asking questions about Portuguese, English, Italian and, as a collective category, "other languages". The evaluation and presentation of data will proceed, in principal, along the same lines, while limiting itself to the key findings and disregarding what were considered to be marginal parameters.

Multilingualism as an Added Value

In general, Luxembourgers have an extremely positive attitude towards multilingualism. A very clear majority of the interviewees (95 %) sees an advantage in being able to communicate smoothly with a large number of people thanks to their language skills. Almost all interviewees (95 %) also regard multilingualism as a cultural enrichment. There are no significant differences in regard to the national, age or milieu-related sub-groups.

Required Language Skills

With respect to the three official languages of Luxembourg, the degree of approval was assessed through the statements whether every inhabitant of Luxembourg should be fluent in three, at least two or at least one language (and passive competences in another or others). A relative majority of 43 % was in favour of a medium requirement level (2 languages), with an equal proportion for Luxembourgers and foreigners. The demand that one should be fluent in all three languages (29 %) and/or in only one (27 %), was expressed by an approximately equal proportion of the interviewees.

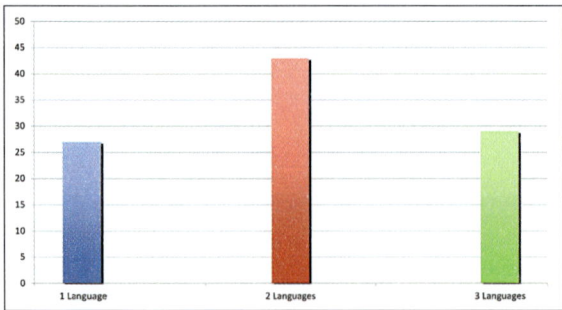

Figure 1: How many of the three national languages should everyone be fluent in?

Postulated Luxembourgish Language Skills

The study reflects a very distinctive loyalty of the interviewees towards the Luxembourgish language. From this we may deduce that the national language is also considered to have an essential significance for social cohesion.

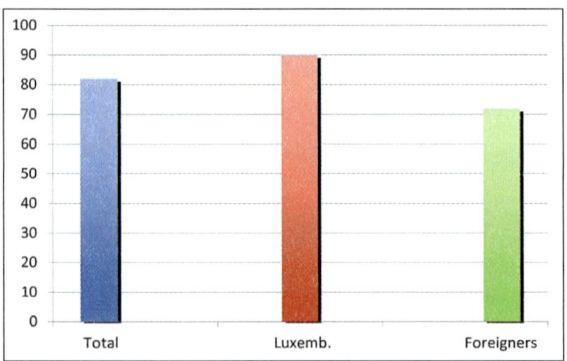

Figure 2: "Everyone should be fluent in Luxembourgish".

This is reflected by the majority opinion (82 %), which supports the demand that all inhabitants of the Grand Duchy should be fluent in Luxembourgish. Differentiated by nationality, approval was, not surprisingly, the highest among Luxembourgers (90 %). But also the overwhelming majority of the foreigners (72 %) agree, in a range between 86 % (Germans) to 63 % (French). Differentiated by milieus and in relation to the entire random sample, the petty bourgeois milieu shows the highest approval rate (86 %), and the privileged liberal milieu the lowest (71 %).

Cross-border commuters are also expected to have at least a passive competence in Luxembourgish. 86 % of the interviewees subscribe to this view, and when graded by age it is the over 60-year-olds that show the highest consent rating (93 %). Distinguished by nationality, the Luxembourgers again score highest (94 %)

followed by the Germans (93 %), while only 73 % of the Portuguese and French respectively approve of the demand that cross-border commuters should least be able to understand Luxembourgish, thereby representing the lowest approval rate.. This is most certainly a reflection of the different systemic distances between Luxembourgish and German, on the one hand, and between Luxembourgish and the Romance languages on the other.

In terms of national affiliation, we can observe certain consistencies in the fact that the approval rate is highest in the petty bourgeois milieu and lowest in the alternative milieu. While there is still a majority of foreign interviewees from the alternative milieu (57 %) demanding passive competence in Luxembourgish for cross-border commuters, a considerable 43 % disagree with this demand.

Language Skills

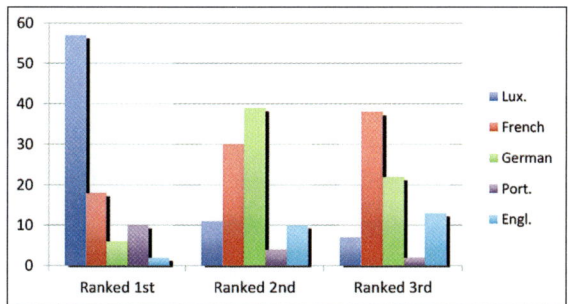

Figure 3: Ranking order of the languages spoken most fluently/overall random sample.

When the interviewees were asked which language they were most fluent in, a majority of 57 % stated Luxembourgish, well ahead of French (18 %), Portuguese (10 %), German (6 %) and English (2 %). When asked which language came second in terms of fluency, a relative majority of 39 % said German (before French with 30 %). As third-ranked language, French collects a relative majority of 38 % (before German, at 22 %).

If we differentiate by national affiliation, the results shown on the chart for Luxembourgers clearly reinforce those in figure 3. 89 % of the interviewees state that they are most fluent in Luxembourgish, while 60 % rank German as their second-best and 54 % French as their third-best language.

In contrast, the linguistic competence of the foreign population is drastically different. Here, Luxembourgish loses its dominant role in favour of French. A relative majority (34 %) names French as the language of greatest fluency, followed by 24 % indicating Portuguese, while Luxembourgish scores a mere 14 %. The second-ranked language in terms of fluency is again French, with a relative majority (32 %), before Luxembourgish (20 %) and German (10 %). English (18 %) occupies the place of the third-ranked language, followed closely by French (17 %), German (16 %) and Luxembourgish (15 %).

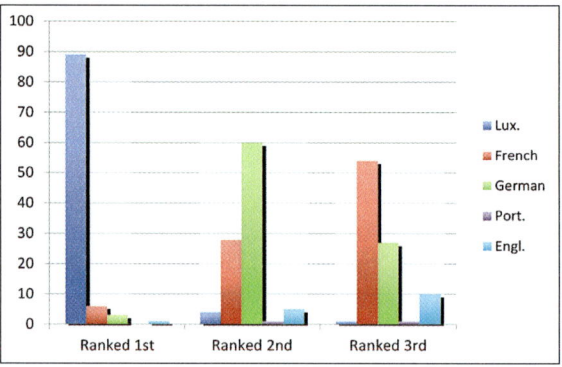

Figure 4: Ranking order of the languages spoken most fluently/Luxembourgers.

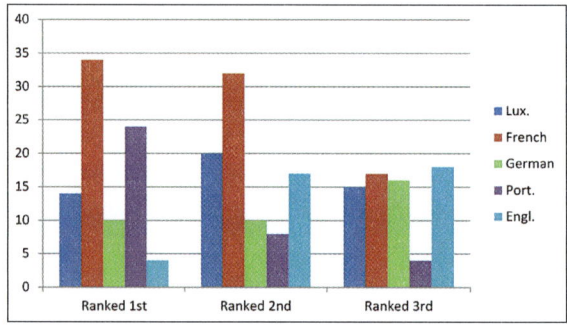

Figure 5: Ranking order of the languages spoken most fluently/foreigners.

All in all, we can therefore observe linguistic orientations that differ significantly between Luxembourgers on the one hand, who show a clear preference for Luxembourgish and for the majority of whom German is their second language in terms of fluency, and foreign residents, on the other. Here, there is a clear preference for French with Portuguese also ranked relatively high. These results coincide with the demographic ratios in the Grand Duchy.

Luxembourgish as a Mother Tongue

The statement "I have several mother tongues" is affirmed by a total of 26 % of the respondents, while 73 % disagree. The affirmation rate of the Luxembourgers is 21 % compared to that of the foreigners with some 33 %, which however reveal a clear spread between 19 % for the Portuguese and 44 % for the Belgians respectively even 55 % for the Italians. The response behaviour of the Luxembourgers indicates that Luxembourgish is accorded a clear (emotionally motivated) privileged position compared with the two other official languages French and German.

Usefulness of the languages in everyday life

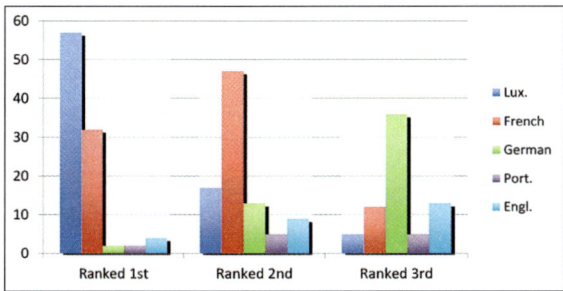

Figure 6: Ranking order of the usefulness of languages in everyday life.

Asked about the most useful language in everyday life, Luxembourgish dominates with 57 %. But a not inconsiderable 32 % of the interviewees named French. All the other languages lag far behind. French dominates as the second most useful language (47 %), while a relative majority of 36 % named German as the third most useful language.

Broken down by nationality and with respect to the most useful language (rank 1), there is a clear contrast. While the Luxembourgers named Luxembourgish, with 76 %, as the most useful language, the (relative) majority of the foreigners (49 %) indicates French as being the most useful language. Differentiated by milieus, and in relation to the overall random sample, only the underprivileged milieu (44 %) and the alternative milieu (40 %) showed proportions of less than half of the interviewees who named Luxembourgish as the most useful language in everyday life.

Most Likeable Language

As the 'most likeable language', Luxembourgish scores highest by a large margin with 56 %, independently of the interviewees' age. A breakdown by nationality, however, reveals clear discrepancies in the distribution of sympathies. Thus the Luxembourgers, with 77 %, rate Luxembourgish as the most likeable language, while only 28 % of the foreigners vote for this language. But here too, a further differentiation brings to light clear national differences. Probably the most noteworthy fact is that a surprising 49 % of the Germans also named Luxembourgish as the most likeable language. In total, however, a relative majority of the foreign interviewees (37 %) consider French to be the most likeable language.

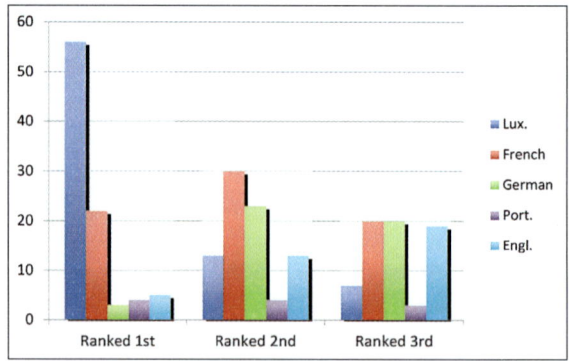

Figure 7: Ranking order of the most likeable languages.

Differentiated by milieu, Luxembourgish achieves the highest sympathy ratings, in relation to the entire random sample, in the status-oriented milieu (68 %), and the lowest ones in the underprivileged milieu (37 %).

The second rank on the 'sympathy scale' is occupied by French with 30 %, followed by German with 23 %. For Luxembourgers, French (34 %) ranks roughly equal with German (32 %) as the second-most likeable language.

In respect of the overall picture, and broken down by milieus, French – with varying degrees of difference – ranks in all milieus before German and only the status-oriented milieu shows a reversal of the ranking order.

Remarkable here, however, is that there seems to be a clear age correlation. Throughout the entire random sample, the sympathy ratings for French decline drastically with decreasing age. The corresponding rate sinks, starting with 46 % for the over 60-year-olds, down to 31 % for the 45 to 59-year-olds, down to 22 % for the 30 to 44-year-olds, down to 23 % for the 21-29-year-olds and all the way down to only 15 % for the 16 to 20-year-olds. With German, on the other hand, the corresponding figures show a clear overall increase with decreasing age, namely from 19 % for the oldest up to 33 % for the youngest age group.

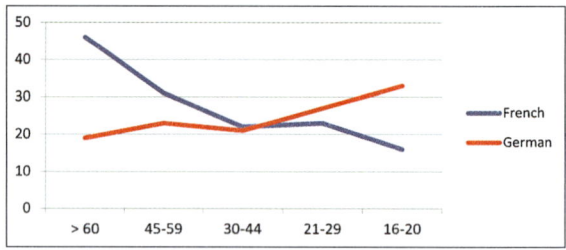

Figure 8: Sympathy for the German and French languages by age groups.

This phenomenon is not simple to explain. One could ask to what extent this is a transitional, i.e. temporary phenomenon, entailing a decline of sympathy ratings for German and a corresponding increase for French with increasing age. A more probable explanation though is that there is a basic change of attitudes towards these two languages in progress. We can also assume that the social stigma of German as a reaction to the occupation of Luxembourg by Nazi Germany during the Second World War is increasingly losing its significance for the younger generations.

Regarding the statements concerning the third most likeable language, the proportions are nearly identical for German (20 %), French (20 %) and English (19 %).

Future Language Importance

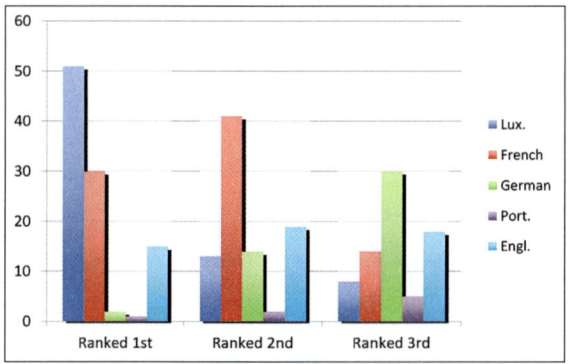

Figure 9: Most important language in the future.

A majority of 51 % of the interviewees state that for them Luxembourgish is the most important language in the future. About one third (30 %) voted for French and 15 % for English. Luxembourgish scored particularly high in the tradition-oriented milieu (61 %), the alternative milieu and the privileged conservative milieu (both 58 %), while the lowest ratings were recorded in the status-oriented milieu (37 %).

The second most important language in the future is – with a clear relative majority of 41 % – French, followed by English (19 %). As the third most important language in the future, German is named by 30 % of the respondents. Here, too, English scores relatively high (18 %).

Differentiated by age, the (predicted) importance of Luxembourgish clearly declines with decreasing age, while French shows a strong increase. Accordingly, the importance of Luxembourgish decreases from 57 % with people over the age of 60 down to 42 % with the 16 to 20-year-olds, whereas that of French increases from 20 % to 43 %.

In particular the Luxembourgers themselves consider Luxembourgish – with 63 % – as the most important language in the future, while the relative majority of the foreigners (42 %) sees French in first place. Here again, the subpopulation of the non-Luxembourgers shows itself to be very heterogeneous. Peak ratings for French are recorded for the Portuguese (50 %) and the French (49 %), while the relative majority of the Germans (48 %) and the group of the not further specified "other foreigners" (46 %) regards Luxembourgish as the most important language in the future.

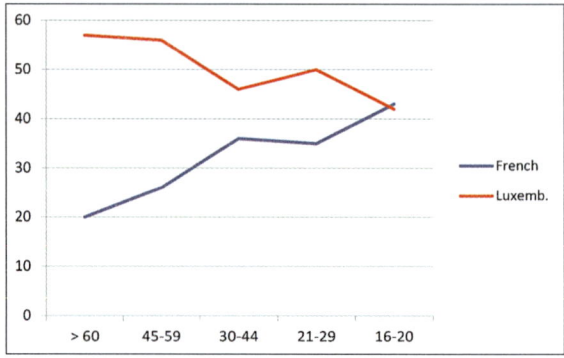

Figure 10: Most important languages in the future according to age.

Most Popular Television Language

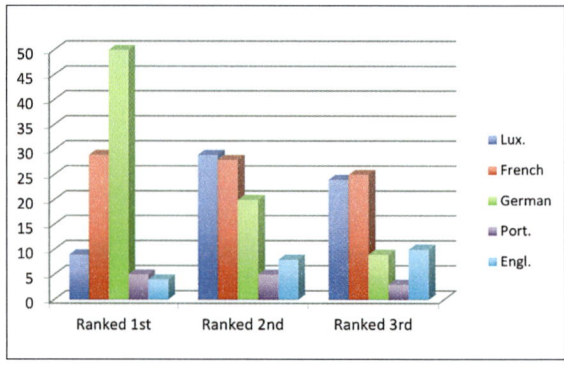

Figure 11: Most popular television language.

German acts, by a significant margin, as the primary language for television consumption: 50 % (in German) compared with 29 % (in French) and 9 % (in Luxembourgish). This ratio is in great part generated by the television consumption of the Luxembourgers (69 % in German, 14 % in Luxembourgish and 13 % in French), while foreign residents clearly prefer French language television (50 %). Here, Germans constitute an easily explained exception, with 91 % preferring German-speaking television, together with members of the unspecified "other nationalities" for whom German (37 %) ranks before French (25 %) and English (16 %).

German is the top television language in all milieus, but in varying degrees. Peak ratings are recorded for the status-oriented milieu (66 %), followed by the tradition-oriented milieu (55 %) and the petty bourgeois milieu (55 %), while the underprivileged milieu (38 %) and the alternative milieu (36 %) showed the lowest ratings.

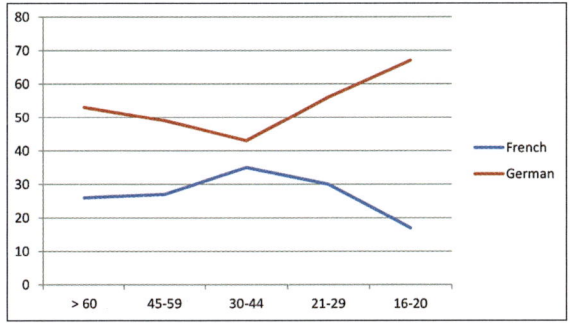

Figure 12: Most popular television language by age.

The diagram in figure 12 clearly shows that the consumption of German language television obviously increases with younger generations. 16 to 20-year-olds exhibit the highest preference for German language television (67 %) and the least for French language television (17 %).

Luxembourgish ranks as the second most popular 'television language' with 29 %, closely followed by French (28 %). The third most frequent language for television consumption, with a maximum of 25 %, is French, barely ahead of Luxembourgish (24 %).

School Situation

Regarding the question whether language lessons at school overtaxed Luxembourgish pupils, 27 % agreed, but a clear majority of about two thirds of the interviewees (65 %) apparently saw no overtaxing – with interviewees with Luxembourgish nationality scoring highest. There is, however, a correlation with educational attainment. A significant difference emerged between interviewees with a university degree, 70 % of whom see no overtaxing, and those with only basic school qualifications, where the figure is substantially lower, at 51 %.

An issue frequently brought up in the educational discussion is that of the educational opportunities of Portuguese pupils, particularly in view of the complex and demanding linguistic situation at Luxembourg's schools and the primary alphabetization by means of the German language. There is a relatively large Portuguese population in Luxembourg as a result of the labour immigration in recent decades, and it significantly outnumbers the other foreign population groups. Regarding the question whether language lessons overtaxed Portuguese pupils in Luxembourgish schools, the picture that emerges is a differentiated one. A relative majority of 49 % answered in the negative; 41 %, however, agreed. The internal differentiation by age groups shows that it is primarily the younger age group (16-20 years) that considers the situation at school the least overtaxing. The Portuguese themselves are (also) ambivalent in their response behaviour: Thus, 48 % of the interviewees do not see any overtaxing, but 50 % hold the view that Portuguese children are indeed overtaxed.

State Intervention

Although state intervention concerning the usage of language is demanded by just about half of the interviewees (48 %), it is also rejected by about the same percentage (46 %) – a clear split into 'two camps'. The highest approval ratings for linguistic regulation by the state are to be found in particular with the inhabitants of the north of Luxembourg (53 %), with the 16 to 20-year-olds (57 %) as well as with assisting family members (72 %), with the underprivileged milieu (57 %), the petty bourgeois milieu and the tradition-oriented milieu (53 % respectively). In terms of nationality, linguistic control by the state is demanded in a relatively high degree by the Luxembourgers (51 %), only exceeded by the Italians (59 %). Again, there is a correlation with educational attainment: The higher the educational level, the less there is a demand for state intervention into the usage of language.

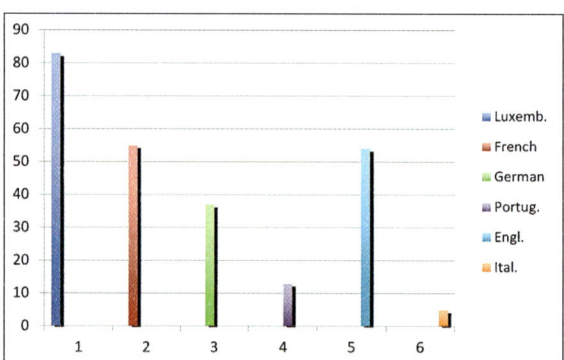

Figure 13: Languages that should be promoted by the state.

With regard to the question which languages should be promoted more strongly by the state, we can again observe a strong loyalty towards Luxembourgish. Thus, a total of 83 % of the group calling for state support would like to see it given to the official language. It is primarily the Luxembourgers themselves who demand this, with 90 %, closely followed by the Germans (89 %), while the Belgians, with

59 %, show the relatively lowest rating. In terms of milieu differentiation, it is above all the tradition- oriented milieu (92 %), the meritocratic-oriented milieu and the privileged liberal milieu (both 88 %) that are in favour of the promotion of Luxembourgish.

Concerning the question which languages should be promoted by the state, French (55 %) and English (54 %) are more or less equal, both clearly before German (37 %) and again clearly before Portuguese (13 %) and Italian (5 %).

Neighbouring Countries: Frequency of Visits

(Regular) visits to the neighbouring countries are apparently common practice among most inhabitants of Luxembourg. About 70 % of them visit France, Belgium and Germany at least several times per year. Differentiated by nationality, Germany emerges as the most-visited neighbouring country for Luxembourgers. Only 17 % of the Luxembourgers state that they travel to Germany either "never at all" or "hardly ever". By comparison, the corresponding percentages for France are 31 % and for Belgium 32 %. With respect to Luxembourgers visiting Germany, the country scores highest both in terms of absolute numbers and of frequency.

Neighbouring Countries: "Feel-Good Factor"

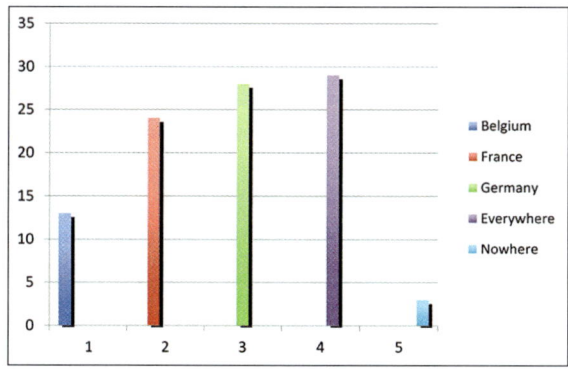

Figure 14: *"In which country do you feel most comfortable?"*

Also concerning the question "In which neighbouring country do you feel most comfortable?", we can observe a certain preference for the German neighbour. While a relative majority of 29 % states "everywhere", when broken up by countries, Germany occupies the front position (28 %), closely followed by France (24 %) and Belgium (13 %).

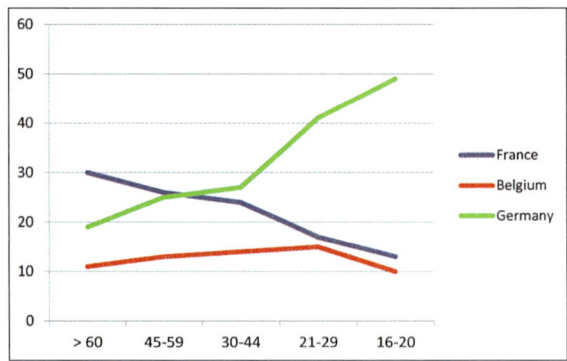

Figure 15: *"Feel-good" factor by age.*

Clear differences emerge in terms of age distribution. Thus, the "feel-good" factor increases continuously and distinctly with decreasing age of the interviewees. Especially with the youngest age groups (up to 29 years of age) Germany is clearly the "favourite". With the 16 to 20-year-olds, Germany scores 49 %, France 13 % and Belgium 10 %. There is however also a pronounced generation shift here, with France receiving the highest approval ratings from the older generations (from 45 years upwards).

Differentiated by nationality, it is also Germany that Luxembourgers consider by far to be the neighbouring country with the highest "feel-good" factor (37 % versus 21 % for France and 9 % for Belgium). Portuguese, French and Italian residents, on the other hand, tend to feel most comfortable in France. It is evident that in the context of this question there is a link between nationality and language.

Conclusion

The evaluation of the collected data shows that Luxembourg's trilingualism is, in general, assessed as stable and positive. In particular, it is considered to have a significant communicative added value, with a pronounced emphasis on Luxembourgish. Luxembourgish (for the Luxembourgers), is *the* mother tongue that is associated with which a high degree of loyalty. It is therefore probably safe to say that Luxembourgish serves a powerful identity-creating function.

The importance of French as the predominant language of public and formal communication is indisputable. At the same time, French clearly emerges as the language of preference for the majority of foreign residents in Luxembourg. While for the Luxembourgers the emotional attachment to as well as the rational relationship with French clearly lags behind that conferred on Luxembourgish, it is, on the other hand, ranked before German, although the ratios currently seem to be shifting (in the younger generation).

To Luxembourgers, German clearly seems to have a high practical value in the more informal aspects of life. Germany is the neighbouring country most frequently visited, with the highest "feel good" factor. In addition, media consumption is dominated by German language television. This preference for German is particularly pronounced with the younger Luxembourgers, whose general assessment of the language is clearly more positive than that of the older generation. At the same time, German is, after Luxembourgish, the language spoken and understood fluently by most people. The emotional attachment to German, however, is weak, at most. The rational assessment of German, too, is low compared to its factual practical value.

4.3 Controversies in Readers' Letters concerning the Linguistic Situation

Preliminary Remarks

The present analysis concerns itself with the readers' letters that have appeared in various Luxembourgish newspapers and discuss the issues 'Language' and 'Multilingualism'. On the basis of this discourse material, we have attempted to draw some tentative conclusions on *appropriated* identities in regard to language. Our basic premise was that languages have an enormous identity-creating potential, particularly in a multicultural and multilingual environment such as Luxembourg. Naturally, Luxembourgish occupied the centre of our interest due to its importance as a constitutive feature that permits distinction from the immediate neighbours Germany and France.

Selection of the Material

First of all, 164 recent articles and 63 readers' letters dealing with language and published in nineteen different Luxembourgish newspapers and magazines were collected and listed for a period of just over a year. Since it is the aim of this study to identify appropriated identities within Luxembourg's population, we decided to focus our attention on the readers' letters. Their analysis provides a vivid picture of the positions and opinions on specific subjects. People who write letters to the editor are not professional journalists, which makes the voices 'from within the population' appear particularly immediate as they address topics that are of particular concern to the letters' authors.

Out of the total number, 54 letters to the editor, which appeared between March 2008 to April 2009 in the newspapers *Tageblatt, Luxemburger Wort, Journal, La Voix, Le jeudi, Lëtzebuerger Journal, d'Land* and *Kulturissimo*, were evaluated. In addition to the classical letters to the editor, in which readers briefly comment on a previously published article, we also considered self-initiated articles or comments by readers that go beyond the usual letter to the editor. It is worth noting at this point that it seems to be a typical feature of Luxembourg's media landscape that anyone who wishes to do so can convey their private or expert opinion to a wider readership. Such articles were also taken into consideration because they allow more comprehensive conclusions on appropriated identities with regard to the topic of language[3].

All the official languages of Luxembourg – Luxembourgish, German and French – are also represented in the readers' letters and remarkably, sometimes the same writers use different languages when writing to different newspapers or on different subjects. What is equally remarkable, and perhaps a specific feature of Luxembourg, is that some letters to the editor were published in several newspapers, which produced multiple counts (in the table presented below, the numbers of readers' letters which also appeared in another newspaper are stated in brackets). A further point worth noting is that only three women wrote readers' letters on the subject of 'language (s)' as opposed to 26 men.

Print Media Selected for the Survey	Language of Article			
	Luxembourgish	German	French	Total
Luxemburger Wort	19 (4)	5	4 (1)	28 (5)
Lëtzebuerger Journal	8 (4)	3	1	12 (4)
Tageblatt	3 (2)	7 (1)	1	11 (3)
La Voix			2	2
Le Jeudi			1	1
d'Land		2		2
Journal	1 (1)	2 (1)	3 (1)	6 (3)
Kulturissimo		1		1
Total	31	20	12	63

In brackets: Number of readers' letters that have also appeared in other newspapers

Table 1: Language of readers' letters in the respective print media.

Even though an analysis of readers' letters permits certain tentative insights into a society's language awarenesss, one should exercise caution and remain mindful of the fact that even a comprehensive evaluation of reader's letters like the present one cannot reflect more than a limited section of interests and opinions existing in society. In terms of the total population, only relatively few people write letters to the editor. Research into this has only been rudimentary up to now and has as yet established no precise author profiles. One can, nevertheless, make a distinction between the spontaneous expression of opinion by laymen on certain subjects which are of special, often personal interest to individual people and the sending of letters to the editor, or articles, by experts in various fields: for example, when

---

3 | In actual fact, more than the analysed 54 readers' letters dealing in a broader sense with the topics of language and multilingualism were published in the period under consideration. Nevertheless, for reasons of objectivity, a number of these letters were disregarded.

a Luxembourger writes a letter to the editor to share her favourable experience with multilingualism when shopping in Trier[4], or when scientists comment on the status of Luxembourgish. In addition, these are often people who regularly write letters to the editor. Here, one also has to distinguish between those who think they are representing a majority opinion and those who quite clearly assume more extreme positions. Moreover, not all letters sent to the editorial staff are published, and if they are, they may appear in an amended or abridged version (see Drewnowska-Vargáné 2001: 2).

Text Type 'Letter to the Editor'

On account of the fact that letters to the editor have not yet been extensively investigated as a text type, there is also no canonical definition for letters to the editor or readers' letters (Drewnowska-Vargáné 2001: 2). There is however a certain consensus about what can be regarded as a typical feature for this text type. A particularly prominent one is intertextuality (see Piirainen/Yli-Kojola 1983: 111), because letters to the editor generally refer to already published articles or to other letters to the editor that they, in turn, comment on, or criticise, or complement. Another characteristic is the specific "emitter-recipient constellation" of readers' letters. Since, in contrast to customary letters, letters to the editor are public, they have a very wide recipient readership. This is not identical with the addressee readership and usually remains unknown to the letter's author (see Drewnowska-Vargáné 2001: 2).

The reviewed material reveals recurring components that are, according to Sandig, constitutive for readers' letters: indication of the subject matter as a main heading, reference to a previous newspaper article as a secondary heading, the text itself and the signature: the writer's name and place of residence (see Sandig 1986: 185). These devices establish a connection to preceding texts, thereby creating *"indirekte Dialoge in schriftlicher Form"*[5] (see Bucher 1986: 147-160). The author also employs a *"Kohärenzmanagement"*[6] (Bucher 1989: 290) by providing the following information:

1. Womit sein Brief zusammenhängt (durch das Zitieren der betreffenden Textstelle oder Angabe des sprachlichen Ausdrucks, auf den er Bezug nimmt); 2. Wie sein Brief gemeint ist (welches Thema behandelt wird und welche Ansichten er verfolgt); 3. "eine Handlung ausführt, die als regelhafte Anschlusshandlung auf den vorausgegangenen Beitrag gilt",

---

4 | See Bauer, Léonie: In welcher Sprache möchten Sie beraten werden? *Tageblatt*, 15./16.03. 2008, p. 72. (Personal translation: "In which language would you like to be helped?").
5 | Personal translation: "Indirect dialogues in written form".
6 | Personal translation: "Coherence management".

z.B. wenn er den Beitrag lobt[7] (Bucher 1986: 149, quoted according to: Drewnowska-Vargáné 2001: 3).

Recent research of readers' letters is increasingly taking contrastive investigations of readers' letters from different communication cultures into account that are based on text-linguistic analysis (see Drewnowska-Vargáné 2001: 3). In this sense, the present analysis could well be the first step on the road to the investigation of Luxembourg's communication culture. Due to the specific circumstances, for instance the manageable scale of the readership and number of letter writers, readers' letters in this country in general appear to be somewhat more personal than, for instance, in Germany. It is for instance by no means rare for someone to close their letter to the editor, written in reaction to another one, with the words: "*Merci fir d'Dokumentatioun vun Ärem Respekt vru menger Aarbecht fir eis Sprooch; ech hoffe just, datt deen esou éierlech ass wéi meng Bewonnerung vun Ärer Leeschtung als Lëtzebuerger Historiker*".[8] The choice of language is also something that carries a particular significance in Luxembourg. Sometimes readers' letters are written in German, presumably to ensure that the addressee understands the arguments or because the debate is continued in same language as it started. There are however also readers' letters which are deliberately or on grounds of principle written in Luxembourgish. For instance, one letter to the editor begins as follows: "*Meng Identitéit als iwerzeechte Lëtzebuerger verbidd mer des puer Wierder op Däitsch ze schreiwen. Mäi Papp a meng Grousspappen genge mer et net verzeien*".[9] A postscript in German then concedes: "*Es wird sich wohl jemand finden, der Herr[n] Müntefering dies zu übersetzen weiß*".[10]

---

7 | Personal translation: "1. What his or her letter refers to (by quoting the respective text passage or indicating the linguistic expression that he/she is making reference to); 2. How his/her letter is meant (what topic is being dealt with and what are his/her views); 3. [... and by performing] "an act that qualifies as a standard follow-up act with respect to the preceding article", for instance, when he/she praises the article".

8 | Personal translation: "Thank you for expressing your respect for my work on behalf of our language; I can only hope that it is as genuine as my admiration for your achievements as a Luxembourg historian" (Roth, Lex:, Keng Hetzcampagne, Här Prof. Dr. Michel Pauly. *Lëtzebuerger Journal*, 31.3.2009, p. 9).

9 | Personal translation: "My identity as a staunch Luxembourger does not permit me to write these few words in German. My father and my grandfather would never forgive me" (Lenz, Guy: Nët esou, Här Müntefering. *Lëtzebuerger Journal*, 21.03.2009, p. 7 and *Luxemburger Wort*, 21.03.2009, p. 21).

10 | Personal translation: "Surely it will be possible to find someone who can translate this for Mr. Müntefering".

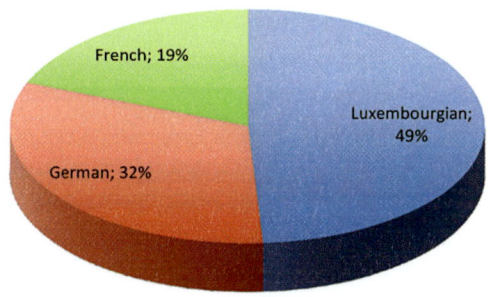

Figure 16: Language distribution of the readers' letters

Topics

In order to draw conclusions on the interrelations between language and identity, only such letters to the editor, which deal with these subjects, were selected. Some are individual letters that refer to an article in an older edition of the newspaper, while there are also entire series of letters, which revolve around one particular subject. This can either be a new law, a bill, issues at the centre of public debate, or,it could be a previous letter to the editor which is being commented on or criticised. This often draws a further response which, in turn, is frequently answered again, creating entire argumental concatenations or even veritable 'feuds'.

The most important subject areas dealing with language are integration, language and identity, the incorporation of Luxembourgish in the constitution, language schools, a momentous slip of the tongue on the radio, linguistic self-confidence, revaluation of Luxembourgish or threat to the language.

Lines of Reasoning and Conflict Lines

In general, the debates on the topic of language in Luxembourg as they appear in readers' letters show four distinct lines of reasoning: There is a) a pro-Luxembourgish, b) a German-critical or c) French-critical and d) a pro-multilingual position. In the following we will discuss these partly very radical sounding categorisations in more detail by providing exact descriptions and illustrative examples.

a) Pro-Luxembourgish

In nearly all letters to the editor, particular importance is attached to Luxembourgish. On the one hand, as an identity-creating feature, for instance when it is stated, as a matter of course: "*[e]is Sprooch ass eis Identitéit*"[11] or when there are calls for teaching more regional cultural topics at school in the Luxembourgish language:

> Ich hatte in letzter Zeit verschiedentlich die Gelegenheit, mich mit Primärschülern der letzten Klasse zu unterhalten. Dabei musste ich feststellen, dass kein einziger den Text geschweige denn die Melodie unserer Nationalhymne kannte. Von andern schönen luxemburgischen Liedern ganz zu schweigen. [...] Was soll in der "Chamber" das große Getue um unsere nationale Identität, wenn nicht an der Basis begonnen wird diese zu lehren? Und gibt es nicht viele luxemburgische Lieder, die einen "Ausflug" in die luxemburgische Geschichte, Geographie und Botanik ermöglichen?[12].

Some readers fear the disappearance of their language, Luxembourgish, and consequently demand that it be included in the curriculum: "*Ich bin 77 Jahre alt und verstehe immer noch nicht, warum in unseren Schulen unsere Sprache nicht gelehrt wird. Denn wenn es so weitergeht, geht unsere Sprache verloren, und das wäre sehr schade*".[13] On the other hand, Luxembourgish is seen as a language of integration that would prove useful to the many foreigners in the country in everyday life. The students of a Luxembourgish course suggest for instance the following: "*Naturellement, si un étranger décide de rester au Luxembourg, la langue luxembourgeoise sera un facteur incontournable qui lui permettra d'atteindre son but: celui de son intégration socio-professionelle*".[14] And the *Communauté Vie Chrétienne au Luxembourg* is of the following opinion: "*Nous ne nions pas le fait que le luxembourgeois reste un facteur important d'integration au Grand-Duché*".[15] Luxembourgish is therefore regarded, in

---

11 | Personal translation: "Our language is our identity" (Weirich, Jos: Eis Sprooch ass eis Identitéit. *Luxemburger Wort*, 09.08.2008, p. 12).

12 | Personal translation: "I recently had the opportunity on several occasions to talk to primary pupils of the upper classes and discovered that not one of them knew the words of our national anthem, let alone the melody. Not to mention other lovely Luxembourgish songs. [...] What's the point in making all that fuss in the 'Chamber' about our national identity if you don't start teaching it right from the beginning? And aren't there a lot of Luxembourgish songs that allow an 'excursion' into Luxembourgish history, geography and botany?" (J. G.: Luxemburgisch an der Basis lehren. *Lëtzebuerger Journal*, 23.10.2008, p. 6).

13 | Personal translation: "I am 77 years old and I still don't understand why our language isn't being taught in our schools. If it goes on like that, our language will vanish, and that would be a great pity" (L.V.E.: Zur luxemburgischen Sprache. *Tageblatt*, 13.2.2009, p. 65).

14 | Personal translation: "Naturally, if a foreigner decides to remain in Luxembourg, Luxembourgish is an essential factor to reach his or her objective, namely social and professional integration" (Letter to the editor by students of a Luxembourgish course: Vivre dans une société multiculturelle au quotidien. *Le Jeudi*,10.07.2008, p. 44).

15 | Personal translation: "We do not deny that Luxembourgish is an important factor for integration in the Grand Duchy" (Communauté Vie Chrétienne au Luxembourg: Lettre ouverte aux députés. *La Voix*, 24.05. 2008, p. 48).

a positive sense, as a language of integration, but it can also be made a condition, for instance when a reader demands *"dass man, dort wo man sein Geld verdient, sich ein bisschen Mühe geben sollte, die Sprache zu erlernen"*.[16] This is demanded particularly emphatically when the topic is about acquiring Luxembourgish citizenship: *"D'Sproochefuerderunge fir Lëtzebuerger ze ginn, hu fir jiddereen ze gëllen, egal wéi laang een hei geliewt huet [...]"*[17].

In the light of the generally high approval rate for Luxembourgish, it is not surprising that most letters to the editor respond favourably to the proposal to incorporate Luxembourgish in the constitution[18]: *"Elo ass jo viru kuerzem d'Proposition op den Dësch komm, eist Lëtzebuergesch als Nationalsprooch an der Verfassung ze verankeren – eng gudd Iddi, wéi mir schéngt"*.[19]

b) German-critical

The acceptance of Luxembourgish is extremely high and there are frequent demands to promote one's native language more vigorously. This promotion of Luxembourgish occurs partly at the expense of the other languages spoken in the country, for instance German. This is reflected in demands for language cultivation, for instance by not needlessly borrowing words from other languages and instead using the ones available in Luxembourgish:

Also missten déi Leit, déi am Radio poteren (inklusiv déi honorabel Politiker a Gewerkschaftler) emol hir Mammesprooch zerguttstert léieren. ‚Innerhalb, ausserhalb, schwul, schwanger, fënnt statt ab ..., im nachhinein, nach wie vor, zumindest, zahlreich, am gesetzleche Rahmen, mindestens' sinn nëmmen e puer Beispiller. Dat ass kee Lëtzebuergesch, dat sinn op Däitsch geduechten an iwwerem braddelen op lëtzebuergesch iwwersate Sätz, déi do erauskommen. [...] An dann och nach dat elei: Wieder, déi et vun Aalst hier am lëtzebuergesche gëtt, musse bleiwen. (Seejomes, net Ameis, Gehaansfénkelchen, net Glühwürmchen, Päiperlek, net Schmetterling). Dat ass jo fir Ekzema an d'Oueren ze kréien![20]

---

16 | Personal translation: "[...] That when someone one earns their money in a certain place, they should also take a little trouble to learn the language".
17 | Personal translation: "The linguistic requirements of becoming a Luxembourger have to be valid for everybody, regardless of how long they have been living here" (Watgen, Fernand: Lëtzebuerger ouni Lëtzebuergesch... *Luxemburger Wort*, 21.05.2008, p. 18).
18 | See Benoit, Jos and Jos Weirich: Eis Sprooch ass eis Identitéit, duerfir eis Sprooch an d'Constitution. *Tageblatt*, 25./26.07.2008, p. 56.
19 | Personal translation: "Now the proposal has recently been put on the table to incorporate our Luxembourgish as an official language in the constitution – a good idea, it seems to me" (lucy lux: Lëtzebuergesch, franséisch, däitsch oder wat? *Journal*, 06.02.2009, p. 6).
20 | Personal translation: "So, the people talking on the radio – including our honorable politicians and union leaders – should learn their mother-tongue first. ‚Innerhalb, ausserhalb, zahlreich, am gesetzleche Rahmen, mindestens' are just a few examples. This is no

Et wär villäicht éischter néidig, dergéint ze protestéieren, datt eis Sprooch am Alldeeglechen vun aflossräiche Leit an och vun de geschwate Medien öffentlech mat engem franséische 'style précieux' oder engem kumpelhaften Däitsch entstallt gëtt, obwohl genuch gutt Lëtzebuerger Wierder parat stinn[21]

There are also complaints that the *"'schnarrende' deutsche Aussprache"* of the *"überwältigende Mehrheit der Schulkinder"* is due to their consumption of German-language television programmes, and *"leider gereicht das dem Luxemburgischen nicht unbedingt zum Vorteil"*.[22]

On the radio, a presenter referred to Luxembourgish as *"Kauderwelsch"*[23], triggering a wave of complaints from readers who demanded a higher level of linguistic self-confidence. One needs to bear in mind here that some readers' resentments against German go back to the German occupation of Luxembourg during the Second World War and the word *Kauderwelsch* automatically provokes the corresponding associations – *"Viru 67 Joër goufe mir Lëtzebuerger schon mat dem Wuert ‚Kauderwelsch' vum Gauleiter Simon a senge Kollaborateuren konfrontéiert an affrontéiert"*, connected with the question: *"Gi mer se wierklech ni lass!?"*[24]. Some comments, therefore, are highly emotional and proclaime: *"[n]ët aleng déi Persoun, och de Radio 100,7 huet sech blaméiert an disqualifizéiert"*.[25] For some Luxembourgers, pride in and the esteem for their own language, appears to be closely tied to the opposition against the German occupiers, for example when one reader writes *"Trotz Repressalien a Prisong, hu mir eis fir ons Sprooch an Onofhängegkeet agesat, déi*

Luxembourgish, these are sentences that were thought in German and then, during talking, were translated into Luxembourgish. And then this: words that exist for eternities in Luxembourgish must remain. [...] That can really give you eczemas in your ears!" (Grethen, Änder: D'Lëtzebuerger an hir Sprooch. *Luxemburger Wort*, 22. 11. 2008, p. 21).

21 | Personal translation: "It would instead be necessary to protest against influential people and the spoken media deforming our language in everyday life through a French ‚style précieux' or a chummy German, although good Luxembourgish words exist" (Thewes, Nico: Eis Sproochen. *Luxemburger Wort*, 24. 03. 2009, p. 14).

22 | Personal translation. "The 'grating' German pronunciation of the great majority of schoolchildren... unfortunately this is not always to the advantage of Luxembourgish" (Roth, Lex: Deutsch und wir. *Lëtzebuerger Journal*,15.11.2008, p. 6).

23 | Personal translation: "Gibberish".

24 | Personal translation: "67 years ago, we Luxembourgers had already been confronted with and insulted by the word ‚gibberish' by Gauleiter Simon and his collaborateurs [...] Will we never get rid of them!?" (Weirich, Jos and Jos Benoit: Eis Sprooch an d'Constitution. *Journal*, 23. 07. 2008, p. 6).

25 | Personal translation: "Not only the person in question but Radio 100,7 too have disqualified themselves". (Weirich, Jos and Jos Benoit: Eis Sprooch an d'Constitution. *Journal*, 23. 07. 2008 p. 6).

mat Blutt bezuelt goufen".²⁶ It may therefore be not surprising that corresponding resentments against German still exist with the older generations.

c) French-critical

Some readers' letters criticise the rapidly increasing predominance of French in Luxembourg. Often, they complain that it is impossible to go shopping without knowing French: *"Wenn ich einkaufen gehe und dann jemanden bitte, mir zu helfen, bekomme ich gleich zur Antwort: 'En français, s'il vous plaît'"*²⁷. This makes some people feel like strangers in their own country. *"Wéi oft hunn sech Lëtzebuerger scho schrëftlech a mündlech driwwer opgereegt, dass een iwwerall mat dem berühmte Satz ‚en français s.v.p.' konfronteíert gëtt?"*²⁸. Especially older people, it is stated, often have problems because a large proportion of the nursing staff in hospitals and senior citizen's homes only speaks French:

Was ich sehr schlimm finde, ist die Situation in den Spitälern, in Altenheimen und überhaupt überall dort, wo ältere Menschen in Pflege sind. Besonders hier müsste das Personal unsere Sprache beherrschen. Oder müssen ältere Leute noch andere Sprachen lernen, damit man sie versteht?!²⁹

It appears that the usage of French in everyday life is not as uncomplicated as one might think if one assumes Luxembourg to be a trilingual country:

Mir perséinlech fällt och op, dass an der leschter Zäit och an den Zeitungen (an zwar net nëmmen an deenen, déi extra op Franséisch veröffentlecht ginn) mee och an deenen traditionellen Zeitungen, déi fréier praktesch nëmmen däitsch Artikelen veröffentlecht hunn, ëmmer méi franséisch Texter optauchen. An och das iergert de richtige Lëtzebuerger, deen zwar ganz gären eppes iwwert dat interessant Thema ging liesen, wat am Titel

---

26 | Personal translation: "In spite of repression and prison sentences, we have committed ourselves to our language and independence, for which we have paid with our blood" (Weirich, Jos and Jos Benoit: Eis Sprooch an d'Constitution. *Journal*, 23. 07. 2008, p. 6).

27 | Personal translation: "When I go shopping and then ask for assistance, I immediately get the answer: *'En français, s'il vous plaît'* ('in French, please')" (L.V.E.: Zur luxemburgischen Sprache. *Tageblatt*, 12. 01. 2009, p. 65).

28 | Personal translation: "How often have Luxembourgers expressed, in writing and orally, their annoyance about being confronted everywhere they go with the famous sentence 'in French, please'?" (lucy lux: Lëtzebuergesch, franséisch, däitsch oder wat? *Journal*, 6. 02. 2009, p. 6).

29 | Personal translation: "What I consider as being very bad is the situation in hospitals, in old people's homes, and generally everywhere where older people are being cared for. Especially here, the staff should be fluent in our language. Or do elderly people really have to learn other languages, just so that they are understood?" (L.V.E.: Zur luxemburgischen Sprache. *Tageblatt*, 12. 02. 2009, p. 65).

ugekënnegt gëtt, awer keng Loscht huet, sech duerch eng ganz Zeitungssäit franséisch Text zu wullen, zumol wenn dat Thema a bësse méi komplizéiert ass[30].

In addition, there is the position of many foreigners working in the country who apparently speak French naturally and also expect this from the Luxembourgers: *"Fir ze wëssen, a watfir enger Sprooch ech mat him misst schwätzen, hunn ech héiflech gefrot 'Vouz parlez français?' wourops ech ganz onfrëndlech ugebaupst si ginn 'Eh bien oui, puisque c'est la langue administrative'. Das ass jo erëm eng Kéier typisch!"*[31]

Some readers explicitly oppose the proposal to continue to incorporate French in the constitution, because it would be *"... politisch onvirsichteg [e]ng friem Sprooch an d'Constitution ze setzen"*.[32]

d) Pro-multilingualism

The pro-multilingual position opposes linguistically one-sided trends and rejects them in favour of practised multilingualism. The constant concentration on Luxembourgish of some letter writers is therefore commented on critically, for instance when a particularly dedicated advocate of Luxembourgish is labelled as *"eisen nationalen Här R[...]"*[33] who *"net iwwert eis däitsch Noperen an hir Sprooch schreiwen [kann], ouni e Gauleiter oder soss eppes vun den Naziën an d'Spiel ze bréngen"*[34] or when the author of another letter to the editor, commenting on the

---

30 | Personal translation: "I personally have noticed that lately more and more French texts have been appearing in the newspapers, and not only in those that are published in French, but also in traditional newspapers that used to publish German articles only. And that annoys the real Luxembourgers, who would like to read about the interesting topic that the heading announces, but who do not want to struggle through a whole page of French text, especially if the topic is a little more complicated" (lucy lux: Lëtzebuergesch, franséisch, däitsch oder wat? *Journal*, 6. 02. 2009, p. 6).

31 | Personal translation: "In order to find out in which language I should talk to him, I asked politely, 'Do you speak French?', whereupon I was snapped at: 'Of course I do, it's the administrative language after all'. This is just so typical!" (lucy lux: Lëtzebuergesch, franséisch, däitsch oder wat? *Journal*, 6. 02. 2009, p. 6).

32 | Personal translation: "Because it would be politically imprudent to establish a foreign language in the constitution" (Thewes, Nico: Eis Sproochen. *Luxemburger Wort*, 24. 03. 2009, p. 14).

33 | Personal translation: "Our national Mr R[...]" (lucy lux: Lëtzebuergesch, franséisch, däitsch oder wat? *Journal*, 6. 02. 2009, p. 6).

34 | Personal translation: "[...] Who cannot write about our German neighbours and their language without bringing up a *Gauleiter* or something else from the Nazis" (lucy lux: Kuerz Äntwort op den Här Roth (*Journal* vum 13. Februar). *Lëtzebuerger Journal*, 25. 02. 2009, p. 6).

proposal to strengthen Luxembourgish at EU level, asks himself: *"Wie weit kann man Nationalismus treiben?"*[35].

One characteristic feature of modern Luxembourg as an international finance and banking centre and as the location of important EU institutions is its multiculturality. This feature is explicitly emphasised by some authors of readers' letters: *"La société luxembourgeoise a choisi de comprendre et d'intégrer les autres cultures. En bref, elle est une société dynamique et hétérogène"*.[36] So besides thoses stances which favour a certain language or want to upgrade and reinforce it in comparison to other languages, there are also those who consider Luxembourg's multilinguality as a significant locational advantage. *"Luxemburg hat drei offizielle Sprachen und wird für diese Sprachegewandheit bewundert"*.[37]

It is only thanks to the Luxembourgers' multilingualism, it is said, that such a small country is assigned almost a key role in the European Union and in the international financial world. Moreover, precisely the good German *and* French skills ensured that Luxembourg can self-confidently assert itself against its larger neighbours Germany and France because it is not exclusively confined to one language and can therefore be ascribed neither to the germanophone nor the francophone side. In addition, multilingualism ensured the good relationship with both neighbouring countries, which is reflected, among other things, by good commercial relations and a trans-border labour market[38].

Conclusion

The fact that, over the relatively short period of just over a year, at least 164 articles and 63 readers' letters were published on the subject of 'language' in a broader sense, points to the presence of a lively discourse on this subject. It is also noteworthy that in letters to the editor, Luxembourgish is very much in the foreground, as well as a topic and as the language of communication, which indicates a strong identification of the letters' authors with this language. This is also something that the letter writers themselves notice: *"Seele wor ons Sprooch esou an der Diskussioun*

---

35 | Personal translation: "How far can one go with nationalism?" (Pütz, M.: Lissabon-Vertrag auf Luxemburgisch? *Tageblatt*, 8. 07. 2008, p. 63).
36 | Personal translation: "The Luxembourgish society has decided to understand and integrate different cultures. In short, it is a dynamic and heterogeneous society" (Letter to the editor written by the students of a Luxembourgish course: Vivre dans une société multiculturelle au quotidien. *Le Jeudi*, 10. 07. 2008, p. 44).
37 | Personal translation: "Luxembourg has three official languages and is admired for its linguistic versatility" (Pütz, M.: Lissabon-Vertrag auf Luxemburgisch? *Tageblatt*, 8. 07. 2008, p. 63).
38 | See Fehlen, Fernand: Wat schwätzt d'Majorité silencieuse? *Luxemburger Wort*, 28. 03. 2009, p. 24.

wéi an de leschte Wochen a Méint. [...] Dat ass och gutt esou".[39] We can therefore assume that Luxembourgish plays an essential role for the Luxembourgers' self-image and thus for their identity.

The analysis of the letters to the editor shows that the subject of 'language' is very emotionally charged. The language is ascribed an important role in forming national identity, statements like "*Eis Sprooch ass eis Identitéit*"[40] are very common. It is consequently not surprising that potential xenophobic leanings should be particularly visible in readers' letters dealing with the subject of language. Many letter writers are unwilling to compromise and to move away from their rigid position, for fear of losing their identity or of 'betraying' their ancestors who had dedicated themselves to the preservation of the Luxembourgish language. This leads some letter writers to become very personal and, in a few cases, even abusive, particularly when they criticise articles or letters to the editor, which express a different position from their own.

On the other hand, however, it is worth pointing out that many letters to the editor address the subject of 'language' and 'languages in Luxembourg' in a level-headed, rational and reasonable way by, for instance, making a distinction between "official language" (Luxembourgish) and "administrative language" (German or French)[41].

Some letters to the editor also take a stance against too polemic positions by correcting false allegations or voicing more temperate opposing views[42]. The authors of these kinds of letters to the editor are however frequently accused in subsequent readers' letters of "betraying" the Luxembourgish language or of simply not being qualified to express an opinion on this subject.

The examples presented above clearly show conflict running along language and language usage lines. One should however bear in mind that there is a "Majorité Silencieuse"[43], as one letter to the editor notes, which is apparently fluent in the languages officially spoken in Luxembourg and uses them quite matter-of-factly. The heated debates in the letters to the editor could therefore in part be mere spurious controversies involving very personal and partly extreme positions.

---

39 | Personal translation: "Rarely has our language been discussed as much as within the last weeks and months [...] That is a good thing" (Grethen, Änder: D'Lëtzebuerger an hir Sprooch. *Luxemburger Wort*, 22. 11. 2008, p. 21).
40 | See Weirich, Jos: Eis Sprooch ass eis Identitéit. *Luxemburger Wort*, 9. 08. 2008, p. 12.
41 | See Watgen, Fernand: Lëtzebuerger ouni Lëtzebuergesch ...? *Luxemburger Wort*, 21. 05. 2008, p. 18.
42 | See also lucy lux: Lëtzebuergesch, franséisch, däitsch oder wat? *Journal*, 6. 02. 2009, p. 6; or Pauly, Michel: Net all Däitsch an een Dëppe geheien. *Luxemburger Wort*, 28. 03. 2009, p. 22.
43 | Personal translation: "The silent majority".

4.4 'Linguistic Landscape':
Public Signage and Multilingualism

Figure 17: Customs at Luxembourg Airport.

Introduction

This paper looks at visual examples of multilingualism as they appear on signs, posters, notices etc. The research field of 'Linguistic Landscaping' (in the following: LL) – a still relatively new approach within (interdisciplinary oriented) sociolinguistics and in part also of visual ethnography – analyses the structure and contextualisation of visible "signs" in public areas (Backhaus 2007: 9) and offers new insights on linguistic policy, multilingualism, language use and linguistic dominance. The prefatory illustration constitutes, to our mind, an almost emblematic condensation of what typifies the language situation in Luxembourg (a) a preference of French and (b) multilingualism where English plays an increasingly important role.

Studies of Visual Multilingualism

In sociolinguistics, the structure of publicly visible text was for a long time, simply ignored. It was only in the 1990s that research into LL began, initially focussing on complex urban areas with a multilingual population. One of the first studies to be published was that by Landry and Bourhis (1997), who directed their attention to the perception of multilingual, public signs in Canada. Here, investigation focusses primarily on language usage in public areas of towns or regions, as exhibited, for instance, on street signs, display boards, street name signs, town name signs, commercial signs and signs in public buildings etc. The analysis of these signs examines issues such as addressee orientation, presupposed linguistic competence, underlying linguistic preference or linguistic attitudes relevant to identity. Furthermore, quantitative results allow the identification of current development trends (e.g., increase/decline of a language, changes in the valence of a language etc.). Backhaus (2007) developed a typology (which we have adopted in our contribution) of multilingual signs which he exemplified in a survey of an urban area of Tokyo. Other research expands the field and analyses signage within a general geo-semiotic framework (for instance, Scollon/Scollon 2003). With Shohamy and Gorter (2009), we have current case studies that examine visual multilingualism and its implications for linguistic policy, linguistic identity and linguistic consciousness.

Methodology and Material

The data base of this case study consists altogether of approx. 600 digital photos which were taken – with student participation – at five different locations (Luxembourg City, Wiltz, Vianden, Esch/Alzette and Junglinster) between October 2007 and June 2009. Here, the objective was to capture all possible visual signs with text segments within a defined area in the town centre. Most of the analysed visual signs were official signs, commercial signs, notices, posters or private signs. The following were excluded: address signs, menus, advertisements for certain products or graffiti (so-called 'transgressive signs'[44]). In the course of our work it became clear that it was not always easy to draw a clear line between institutional notices and actual advertisements. For instance, is an information board pointing out specific services of the railway company *Sociéte nationale des chemins de fer luxembourgois* CFL to be classified as a top-down sign[45] or as advertising? Here, finer analytical grids need to be developed in the future.

In the following quantitative analysis, we concentrated our investigation on the linguistic distribution and the roles the different languages play. We subsequently interpreted the results with regard to the linguistic situation of the country and its linguistic profile.

Corpus Analysis

The signs are first subdivided according to whether they are monolingual or multilingual signs.They are further differentiated by authorship: Top-down signs are signs that are provided by state or quasi-state institutions (e.g. information notices issued by the authorities, town entrance signs etc.). Bottom-up signs, by contrast, are provided by private individuals, shops or companies. As will be

---

44 | Signs that intentionally and without authorisation disturb the real semiotics of the place, e.g., graffiti, tags, intentionally discarded garbage.
45 | Centrally and mostly uniformly provided signs: e.g. information notice boards, offer boards or advertising campaigns (internal and external producers).

shown, this type of differentiation constitutes an essential controlling factor for the linguistic structure of the signs.

On the basis of these criteria the corpus is composed as outlined in table 1.

	Top-down signs (institutional signs)	Bottom-up signs (commercial, private)
Monolingual	95	227
multilingual*	103	159

Table 2: Distribution of monolingual/multilingual and top-down/bottom-up signs (* bilingual or trilingual).

What is clear at first glance is that bottom-up signs are less often multilingual than top-down signs. In the case of the-top down signs, however, the ratio of unilingual to multilingual signs is almost equal.

Analysis of Monolingual Signs

The quantitative distribution of monolingual signs is as follows:

	Luxembourgish	French	German	English	Portuguese	Italian	Chinese	Total
Top-down signs	16	64	6	8	1	0	0	95
Proportion in %	16.84	67.37	6.32	8.42	1.05	0.00	0.00	100.00
Bottom-up signs	30	132	25	33	2	3	2	227
Proportion in %	13.22	58.15	11.01	14.54	0.88	1.32	0.88	100.00

Table 3: Language distribution on monolingual signs.

As is to be expected, French is most frequent (67 %), while Luxembourgish – by a considerable margin – generally occupies second place. A typical feature is that, for the top-down signs, French is represented 10 % more often than in the bottom-up category. The stronger presence of German and also of English in the bottom-up area can be explained by the high degree of globalisation. At the airport of Luxembourg in particular one finds many exclusively English language signs.

In spite of French dominance, the language distribution of the monolingual signs shows ample evidence of mutlilingualism, since the rarer languages (Luxembourgish, German, English) are also represented in no small degree.

Figure 18: Notice board of the city of Luxembourg: Top-down, unilingual, French.

Figure 19: Road sign in the city of Luxembourg: Top down, unilingual, Luxembourgish.

Analysis of Multilingual Signs

For an analysis of a large number of multilingual signs to lead to a uniform and unequivocal evaluation it is necessary to simplify the terminology. This obtains particularly for multilingual areas or countries with a high level of linguistic contact. In the following, we will examine aspects of linguistic preference and of sign types.

Examining Language Preference

By this, we understand the order and general presentation of the languages on multilingual signs. A particular language is often emphasised by the manner of spatial arrangement and/or by the graphic design (including size, colour, typeface) which indicates a certain rank order and valence of the language in question. It is beyond the scope of our study to factor in this code preference in a systematic way, something that will have to be carried out in a subsequent investigation. Typical for Luxembourg are the place-name signs, which display the French name at the top in boldface and capital letters, and underneath the Luxembourgish name in italics and a smaller font.

Figure 20: Place-name sign of the city of Luxembourg.

The distribution and order of the languages are examined more thoroughly in the following sections. The tables show the distribution of the language combination for bilingual and trilingual signs. The order of the language codes corresponds to the order on the respective sign.

	FR-LU	LU-FR	LU-GE	FR-GE	GE-FR	FR-EN	EN-FR	GE-EN	FR-NL	other	Total
Top down signs	4	10	0	40	3	13	7	0	0	3	80
Proportion in %	5.00	12.5	0.00	50.00	3.75	16.3	8.75	0.00	0.00	3.75	100.00
Bottom up signs	16	5	0	25	4	18	13	6	15	26	128
Proportion in %	12.50	3.91	0.00	19.53	3.13	14.06	10.16	4.69	11.72	20.31	100.00

Table 4: Language distribution on bilingual signs.

	FR-GE-EN	FR-EN-GE	EN-FR-GE	EN-GE-FR	other	Total
Top-down signs	12	3	2	2	4	23
Proportion in %	52.17	13.04	8.70	8.70	17.39	100.00
Bottom-up signs	11	1	3	4	9	28
Proportion in %	39.29	3.57	10.71	14.29	32.14	100.00

Table 5: Language distribution on trilingual signs.

Conspicuous at first glance is the language combination: While for the top-down signs, the combination FR-GE (50 %) or FR-GE-EN (52 %) is the most frequent, the bottom-up signs display a greater level of heterogeneity. They very clearly show the heterogeneous multilinguality that is a feature of Luxembourgish sign-posting (see also the high proportion in the category 'other' which subsumes all other possible linguistic combinations). Conversely, the proportion of Luxembourgish-French signs in the top-down category is greater than in the bottom-up one (12.5 % versus 3.9 % with the bilingual signs). On most signs, French is the first-used language, while German is practically never found in this position; in fact, English is found more often in the first position.

In table 6, the linguistic occurrence on bilingual and trilingual signs has been added up, regardless of the order, to get an impression of the usage frequency of the individual languages. The leading position of French, which is represented almost continuously in all categories, is very obvious. With bilingual top-down signs, German is found in approximately half of the cases, while this portion is lower in the case of the bottom-up signs which favour English.

	FR	LU	GE	EN	Total
bilingual top-down signs	79	14	44	20	80
Proportion in %	98.75	17.5	55.00	25.00	
trilingual top-down signs	23	2	22	21	23
Proportion in %	100.00	8.70	95.65	91.30	
bilingual bottom-up signs	105	21	40	40	119
Proportion in %	88.24	17.65	33.61	33.61	
trilingual bottom-up signs	30	4	26	27	31
Proportion in %	96.77	12.90	83.87	87.10	

Table 6: Occurrence of the four most frequent languages on multilingual signs.

Therefore trilingualism – made up of French, German and English – is a feature of both sign types, while Luxembourgish is used only in 8 and 18 % of the cases. The figures clearly prove that English has already firmly established itself.

Analysis of the Different Sign Types

In this section we will examine the multilingual signs in terms of how the individual languages represented on them relate to each other. Following the model developed by Backhaus (2007) we distinguish three different types of signs:

1. *Homophonic signs*: The entire information presented on the sign is translated into several languages. The language distribution on such signs is ideal, as it were, because no language is preferred over another except by the order in which they are listed. A homophonic sign requires no multilingual competence from the reader because the information is available in 'his or her' own language.
2. *Mixed signs*: On such signs, only part of the information is translated.
3. *Polyphonic signs*: These signs contain information which is distributed among several languages without translation. Even more so than with the mixed signs, multilingual competence is necessary for understanding polyphonic signs.

Our Luxembourg sample reveals interesting differences between the top-down signs and the bottom-up signs, because the proportion of homophonic signs is clearly higher in the former group, whereas the latter contains more polyphonic signs (57 % and 31 %). While on homophonic signs, the information is identical in all languages represented on the sign and therefore democratically available to all population groups, readers of polyphonic signs must be conversant with the languages used in order to decode the entire information. It is evident that polyphonic signs require higher multilingual competence than homophonic ones.

	Top-down signs	Bottom-up signs
mixed	17	14
homophonic	57	31
polyphonic	26	55

Table 7: Sign distribution according to type.

Figure 21: Police sign: homophonic, top-down, trilingual (Luxembourg train station).

Figure 22: Hotel in Vianden: Homophonic, bottom-up, four-lingual.

The examples shown in figures 21 and 22 represent the classical situation of the homophonic sign on which the contents are translated completely into the other languages. Often, this is also supported by a corresponding graphic design.

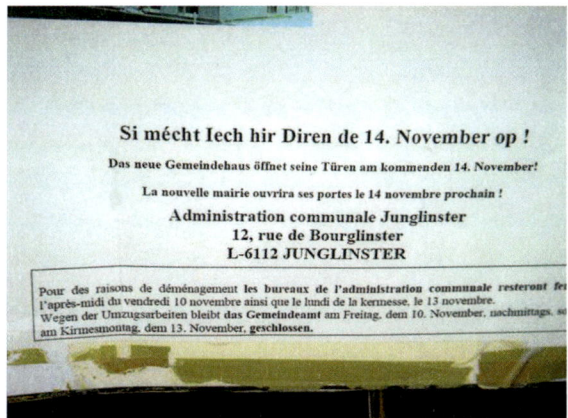

Figure 23: Notice by the Junglinster municipality: mixed sign, top-down, trilingual (Junglinster).

While the upper portion of the notice at Junglinster city hall shown in figure 23 has homophonic characteristics, the 'small print' in the bottom part is only available in French and German.

Figure 24: Advertising poster in Junglinster: polyphonic sign, bottom-up, trilingual (Junglinster).

In order to understand all the information on the sign in figure 24, the reader must have at least a passive knowledge of French ('Expo', 'Bourse'), German ('Modellbau, Tauschbörse') and Luxembourgish ('Auer'), where opening times are mentioned).

Conclusion

The analysis of the text types present on public signs and notices, up to now largely neglected by research, produced the following results:

- In quantitative terms, about half of public sign-posting is multilingual. When signs are monolingual, French dominates, while Luxembourgish, English and German are represented clearly less often as sole language.
- On multilingual signs, French is represented almost throughout. The most frequent combination is 'French/German' and 'French/German/English'.
- Top-down signs are more frequently multilingual than bottom-up signs. Here, we can discern an element of official language policy that wishes the country's multilinguality to be reflected also in the official sign-posting.
- The occurrence of English is particularly interesting: If there are three languages on a sign, the third one is always English. Luxembourgish as the third language does not seem to be an option.
- Top-down signs tend to reproduce identical information in all the languages represented (homophonic signs), still, however, reflecting a certain bias by the frequent first position of French. Bottom-up signs, in contrast, show a bigger heterogeneity in language choice and also in dealing with the translation, meaning that polyphonic signs are more frequent in this category, requiring a higher level of multilingual competence for their decoding.
- In general, Luxembourgish is used relatively rarely on public signs and occurs more frequently in the bottom-up than in the top-down category. For many Luxembourgers, standard German is still the main written language, so that a parallel use of the closely related languages of German and Luxembourgish is considered to be redundant.

With regards to identity constructions, our LL case study seems, at first glance, to contradict both the results of the questionnaire survey presented earlier and of the analysis of the letters to the editor which clearly established the enormous significance of Luxembourgish in identity formation processes. In fact, public signage is marked by the dominance of French or by multilingualism without the participation of Luxembourgish. There are various reasons for the widespread absence of Luxembourgish, the country's official language: due to the still very dominant medial diglossia the use of Luxembourgish is restricted primarily to its oral form and it manages to penetrate only rather haltingly into those areas of the public domain where the written language prevails. The fact that Luxembourgish is still only moderately standardised is often seen as a further obstacle to using this language on public signage. There is too much uncertainty about committing an error. Although German is not represented on signs as rarely as one might think, it never occurs as the sole language (monophonic signs); rather, it is accompanied by French and also by English. The probable reason for this is the radical rejection of anything German immediately after the end of the Second World War .

4.5 Conclusion: Linguistic Polynomia as an Opportunity

The results presented emphatically confirm the relevance of the subject of multilingualism in Luxembourg. The co-existence, juxtaposition and occasional opposition of different languages is one of the constitutive conditions of Luxembourg's society. The complexity of the linguistic subject matter is demonstrated, for instance, by the way in which on the one hand outstanding importance is attributed to Luxembourgish, whereas this is only reflected to a very limited extent in public usage. Perhaps it seems, not least for this reason, Luxembourgish achieves its function as an identity forming language – an added value that neither French nor German can claim for itself. Despite having been used in the Grand Duchy for centuries and therefore being influential in school, press and administrative settings, these are considered by large parts of the population not as (other) mother tongues and therefore legitimate linguistic property but rather, as the languages of the neighbours.

Nonetheless, (specifically) Luxembourgish multilingualism is certainly recognised as being advantageous for the cultural and economic interests of the country. It represents a unique defining feature that makes Luxembourg a European, if not global, linguistic model. This too, as the study shows, is a fundamental element of Luxembourgish identity.

Luxembourg cannot function as a monolingual country but only on the basis of a linguistic consensus, which includes (at least) the country's three official languages. Only under this condition can the communicative efficiency of the country and the inclusion of the large foreign population groups be ensured – notwithstanding issues in the detail. However, one cannot speak of a linguistic conflict in Luxembourg, as exists, for instance, in Belgium, South Tyrol or the Basque Provinces.

In line with the premises of this investigation, identity is always to be understood in terms of continuously updating identity structure(s), drawing nourishment from public and private discourse. An essentialist approach to identity is aporistic and is not conducive to the current investigation. The society of (not only of) Luxembourg is so complex in its structure that a simple equation between language and identity is not possible: nominating Luxembourgish as the national language does not automatically mean that all inhabitants speak this language, that the state translates this linguistic-political decision into educational policy or that all sections of the population will interpret the first clause of the Language Act of 1984 ("*La langue* nationale des Luxembourgeois est le luxembourgeois"[46]) in the same vein. The same goes for the general principle of multilingualism: while the quantitative results in section 4.2 show that multilingualism is seen as a central cultural and social constant by almost all Luxembourgers, the same results also show that significant differences exist in terms of the manner in which to bring about this multilingual facility: thus the majority (43 %) is of the opinion that bilingualism is sufficient, while only 20 % are in favour of (the officially championed) trilingualism. This contradiction and heterogeneity is not solely due to the high proportion of foreigners, but rather it becomes evident that all parameters of social and cultural differentiation (i.e. milieu affiliation, age, gender etc.) can lead to constantly changing identity structures in which conflicts between 'appropriated' and 'attributed identities' can emerge. This inevitably leads to divergent notions about a 'good' and 'correct' structure of multilingualism, as the discussion of the letters to editors discourse has demonstrated. A linguistic identity, therefore, arises not from the languages involved but from specifically divergent notions as well as communicated and mediating discourses *about* the languages: "In this view, processes of identification take place through practice, which is not limited to the use of language, but includes representations of language (like discourses of endangerment)." (Jaffe 2007: 70)

Now, it may well be a matter of regret that no simple equation can be made between language (s) and identity and that, also in the case of Luxembourg, no simple formula exists for a national identity, however constituted. In point of fact, any society requires flexibility. Particularly in the case of multilingual communities with small regional languages, there is evidence to show that linguistic and therefore also social conflicts can be avoided if 'polynomia' (Marcellesi 2003) is permitted, i.e. the social acceptance of different linguistic standards and multilingual constellations.

4.6 References

Backhaus, Peter. 2007. Linguistic Landscapes. A Comparative Study of Urban Multilingualism in Tokyo. Clevedon: Multilingual Matters.

Bucher, Hans Jürgen. 1986. Pressekommunikation. Grundstrukturen einer öffentlichen Form der Kommunikation aus linguistischer Sicht. Tübingen.

Bucher, Hans Jürgen. 1989. Zeitungen und Leser im Dialog. Ein Beitrag zur kommunikativen Analyse von Pressetexten. In Dialoganalyse II. Referate der 2. Arbeitstagung Bochum 1988. Vol. 1, ed. Edda Weigand and Franz Hundsnurscher (1989): 287-303.

Bucher, Hans Jürgen. 1986. Media release. Grundstrukturen einer öffentlichen Form der Kommunikation aus linguistischer Sicht. Tübingen.

Drewnowska-Vargáné, Eva. 2001. Kohärenzmanagement und Emittent-Rezipient-Konstellationen in deutsch- polnisch- und ungarischsprachigen Leserbriefen.

---

[46] | Personal translation: "The Luxembourgers' national language is Luxembourgish".

In Zur Kulturspezifik von Textsorten, ed. Ulla Fix, Stephan Habscheid and Josef Klein, 89-108 Tübingen: Staufenburg Verlag.

Gilles, Peter. 1999. Dialektausgleich im Lëtzebuergeschen: zur phonetisch-phonologischen Fokussierung einer Nationalsprache. Tübingen: Niemeyer.

Gilles, Peter and Claudine Moulin. 2003. Luxembourgish. In Germanic standardizations – Past to Present, ed. A. Deumert and W. Vandenbussche, 303-29. Amsterdam: de Gruyter.

Jaffe, Alexandra. 2007. Discourses of endangerment. Contexts and consequences of essentializing discourses. In: Discourses of Endangerment: Ideology and Interest in the Defence of Languages, ed. Alexandre Duchêne and Monica Heller, 57-74. London: Continuum.

Joseph, John E. 2004. Language and identity. National, ethnic, religious. Houndmills: Palgrave Macmillan.

Kraemer, Jean-Pierre. 1993. Luxembourg. In Sociolinguistica 7 (Multilingual Concepts
in the Schools of Europe), 162-73.

Landry Rodrigue and Richard Y. Bourhis. 1997. Linguistic Landscape and Ethnolinguistic Vitality. In Journal of Language and Social Psychology, Vol. 16, No. 1: 23-49.

Marcellesi, Jean-Baptiste, Thierry Bulot and Philippe Blanchet. 2003. Sociolinguistique: Epistémologie, langues régionales, Polynomie. Paris: L'Harmattan.

Mattheier, Klaus J. 1991. Standardsprache als Sozialsymbol. Über kommunikative Folgen gesellschaftlichen Wandels. In Das 19. Jahrhundert. Sprachgeschichtliche Wurzeln des heutigen Deutsch (Yearbook 1990 of the Institut für deutsche Sprache), ed. Rainer Wimmer, 41-73. Berlin/New York Verlag.

Moulin, Claudine. 2006. Grammatisierung und Standardisierung des Luxemburgischen. Eine grammatikographisch-sprachhistorische Annäherung. In Perspektiven einer linguistischen Luxemburgistik, ed. Damaris Nübling and Claudine Moulin, 277-311. Heidelberg: Winter Verlag.

Naglo, Kristian. 2007. Rollen von Sprache in Identitätsbildungsprozessen multilingualer Gesellschaften in Europa. Eine vergleichende Betrachtung Luxemburgs, Südtirols und des Baskenland. Frankfurt: Peter Lang.

Piirainen, Ilpo Tapani und Anneli Yli-Kojola. 1983. Untersuchungen zur Sprache der Leserbriefe im Hamburger Abendblatt. Vaasa.

Sandig, Barbara. 1986. Stilistik der deutschen Sprache. Berlin/New York: de Gruyter.

Scollon, Ron and Suzie Scollon. 2003. Discourses in place: language in the material world. London: Routledge.

Shohamy, Elana and Durk Gorter, ed. 2009. Linguistic Landscape. Expanding the Scenery. New York, London: Routledge.

Wagner, Melanie and Wini V. Davies. 2009. The role of World War II in the development of Luxembourgish as a national language. Journal of Language Planning and Language Policy.

5. Spaces and Identities

MARION COLAS-BLAISE, SYLVIE FREYERMUTH, SONJA KMEC,
GIAN MARIA TORE, CHRISTIAN SCHULZ

5.1 INTRODUCTION: GEOGRAPHIC DISCOURSES AND TOURISM PRACTICE

While questions of spatial dimension have since long been central topics of (social-) geographic identity research, they have only been approached by human and social sciences in recent years (see Döring/Thielmann 2009; Lossau/Lippuner 2004). In parallel to this interest for the conceptual foundations of geography, also known as 'spatial turn', geography, conversely, performed a 'social' or 'cultural turn', i.e. an increasing import of conceptual and methodological perspectives from the relevant neighbouring disciplines. All in all, this has led to a wide diffusion of discourse-analytical and semiotic approaches with a decidedly spatial perspective (see Blunt et al, 2003; Gebhard et al. 2003; Glasze/Matissek 2009; Shurmer-Smith 2002).

According to Weichhart's very sociopsychologically inspired concept of space-related identities (1990), one can distinguish between two basic concepts: One is the 'identity of a space', i.e. the cognitive-emotional representation of the identity of a certain segment of space, which is perceived individually or collectively (e.g. specific features of a border region in the perception of its population). Secondly, there is the concept of 'space as a component of individual and/or collective identities', i.e. those mental representations and emotionally affective assessments of a space segment which become a part of the individual 'self-concept' respectively the collective 'we-concept' – or determine external group identity as a 'they-concept' (e.g. the everyday relevance of the specific features of a border region forms the basis for specific group identities, for instance: "We/The cross-border workers").

In both cases, the physical and material specificities of the space are secondary or serve – in their selective perception – primarily as a projection screen for assignments of meaning. These are constituted by patterns of action as well as from discursive practice – both in the sense of "everyday regionalisations" – according to Werlen (1995/1997). Spatial identity aspects thus becomes, via social practices, an element of symbolic social systems and therefore part of social constructions of reality (Berger/Luckmann 1966). Here, the consciousness-shaping discourse is not only constituted by elements of social communication about space (language, including literature, film etc. as well as maps, statistical data etc.). It can also be influenced by material environments (e.g. the building fabric of a city district, the aesthetics of a landscape, traffic congestion) without these assuming a deterministic character. Other semiotic elements are also included, such as direction-signs, flags, emblems, architectural stylistic elements etc. In view of this wide range of corpora and perspectives for possible investigation, the aforementioned authors stress the added value of interdisciplinary investigation designs that are better equipped to meet the conceptual and methodological demands of contemporary research requirements than purely disciplinary approaches.

The current chapter explores such 'geo-graphical' issues from various angles, shedding light on the different ways in which Luxembourg is described, depicted and signified as a space. It seeks to analyse precisely those discourses that 'produce' Luxembourg as a space, thus defining and designating it as such. How then is Luxembourg conceived as an urban, regional, national or international space? How are the different components of this space organised and how can they be reassembled into a unity? How does this space lay claim to autonomy and in which way can it be put into relation with an exteriority? How are itineraries and borders signified, and how are issues concerning the country's size and its ties with other countries put to the fore? The extraordinary diversity of discourses performing this function constitutes an enormous obstacle for conducting a comprehensive study or even a representative one. However, these multiple discourses may be reduced to a limited number of possible practices: the spatial segment 'country' is either a subject matter of language or is it beeing constituted only through language, in particular when one is dealing with practices relating to the fields of politics, economy, education and tourism. Space becomes a subject of discussion, when it involves planning for it, teaching about or promoting it. This chapter examines the manner in which space is vested with value through discursive uses of tourism practices.

There are two main reasons for choosing to focus on tourism. First of all, it appears to be a defining feature of tourist discourses to talk about space as such, whereas in politics or education, for example, space is only one of many discursive topics. More precisely, tourism aims in particular at enhancing, defining and characterising space in a way more direct and explicit than is the case in politics or education. In short, as a subject matter for investigation, tourism is of immediate significance when we direct our attention to questions of identity, in this case to the dynamics of discursive production in defining what is 'Luxembourg'. For the aim is to advertise the country, whereas it should be to describe, to explain, to illustrate it. In other words: the tourism discourse has to convince others of the country's worth, whereas it pretends to provide a mere status report. This explains the significance that tourism discourse has for a study of the attribution of meaning: they *inform* about something by emphasising its importance, singularity or authenticity *through argumentation*; here 'objectivity' is thus quite clearly constructed and negotiated.

Finally, the theoretical interest in a study of tourism discourses has been reinforced by the corpus analysed here: the collection of tourist maps, guides, brochures and books is – despite its wealth and variety – rather homogeneous and clearly delineated in character, thus ensuring the validity of the sample. The eclecticism of the various approaches used here does not call into question the overall structure. Rather, the different strands of analysis converge as they focus on one common discursive 'object'.

The Levels of Scale

The foremost reason for the (relative) heterogeneity of approaches we chose to study tourism discourses in Luxembourg lies in how the corpus is structured. Indeed, in reviewing the materials under investigation it quickly became clear that, in terms of discourse, Luxembourg 'exists' on at least five different levels: the districts of the city, the city as a whole, the regions, the national unit and the country's position within the Greater Region. However, each of the above-mentioned questions (borders, internal composition, identifiable itineraries, characterisations, etc.) poses itself in a completely different way; moreover, the corpus and textualities change with each level. Consequently, the approaches too had to be differentiated and adapted to the respective corpora and to the questions addressed.

In all cases, the aim was to analyse the representation of space in tourist texts, namely in how far the presentation of places and territories of Luxembourg make sense and carry significance. The smallest geographical level of scale we examined, that of the districts of the capital city, is textualised in the brochures and booklets of the *Luxembourg City Tourist Office*. They present and praise the various areas of Luxembourg City by the means of itineraries illustrated by maps and commented by verbal texts. We therefore needed to examine the interdependency of verbal and visual representation and their underlying contents. For this purpose we employed the tools of semiolinguistics as well as those of pragmatics and speech act theory. We were thus able to study the congruity between the 'official' discourse (which utilizes the epideictic genre of praise and the advisory genre of recommendation) and the 'spontaneous' discourses of respondents in two surveys, one quantitative and the other qualitative. The next geographical level of scale, that of Luxembourg City, is examined primarily with regard to a collection of maps of the capital. Here the methods of choice are those of visual semiotics that allow us to analyse the tabular and iconic strategies of representing the city, i.e. its reduction to a one-dimensional surface and its visualisation, plus occasional paratexts comprised of photographic or drawn images. Subsequently, the coherence of such a collection of visualisations, its stability and consequently its efficacy was correlated to questions concerning its communicative value.

The regional level of scale was investigated on the basis of the discourses developed by brochures released by the *Office National du Tourisme*, focussing on both their verbal and iconic contents. The compositional analysis draws on stylistics, rhetoric and discourse analysis. In applying the tools of these three connected fields, we were able to clearly reveal the interaction that links writing and visual iconicity with the essence of a relationship that is based on redundancy and the production of prototypes. This is achieved notably by a subtle use of colours and hyperbolic speech acts.

The national level of scale was examined using a corpus composed of a series of guides that reflect how the Grand Duchy of Luxembourg has been represented over time. This requires a historical discourse analysis that takes into account representations of national identity, as seen by other countries, or in relation to these. This approach reveals an image of Luxembourg that is multilayered and often paradoxical.

Finally, we scrutinised the level of scale of the Greater Region by analysing and comparing some hybrid works about that area. These books are both promotional and descriptive; they seek to defend a 'geographical reality' that is neither stable nor fully recognised and whose study assesses the intricate interplay of the given representations.

While the topics addressed at each level of scale are different, the way they are emphasised follows argumentative strategies. Thus, each microanalysis of maps, brochures, guides and books had to take into account the way in which identities of places are *projected*, as opposed to the way in which the residents themselves *appropriate* those same places, in other words how they conceive them, characterise them and which value they accord them in their own lives. In order to incorporate in particular this last aspect and dialectise the studies on tourism textualities, each analysis of the five geographical levels of scale was compared to the results of the qualitative and quantitative surveys conducted with the residents of Luxembourg.

5.2 Between Seduction and Reality: Luxembourg City and its Discourses

"*Le mode selon lequel j'écris – ou même rêve – l'espace, rien ne saurait en dire plus long,*" wrote François Wahl (1980: 46), "*sur le mode que j'ai d'habiter mon lieu*".[1] How do the respondents of the quantitative survey transform the districts of Luxembourg City into a 'place'? How do 'spontaneous' discourses, captured during the qualitative surveys, which provide an insight into 'appropriated' identities, differ from

---

1 | Personal translation: "With the way I write – or even dream – about space, nothing could say more about the way I inhabit my place".

representations communicated through the 'official' discourse of tourism, which is the source of 'attributed' identities? Targeted at foreigners, the latter attempts to convey knowledge, but also to make things tangible and initiate activities by encouraging a pragmatic attitude.

Observations relating to these questions fall into two categories: (1) the comparison of individual responses to the question on 'places one shows to friends from abroad as a matter of priority' with the frames of reference of Luxembourg City presented in two pamphlets and two leaflets published by the Luxembourg City Tourist Office[2]; (2) the comparison of images of the Bonnevoie area, the Grund and Limpertsberg quarters and the Kirchberg district, as described by the interviewees, with the corresponding 'official' texts[3].

To this end we shall make use of semiotics, rhetoric, pragmatics, and the linguistic speech act theory. To show how the image of the city is shaped by the laudatory discourse of tourism, one must investigate the consistency between content and expressive layers in terms of its verbal and visual expression.

If Someone Were to Show Me Luxembourg City ...

The questions asked in the quantitative survey immediately implies an elective strategy (Fontanille 1999: 41-61): the viewpoint from which specific aspects of a country are perceived and which frames the interaction between the subject and the object in question determines the 'best possible example', the contribution which is representative due to its inherent 'radiance', the symbolic 'place' which stands for all others. The point here is not to settle for a single feature, even if it is considered picturesque, nor to surprise, but rather to determine that one specific aspect which can be associated with an 'identifying' value: thus the particular aspect, combining the glamour of the spectacular with the stability of time, should draw the stranger's attention to something unique and create a 'recognition' value.

It is not insignificant that 71 % of those questioned generally preferred Luxembourg City to the rest of the country, or in order of preference, the Old Town (51 %)[4], Grund/Corniche (7 %), the grand-ducal Palace (5 %), the Bock Casemates/Clausen (3 %), the Pétrusse viaduct, the cathedral, the museums and Philharmonic Concert Hall, the Kirchberg district and the *Gëlle Fra* Monument of Remembrance

---

2 | The brochures *Luxembourg la ville, bonjour!*, *Luxembourg, Vivez la ville!* as well as the two leaflets: *Panorama City Map* and *City Promenade*.

3 | See the leaflets *Le circuit des roses du Limpertsberg 'RosaLi'* and *Luxembourg, une capitale européenne*. For the purposes of this study we refer only to the French language versions.

4 | Vianden received 6 %, Little Switzerland/Müllerthal 3 %, Northern Luxembourg (*Éisléck*), Remich/the Moselle, Echternach, the Upper Sûre and Southern Luxembourg 2 % each; Diekirch and Clervaux each scored 1 %.

(1 % each)[5]. Without ignoring the risk of over-interpretation arising from the lack of more significant differences, one notes that this emphasis encompasses several dimensions and subordinates the effects of identity to an ethical and aesthetic sense. Certain tendencies are indeed apparent: the selection takes in a broad spectrum of the historical past (the cradle of the city, listed as a UNESCO World Heritage Site, but also the Gëlla Fra, albeit with less emphasis) before turning to the present (namely to the Kirchberg district); in general, tradition, continuity and the wish for unification (like the grand-ducal Palace or the cathedral for instance) appear to win out over modernity and the opening up to Europe; the beauty of the landscape (the Pétrusse and the viaduct) and focal points of the arts (the museums, the Philharmonic) receive equal emphasis.

The comparison of these data with the discourse of tourism must take into account the pragmatic objectives of the various pamphlets and leaflets published by official bodies. As these are designed to advertise the city in the manner of marketing texts, they are, in the words of Marc Bonhomme, expressed in terms of *"deux genres rhétoriques de discours"*[6]:

[...] d'une part, le discours épidictique, fondé sur le macro-acte de l'éloge et axé sur le présent de la célébration du produit proposé. D'autre part, le discours délibératif, [...], qui repose sur le macro-acte du conseil en vue d'une décision future du récepteur quant à l'achat/utilisation du produit en question[7] (Bonhomme 2003: 13).

As such they make use of three speech acts for the basic 'schematisation' of the city: in addition to the selection and the symbolisation – both also targets of the quantitative survey – 'streamlining' increases the recognisability of the area; as a thymic correlate, it has a feeling about it of being in control of the territory and conveys a sense of safety (Bonhomme 2003: 14-15).

Because the pamphlets *Luxembourg la ville, bonjour!* and *Luxembourg, Vivez la ville!* are aimed at potential 'consumers', they combine elective and comprehensive

---

5 | Taking age into consideration, one notes that these places were chosen by 74 % of the over 60s, with the majority being women. Youths (16-20 years) and 30 to 44 year olds came in second at 68 %. One notes further that these places were nominated by 77 % of those belonging to the status-oriented milieu, compared with 73 % from the privileged conservative milieu, 72 % from the privileged liberal milieu, 71 % from the petty bourgeois milieu and 70 % from the meritocratic-oriented milieu; 69 % belonged to an alternative milieu, whereas 67 % belonged to an underprivileged milieu; the hedonistic milieu (62 %) lies ahead of the tradition-oriented milieu (58 %).

6 | Personal translation: "Two rhetorical genres of discourse".

7 | Personal translation: "On the one hand the epideictic discourse which reposes on the macro-act of praise and is aimed at the present appraisal of the proposed product; on the other, the deliberative discourse [...], which reposes on the macro-act of advice with view to the recipient's prospective decision to purchase/utilise the product in question".

strategies: by taking a broad-brush approach, they aim less at a comprehensive enumeration of every feature than at oscillating between attention-grabbing detail and integration into a greater whole more conducive to the creation of coherence. It is about enabling the visitor to understand the city 'at a glance' while at the same time inviting him or her to appropriate the 'reality' on offer, by making a cognitive, but also a pathemic and somatic – in other words an affective as well as a physical – experience of the localities. This is also the general structure of the pamphlets, which, by specifying a marked-out route[8], work their way comprehensively through a set of points arranged into paradigmatic categories either in the introduction or the cover pages.[9] In this way one can see that, in terms of contents, antithetic concept pairs are used systematically and repeatedly: past versus present; tradition – for example, in the context of folk festivals – versus modernity; culture versus nature; art versus finance or commerce, and national versus international. At the same time the 'narrator' appeals to the axiological realms of the good, the beautiful and the real. On the level of expression, systematisation and aestheticisation go together: more likely to be descriptive or prompting, titles, leaders and eye-catchers multiply the rhetorical resources (metaphor, generalisation, hyperbole); these are supported by the color scheme[10] and by full-page illustrations or small decorative images positioned next to small text boxes, which also attempt to serve the logic of the laudatory discourse[11], in particular through the use of evaluative adjectives and quotes from well-known personalities.

---

8 | See the cover of *Luxembourg, Vivez la ville!* which, with the aid of an arrow sign, creates an expectation for the rest of the pamphlet.

9 | The four strips of images arranged on the front and back covers of the pamphlet *Luxembourg la ville, bonjour!* show the big wheel of the *Schueberfouer*, the Luxembourg City Historical Museum, the National Archives with Corniche and a part of Grund with the Alzette River.

10 | The pamphlet *Luxembourg la ville, bonjour!* uses a different colour for each subject discussed.

11 | See the following examples in particular: "Gibraltar of the North", "A financial centre of international standing" (see *Luxembourg la ville, bonjour!*); "Solid walls, UNESCO World Heritage Site. Experience 1 000 years of fortress history!", "International meeting point. Experience a city of finance, congresses and dynamic commerce!", "The cradle of European unification. Experience a capital city open to the world!", "Festivals and traditions. Experience events galore!", "Trips to the 'green heart'. Experience nature in its purest state!" (see *Luxembourg, Vivez la ville!*). Moreover, the subjective adjectives that refer to the (anonymous) narrator while assuming agreement and consent on the part of the reader are numerous: "[...] you, dear guest, will undertake glorious hikes", "well-known architects are responsible for designing some of the most remarkable buildings in the capital" (see *Luxembourg la ville, bonjour!*).

What is noticeable is the broad convergence between preferences expressed by respondents and the selection used in tourism discourse[12]. Not only does the latter mention all of the verbally selected 'identification candidates', but it also enhances their recognition value by providing illustrations[13]. In particular, the two pamphlets open up with large format photographs of Corniche and the Old Town (spread across more than one A4-size page)[14]. If precisely those variables considered to be the essence of the 'style' of the City of Luxembourg are thrown in here and there, they are not only designed to establish those contrasts that are considered important ("small country, strong attraction": see *Luxembourg la ville, bonjour!*; "Vivez une ville pleine de contrastes!": see Luxembourg, *Vivez la ville!*), but also to assign the relicts of the past a position of choice by inserting them in a narrative or even in a fictional account[15]. The fact that the choices of one side are, so to speak, on the same wavelength as those of the other can create the impression that the idealisation of the staged remnants of a turbulent, even spectacular history presented to the foreign visitor is founded upon a broad consensus: history; along with it the actual staging the city's development, reconstructed step by step with the help of outlines and layers, seems to be considered a very convincing 'gateway'.

Ultimate proof of this convergence of outlooks can be found in the leaflet entitled *City promenade*. Not only does the introductory statement conform to the rule, opting for the historical narrative while incidentally making use of familiar metaphors – "the cradle of Luxembourg City", "the European power game" – or borrowing formulations from historians that are thought to hit the mark ("Gibraltar of the North"). Above all, the map, which takes up the second and third pages, re-establishes 'reality' (see Marin 1994) by showing enhancements: for certain places and buildings in the city centre it offers a representation 'in perspective', which contrasts with the otherwise two-dimensional drawings. This essentially concerns locations mentioned spontaneously by the respondents: the Bock Casemates, Corniche, Grund, the grand-ducal Palace, the Cathedral of Our Lady, the Former Jesuit College and the *Gëlle Fra* monument. Thus the high density of references

---

12 | See Linden & Thewes on the subject of a "convergence between tourism publicity and national advertisement, using 'premium' sights and idealised self-perception". They add: "Not only do these representations influence tourists' views, in the final analysis they also determine the perception that Luxembourgers have of their own country, its past and its geography" (Linden/Thewes 2007: 44).

13 | However, at the pictorial level the *Panorama City Map* includes neither the Place de la Constitution nor the *Gëlle Fra* which is situated there.

14 | In the pamphlet *Luxembourg la ville, bonjour!*, the smaller of the photographs of the Corniche and of the Old Town overhang a strip of two small-format photos; the first shows the Place de la Constitution, the second the Town Hall.

15 | Thus one reads in the pamphlet *Luxembourg la ville, bonjour!*: "These angular streets echoed to the sound of cannon fire and the clanging of swords in the days of yore. Today, visitors can tread in the footsteps of cunning conquerors and heroic defenders [...]".

reinforces the 'referential illusion' and, by facilitating (re)-cognition – for instance one is not just looking at a generic cathedral, but rather at that of Luxembourg – creates a sensory perception. Even before conceptualisation, attention can be focused on the tangible characteristics of the 'concrete image'.

Figure 1: Le circuit des roses du Limpertsberg 'RosaLi' (cover page), with the kind permission of the Luxembourg City Tourist Office.

Figure 2: City promenade (cover page), with the kind permission of the Luxembourg City Tourist Office.

The City Centre and its 'Beyond'

What does one call the areas beyond the railway tracks, the green belt, the upper part of town and the Grand Duchess Charlotte Bridge? Comparing the discourses of tourism and 'spontaneous' oral descriptions in relation to the Bonnevoie area, the Limpertsberg and Grund quarters and the Kirchberg district[16], one can expect significant shifts in emphasis: 'spontaneous' discourse reflects more something experienced, appropriated identities, and at least partially avoids the rhetoric of laudation, which official bodies tend to use, thereby attributing identities.

First of all, we come across a double divide: the external one makes for a differentiation between residential districts (Bonnevoie and Limpertsberg) and those that could sooner be considered areas of transit or encounter (Grund and Kirchberg); the internal differentiation establishes two zones within each residential district based on a spatial differentiation: firstly the upper part and the lower part of Bonnevoie, and secondly Limpertsberg and the Glacis, the latter belonging more to the zone of transit and encounter, largely considered non-residential due to its annual funfair, its bars, cafés and restaurants, and its cinema and theatre.

Let us begin with the Bonnevoie area, which is not mentioned in our tourism discourse. The interviewees consistently mentioned conceptual pairs whose antithetical aspects result almost automatically: for them, the lower part of Bonnevoie is a place for the ordinary people, somewhat run-down in parts, a place with a mixed population, including older people, foreigners (Portuguese, Africans…) and homeless. For some it is a red light district as well as a drug and crime zone, while others see it as an environment conducive to community life. By contrast, the upper part of Bonnevoie is described as the exact opposite: upper class and remodelled, this zone is inhabited, we are told, by people of all ages belonging to the bourgeoisie, and mostly Luxembourg nationals. Could one assume that this selective image does not reflect a reality as much as reproduce rigid representations? Some respondents did not exclude the possibility that they were simply repeating the stereotypes used by the media.

With regards to Limpertsberg, it is considered, in the collective imagination, to be a primarily residential quarter whose green areas increase the quality of life, bourgeois, chic and expensive, located close to the town centre, shielded from abrupt changes. While (too) calm at weekends, it is a busy district on weekdays due to the many schools located there.

In contrast to other residential quarters, one tourist leaflet is dedicated to Limpertsberg: *Le circuit des roses du Limpertsberg 'RosaLi'*. The title is characteristic of a desire for aestheticisation that, instead of obscuring the other facets, puts them in a specific perspective[17]. The introductory text on the 19th century rose-growing operates with an objectivising distancing ('débrayage'); the visitor is then encouraged by means of the presentation of the walking tour in the form of a

---

16 | Contrary to Limpertsberg and Kirchberg, the Bonnevoie area is not the subject of a pamphlet or leaflet published by the Luxembourg City Tourist Office. There is also no mention of this area in the pamphlets *Luxembourg, Vivez la ville!* and *Luxembourg la ville, bonjour!* (by contrast to the Grund district). In comparing these different districts, we use the criteria on the basis of the selection made.

17 | For example, the University Campus of Limpertsberg is called *'the Campus des Roses'*.

map, the verbal final comment which elucidates the points mentioned, but also the large and medium-sized illustrations, to appropriate the area not only as a cognitive concept, but also somatically, pathemically and aesthetically[18]. The map and the encouraging discourse embody a 'means' in terms of the action to be carried out by the visitor; he or she follows a path corresponding to the map's guidelines, thereby making it into a 'route'.

Ought one to criticise the difference between the quarter's attributed identity set out in the leaflet and the lived identity? They correspond to different experiences of location, but in both cases the individual establishes an intimate relationship with the space.

As far as the Kirchberg plateau is concerned, it is, on the one hand – in contrast with the residential districts of 'old' Kirchberg, Weimerskirch or Weimershof – considered to be distant from the centre, expensive, impersonal, congested during the day, deserted at night, in short, not particularly congenial. On the other hand, the European institutions are emphasised, the international importance of RTL[19] and the banks, in the same way as those places relevant to consumption (Auchan shopping centre, exhibition grounds) and entertainment facilities (cinema). The Philharmony and the *Mudam*[20] lend the district an undeniable artistic ambiance, although slightly more space would show the buildings in a better light.

The Kirchberg plateau appears therefore to have its set place in everyday life,[21] although, as it is exposed to a constant coming and going, its structure is not predispose to be a residential area. In certain instances it can function as a go-between, or even as a meeting point between the foreigners employed in the offices of the European institutions and the rest of the population.

The leaflet *Luxembourg, une capitale européenne*[22] deals with the European dimension at the expense of the others: the laudatory discourse obscures the 'non-European' component, whose importance was, however, emphasised by those interviewed. To better understand its peculiarities, we will compare this leaflet to *Le circuit des roses du Limpertsberg 'RosaLi'* in terms of the map positioning, the images and the personal references.

While the map in the leaflet *Le circuit des roses du Limpertsberg 'RosaLi'* is sandwiched between the text passages, in *Luxembourg, une capitale européenne* it is

---

18 | See the uniform colour scheme in which the colour pink is used for the map and to frame the images.
19 | *Radio Télévision Luxembourg.*
20 | *Musée d'Art Moderne Grand-Duc Jean* (Grand Duke Jean Museum of Modern Art).
21 | The hospital is repeatedly mentioned. Some respondents emphasised the green spaces.
22 | We count 12 locations: Town Hall, Municipal Circle, *House of Europe*, the *Robert Schuman House*, the *Council of the European Union*, the *European Court of Auditors*, the *European School*, the *European Commission*, the *European Court of Justice*, the *European Investment Bank* and the *Robert Schuman Monument*.

located at the end of the leaflet and graphically emphasised by a thick border; it is accompanied by a list of place names. If one relates the content and presentation layers one can assume that the map in *Le circuit des roses du Limpertsberg 'RosaLi'* contributes actively to the walker's spatial perception of the area, in that the map constantly suggests new options and the accompanying text lists the sites. Significantly, the tour's destination point does not coincide with the starting point. The route is a function of this gap and the resulting tension.

In *Luxembourg, une capitale européenne*, the map provides summary access to an objective 'reality'. In a general view from above – the objective being to provide an 'overview of the European Union' – and therefore also with the possibility to be cognitively in control of the space, the map takes on a primarily didactic function: it aims to present that which suggests itself on the grounds of self-evidence. It comes as no surprise that the tour ends where it starts, the route makes full circle and the initiative of the rambling reader is circumscribed.

This impression is reinforced by the images. The leaflets contain picture strips, those in *Le circuit des roses du Limpertsberg 'RosaLi'* on the lower border and those in *Luxembourg, une capitale européenne* on the upper edge. The function of the photos is fundamentally different in each case. The six-sided fold-up leaflet *Le circuit des roses du Limpertsberg 'RosaLi'*, enables the rambling reader to discover the photos in motion and to continuously adjust his or her gaze[23]. Based on his or her observations en route, the reader is directly involved in determining the course, which is not uniformly structured, but includes changes of tempo and tension (see Fontanille/Zilberberg 1998; Zilberberg 2006).

The leaflet *Luxembourg, une capitale européenne*, on the other hand, is presented as a booklet with its pages carefully stapled in the middle. Most of the images conform to semi-wide or wide shot formats (they depict buildings with or without adjacent surroundings), serving a primarily descriptive function with no dynamic visual demands.

Finally, the analysis is confirmed in particular through the use of personal pronouns (see Benveniste 1966). Through the use of the formal *'vous'* (you) in the French text to address the reader and through the frequent use of the imperative, the discourse in the leaflet *Le circuit des roses du Limpertsberg 'RosaLi'* acquires a clearly encouraging and prompting character: it is about encouraging those readers with the required skill to 'reinvent' the space, and to give it a new form through a different kind of characterisation. In contrast to this, one notices in the leaflet *Luxembourg, une capitale européenne* the dominance of the pronoun 'we' ("*Au rond-point, nous pouvons décider de parcourir le chemin d'environ 2 km menant, à travers le parc, jusqu'à*

---

[23] | Moving from a close-up of a rose to medium close-ups (e.g. the top of a tombstone), but also to medium-long shots (a sculpture) and wide shots, with the central building of the university as the focal point, then another close-up, followed immediately this time by a photograph of a water tower. The rest of the leaflet displays the same pattern of alternating close-ups and wide shots.

l'École européenne [...]"²⁴). The process of objectivising distancing ('débrayage'), the dissolution of the 'I-realm' and the creation of distance is blocked by a strictly first-person oriented referential system. According to Emile Benveniste, the 'we', which augments the 'I' with a "non-differentiated totality of other people [...] expresses an extended and less precise person"²⁵ (Benveniste 1966: 235). Thus the author of the pamphlet and the reader are caught up in an interpersonal web designed to ensure consensus, even agreement and empathy between them. In particular, the use of the infinitive (*"Quoi de plus logique que de commencer au tout début, dans le système scolaire?"*²⁶), which implies neither time nor person, is conducive to an enunciating (in)differentiation that leaves the addressee of the utterance no other choice than to embrace the opinion of the enunciator – consent by enunciative continuity. Although the European institutions are striving for openness, the leaflet attempts to trap the reader in a diffuse 'we': instead of accompanying the reader on his or her walk, rather than constructing the 'European city' step by step, it purports to describe something that already exists, the various facets of which it enumerates. The map provides a complete overview of this, independently, as it were, from the visit itself. From that point on, it is about situating oneself within a sphere, tightly circumscribed by visual and verbal statements; perhaps the imaginery can unfurl from this position. Indeed, given the 'we' that encompasses both the narrator charged with conducting the discourse of tourism and the walking reader, one can assume a non-represented addressee: the addressees belong to Europe and are to be assigned to a world that the 'we' is just in the process of *imagining*.

Based on these brief considerations one is able to see that even if there is no complete overlap between the opinions of the interviewees and the corresponding leaflets, between the appropriated and the attributed identities, there is a basic 'concordance': the experience achieved by the strolling reader in Limpertsberg gives an idea of the relationship of the intimate complicity which connects the resident with his or her place of residence; similarly, by subsuming 'you' in 'we', thereby preventing the recipient from exteriorisation, the leaflet *Luxembourg, une capitale européenne* attempts to generate a consensus, or even a sense of empathy towards the addressee which is never explicitly expressed (Europe and the world); certainly this is not in contradiction to the nature of the Kirchberg district, which is often spontaneously experienced as being an international place and an impersonal one at the same time.

And finally, in the case of the Grund quarter, clear congruities in attitudes are evident: even outside the 'Blues 'n' Jazz Rally', the lower town with its terraces

---

24 | Personal translation: "At the roundabout, we can decide whether to take the 2km long road through the park, up to the European School [...]".

25 | Original version: "[Le 'nous'] annexe au 'je' une globalité indistincte d'autres personnes [...] exprime une personne amplifiée et diffuse."

26 | Personal translation: "What would be more obvious than to start right at the beginning, namely with the school system?"

invites a "moment of relaxation" (see *Luxembourg, Vivez la ville!*); respondents across the spectrum confirmed this, highlighting less the residential character and more the congenial side of this renovated neighbourhood, which attracts many (often anglophone) foreigners. To some extent, the cultural offering is also considered a distinctive trait, as is the beauty of the area, which tempts one to take a stroll.

At the end of this swift tour two things are apparent: on the one hand, the logic of the tourism discourse and the realisation of this discourse when someone shows Luxembourg City to a foreign friend are both aspects of the same macro-act of laudatory positivisation or, more specifically still, of aestheticisation. It is clear that, for the most part, preferences voiced in both cases concur and that, at least for a part of the population, the fortress and the Old Town are the first choices. On the other hand, and as far as the city districts are concerned, certain differences between the richly-filled daily life and the tourism-related schematisation were predictable; this is due to the fact that survey respondents were not in the same situation as the spokesmen of the tourism discourse. One notes in particular that leaflets dedicated to Limpertsberg and Kirchberg primarily emphasise aesthetic criteria and also the differences between 'tradition and modernity', 'national and international', which substantiate the official discourse about Kirchberg. The Bonnevoie area is excluded from this characterisation; it is not among the places 'worth visiting'.

In all cases, the discourses are internally coherent. Whether it is about attributed or appropriated identities, in the final analysis they create, each in its own way, artefacts in which 'reality' and representation are blended.

5.3 Representing and Revaluating the City: the *Geo-Graphy* and Visual Identity of Luxembourg City

Preliminary Remark: the City as a Semiotic Construct

A city is not the sum of its streets and buildings, its green spaces and places; instead, it represents a framework within which it becomes possible to consider all of these as belonging together, as parts of a whole. The city is a semiotic construct: a view in which several elements are unified, and which re-unifies them as aspects of one and the same identity. One could make the mistake of thinking that the existence of the city is simply the result of a territorial allocation by a recognised authority, whereby a place is specified: 'the city begins or ends here'. Yet even in such a narrow view (which sees it as sufficient to delineate something to give it an identity), it is still a question of a 'semiotic practice': our starting point was that one needs to specify a location; to mark a space; one also requires an authority to which one can turn for the formulation of such a discourse. Even at this level, one is a long way away from the mere physical presence of a building or a crossroads.

We will address this question in more depth in the following pages. We will investigate how one displays a city with the aid of that special semiotic practice, which we call 'geo-graphic representation'. We will analyse how various tourism bodies represent Luxembourg City in their maps. Even at this stage it is important to highlight the term 'representation', as 'representation' is about simulating something (re-presenting it) or (re)-producing it. Because a map does not find a ready-made city, it must reproduce it using a series of visual tricks; in this way the map represents a construction space for reading-orientated seeing.

A map is a text; the maps we shall be investigating "textualise" (Greimas/Courtés 1979) Luxembourg City. This means that the so-called physical reality of the 'City of Luxembourg' (that maps, like other semiotic mediations, are allotted the task of representing and reproducing) has been transposed onto a two-dimensional surface of finite extent, and then confronted with the following semiotic constraints: it must be bordered in, before it can represent a specific number of the city's symbolic elements, which must fit together and be read (see Shapiro 1969). Altogether, 'Luxembourg City' is permeated by a series of semiotic constraints arising from the medium of the geographical map media and how it is used (see Goodwin 2003) – which in turn affect the very 'essence' of 'Luxembourg City'. Everything that appears within the framework of the map, which is coloured in specific shade, orientated on a specific alignment, arranged in terms of a specific typeface, graphically represented by a symbol, all of this creates the City of Luxembourg in a 'performative' way[27] (Austin 1972; Ducrot 1984). Employing its own means, the tourist map takes on an active role in producing an ensemble which it refers to as 'Luxembourg City'; it contributes to the public game of 'permissible identifications' of that which constitutes the city.

We shall approach the manner in which the City of Luxembourg is textualised in the form of a touristic map in this double sense. For one thing we shall focus on the series of 'objectifications' of the city: which of Luxembourg's features have been considered and used to produce the maps; which aspects and perspectives were selected during adaptation and orientation? At the same time we are interested in the possible emergence of a 'subjective city' as a result of those features that one selects to represent the city: which 'essence', or at least what structure and what model of the city can be glimpsed behind the individual partial embodiments? To sum it up and to put it simply, one could say that we shall be investigating both the 'drawn' city and the 'intended' city (see Marin 1983).

To this end we shall be examining a body of evidence, which, whilst not exhaustive, is at least representative: a varied collection of maps of Luxembourg that appeared over the past two decades and address different touristic objectives – sometimes the general exploration of the country by a visiting foreigner; sometimes the cataloguing of important locations for consumers resident in Luxembourg;

---

27 | 'Performative' means: to create something through a speech act. Thus, a promise exists because someone promises, a name exists because someone names; but also a love, because (by various and multimodal speech acts) someone declares and promises.

sometimes the provision of a simple road map of the capital[28]. Sometimes the map is a street map of the city; sometimes it constitutes a page in a guide. We ignored these differences, because, as we shall see, the semiotic effects produced are related. By contrast, we did take the images, whether photographs or paintings, into consideration. They accompany the maps and therefore, together with the map, make a contribution towards the (re)-presentation of the city. If the map and all the figures it contains constitute a 'text', then the images and the figures preceding them constitute a 'paratext' (Genette 1987).

The Profile of Luxembourg City Mirrored in its Maps: 'the Ascent to the Enclave'

The first approach to the re-presentation of the city centres on the way in which it is 'profiled'. In this regard, it is astounding to see how the city is systematically given merely one single 'profile': it is represented as an 'ascent to an elevated island' (where 'the island' in question denotes the city centre, the so-called 'upper town').

Constants and variables are used which all tend to produce the same idea. In terms of this constant tactic it can be observed that: (i) the paratext (i.e. the photos or drawn images that accompany the map) always contains a bridge or bastion; (ii) the text (i.e. the map itself) invariably shows the way into the city centre.

A paratext diverts the reading away from the text it accompanies. The figures of bridge and bastion reveal a clear semiotic intention: the paratext carries the notion of 'entrance to a raised, enclosed place.' As we shall see, the map-text repeats precisely the same content, however using other means. What remains constant is the representation of the 'gateway' to the centre: rather than showing the city centre itself in its entirety, the map shows the gateway to it. Other than that, the map often shows the south-eastern part of the city centre; or alternatively it will show the city centre along with the district surrounding the railway station, Belair, Kirchberg, Grund, etc. One notes also that the bridges and bastions are not the preferred signs in the map's text: either they are just vaguely indicated, or they are omitted altogether. One discovers also that the provision of the means of re-presenting the 'city' is not obvious: the variability of its signifier is recognisable, as is the interplay between various semiotic approaches that characterise the city and enhance it in a specific way.

---

28 | The documents (maps or guides with maps) studied were: *Baedekers Allianz Reiseführer. Luxembourg,* Ostfildern-Kemnat: Mairs Geographischer Verlag, 1990; *Discover Luxembourg,* 1995; *Marco Polo. Luxembourg: Reiseführer mit Insider-Tips,* Ostfildern: Mairs Geographischer Verlag, 1995; *Luxembourg. Ni vu ni connu,* Luxembourg City Tourist Office, 2000; *Michelin. Belgium/Luxembourg,* Zellik: Le Guide Michelin, 2007; *Panorama City Map. Luxembourg: La ville,* Luxembourg City Tourist Office, 2008; *Plan de la ville de Luxembourg,* Luxembourg City Tourist Office, 2008.

But let us move on to deal with the variable approaches that all converge on the same objective, that is, to depict the centre as an 'isolated enclave toward which one is drawn'. The approaches to visualising something within the map can be categorised as one of three types: (i) chromatic, (ii) iconic and (iii) eidetic. That is, the various approaches display information using (i) colours, (ii) iconic representation and (iii) the lines and axes that structure the surface of the text.The use of colour shows the city as an 'isolated enclave'. A more or less black, but always visible line, which symbolises the railway line, produces the effect of enclosing the centre of town in the east. A band of green, also incorporating a number of very different shades, symbolises the park and appears to round off the city centre to the west. Depending on the map, the green area representing the park will show different dimensions from west to north: this means that it is not so much about depicting a physical reality than about reproducing the city in a certain way.

The iconic approaches have a dual objective: not only do they constitute a complimentary effect of 'isolating' the 'enclave' of the centre, but they also express the 'being drawn' towards this location. With regard to the first objective, one can see that the representation of the walls and bastions, when located to the *south* of the centre, is quite pronounced (this varies by map), whereas the same walls and bastions, when not surrounding the centre, are hardly sketched in, often virtually absent. On the other hand, all the monuments in general, when rendered in three dimensions, are always shown with a south-north orientation, from the bottom up: this reflects the concept of the ascending orientation of the city, of a route that visibly leads upwards.

The eidetic strategies, finally, enclose the centre, making it into a point of convergence. On the one hand everything looks as if the depiction and the highlighting of particular streets signify a rigid enclosure of the centre. In some cases the box containing the detail enlargement of the city centre fulfils the same function. On the other hand, the name 'Luxembourg' does not appear above the whole city map but rather near to the centre. It almost seems as if it serves as a legend only for the city centre, as if it creates the city of Luxembourg as a point of convergence by way of antonomasia.

In conclusion one can note that this variety and redundancy of semiotic devices (chromatic, iconic, eidetic), which are combined in various ways, all pursue the same aim.

The Profile of Luxembourg City Mirrored in its Maps: the Absence of a Strong Identity

The first approach to the re-presentation of the city sought to show how it is structured and shaped, how it is approached in every instance as a 'phenomenon'. The second approach will now turn to the emphasis of an object 'the city' as a purely intellectual concept, a 'noumenon': not an aggregation of features but rather a model; a sketch rather than a set of intentions. It is here that we have the perhaps most astonishing result of the corpus analysis: a conceptual model for Luxembourg does not seem to exist. Everything evokes the impression that there is no intent, no idealised concept and no strong identification with the city itself behind the plethora of drawings and landmarks of the city.

To comprehend such a semiotic effect, it is important to distinguish between the two, albeit complementary, approaches to re-presentation. Until now, we have dwelt upon the concept of an 'ascent to an elevated island' – an ascent both difficult and steep: the city is grasped, endowed with meaning and enhanced by virtue of this ascent. And it is this representation that shows the city, depicts it. We shall now attempt to develop a model that renders the city 'legible', one which symbolizes it. The first approach concentrated on *spatialisation* (a conceptualisation 'process', and thus a process of reproduction of a specific space); the second is focussed on a topology (on a 'state' that abstracts the routes from the phenomenal properties, i.e. the routes, and provides a system instead: 'city' as a kind of absolute object, an 'essential' city)[29].

The conceptual model of Luxembourg City as a representation seems not to exist. Firstly, there is only one place that is not only a spatial reference point, but can consistently represent and therefore also symbolise the city: the cathedral. Secondly, the delineation of the city is rather vague: every map centres it in a slightly different way – we have seen that the only constant is the fact that one or several entry points to the centre are shown; the centre itself is not assigned to a fixed location within the text of the maps. Thirdly, the contours of the city are also defined in quite a vague way; one could even describe them as virtually undefined: although the City of Luxembourg is always represented as an ascending route leading to the centre, the city limits of Luxembourg, as well as its extent and margins invariably remain vague.

Conclusions: Problems in Communicating 'the City'

We often know the form of a city and know how its nucleus is built around a set of reference points (monuments, places, crossroads, etc.) This kind of city allows the forms, structures and reference points to communicate effectively, and, in so doing, accords itself the meaning of a city. It promotes a model of its 'city essence' – a model that every map, but also every logo, every photo, and every image combined, strive to reproduce in as many variations. Yet for Luxembourg, this attribution of meaning, which produces 'the City' together with a "visual identity" (Floch 1990; Floch 1995) seems to be missing.

---

29 | This refers to Ricœur's theory of identity (1990), which problematises identities by distinguishing between an *'ipse'* identity (an identity accepted in spite of a series of changes, e.g. in a promise: even if my mood or my life circumstances change, I will always be the one who owes you that which has been promised you) and an *'idem'* identity (a structural, profound, immutable identity, e.g. that of a name, a genetic code, etc.).

'Geo-graphy' is always a communicative practice, in the broadest sense of the term. It is a written artefact, a textualisation, and therefore a conceptualisation and thus a meaning and enhancement. 'Re-production' is a speech act that entails showing; we have seen that it involves a totality of coordinated approaches. This is why the geo-graphy of a city and its re-presentation on a map produce a certain visual identity that is suited to serving as the incentive for more general 'cultural strategies'. With regard to the representation of the City of Luxembourg that we have discussed, one can raise questions as to their adequateness, their effectiveness and their optimum expression (Fontanille 2008). In other words, is 'access to an elevated island' (i.e. the 'tension to be overcome' on the one hand and the 'isolation' of the central object on the other) appropriate? Based on what city-enhancement strategies? And is the absence of a conceptual model of the city and of an 'essential' identity also of use? If so, then why and to what end?

5.4 Between National Unity and Regional Individualism 'Sways the Heart of Luxembourg'

Enlisting the contiguous fields of rhetoric (see Perelman/Olbrechts-Tyteca 2000), stylistics (see Adam 1990; Adam 1997; Herschberg-Pierrot 2003) and discourse analysis (see Adam 1999; Amossy/Maingueneau 2003), the study of three tourist brochures[30] from Luxembourg conducted here takes a vigorously compositional approach, which also plays a factor in the interaction between the written entity and the iconic dimension. The two procedures of encoding and decoding investigated here presuppose an intention to exert a specific influence on others, which also establishes a link with pragmatics (see Bonhomme 2005; Bonhomme 2006) and speech act theory (see Ducrot 1984; Searle 1972). What will interest us in this context is the meaning produced by this tourism discourse and how it is generated (see Bonhomme/Adam, 1997), while at the same time avoiding the pitfalls of radical constructivism. Our aim, therefore, is to comprehend the workings of a discourse originating from the *Office National du Tourisme*[31] (attributed identities) as well as to gauge how the output of this institutional body is shaping personal notions of the country (appropriated identities).

---

30 | Luxembourg National Tourist Office. 2006. *Les Produits du Terroir et les Métiers d'Art*. Mersch: François Faber; Luxembourg National Tourist Office. 2008. *Hôtels Restaurants et Arrangements* (11/2007 for the year 2008), Luxembourg: Saint-Paul; Luxembourg National Tourist Office. *Sites et Attractions*. (12/2007 for the year 2008), Luxembourg: Saint-Paul.
31 | Personal translation: "National Tourist Office".

Apparent Uniformity, Definite Complementarity

The manner in which the two publications *Hôtels Restaurants et Arrangements* and *Sites et Attractions* present their information only appears to be a neutral one: the editing and presenting of information by regions creates the impression of a ranking according to size with the Luxembourg City region and the centre at the top in a descending order down to the south and the Minette region. By contrast, the third publication considered here, *Les Produits du Terroir et les Métiers d'Art*, favours a thematic classification over an alphabetical or regional one. However, the three brochures share one common aspect: they use the same map of the country, with the different regions set off from each other by colours (we will return to this particular point below). The three thematic areas, which are treated in a complementary fashion, seem to cover all the information likely to be of interest to the curious and pragmatically oriented tourist, while the complementarity of these sources of information also appears to guarantee the coherence of these multiple actualisations of an attributed identity. Linden and Thewes hold that already at the 1937 World Exhibition *"promotion nationale, touristique et économique s'entremêl-[ai]ent [...] dans un vaste effort de synthèse"*[32] (2007: 44).

As is already apparent from the corpus, this study is positioned at the interface between the country and the region, and we will show that the quantitative analysis confirms this extreme fragmentation, which is all the more surprising at a time where there is much talk of building the Greater Region. In other words, we will see how attributed and appropriated identities enter into a dialogue.

A Regional or Regionalist Approach?

The quantitative survey reveals that the respondents attach great value to the notion of proximity, a remarkable attitude in a country where, on account of its small size, almost everything is in relatively close proximity. From the interviewees who responded with "several times a week" to the question, "How often do you visit the following places in your free time?" (the place in this instance being the Oesling, a wooded region in the north of the country), 46 % live in the north and essentially belong to atypical milieus on the fringe of 'mainstream society'[33]. The rest of the population never, or almost never, visits this area[34] with a particularly high percentage among residents in the east (51 %), who themselves have beautiful scenery right in front of their doorstep, followed by residents of Luxembourg City

---

32 | Personal translation: "Advertising for the country, tourism and economy blend[ed] in a broad endeavour to attain conflation".

33 | Status-oriented milieu: 12 %; underprivileged, meritocratic-oriented and alternative milieus: each 10 %. Respondents in these categories are divided almost evenly between men (47 %) and women (45 %).

34 | Again, division by gender is even, with 34 % men and 37 % women.

and the south (each at 40 %)[35]. The percentages of residents of the capital who visit several times per year and those who never or rarely visit are relatively balanced, at 51 % and 40 % respectively.

This tendency to favour one's home region can be detected in the Minette region, the southernmost region of the country, in Luxembourg City and in the Moselle region. Accordingly, 53 % of those surveyed who visit the Minette region several times per week in their free time live in the south[36], as opposed to 3 % in the north; 41 % of these are of Italian origin, presumably on account of it being a former mining region that had experienced large-scale economically motivated immigration from the Italian peninsula. Only 8 % of regular visitors to this region come from Luxembourg City, which after all is not that far away. Of the respondents, 57 % of residents from the north and 45 % from the east never or rarely visit the Minette region[37]. The same applies to residents of the Moselle region, in the southeast, 49 % of whom frequent their region in their free time[38], whereas inhabitants from the north rarely if ever go there (39 %). However, one should note that more than half of the nation's population visit this wine region several times per year. By contrast, the figures are reversed for Luxembourg City: a mere 4 % of all respondents never or rarely travel to the city, and of these, 10 % live in the north, 4 % are men and 9 % are women of 60 years and older. Regarding frequent visits to Luxembourg City during spare time, an unsurprising 66 % of respondents live in the city, 44 % in other places of the central region, 31 % come from the south, 28 % from the east and 12 % from the north. The largest share of visitors comes from the privileged conservative milieu (51 %), as opposed to 10 % from the tradition-oriented milieu. Here again, Luxembourg City clearly stands out, which is not entirely surprising given the cultural and economic resources a capital city commands.

In terms of the tourism discourse, the order in which the regions are discussed in the brochures (starting clockwise from Luxembourg City and the surrounding area) is confirmed by the respondents' answers, particularly with regard to the prominent position of the capital and the surrounding area. The attributed identities emerging from the information contained in these publications combine to create an image of a metropolis with marked centralistic traits, yet geographically shifted toward the south. These identities reappear, internalised and appropriated, in the surveys. They are reflected in the pronounced interest directed towards Luxembourg City, at the expense of other places. On the other hand, the regionally

---

35 | Among them, 46 % originate from the tradition-oriented milieu and 44 % from the underprivileged milieu.
36 | Divided as follows: 28 % from the hedonistic milieu, followed by 27 % from the petty bourgeois and tradition-oriented milieus.
37 | The majority (36 %) of which are from the tradition-oriented, underprivileged and privileged liberal milieus.
38 | The hedonistic and alternative milieus provide the most visitors to the region, as opposed to the scarcely represented traditional milieus.

oriented manner of perceiving the national territory, which attributes identities, conveys the impression of a far-reaching fragmentation. Considering how this is mirrored in the appropriated identities, this suggests the presence of a regionalistic attitude among the respondents. We were indeed able to establish that the preferred destinations for leisure-time visits were primarily located in the respondents' home region and that there was a marked lack of interest in the other parts of the country (except for the capital), which, given the country's limited size, would not take much time to reach. This tendency towards withdrawal shows certain similarities with regionalistic behaviour. In other words, the official regional tourism discourse corresponds to individual regionalistic attitudes. Linden and Thewes arrived at the same conclusions for the field of advertising:

En dépit de la superficie très limitée du Luxembourg, les campagnes publicitaires distinguent plusieurs régions spécifiques [...]. Ces représentations n'influencent pas seulement la vision des touristes. Elles finissent par déterminer la perception que les Luxembourgeois ont de leur propre pays, de son passé et de sa géographie. La propagande touristique reflète finalement les histoires que les Luxembourgeois aiment raconter sur eux-mêmes, tout autant qu'elle leur sert de moule[39] (2007: 44).

We will now turn to the question whether the analysis of rhetorical devices and their interaction with the visual information will confirm this first conclusion.

Matching Colours

In all three brochures examined, the use of colours aims at reinforcing the regional representation of the country. The colours are charged with a symbolic meaning which acts as a mnestic device. This procedure contributes to creating the particular redundancy that marks the discursive style of these publications.

Each of them contains the same map of the Grand Duchy: the 'Ardennes and nature parks' region is assigned the colour green, particularly suited for representing nature and flora, this region's major attraction. The region Müllertal is coloured in the sandy brown of its rocks, while the City of Luxembourg and its surroundings are shown in the colour gold. The Moselle region takes its blue from the river reflecting the sky on a sunny day, whereas the mining region of Terres Rouges, is imbued with the brick colour of its ore, as if the mineral wealth reaped from its depths permitted the choice of no other colour. This association is essentially

---

39 | Personal translation: "Despite Luxembourg's very limited surface area, advertising campaigns distinguish several specific regions [...]. These representations not only influence tourists' perceptions, in the final analysis they determine the image Luxembourgers have of their own country, of its past and its geography. Tourist propaganda ultimately reflects the stories Luxembourgers like to tell about themselves, as well as providing them with a template".

based on a prototypical representation of the regional colour scheme and fosters in the reader a simplified perception of the regional differences, by highlighting each region's most representative feature. This is confirmed in the downsized reproduction of each region at the bottom of the page, named in four languages (French, German, Dutch, and English), shaded in each region's symbolical colour.

In the case of the two publications *Hôtels Restaurants et Arrangements* and *Sites et Attractions*, the exemplary significance of the map's colours is resumed both in the table of contents for the regions and in the page numbering (upper corners, left and right), enclosed in an off-centre square in which the entire country is reproduced in outline. The section of the contour drawing illustrating the region discussed on that page is colour-highlighted according to the colour allotted to that region on the larger map of the country. We noted that this square creates a link between the guide's contents and its cover: it is present on the strip of the three cover pages, playing with a switch between positive and negative mode (red letters on white background, white letters on red background), clearly setting off the abbreviation *lu* in the internet address. The two-coloured index reference of *Hôtels Restaurants et Arrangements* alternating between blue and white, is developed further in *Sites et Attractions*: the locations can be linked to the appropriate region at a glance with the help of symbolic colours. The guide *Les Produits du Terroir et les Métiers d'Art*, by contrast, uses these fine distinctions in a different manner; instead of indicating regions, they refer to the nature of a product (which in a semiotic sense constitutes partial motivation). For example, the clear green indicates viticultural products, whereas the warm orange colour symbolises brandies and liqueurs, and ochre (a variety of orange) the domestic beers. A comparison of the cover with the contents of the brochure shows that the colours used correspond precisely with those in the cover photo, each slightly modified with a tone-on-tone effect.

The colours almost act as a weapon of persuasion. An analysis of how they are used reveals a schematic treatment of the country which is no longer based on a regional (pragmatically neutral) perspective but on a regionalistic (pragmatically biased) one, and whose purpose it is to facilitate the reader's assessment of the space by streamlining it. Bonhomme demonstrated this convincingly in a study of a tourist brochure of the city of Bern: "*Schématiser la ville, c'est en retenir les aspects les plus typiques à travers trois actes énonciatifs [:] a) Sélectionner [...] b) Emblématiser [...] c) Rationaliser [...]*"[40] (2003: 14). The Luxembourg publications base their use of colours on particulars from which they extract prototypical features[41] and guide the reader's decoding effort by employing a redundancy technique that even includes a referential link between the publication's cover and contents. This procedure is

---

40 | Personal translation: "To create a schematised representation of a city one has to capture the most typical aspects in three enunciative acts [:] a) selecting [...] b) symbolising [...] c) streamlining [...]".

41 | For example, the colour of the iron ore for the aptly named Terres Rouges or the colour of vegetation for the natural park region.

an element of rhetoric that has been expanded to include pragmatics, as conceived by Perelman and Olbrechts-Tyteca (2000), as a specific manner of constructing the object with the intention of guiding the reader's interpretation. Georges Molinié succinctly emphasises the significance of the perlocutionary effect of rhetoric when he writes: "[E]lle vise à faire penser ou croire aux gens ce que spontanément ils ne pensent ou ne croient pas, [...] à leur faire même désirer ce qu'ils n'imaginent même pas de désirer"[42] (1993: 2). It therefore requires little to operationalise this type of epideictic discourse for the advertising discourse, which praises an object in order to recommend its consumption.

The analysis of the covers, which may not be elaborated here further, not only convincingly reaffirmed the use of colour symbolism, guide lines and perspectives, which, in the photos, were literally orchestrated with carefully calculated framings. The space which has been structured in this way guides the reader's eye thereby transporting an ideology that attempts to reconcile antithetical meanings: on the one hand a strong and conservative attachment to one's own roots, and on the other, the temptation to yield to the allure of spaces dominated by futuristic vistas.

The Rhetoric of Tourism

As is clear from the above, the three tourist brochures display a highly skillfull application of images, but this is not the only feature that characterises their modus operandi. The rhetoric employed here also plays a significant role, as shown by the text analysis of *Luxembourg, la capitale et ses environs*, which is representative of the style used in the publications studied. Thus the guides *Hôtels Restaurants et Arrangements* and *Sites et Attractions* have similar introductory texts which are clearly marked by poetical tourist clichés.

Luxembourg, aux contrastes enchanteurs, est une ville chargée d'histoire, débordant de trésors artistiques et culturels qui ne demandent qu'à être admirés, regorgeant de sites intéressants et de coins pittoresques qui ne demandent qu'à être explorés, truffée d'anecdotes et de légendes qui ne demandent qu'à être racontées.

Et puis, quelles sont les autres capitales européennes qui peuvent se targuer d'être à quelques jets de pierre seulement de paysages verts impressionnants, où d'accueillants villages ont conservé leurs caractères?

A ce propos, le Prix Europa Nostra décerné au village restauré d'Useldange ne doit rien au hasard. Comme son nom l'indique, la Vallée des Sept châteaux invite à un périple à travers

---

42 | Personal translation: "[I]t tries to make people think of or believe in what they do not naturally think of or believe in, [...] to make them even want what they did not even imagine they wanted".

l'histoire et la nature, depuis Koerich et son église baroque jusqu'à Mersch[43] (11/2007: 10 and 12/2007: 6).

The lyricism apparent in these few lines of text uses in the first passage a ternary rhythm that involves the syntactic, morphological and lexical levels. It creates a movement that conveys a soothing and harmoniously balanced pace to the reader.

The mention of the city at the very beginning is made in the form of a personification based on its properties and qualities, which are themselves personified via their verbs. For example, the treasures that embody the capital's historic and artistic heritage are endowed with a veritable soul: they solicit the tourist's attention and the assistance from whoever is willing to bring them to life via the language. This interlacing is produced by a ternary concatenation. First, Luxembourg is named in its integral entirety together with one of its salient features, the "enchanting contrasts" (1); this is followed by a reference to its rich history (2), itself composed of the sum of its "artistic and cultural treasures" (3). These are themselves characterised by three distinctive features, creating the effect of a saturation of information that seeks to be as comprehensive and attractive as possible. As Bonhomme (2003: 18) reminds us, "*Loin d'obéir à des procédures logico-déductives plus ou moins complexes (du genre Démontrer à Convaincre), cette orientation persuasive est de nature empathique, faisant appel à la séduction (Grize 1981) et à l' 'évocation' (Dominicy/Michaux 2001)*"[44]. However, it is doubtful whether the introductory text actually achieves the intended result, for it resembles more a caricature of a panegyric, as we will presently show.

The first paragraph, constituting half of the introductory text, is one single compound sentence:

[*Luxembourg*], [first-order apposition: *full of enchanting contrasts*], [copular verb establishing the link between the city and its feature: *is*] [nominal group establishing the strict

---

43 | Personal translation: "Luxembourg, full of enchanting contrasts, is a city steeped in history, brimming with artistic and cultural treasures that are waiting to be admired, overflowing with interesting sites and picturesque corners that are waiting to be explored, larded with anecdotes and legends that are waiting to be told. And then, which other European capitals can boast of being only a stone's throw away from impressive green landscapes, where hospitable villages have retained their character? Speaking of which, the restored village of Useldange did not receive the Europa Nostra Award for Cultural Heritage by chance. And as the name suggests, the Valley of Seven Castles invites you to take a journey through history and nature, from Koerich's baroque church to Mersch".

44 | Personal translation: "Far from obeying logico-deductive procedures of varying complexity (such as to prove in order to convince), this persuasive orientation is of an empathetic nature, appealing to seduction (Grize 1981) and 'evocation' (Dominicy/Michaux 2001)".

equivalence between the city and the fact of it having a rich history: *a city steeped in history*]

This statement, which could have been expressed with a simple sentence, instead serves as an opening for three participial constructions for which it acts as a distributor. Redundancy is achieved by the repetition of two forms of the present participle ("brimming with/overflowing with") and one form of the past participle ("larded with"), creating a ternary rhythm. Each of these participles transports a set of objects, and each of these, in turn, is formed on the same pattern, which produces the tree structure mentioned above. The three objects are introduced with the preposition "with": in the first segment, the noun "treasures" is specified by two co-ordinated adjectives; the second segment consists of two co-ordinated nouns, each qualified with an adjective; lastly, the third and final segment is constructed of two co-ordinated nouns. Together, these segments combine to form the following pattern[45]:

[with artistic *and* cultural treasures] = 1 N + 2 co-ordinated adj.
[with interesting sites *and* picturesque corners] = 2 SN + co-ordinated adj.
[with anecdotes *and* legends] = 2 co-ordinated N

Here we see how the binary rhythm of each syntagm is combined into the ternary rythm which homogenises the sequence. In this way, the power of the information is supported by the reading pace, which facilitates the assimilation of the contents. From a lexical viewpoint, the narrator has produced a hyperbolic discourse containing certain expressions that border on the trivial ("Luxembourg is brimming with", "overflowing with", "larded with"). Everywhere there is profusion, even overabundance, a wealth that is inversely proportional to the size of the country. This lavishness is also sustained by the ternary rhythm. The three sets of objects (whose syntactic structure is described above) are each expanded by an identical relative clause ("that are waiting to …"), which, in turn, is complemented by a passive infinitive ("to be admired", "to be explored", "to be told"). This structural redundancy (three instances in four and a half lines) appears counterproductive and is more likely to disorient than create the intended attraction.

The text that follows changes to a radically different style: instead of lyrical hyperbole we now have a discourse affecting spontaneity; the sentences are shorter, they address the reader through the illocutionary effect of the interrogative and seem to digress heavily. This effect is produced by the connectors of a textual 'signposting' (see Freyermuth 2003) – e.g. "and then", "speaking of which" – which point to a pronounced oralisation of the discourse. The second paragraph takes on a more demanding tone, because it addresses the reader, prompting him to

---

45 | For the commentary on the syntax of the text, the abbreviations used are as follows: N = noun; adj. = adjective; SN = nominal syntagm; V = verb.

answer the pragmatic question (see Searle 1982; Kerbrat-Orecchioni 1991) and requesting that he recognise the legitimacy of the advantages offered by the capital of the Grand Duchy. The need to resort to this type of speech act has a negative implication, as if the narrator anticipated a certain reluctance on behalf of the reader to endorse this laudatory device[46]. The manner in which the question is formulated obscures one of the reasons for the proximity of Luxembourg City to the 'impressive green landscapes': for example, the very idyllic and romantic little town of Esch-sur-Sûre (in the northern part of the country) is less than 50 km from the capital. To put this otherwise would risk diminishing, in the eyes of the potential tourist, the importance of the country regarding its size. This paragraph ends with a mention of the strong character of the surrounding villages. This constitutes a perfect transition to the third and final paragraph, which resumes the previous one with the anaphoric expression 'Speaking of which'. The involvement of the reader, who continues to be engaged in a conversation about this and that, is taken to a further level: the Europa Nostra Award is used as supplementary proof of the historical value of Luxembourg's architectural heritage.

Lastly, the text's lexical elements reinforce its heterogeneity. No cliché of pseudo-poetic rhetoric is omitted[47], whether it be "enchanting contrasts", "picturesque corners" "green landscapes" and other "hospitable villages". These commonplaces are exacerbated by multiple instances of awkwardness in the use of register and display a degree of triviality that impairs the ostensibly refined stylistic effects of the preceding lines. In short, the brief text, hyperbolic and overburdened in its first half, turns into a tonal and lexical patchwork in the second half, which risks jeopardising the aim of these brochures, namely to attract potential tourists.

To sum up, this (too) brief analysis of three publications released by the Luxembourg Tourist Office reveals a tendency for redundancy, supported moreover by a process of streamlining and reduction of information into prototypical formulae, with the aim to facilitate access to the facts. Yet the simultaneous use of hyperbole, both scriptural and iconic, impairs the intended aid and betrays the perhaps too overzealously expressed desire to promote and advertise at all costs.

5.5 THE IMAGE OF LUXEMBOURG AS A 'MELTING POT'

The representation of the territory of Luxembourg in tourist guides also requires a diachronic analysis. This section focuses on the evolution of this projected identity in the tourism discourse throughout the 20th century and examines its continuities and discontinuities. At first glance, the tourist guides do not seek to lay down borders, but to cross them by encouraging international flows of people and

---

46 | This tendency is related to what is referred to as the "Theory of Mind", which can also be described as the "Theory of Mental Representations" (see Freyermuth 2008).
47 | See section 5.5.

capital. However, before these borders can be crossed, they must first be discursively constructed. Luxembourg is 'different' on two levels: on the one hand, the country is endowed with an aura of authenticity linked to the significance of its rural past and its small size; on the other, it is distinguished by its economic modernity and its open culture. These paradoxical traits confer upon it a uniqueness, which according to guides explains the tourists' interest. This representation of the authenticity/modernity paradox is evolving over time, becoming more and more dissonant while – at the same time – the image of an interstitial existence between the German and French 'cultural spaces' is becoming increasingly preponderant and depicts Luxembourg as a role model for Europe.

The historical analysis conducted here is based on a selection of six tourist guides, chosen for their widely differing production contexts: the golden age of the railroad[48], the eve of World War I[49], the inter-war years[50], the 1960s, marked by celebrations of the thousand-year anniversary of Luxembourg City in 1963[51], along with the years of energetic tourism campaigns 1995 (*Luxembourg – European Capital of Culture*)[52] and 2007 (*Luxembourg and Greater Region – European Capital of Culture*)[53]. A second criterion of selection was the ability to trace the evolution of the representation of Luxembourg through the 20th century in the *Woerl* (1914, 1934) and *Merian* (1964, 1995, and 2007). The selection is rounded off with Luxembourg's first tourist guide, published in 1861 by Mathias Erasmy, and by a brief presentation of the country appearing in a 1967 edition of *Reader's Digest* that was printed in 13 languages[54]. Except for Erasmy's work, these texts were written from an external perspective (German for the most part), even if the 1967 *Merian* also included

---

48 | Erasmy, Mathieu. 1861. *Le guide du voyageur dans le Grand-Duché de Luxembourg.* Luxembourg: V. Bück; Anonymous (1892): *De Luxembourg en Écosse. Guide du Touriste à travers Le Luxembourg. – L'Ardenne Belge. – Les Flandres. La Mer du Nord et la Manche. Le Comté de Kent. – Le Pays de Galles. – Les Lacs Anglais. L'Écosse. Avec 100 dessins originaux de MM. Hoeterickx, Van Gelder, etc.* Published by S. de Ruette for London Chatham & Dover Railway [Brussels], with the approval of the London & North Western Railway, London Chatham & Dover Railway, the Chemins de fer Prince-Henri and the Chemins de fer du Nord de France companies. Luxembourg: Pierre Bruck.
49 | Renwick, George. 1913. *Luxembourg. The Grand-Duchy and its People.* London: T. Fisher Unwin; Anonymous. 1914. *Woerl's Reisehandbücher. Illustrierter Führer durch das Großherzogtum Luxemburg. Mit Plan der Stadt Luxemburg, 7 Kartenbeilagen und 65 Abbildungen,* 2nd ed. Leipzig: Woerl's Reisebücher-Verlag. Kaiserl. u Königl. Hofbuchhandlung.
50 | Anonymous. 1934. *Woerl Reisehandbücher. Großherzogtum Luxemburg [mit Plan der Stadt Luxemburg, 7 Karten und 29 Abbildungen],* 3rd ed. Leipzig: Woerl's Reisebücher-Verlag.
51 | Merian. 1964. *Luxembourg.* Merian XVII/7.
52 | Schröder, Dirk. 1995. *Merian live! Luxembourg.* Munich: Gräfe und Unzer.
53 | Merian. 2007. *Luxembourg.* Merian 60/03.
54 | Schisgall, Oscar. 1967. *Le Luxembourg, pays de paradoxes.* Selection from Reader's Digest. 01/1967, p. 62-69.

articles by Luxembourgish authors. The guides were not published by the National Tourist Office; they therefore do not attempt to achieve the maximum number of visitors to Luxembourg, but rather to reach the greatest number of readers. The 1892 guide does seek to promote the railroad, but the 'product' is not Luxembourg, even though the same guide must seduce, attract and sell.

This corpus will be compared to qualitative surveys and in particular to the collected responses concerning the European institutions based in Luxembourg. They allow us to decipher the reception of the image of Luxembourg as a role model for Europe and as a space that is open and multicultural. The other side of the coin, the rustic image of a country bound to its traditions, does not appear in the interviews. Comparing the projected collective spatial identities (representations conveyed by tourist guides, among other things) and appropriated individual spatial identities is difficult due to the dissymmetry of the sources. If limited – as we have done – to qualitative surveys, the comparison can only weigh the individual expressions of spatial identity against the most recent guide, that from 2007. All we can do is examine whether the respondents repeat the stereotypes presented by this guide (or other, even older ones) or if their judgments differ from those of the tourist guides.

This research question is new, as most historical, sociological or anthropological studies of tourism tend to evaluate economic impacts and tourism practices. These studies are often concerned with remote tourism, analysed from an angle of meeting the Other (see Cohen 2004: 229-316), whereas tourism in Western Europe is rarely studied from this perspective. Yet more that more than two-thirds of the tourists visting Luxembourg are from an adjacent country (Belgium, France or Germany), the Netherlands or Great-Britain; only 10 % come from a non-European country. These numbers have hardly changed between 1980 and 2006 (Statec 2007: 213, 228). Nevertheless, the Luxembourg tourist guides provide an 'exotic' gaze, for the primary objective of the tourist is ultimately to have a different physical and mental experience (see Hennig 1997). The guides implicitly fulfil tourists' expectations by proposing they visit 'extraordinary' places that offer contrast to the working world – places they can capture on film and then turn into landscapes (Urry 1990: 2-3). Urry and MacCannell moreover consider the tourist experience – characterised by the search for authenticity – emblematic of (post)modernity turning to the past (linked to the emergence of museums) and to other countries where life is imagined to be simpler, more pure (Urry 1990: 82, 104-134; MacCannell 1976: 103, 48; Cohen 2004: 159-178). Therefore, one of the functions of tourist guides is to quench the thirst for authenticity. Our analysis will first show in what terms this *genius loci* is described and will then examine whether the 'natives' subscribe to this description and identify with it (or not).

The Quest for Authenticity

The projected identity of Luxembourg as the last peaceful corner is pushed to the extreme by Renwick's work, in which the first chapter, entitled "A Ruritania of today", is marked by a nostalgia for a lost world: "The world appears to be fast outgrowing its Ruritanias [...] The Empire of Speed [...] is wrecking Arcadia" (Renwick 1913: 13). Very much in contrast to the cult of speed and modernity launched by Marinetti's *Manifeste du futurisme* (1909), the author proposes trips without haste, without maps or directions, and above all without guided tours: "This tiny paradise, this little unspoiled corner of earth which has known Nature's most happy inspirations, is for those whose guide is *Wanderlust*" (Renwick 1913: 14). Industrialisation, however, is not demonised. The verdict, "the canton of Esch is blackened and blurred by furnaces, forges and foundries" does not lack in poetry (alliteration) and admits that the Grand Duchy produces no less than one fortieth of the world's steel, "an extremely large proportion" (Renwick 1913: 19). This paradox had deepened in the description of Luxembourg printed in *Reader's Digest* at the end of the 1960s: Luxembourg is presented as "a modern and prosperous nation that is the seventh largest steel producer in Europe" and is the seat of European institutions, yet remains an "idyllic land", straight out of a fairy tale. It is the last refuge of tranquillity: *"Le monde d'aujourd'hui a grand besoin d'un pays comme le grand-duché, ne serait-ce que pour prouvez qu'il est encore possible de vivre tranquille sur notre planète"*[55] (Schisgall 1967: 64).

By contrast, this notion of tranquillity is ridiculed by Gliedner (see *Merian* 1964). His essay "Ellinger Blätter" denounces the provinciality and the sluggishness (*"Biertischgemütlichkeit"*, *"Fettbäuche"*, *"bourgeoise eingemachte Gurkenideen"*) of the Luxembourgers. The land only remains fertile with chemical fertilisers and the landscape is so lyrical in itself that the poets are considered superfluous. Gliedner's essay is included towards the end of the 1964 *Merian* edition, in which the iconography introduces a subtle division between 'tradition', illustrated by photos of castles and shots of the Old Town, and 'modernity', intersected by representations of factories and advertisements. The historical past is contrasted with economic progress. In the middle of the brochure, the 'traditional' type of representation reaches its peak: a black-and-white photo of an old woman, evocatively entitled *"Beim Kartoffelschälen – Küchenidyll in einem alten Öslinger Bauernhaus"*[56], on the left page, across from the essay *"Mir wële bleiwe wat mir sinn"*[57] by the ethnographer Joseph Hess on the right page (*Merian* 1964: 58-59). Hess states that the Luxembourgish mentality is still rustic and honest, *despite* prosperity and urbanisation. The aspect of 'tradition' thus dominates the 1964 *Merian*, as evidenced also by the picturesque map of the

---

55 | Personal translation: "The world today is in great need of a country such as the Grand Duchy, if only to prove that it is still possible to live in peace and tranquillity on our planet".
56 | "Peeling Potatoes – Idyllic Kitchen Scene in an old Ösling Farmhouse".
57 | "We want to remain what we are".

country, decorated by the coat of arms and icons representing castles, churches and industrial sites in the same colours and style, so that one cannot distinguish them at first glance. The industrial sites are incorporated into the Arcadian image of Luxembourg despite the dissonances introduced by some authors.

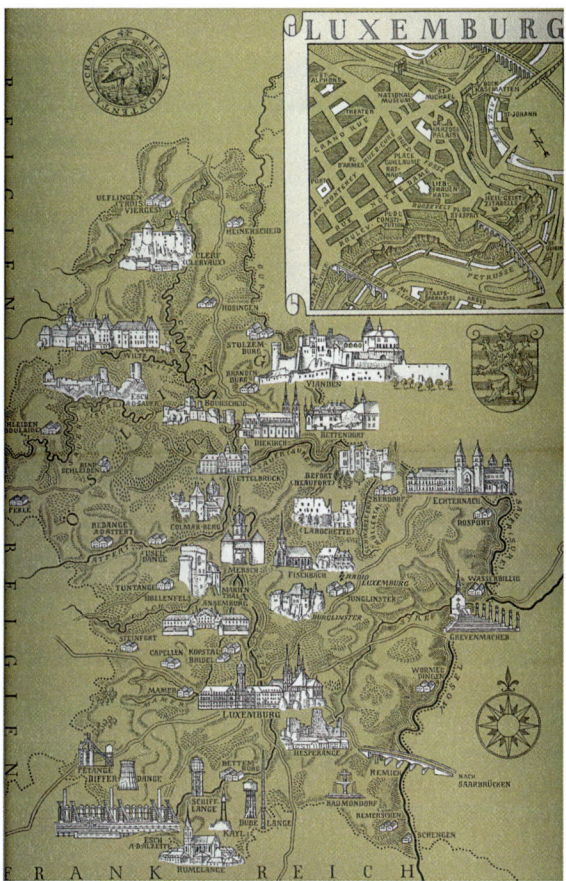

Figure 3: Picturesque map of the country (Merian 1964: 97).

The 1995 *Merian* repeats the advertising strategy of the *Syndicat d'initiative touristique* (now the *Office national du Tourisme*), which has been promoting both 'soft' local tourism and 'hard' business tourism since the 1960s. The slogans "*Découvrez Luxembourg, le cœur vert de l'Europe*"[58] and "Luxembourg, a Must for Congress and Incentive" (Pinnel 1989: 951) are reflected in the juxtaposed images of the façade of a shiny bank ("*Am Boulevard Royal, auch 'Wall Street' genannt*"[59])

---

58 | Personal translation: "Discover Luxembourg, the Green Heart of Europe".
59 | Personal translation: "On the Boulevard Royal, also referred to as 'Wall Street'".

and of cows on a lush meadow ("*Beschaulich: Idyll im Ösling*"[60] [both Merian 1995: 6f.]). This idyllic and pastoral landscape, a symbol of authenticity and innocence, is no longer presented at face value in 2007. Rather, hyper-reality is introduced by romantic clichés, swans and floating mist included, reminiscent of the hamlet of Marie-Antoinette or Castle Neuschwanstein (see Baudrillard 1994). The most bucolic article, both by its illustrations and by its title "*In der Ruhe liegt die Kraft*"[61], has the subtitle "*Sinnlich, still und leise zeigt Luxemburg seine Stärken: ein Land zum Auftanken*"[62] (*Merian* 2007: 86), introducing refuelling (the literal meaning of *Auftanken*) – at least by association – and thus the automobile and "the Empire of Speed" rejected by Renwick. The underlying irony is repeated by subtitles such as "*Burgen-Land*"[63], an allusion to the Austrian federal province of Burgenland (*Merian* 2007: 5), or Stölb's article "*Das Land der Schlichter und Banker*"[64], a reference to Germany as "*Land der Dichter und Denker*"[65] (*Merian* 2007: 14-15). Like the 1964 *Merian*, the 2007 version juxtaposes heritage and innovations, but in reverse order, commencing with the modern and cosmopolitan ("*Kulturhauptstadt*", "*Banker*",

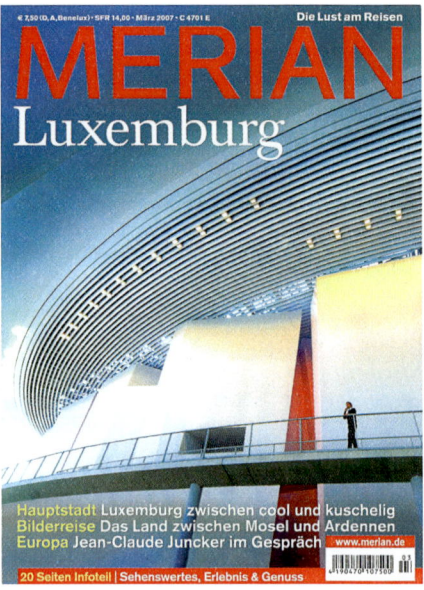

Figure 4: Cover of the 1964 Merian   *Figure 5: Cover of the 2007 Merian.*

---

60 | Personal translation: "Tranquil: Idyllic Ösling Landscape".
61 | Personal translation: "Strength lies in Silence".
62 | Personal translation: "Luxembourg's strong points: sensuous, calm and quiet – a country for recharging your batteries".
63 | Personal translation: "Castle-Land".
64 | Personal translation: "The Land of Mediators and Bankers".
65 | Personal translation: "The Land of Poets and Thinkers".

"weltoffen", "feiern", "Nassauer", "Kirchberg", "Europa", "Migranten", "berühmt"[66]), followed by the past ("Familienerbe", "Sigismund", "Ruhe", "Sattel", "Steinzeit", "Vianden," "bodenständig"[67]) in the next section (Merian 2007: 4). Yet these keywords derived from the titles of the articles presented in the table of contents are ironic: the "Stone Age" indicates to the early stages of RTL, prehistory does not refer to the time before the invention of writing, but before the emergence of modern media.

Contrary to the cover of the 1964 Merian, which displays an element of the fortress, the cover of the 2007 version depicts the interior of the Philharmonic[68] and emphasises the headline "Luxemburg zwischen cool und kuschelig"[69] by the choice of colours: blue (a cool colour for cool), and red (a warm colour for kuschelig). Associated with the white pillars, this results in the national tri-colour red-white-blue. The projected identity is one of a country either in transition, or wedged in an interstitial space between traditions and ambitions. This in-betweeness is not only temporal (between the past and the future), but also spatial (between the local and the global), even mental (between withdrawal and opening). The image of an 'open' country is based on the representation of being linguistically and culturally in-between (Germany and France), which is highlighted as an 'extraordinary' feature that characterises Luxembourg.

Image of an Open and Multicultural Country

The hybrid character of Luxembourg is a topos that dates back to the first tourist guide. Even if Erasmy defines Luxembourgers as a *"race allemande d'origine germanique"*[70], he insists on the 'intermingling' of peoples and judges their mentality as 'imitating' that of their neighbours a bit too much. Even the physical space is closely linked to adjacent spaces:

> Les montagnes luxembourgeoises appartiennent au système des Ardennes et des Vosges [...] Le noyau des Ardennes se trouve dans le Luxembourg belge [...] Les sources des fleuves entre les bassins du Rhin et de la Meuse. La principale chaîne de montagne franchit la frontière et rattache Ardennes à Eifel[71] (Erasmy 1861: 3).

---

66 | Personal translation: "Capital of culture, banker, cosmopolitan, celebrate, Nassauer, Kirchberg, Europe, migrants, famous".
67 | Personal translation: "Family heritage, Sigismund, tranquillity, saddle, Stone Age, Vianden, down-to-earth".
68 | See section 5.4.
69 | Personal translation: "Luxembourg, between cool and cuddly".
70 | Personal translation: "German race of Germanic origin".
71 | Personal translation: "The mountains of Luxembourg belong to the Ardennes and Vosges system [...] The core of the Ardennes lays in Belgian Luxembourg [...] The sources of rivers between the Rhine and Meuse basins. The principal chain of mountains forms the border and links the Ardennes to the Eifel".

Renwick also emphasises the intermingling of peoples and languages. According to him, the Luxembourger is bilingual (French and German) and uses moreover a strange dialect:

And what a mixture that patois is! Just as the country itself carries traces of all the peoples who have swept across it and dwelt in it, so the people's language has borrowed from at least a dozen tongues [...] Spoken, the patois sounds like curious Dutch and bad German coming from a worn gramophone (Renwick 1913: 21).

The 1964 *Merian* combines multilingualism with Europeanism, personified by the 'great European' Robert Schuman, born in Luxembourg. In his contribution titled "Unser Europa begann in Luxemburg"[72], Friedländer formulates it as follows:

Diese [moselfränkische] Mundart war wohl seine eigentliche Muttersprache, denn er sprach deutsch nicht ganz wie ein Deutscher und französisch nicht ganz wie ein Franzose. In Schuman waren zwei nationale Kulturen verschmolzen[73] (Merian 1964: 70).

In the same issue, writer Nic Weber, co-founder of the *Cahiers luxembourgeois* and the *Journées littéraires de Mondorf*, describes the cultural in-between in a humorous fashion as a "*Löwe zwischen Geflügel*"[74], accompanied by a pen and ink drawing showing the heraldic lion of Luxembourg quibbling with the French cock and the German eagle (*Merian* 1964: 5). There is no trace of conflict in the 1995 work, which presents Luxembourg as the birthplace of the "*Vater des europäischen Gedankens*"[75], Robert Schuman, "*überzeugt vom Geist eines gemeinsamen Europas*"[76], and deducts that "*der europäische Geist ist tief verwurzelt*"[77] in Luxembourg (Schröder 1995: 8) and that the cultural borders have been abolished (Schröder 1995: 7). The first chapter is logically titled "*Eine Region stellt sich vor*"[78] (Schröder 1995: 4-9) and not 'A country presents itself'. The natural borders have also been abolished: the Moselle is cited as a typical example of a border that does not separate, rather unites (Schröder 1995: 6). In the brief chronology, the year 1995 – in which Luxembourg is the European Capital of Culture – is summarised as follows: "*Mit dem grenzüberschreitenden Programm spiegelt sich der Gedanke einer multikulturellen Gesellschaft in Kunst und*

---

72 | Personal translation: "Our Europe began in Luxembourg".
73 | Personal translation: "This (moselle-frankish) dialect was his actual native language, for he did not speak German quite like a German, nor French quite like a Frenchman. In Schuman two national cultures coalesced".
74 | Personal translation: "Lion between fowls".
75 | Personal translation: "Father of the European idea".
76 | Personal translation: "Imbued with the spirit of a common Europe".
77 | Personal translation: "The European spirit is profoundly rooted".
78 | Personal translation: "A region presents itself".

Kultur wieder"[79] (Schröder 1995: 123). The 2007 *Merian* includes the Portuguese of Luxembourg in this multiculturalism, but presents them from an ethnicised angle, *"Saudade an der Sauer"*[80] (60-68). The editorial states that Luxembourg is a country in-between (*"Zwischenland"*) and the cover title *"Bilderreise: Das Land zwischen Mosel und Ardennen"*.[81] Imagery of bridges, mediation and intermingling is recurring and presented as typically Luxembourgish (4). Europeanism is one of the key themes in the 2007 *Merian*. The cover announces an interview with Jean-Claude Juncker about Europe. In the table of contents, the Prime Minister is presented as a *"Visionär"*[82] who *"für ein vereintes Europa kämpft"*[83], illustrated by a profile portrait, looking straight ahead and flanked by the European flag (5). The interview itself is titled *"Grenzen in Europa? Ein Horror!"*[84] and ends with a history of relations between Luxembourg and the EU titled *"Das Zugpferdchen – Luxemburg ist Vorreiter der Europäischen Union und einer seiner stärksten Antreiber"*[85] (58). We have highlighted the projected identity formulated in the guide published in 2007, as it is the only one that could be compared to the appropriated identity discourse as it appears in the qualitative interviews.

An Ambivalent and Politically (In)Correct Image

The Eurobarometer surveys show that Luxembourg's commitment to the European Union is relatively high. In early 2009, 74 % responded positively to the question, "Generally speaking, do you think that [your country]'s membership of the European Union is...? A good thing", compared to the European average of 52 % (see European Commission 2009: 85). However, this general appreciation conceals the discontent and much more ambivalent assessments, which are articulated in the qualitative interviews with a, "Yes, but...". They largely overlap with the results of a study from 2006 on the vote for or against the Treaty establishing a Constitution for Europe, which received 56.52 % of the vote in July 2005 (Dumont et al. 2007). The analysis of four focus groups, particularly regarding the response strategies seeking to position themselves in relation to the 'politically correct' (Dumont et al. 2007: 150), facilitates a comparison with the opinions offered in qualitative surveys conducted in Spring 2009. Thus, a question in our study that

---

79 | Personal translation: "The crossborder programme reflects the spirit of a multicultural society in art and culture".
80 | Personal translation: "Saudade on the Sûre".
81 | Personal translation: "A Journey in Pictures: The Land between the Moselle and the Ardennes".
82 | Personal translation: "Visionary".
83 | Personal translation: "Fights for a united Europe".
84 | Personal translation: "Borders in Europe? Utter horror!"
85 | Personal translation: "The Little Draught-Horse – Luxembourg is leading the charge for the European Union and is one of its strongest driving forces".

was considered 'delicate' – i.e. "What significance do the European institutions in Luxembourg have for you?" – received some reticent responses, considered unspeakable ("forbidden" or "horrible") or preceded by an apology:

Mit zunehmendem Alter denke ich, hm [zögert] ist's... normalerweise streng verboten, man ist sofort in der rechtsextremen Kiste, ausländerfeindlich und und und. Ich seh trotzdem nicht, wo denn die Gemeinsamkeiten zwischen hier, den Luxemburgern, den Deutschen, den Franzosen hier von Nordfrankreich, den Belgiern und so weiter *und* den Portugiesen zum Beispiel sind. Weder in der Kultur noch in der Sprache noch in gar nix. Außer, dass alle gute Christen sein sollten[86] (Female, 50 years old, Luxembourger, Rambrouch).

Voilà, mais avec des interférences aussi qui ne sont pas sur le plan politique non plus, mais sur le plan très concret. C'est-à-dire que euh [rire gêné], mais, ah, mon dieu, c'est horrible de dire ça comme ça, mais c'est, euh, quand on cherche un appartement à Luxembourg-Ville, euh, euh, dans, dans, de discu, enfin, je sais pas si c'est une légende urbaine ou si c'est authentique, que certains prix élevés de l'immobilier à la location au Luxembourg vient également de la présence de ces fonctionnaires européens[87] (Male, 30, French, Esch-sur-Alzette).

These responses reveal two recurring elements: insistence on cultural diversity, considered threatened by Europeanisation, and more concrete grievances tied to the impact of European officials on the real estate market. Of 28 persons asked about the European Union, half had a favourable opinion, a quarter were sceptical and a quarter ambivalent. This sample is not representative, but allows – by qualitative methods – to further examine the arguments that have been advanced. Amongst the positive evaluations of the European institutions in Luxembourg, two arguments prevail. The first is linked to the image of Luxembourg, a small country particularly recognised as the seat of some institutions and as a founding country. This thought perfectly overlaps with the tourism discourse. The second argument is more common: the institutions are considered an important creator of jobs and

---

86 | Personal translation: "As I get older, I think, hm [hesitates] it's... usually strictly forbidden, you're automatically in the right-wing extremist camp, xenophobic, and and and. I still don't see what they're supposed to have in common, the Luxembourgers, the Germans, here the French from Northern France, the Belgians and so on *and* the Portuguese, for example. Neither in their culture, nor in their language, nor in anything. Except that they should all be good Christians".

87 | Personal translation: "Well, but there are also interferences which also aren't on a political level, but on a very concrete one. That's to say that, uh [embarrassed laugh], but, uh, my God, it's horrible to say it like that, but it's, uh, when you're looking for a flat in Luxembourg City, uh, uh, in, in, in conversation, after all, I don't know if it's an urban legend or if it's real, that some high prices for renting properties in Luxembourg are also because of the presence of these European officials".

'advantageous' for the country or the state. This argument is also advanced by the 'ambivalent' respondents, who qualify the remark by saying, for instance, that the benefits are limited to the "upper layers" (Male, 39 years old, Portuguese, Strassen). In addition, Luxembourg's European and multicultural character is called into question:

> Die normale Bevölkerung identifiziert sich nicht damit. Das ist eine einzelne Gruppe von Europäischen Bürgern, die da arbeiten, die sich unter sich aufhalten und selten integriert sind. Oder sich integrieren wollen. Und deshalb ist auch wenig Kontakt dann da, von Menschen die da arbeiten mit der richtige Bevölkerung. Und deshalb, ja, das sind zwei Welten, die so parallel laufen. Ja, habe ich den Eindruck.
> *Und meinen Sie denn, dass das für das Land selber eher vorteilig oder nachteilig ist?*
> Ist schade, eigentlich – finde ich. Es ist zu verstehen, aber es fordert sicher nicht die multikulturelle Gesellschaft und Akzeptanz von Ausländern in Luxemburg. Macht das eher noch wieder ein Beispiel mehr, wo keine sich integriert und sich nicht anpasst. Ich glaube die Bevölkerung ist da eher... Ja, es bringt... Luxemburg ist mal wieder in den Schlagzeilen, wenn da irgendwas los ist. Aber sonst?[88] (Female, 30 years old, Dutch, Lintgen).

The idea of parallel worlds is also repeated by another respondent, who feels:

> C'était, un moment donné, j'avais lu, c'était à propos des Etats-Unis où ils disaient: 'le melting-pot est terminé, on est passé à un système de mosaïque.' Et, j'avais l'impression que ça faisait un petit peu pareil sur le Luxembourg où il y avait une petite mosaïque euro, euh, dans la mosaïque, il y avait des petits bouts européens qui ne se, à côté il y avait les gens de la finance ou les, ou les Portugais, les Français, les Luxembourgeois de souche, et les Belges. Et ça vivait côte à côte de manière sympathique et sans accrocs. Mais côte à côte, pas ensemble[89] (Male, 30, French, Esch-sur-Alzette).

---

88 | Personal translation: "The normal population doesn't identify itself with it. It's a single group of European citizens who work there, keep to themselves and are rarely integrated. Or want to integrate. And that's why there's so little contact between people who work there and the actual population. And that's why, yes, those are two worlds running parallel. Yeah, that's the impression I get". *So do you think that this is good or bad for the country itself?* It's unfortunate, actually – I think. It's understandable, but it certainly doesn't help this multicultural society or foreigners being accepted in Luxembourg. It actually just makes it another example of no one integrating or adapting. I think people think... sure, it draws... Luxembourg makes the headlines once again if something happens. But otherwise?"

89 | Personal translation: "There was, one time, I read, it was about the United States where they said, 'The melting pot is over, it's become a mosaic.' And I had the impression that was kind of like Luxembourg where there was a small European mosaic, uh, in the mosaic, there were little bits of Europe that didn't, nearby there were the finance people, or the, or the Portuguese, the French, or the native Luxembourgers, and the Belgians. And they lived side by side so nice and smoothly. But side by side, not together".

Most respondents who consider the 'level of integration' low and society as compartmentalised often live themselves in mixed marriages and complex multilingual milieus. The responses – mixing experiences, prejudices and received images – can differ from the tourism (and political) discourse of Luxembourg, which sees it as a model for Europe (see Majerus 2007) and considers its history an intercultural success story.

Since the first tourist guides in the 19th century, Luxembourg has been presented as an oddity. The authors (all male) see themselves as explorers, ethnologists or sociologists studying a country and its residents who live on an island of tranquillity and/or prosperity. This image finds itself in apparent contradiction with that of a cultural intersection (Germanic and Romance), of a linguistic and ethnic melting pot. However, the two clichés are combined to emphasise Luxembourg's exceptional character. The paradox lies rather in the opposition between the small size of the country (particularly described in pastoral terms) and its economic and political force within the European Union. This paradox is deepening over the years, but this diachronic analysis reveals in particular the surprising continuity of the projected identities. As for the appropriated identities, we were only able to analyse the attitudes towards Europe, and it is clear that the opinions collected are far more diverse and more critical. If some people subscribe to the image of an open and tolerant Luxembourg, others observe the emergence of parallel societies, with no contact between them.

5.6 The "Greater Region" – Spatial Constructions between Desire and Reality

Any investigation into tourist discourses in Luxembourg must necessarily also deal with the question of how the cross-border cooperation area, the so-called 'Greater Region'[90], is represented within the discourse, negotiated and appropriated. For this – in contrast to the local, regional and national levels – there is no large corpus of established tourism literature available consisting of general guidebooks, tourist maps and plans and special themed guidebooks. Nevertheless, it is precisely this corpus, focussed as it is on the external representation and image construction of a newly set out region that seems to be particularly suited to the current study, given that it is strongly implicated in identity attribution processes.

---

90 | The 'Greater Region' refers to a cross-border area of cooperation, which, next to the Grand Duchy includes the French region of Lorraine, the German federal provinces of Rhineland-Palatinate and Saarland and the Belgian Wallonia region (including the German- and French-speaking communities). With over eleven million inhabitants and an area of 65,000 km^2, it is the largest sub-state cooperative zone in Europe: see also www.grossregion.net

Corpus of Investigation and Conceptual Preliminary Remarks

Despite many years of efforts aimed at a stronger cross-border coordination and orchestration of tourism marketing and management, there are very few overviews that could be used for this study. For this reason this microanalysis is focussing on two recent works. One is a concise tourist guide[91] published by a Luxembourgish publishing company to mark the year in which Luxembourg was the European Capital of Culture (*Luxembourg and Greater Region – European Capital of Culture 2007*). The other is a rather essayistic anthology comprising a multi-faceted portrait of the Greater Region[92] collated by a team of authors consisting of scientists, people engaged in the cultural sector and journalists with cross-border commitments. Whilst the work of Mendgen et al. (*Im Reich der Mitte/Le berceau de la civilisation européenne. Savoir-faire/savoir-vivre*, henceforth to be referred to as the 'IRDM') is a richly appointed collaborative opus, the first source (*Die Großregion entdecken/ Découvrir la Grande Région*, or the 'DGRE' in the following) was masterminded by a single author. Both are bilingual works written in German and French, whereby, in the IRDM, the manuscript language of the authors varies, while the DGRE was written entirely in German and was then translated. The further analysis is based on the respective original version (on issues relating to bilingualism: see below).

The DGRE is a handy travel guide that was published as 'official contribution' to the Capital of Culture 2007. The IRDM can best be understood as a 'background contribution', the editorial part of which exceeds the scope of the DGRE, and which can only be considered a part of the tourism discourse in the widest sense of the term. Notwithstanding this fact it does at times lapse into a style characteristic of 'promotionally' oriented texts, due not in a small way to the emphasis and institutional positions of some of the authors.

Given that the identities examined here tend to be appropriated, this section also includes the results of the qualitative interviews as well as the standardised survey.

The basis of the micro-analytic examination of the two works, both from the perspective of human geography and the cultural geography, is based on a (de)constructivist outlook and a pragmatic concept of discourse. In a further development of Foucault's rather holistic concept of discourse, the latter is limited to discourse practices relevant to the research subject (see Hajer 1995 and 2003) as manifested for example in written texts or spoken language, and which can lead to the development of specific discourse strands ('story lines','narratives'). These are made up of selective discursive events (e.g. a politician's speech) or discourse fragments (e.g. discourse pattern of a publication) and through reproduction and/

---

91 | Scholz, Ingeborg. 2007. *Die Großregion entdecken / Découvrir la Grande Région*. Luxemburg: Guy Binsfeld.

92 | Mendgen, Eva , Volker Hildisch and Hervé Doucet, eds. 2007. *Im Reich der Mitte / Le berceau de la civilisation européenne. Savoir-faire / savoir-vivre*. Konstanz: Hartung-Gorre.

or interlinkage, achieve a dominant and therefore, in the current case, identity-forming character (see Strüver 2005; Mattissek 2007). Furthermore, from a methodological point of view, a pragmatic form of critical discourse analysis was chosen, which essentially operates at a semiotic and/or content-associative level to identify specific 'story lines' or narrative patterns based on recurring concepts, metaphors and discourse fragments (see key quotations) and to attempt an initial interpretation[93].

The main focus of the analysis was a review of those editorial parts relevant for the question, i.e. in the IRDM above all the contributions by Mendgen/Hildisch (p. 13-20) and Gengler (p. 67-73), and in the DGRE primarily the introductory passages (p. 8-13).

The Dominating Topoi of Identity Attribution

An initial review of both works quickly reveals a series of recurring discourse elements in the form of interdiscursive metaphors and images[94], which can essentially be summarised under the following topoi: 'centrality', 'space appropriation', 'uniqueness' and 'showcase character'. Following Weichhart (1990), this concerns 'identity features of the space', meaning cognitive-emotional representations of the Greater Region in processes related to the consciousness of an individual or a group of individuals (space-centric perspective), and the 'space as a constituent part of individual or collective identity patterns', i.e. those conceptual representations and emotional-affective assessments of the Greater Region which become a part of the individual 'self-concept' and/or collective 'we-concept' (person-centric perspective).

'Heart', 'Navel', 'Back' – On the Anatomy of Europe and the Greater Region

An almost inflationary use of paraphrases is made in both sources, designed to invest the Greater Region with a special geographical, cultural or even political economic significance within Europe. At the same time the purely geometrical location is often given an additional qualitative nuance in the sense of a surplus of significance compared with other regions of Europe. Already the immodest title of the German version *Im Reich der Mitte* ("Middle Kingdom") seems like a tongue-in-cheek reference to a disproportionately larger cultural region. The French version *Le berceau de la civilisation européenne* ("The cradle of European civilisation") clearly resonates with ambitious positioning attempts. By contrast, the English title *The Center at the Edge* seems comparatively restrained and almost like a geographical concept. What remains more or less implicit in the various titles is presented

---

93 | This approach cannot and does not aspire to meet the demands of, for example, a linguistic discourse analysis in the narrower sense.
94 | See also chapter 6.

explicitly in the main body of the text as a portrait "of the real geopolitical and historical heart[95] of Europe" (IRDM: 14). According to this view, the Greater Region is undoubtedly a *"Teil des dicht besiedelten 'europäischen Rückens'"*[96] (DGRE: 8). The latter possibly derives from the French, *"dorsale européenne"*[97] (Brunet, 1989), better known in Germany as *'Blaue Banane'*[98], an area with the highest density of economic activities and urban spaces in Europe.

As if the civilisation-historical significance of being part of the 'centre' needed further underlining, a quote made by the Romanian theologian and philosopher Mircea Eliade in 1957 is pressed into service in a very prominent position: *"l'Homme de la société pré-industrielle souhaite vivre aussi près du centre du monde. Il sait que sa patrie se situe vraiment au centre de la Terre, que sa ville est le nombril de l'univers"*[99] (IRDM: 225). It remains unclear in this context whether this pre-modern mentality is also intended as a maxim for the present.

Processes of Appropriation – or: *"Une réalité vécue"*?

A remarkably vigorous 'person-centric perspective' is adopted in both sources to emphasise patterns of perception and identity attributed to the Greater Region – in some cases with the addition of an almost programmatic imperative. Non-substantiated statements like "The people accept this borderless Greater Region as something completely natural" (IRDM: 16) or, *"'SarLorLux' est une réalité vécue"*[100] (IRDM: 67), culminate in the announcement of a newly discovered species which has almost an ethnographic ring to it:

A l'instar du 'SarLorLux', il existe le 'SarLorLuxois' ou la 'SarLorLuxoise'. Depuis de nombreuses années, des centaines de milliers d'individus assimilent cette vaste étendue à une véritable région. Ce chiffre ne cesse pas de croître et nous voyons, nous entendons, nous rencontrons partout ces personnes[101] (IRDM: 67).

The DGRE is significantly more restrained in this respect:

---

95 | The collective symbolism of the heart metaphor also has an important inter-discursive role in the representation of Luxembourg in the international media (see Parr 2009).
96 | Personal translation: "Part of the densely-settled 'back of Europe'".
97 | Personal translation: "European backbone".
98 | Personal translation: "Blue banana".
99 | Personal translation: "Man in premodern societies wants to live as close as possible to the centre of the world. He knows that his country really is at the centre of the Earth and that his town constitutes the navel of the universe".
100 | In English something like: "The SarLorLux concept is a lived reality".
101 | Personal translation: "Just as there is the 'SarLorLux', there is the 'SaarLorLuxois' or the 'SaarLorLuxoise'. Since many years hundreds of thousands of people have equated this huge expanse with a veritable region. Their numbers are increasing, and we see, hear and meet these people everywhere".

Qu'est-ce que les habitants de la Grande Région savent les uns des autres? Existe-t-il une conscience identitaire commune? L'absence – provisoire – de cette dernière est assez souvent regrettée. Ce petit guide touristique ne doit toutefois pas servir aux lamentations. Mieux vaut se préoccuper des opportunités de forger une conscience identitaire. Une identité n'est pas une saute d'humeur, mais un sentiment qui résulte de l'expérience, du contact, de la communication et de la connaissance[102](DGRE: 13).

According to this, a common cross-border consciousness of identity is still to be created and/or "forged", although "experience and contact [...] on a broad scale are already the current reality in the Greater Region" (DGRE: 12).

Unique Showcase Region and "Laboratoire de l'Europe"

Closely linked to the topos of centrality is the just as frequently emphasised special character or even uniqueness of the Greater Region. Superlatives – "the first cross-border capital of culture" (IRDM: 13) – are just as enthusiastically pressed into service as arrogant characterisations, for example, when the (romanticised) population is attested a "multi-lingual facility and innate intercultural competence" (IRDM: 16). Here, too, an appeal is made to the "common" historical perspective to identify present needs:

2.500 Jahre gemeinsamer Geschichte verbinden die einzelnen Regionen miteinander. Da mutet die Bezeichnung 'Großregion' für ein Gebilde derartiger kultureller Reichtümer an wie ein blasses Provisorium – und das ist es auch. Versuche einer klangvolleren Namensgebung sind bislang gescheitert. So muss die Großregion weiterhin mit ihrem nüchternen Namen leben, kann ihre Energien aber nun darauf verwenden, sich selber und der Mitwelt zu vermitteln, wer sie eigentlich ist (DGRE: 8).[103]

In this context, uniqueness is often clearly understood as a value in itself, in the sense of an exemplary pioneering region standing for cross-border integration. Paraphrases such as "mini Europe", *"laboratoire de l'Europe"* etc. are very often encountered. Even when the Greater Region as a whole is not attributed showcase

---

102 | Personal translation: "What do the inhabitants of the Greater Region know about each other? Is there a common consciousness of identity? The latter's absence – so far – is often lamented. However, the limited space of this travel guide should not be misused for such lamentations. Let us better ask: What potential is there for forging an identity? Identity does not drop miraculously into our laps, rather it is something that is born from experience, contact, communication and knowledge".
103 | Personal translation: "2,500 years of a common history link the individual regions. Seen in this light, the term 'Greater Region' seems a feeble, provisional term for a polity of such cultural richness – and so it is. Attempts to create a more illustrious sounding name have so far failed. Thus the Greater Region must continue to live with its sober name, but can now direct its energies into showing itself and the rest of the world who it really is".

character, at least a part of its population is: "Experts consider the cross-border commuters as a veritable avant-garde of the Greater Region" (DGRE: 12).

As already implied above, the bilingual layout of the two works analysed raises further questions, and not only in terms of methodology. The caution that needs to be exercised as a matter of course in taking a discourse-analytical approach to a multi-lingual corpus applies all the more when sense-extending or sense-distorting divergences exist between the two language versions. By way of example, the following table contains some chapter headings and subheadings from the IRDM; the original version in each case is emphasised in italics:

German version	French version
Im Reich der Mitte (Personal translation: In the Middle Kingdom)	Le berceau de la civilisation européenne (Personal translation: The cradle of European Civilisation)
Eine (Groß-)Region rauft sich zusammen (Personal translation: A (Greater) Region is wrestling to find common ground)	*La Grande Région – un terrain d'entente?* (Personal translation: The Greater Region – a common ground of agreement?)
Renovatio Lotharingiae? (Personal translation: The rebirth of Lotharingia?)[104]	*Renovatio Lotharingiae ou l'affrontement définitif* (Personal translation: The rebirth of Lotharingia or the final confrontation)
Erste Phase der Industrialisierung (Personal translation: First phase of industrialisation)	*Un esprit nouveau* (Personal translation: A new spirit)
Lothringen, zwischen Frankreich und Deutschland (Personal translation: Lorraine, between France and Germany)	*Entre France et Allemagne, la Lorraine déchirée* (Personal translation: Between France and Germany: a torn Lorraine)

Table 1: Examples of discrepancies between the German and French versions of IRDM (original version emphasised in italics).

Since nobody would accuse either the translators or the publishers of acting intentionally and since it is only a matter of a few divergences, primarily on the level of the (sub) headings, these effects should not be overrated. Only a systematically comparative fine analysis, which was neither intended nor possible within the

---

104 | Lotharingia: Lotharingia is the name given to the kingdom of Lothair II (855-869) and to a duchy in the 10th century that geographically overlap with today's Greater Region. The only other historical periods when these composite territories were under the same rule were under Napoleon and the National Socialist Occupation, which are difficult to use as historical antecedents.

present framework, could show whether divergences could be detected here that might serve different discourse strands within the two languages.

In summary, the preeminent pattern of discourse in both sources is the obvious attempt to stress the qualitative peculiarities (historical importance, linguistic-cultural complexity, pioneer character etc.) and the 'centrality' (geographic, political, commercial, cultural) of the Greater Region. The frame of reference is a more or less abstract Europe (continent/the EU/'cultural zone') within which the Greater Region and its inhabitants are attributed a special, exemplary role. The sources evaluated in the following enable a first empirical review of the sensitivities of the inhabitants of Luxembourg, frequently labelled as model Europeans.

Perception of the Neighbouring Regions

Starting with the assumption that individuals can hardly establish cross-border identity patterns without personal experiences with or in the respective neighbouring regions, a part of our questionnaire and the qualitative interviews first dealt with behavioural routines, perception and attitudes with respect to the surrounding subregions of the Greater Region. By way of example, the frequency with which respondents to the standardised questions visit the neighbouring countries is about the same for all of them, albeit slightly higher for the bordering states of Rhineland-Palatinate and Saarland, whereby the age and gender of the those questioned does not influence visiting frequency. Neither are there appreciable differences between the various milieus (see below) in this respect. In terms of personal preferences regarding 'a sense of wellbeing' during visits to neighbouring countries, the interviewees tend to make balanced statements. In this respect though, a clear age gradient is evident in that statements by older interviewees were more likely to indicate positive feelings towards France whereas it was primarily younger interviewees who indicated positive opinions about Germany[105]. This may be related to age-specific consumer and leisure behaviour, but may also reflect historically conditioned prejudices and resentments. However, this gradient is not evident in answers to the counter question about feeling uncomfortable, which produced even more balanced results.

More evident still than the age gradient, however, are the milieu-specific preference patterns that, for instance in the case of the tradition-oriented milieu, are clearly in favour of Germany (42 % as opposed to 18 % for France, 15 % for Belgium and 18 % non-specific). This applies in equal measure the alternative (32 % for Germany, 16 % for France, 8 % for Belgium and 36 % non-specific) and the status-oriented milieu (41 % for Germany, 26 % for France, 7 % for Belgium and 19 % non-specific). Here, too, the answer pattern to the counter question is more balanced, although the underprivileged milieu (28 % for Germany, 23 % for

---

105 | See in-depth Section 4.2.

France and 17 % for Belgium) and the privileged liberal milieu (23 % for Germany, 15 % for France and 19 % for Belgium) clearly feel less comfortable in Germany.

However, the findings of the qualitative interviews show that, in many cases, answers and comments were very nuanced, as illustrated by the following selection of quotes:

Nee, ich bin jetzt am Überlegen, ob's Deutschland oder Frankreich ist. Wenn ich ausländerfeindliche Sachen in Deutschland beobachte, dann sage ich mir, oh, Gott sei dank wohne ich hier nicht. Und die gibt's auch in Trier. Und in Frankreich, da laufen manchmal so Gestalten rum, wo ich sage, hm, der wird Dir ja jetzt nicht was tun. Also, ich würde sagen, in beiden fühle ich mich nicht unbedingt wohl[106] (Female, 32 years old, Luxembourger, Leudelange).

Also während der Zeit, wo ich arbeitete, hab ich mich am wohlsten gefühlt in Belgien. Und wenn ich dort arbeiten und leben müsste, noch heute, wäre ich nur aus persönlichen, mir persönlichen Gründen, hätte ich mich wahrscheinlich in Belgien etabliert. Aber durch meine Frau, die mag das nicht. Nein. Aber, und wenn ich hier wählen könnte, heute, würde ich auch nicht in Luxemburg leben. Würde ich auf der deutschen Seite leben. Und ich hab in Deutschland, bekomm ich relativ schnell Kontakt, egal, wie man das jetzt sagt. Und in Belgien auch. Fran... nach Frankreich will ich nicht gehen. Auf keinen Fall. Das ist etwas ..."[107] (Male, 67 years old, Luxembourger, Echternach).

Ça a toujours été [la France], même en tant que gosse. On est parti souvent en, en France en vacances avec mes parents. Moi, je me sens bien en France. Les gens sont beaucoup plus relax qu'en Allemagne. En Allemagne, c'est toujours ehem, il faut que ce soit comme ça euh. Je ne sais pas, ils sont... deutsche Gründlichkeit, ne?[108] (Female, 54 years old, Luxembourger, Walferdange).

---

106 | Personal translation: "No, I'm trying to think whether it's Germany or France. When I see xenophobic stuff in Germany, I say to myself, oh thank God I don't live here. And they do have it in Trier. And in France, you get these weird characters walking about at times, where I say, hmm, bet he's going to do something bad to me now. So, I would say, I don't feel totally comfortable in either".
107 | Personal translation: "Well, at the time when I was still working, I felt most comfortable in Belgium. And if I still had to work and live there today, for personal reasons, personal to me, I would probably have settled down in Belgium. But because of my wife ... she doesn't like it. No. But ... and if I had the choice here and now ... I also wouldn't live in Luxembourg. I'd live on the German side. And in Germany, I've got ... can get contacts relatively quickly, or however you say it. And the same in Belgium. Fra ... I don't want to go to France. No way. That's something ..."
108 | Personal translation: "It's always been [France], even when I was a kid. We often went to, to France on holiday. I like being in France. People are much more relaxed than in Germany. In Germany, it's always, uhm, everything has to be like this, ah. I don't know, they're ... *deutsche Gründlichkeit*, [German thoroughness], you know?"

Whilst such sweeping general judgments about the nation in question, are mostly influenced by personal biography or social status, and range from romanticised generalisations derived from positive memories of childhood and holidays to overrating specific negative experiences (as a tourist at a holiday resort for instance), opinions about the directly adjoining regions are more differentiated and less stereotyped. Numerous interviewees stress the differences in their attitudes to the respective border region and to the rest or centre of the neighbouring country (for instance, South Wallonia versus Flemish North Sea coast or Brussels, Lorraine versus Côte d'Azur or Paris), whereby positive and negative judgments are encountered with about equal frequency. With conspicuous frequency, Belgium or the Belgian population are used as a reference to describe what one dislikes about the two 'big' neighbours, France (often) and Germany (here more seldom). In this respect, affection for the relatively small neighbour may be as significant as historical links, inter-family relations or a feeling of familiarity from 60 years of Benelux cooperation.

Less often, regional variation leads to an integrative judgment about similarities and links of the whole border region (without necessarily meaning the Greater Region within its above-mentioned boundaries). Here, it is primarily commonalities of language as well as other links due to affinities in culture or mentality that tend to be brought to the fore:

[...] d'Grenzregioun einfach. Also déi eicht 50 km iwwert d'Grenz ass dat nämlecht wéi fir d'Belsch. Et kann een net vergläichen Frankräich ass een ganz groussst Land, et kann een net vergläichen mat Marseille, Nice, oder...[109] (Male, 36 years old, Luxembourger, Redange).

Dat ass zum Beispill, hei [...] an all di Streecher do, ass d'Grondsprooch vun deenen Aalen ass nach Lëtzebuergesch, also awer wierklech dat aalt Lëtzebuergescht, also di hu nach Ausdréck dran, wou nach just den Alain Atten mol op dem Radio seet, wou dohannen bei deenen Aalen, d'Fransousen hei vir, deen aalen Loutrénger nach Gang und Gebe sinn. An esou ass et och an der Belsch. Bon, d'Belsch, 't ass e Land 't ass no bei eis[110] (Male, 65 years old, Luxembourger, Dudelange).

---

109 | Personal translation: "[...] simply the border region. These first 50 km after the border, it's just the same there as in Belgium. It's just not comparable, France is a very big country, one can't compare it to Marseille, Nice, or [...]".
110 | Personal translation: "It's for example, here [...] in all these areas the old people's main language is still Luxembourgish, – the really old Luxembourgish, like, they still use the sort of expressions that Alain Atten, if anyone, might use on the radio once in a while, but that are still in everyday use over there among the old folks, with the French over this way, or among the older people in Lorraine. And in Belgium it's the same. Well, Belgium is a country that is close to us".

Mä wann een awer éischter sou an Baden Baden rageet oder alles wat bei Berlin, München an sou Saachen leit. Dass eppes ganz anescht wei hei an der Géigend, well hei alles wat Moselfränkesch ass dat ass jo am Fong, Groussregioun [sic!] nennen ech dat, fir mech ass dat een Land. Och wann een seet Lëtzebuerg, Däitschland an sou mä et gehéiert zu engem Ensemble. An mä wann een awer wierklech bei hinnen eran geet, et sinn aner Leit, sinn fréndlech, sinn ganz op, si laachen gären[111] (Male, 21 years old, Luxembourger, Esch-sur-Alzette).

All the same, statements like the latter are rather the exception. There was far less talk of commonalities and uniting features than of that which separates and repulses or of the, occasionally attractive, 'other'. Whilst one can often discern a certain awareness of Luxembourg's position within a complex border region situation, indications of an increasing self-understanding as, for instance, a 'Saar-Lor-Luxois'[112] can hardly be found, even implicitly.

Even the blank map (i.e. without captions) of Western and Central Europe[113], used during the interviews, generated few comments on the transnational dimension of feelings related to homeland and belonging. The low number of relevant interview passages justifies only a very careful classification of the findings, but does allow initial inferences concerning appropriated identities.

The inclusion of neighbouring regions within drawings and verbal statements without explicitly referring to the institutionalised Greater Region is an expression of identification with the whole region that is not bound by national borders. In one case, the chosen drawing is deliberately used to move away from nationalistic interpretations:

---

111 | Personal translation: "But if one were to go to, say, Baden-Baden, or to the areas around Berlin or Munich. That's totally different to the way it is around here, because everything that is Moselle-Frankish is, basically, Greater Region, that's how I call it, to me it's all one country. Even if one speaks of Luxembourg, Germany and all that, it still all belongs together. And if you really go there, they're different people, friendly, very open and they like to laugh".

112 | The bulkiness of this neologism as well as its barely possible translation into English (see above) indicate that its suitability for everyday use is very limited and that a diffusion of the term cannot be empirically verified.

113 | When choosing 'mental maps' as a complementary method, the authors of this chapter were aware of their restricted applicability and the issues relating to the hypostasising region concept upon which it is based. Their use therefore is to be understood rather as an interview stimulus than as an independent and supportable approach. However, it was precisely the interviewees' limited drawing-based abilities that had a marked narrative-generating effect (see the following quotes). Nevertheless, the results of the graphic representation are usually of a specific nature and are limited to Luxembourg or the place of residence. We shall forego a separate description here.

Und da ich nicht so orientiert bin, dass ich nur sage: 'Luxemburg ist gut oder so', das ... das bin ich nicht. Da mach ich den Kreis ein bisschen grösser[114] (Female, 55 years old, Luxembourger, Lintgen).

At the same time, in terms of cross-border categorisation, a distinction needs to be made between a rather pragmatic, functionally based *familiarity with* the neighbouring regions which can result in a less rigid demarcation, and a qualitatively more significant, identity-forming *relationship with* the neighbouring regions. Frequent visits to neighbouring regions for professional or private reasons does not necessarily say anything about the emotional relationship with the respective region or must be viewed in a nuanced manner as the following quote makes clear:

L'Allemagne. Oui, bon, on y va régulièrement. C'est pas que je me sens pas bien là-bas, ça c'est pas le cas[115] (Female, 54 years old, Luxembourger, Walferdange).

Often, special affinities with foreign regions, which do not share a border with Luxembourg are spontaneously addressed in several interviews. The likes and dislikes formulated in this context are not always free of clichés or idealisations based on holidays, but they often go beyond this, apparently mostly for biographical reasons (familial links, business trips and other personal experiences). The interviewees sometimes make use of the large-scale layout of the blank map to establish corresponding relational connections with more distant regions.

Lëtzebuerg, an dann wou ech mer nach elo kéint virstellen dat misst dann méi sou heierouter... Am Elsass. [...] An dann eh, och ech weess net, jo vläicht och an der Schwäiz, ech weess et net. [...] Éischtens emol well ech schonn oft am Elsass war, an ech fannen déi Leit hunn och eng aner Mentalitéit wéi lo, also wat hei d'ganzt Louthrengen hei ubelaangt, also do kann ech mer virstellen datt ech mech doudsécher net géif do doheem fillen, hein. Well eh also déi Mentalitéit déi, déi leit mer guer net. An dann och vun der Landschaft hier, ech nee, do géif ech mech net doheem fillen. D'Elsass kéint ech mer eventuell nach virstellen do, do ze wunnen. An dann och, an dann och d'Schwäiz. Jo vun der Mentalitéit hier, awer lo net iergendwéi, well do lo d'Bierger sinn oder, oder[116] (Female, 37 years old, Luxembourger, Bascharage).

---

114 | Personal translation: "And since I'm not the sort to just say: 'Luxembourg is good or something like that', that ... I'm not like that. So I'd make the circle a bit bigger".
115 | Personal translation: "Germany. Yes, we go there regularly. It's not that I don't feel comfortable there, that's really not the case".
116 | Personal translation: "Luxembourg and where I could imagine myself as well would be more down here. In Alsace. [...] And then, oh I don't know, well maybe also in Switzerland, I don't know. [...] For one thing, because I've often been to Alsace, and I think people there also have a different mentality than here, meaning as far as the whole of Lorraine is concerned; well, I'm dead certain I wouldn't feel at home there, no way. Because, uh, the

Divergence or Convergence within the Patterns of Discourse?

In spite of a relatively small corpus of textual evidence as well as findings from standardised questioning and qualitative interviews that can only be partially generalised, it was obvious how little correspondence seems to exist between the postulated everyday relevance of the Greater Region or the international inter-connections on the one side (attributed identities), and, on the other, the peculiarities of this living space, actually perceived as being relevant in terms of behaviour and consciousness (appropriated identities). At the same time, several interview passages indicate to what extent the unsolicited internal differentiation in terms of an assessment of neighbouring countries primarily supports the construction of alterity, but, in an inversion of the argument, also evoke (cross-border) identity characteristics and a – variously justified – concept of togetherness. A fundamental sensibility for having something 'in common with the other' beyond the border can often be recognised. However, whether the trend is more towards divergence or convergence, i.e. a drifting apart or coming together of the discourse patterns, cannot be established with reference to the body of evidence available. Only diachronic long-term studies with a clear focus on the border-regional aspects of identity formation and the relevant methodological tools could produce answers to this question that would lead to further insights. However, it can be taken as read that *the* 'Saar-Lor-Luxois' does not and cannot exist just as one cannot define *the* Luxembourger or any *one* national identity. Whilst tourism marketing's extra-regional target audience may be more receptive to stereotypes and clichéd portraits of a population with which they are not particularly familiar, the, on occasion, very far-reaching constructions of border region identities postulated here are partially contradicted by the empiric findings from the region. Whether 'performing' identity happens intentionally to generate special interest in the region by exaggeration or whether it is rather due to the personal enthusiasm of individual authors cannot be conclusively determined here.

5.7 Conclusion: Spatial Identities – Multiple Readings?

The analysis of geographical representations of Luxembourg through the lens of five micro-analyses was inspired foremost by the tourism practice itself, which uses five different spatial scales: the quarters of Luxembourg City, the city itself, the regions of Luxembourg, the country as a whole and finally the country 'at the heart' of the Greater Region. However, what the micro-analyses have revealed

---

mentality there, well, it really doesn't agree with me. And then also the landscape, I, no, I wouldn't feel at home there. Alsace though, I could maybe just imagine myself living there. And also there, and then in Switzerland as well. Yes, because of the mentality, but not because it's got all those mountains or anything".

is far removed from a mere scalar distribution; instead, we are faced with five distinct 'geo-graphies' that are as much distinct categories of representations of 'Luxembourg space' as differentiated collections of semiotic values and strategies.

This diversity can undoubtedly be attributed to differences in the tourism discoursive practice itself: the notion of the Greater Region does not engage the same actors, temporalities and lifestyles as those in the various districts of the city; information about exploring the country's regions does not quite satisfy the needs of those who, coming from afar, are merely passing through Luxembourg, or who simply want to be informed about the country in general. This also explains the variety of texts that 'support' each level of the touristic practice: in towns and cities, brochures, booklets or maps are sufficient to satisfy the visitor eager for discovery, whereas it takes rather more to explore or familiarise oneself with the country or its regions; as for the Greater Region, it is not so much destined for ramblings and explorations than for people to live and, increasingly, work in. This is what the supporting texts demonstrate. It thus becomes clear that what emerges beyond the different methods of practical and cognitive understanding is Luxembourg's diversity, multiplicity and even instability.

Nevertheless, even if the five analyses of the various levels underscore this variety and this heterogeneity, we may ask ourselves, in view of the general research subject addressed in this volume, whether anything actually emerges that can be called an 'identity': Something recurrent, stable or some kind of thematic unity, perhaps even a system of values on the one hand, and a congruence of forms of internalisation, styles of representation and argumentative tactics on the other. In other words: following the analyses in this chapter, can we maintain that the five spaces of Luxembourg or the discourses depicting them share some essential commonality? Before we can answer such a question, we must first answer the one raised by each of the five microanalyses concerning the internal cohesion of their respective 'geo-graphical' objects of investigation: what are the 'discursive touristic identities' of the districts of Luxembourg City, of the capital itself, of Luxembourg's regions, of the country as such and of the country within the Greater Region? The answer seems to lie in the fact that the identifying features – if there are any – are to be found not so much in the topics or values as in the manner in which the country and its various levels are topicalised and emphasised. This would mean that there is little discursive national identity in evidence, or even none at all, only a certain amount of homogeneity of discursive strategies, quite often centred on the local, the distinct and the singular. Consequently, not only is Luxembourg portrayed differently according to the five levels of scale examined here, but even within these categories, geographical and historical differences emerge, boundaries and borders are erected and emphasis is laid on the exceptional, the distinctive and even the exclusive.

From this perspective, the analysis of the districts confirms that the touristic practice on this level is based on the same macro act of emphasising and, specifically, of aestheticising. The results of the survey asking residents which place they would first show a friend from abroad corroborate the results of the leaflet and booklet analysis, both in regard to key locations such as the fortress and historic city center and to the general approach to aesthetic appreciation. Even the predictable divergences between tourist texts and the respondents' statements implicitly reflect the same requirements: the Bonnevoie district is not accorded the status of an 'attraction', because it does not lend itself, as Limpertsberg does, to an aesthetisation, nor can it draw from the contrasts 'tradition vs. modernity' or 'national vs. international' as the official discourse on Kirchberg does.

The analysis of Luxembourg City through its maps and leaflets also reveals that the emerging question pertains to a selected and distinctive emphasis of the city in general. This means, it is represented only in parts and with a certain remove: on the one hand, it is constantly and with particular emphasis displayed as an access to the centre, and on the other, the latter is presented as an elevated island to which one has to ascend. We therefore have neither a depiction of a totality (since only a part was selected, namely the route to the centre) nor, ultimately, a stable and recognisable reality, since what matters is only the access to the city centre and not the centre itself, let alone the city as such, which appears to contain relatively few historical monuments and to lack a characteristic profile.

The absence of a national discursive identity in favour of singularising discursive strategies is confirmed and reinforced when we analyse regional tourism discourses. The study of three booklets from the National Tourism Office sheds light on the rhetoric, which presses the combination of images and text into the service of redundancy and hyperbole. Certainly this is designed to streamline the reader's work as much as possible by allowing selected information to be accessed directly; however, the extreme regional prototyping, conveyed via an exceedingly fragmented structure, has the immediate effect of promoting a country whose diversity would be inversely proportional to its surface area. The results of the quantitative survey undeniably bear out this perception of a both virtual and differentiated entity at the interface between the region and the country.

The national space too, whose touristic representations were analysed along diachronic lines, appears to lack unity; at the same time, the strategies used to explain and enhance remain the same. On the one hand, Luxembourg is seen as an open, welcoming, familiar space that conveys a sense of security; on the other, it is described as unique, different and exotic. Particular emphasis is laid on the specific feature that typifies Luxembourg as a place marked by distinctiveness and difference, given its multicultural and multilingual character, while also stressing calm and tranquillity as the country's salient traits. Therefore Luxembourg is regarded both as modern and traditional, innovative and authentic. The semantic tension is even embraced and emphasised: Luxembourg is regularly depicted as a 'country of contrasts', characterised by its smallness and its great ambitions – first industrial ones, then, in the framework of the European Union, also political ones. This European vision – show-cased in the recent *Merian* guides from 1995 and 2007 – is reflected in half of the interviews conducted by us, whereas the other half of the respondents was more sceptical, emphasising the dissenting character of their opinions.

The discrepancy between attributed and appropriated identities becomes even more visible at the level of the so-called Greater Region and its respective tourism discourses. The idealising character of the examined publications seems to deviate considerably from discourses observed among residents and their cross-border practices and attitudes. Nevertheless, the majority of the residents reveal elements of identity that reach beyond the national borders of the Grand Duchy. This aspect merits closer investigation, taking into account the context of Europeanisation and globalisation.

Looking at the entirety of levels examined in this study, we are aware that an 'official' tourism discourse, as reflected in most of the documents analysed, is always directed at the enhancement of a particular space. This means it generates strong projections of a common identity. This is why we directed our interest to the strategies of enhancement that were used: to better comprehend the *attributed* identities and assess how they differ from the ones *appropriated* by the people living in these spaces – in Luxembourg City, in the country and in the Greater Region.

5.8 References

Primary Sources

Anonymous. 1892. De Luxembourg en Écosse. Guide du Touriste à travers Le Luxembourg. – L'Ardenne Belge. – Les Flandres. La Mer du Nord et la Manche. Le Comté de Kent. – Le Pays de Galles. – Les Lacs Anglais. L'Écosse. Avec 100 dessins originaux de MM. Hoeterickx, Van Gelder, etc. Pub. by S. de Ruette, representing the London Chatham & Dover Railway [Brussels], with approval of the London & North Western Railway, London Chatham & Dover Railway, Chemins de fer Prince-Henri and Chemins de fer du Nord de France companies. Luxembourg: Pierre Bruck.

Anonymous. 1914. Woerl's Reisehandbücher. Illustrierter Führer durch das Großherzogtum Luxemburg. Mit Plan der Stadt Luxemburg, 7 Kartenbeilagen und 65 Abbildungen, 2nd ed. Leipzig: Woerl's Reisebücher-Verlag. Kaiserl. U Königl. Hofbuchhandlung.

Anonymous. 1934. Woerl Reisehandbücher. Großherzogtum Luxemburg [mit Plan der Stadt Luxemburg, 7 Karten und 29 Abbildungen], 3rd ed. Leipzig: Woerl's Reisebücher-Verlag.

Baedekers Allianz Reiseführer. Luxembourg, Ostfildern-Kemnat: Mairs Geographischer Verlag, 1990.

Discover Luxembourg, 1995.

Erasmy, Mathieu. 1861. Le guide du voyageur dans le Grand-Duché de Luxembourg. Luxembourg: V. Bück

Luxembourg City Tourist Office. Panorama City Map. In Luxembourg la ville, die Stadt, the city, bonjour!, ed. Luxembourg City Tourist Office. Luxembourg.

Luxembourg City Tourist Office. 2000. Ni vu ni connu. Luxembourg.

Luxembourg City Tourist Office. 2003. Luxembourg la ville, bonjour! In Luxembourg la ville, bonjour!, ed. Luxembourg City Tourist Office. Luxembourg: Éditions Guy Binsfeld.

Luxembourg City Tourist Office. 2006. Le circuit des roses du Limpertsberg 'RosaLi'. In Luxembourg la ville, bonjour!, ed. Luxembourg City Tourist Office. Luxembourg.

Luxembourg City Tourist Office. 2007. Luxembourg, une capitale européenne. In: Luxembourg la ville, bonjour!, ed. Representation of the European Commission to Luxembourg & Luxembourg City Tourist Office. Luxembourg: Binsfeld Communication.

Luxembourg City Tourist Office. 2007. City Promenade. In Luxembourg la ville, bonjour!, ed. Luxembourg City Tourist Office. Luxembourg: Éditions Guy Binsfeld.

Luxembourg City Tourist Office. 2007. Luxembourg, Vivez la ville!. In Luxembourg la ville, bonjour!, ed. Luxembourg City Tourist Office. Luxembourg: Éditions Guy Binsfeld.

Luxembourg National Tourist Office. 2006. Les Produits du Terroir et les Métiers d'Art. Mersch: Imprimerie François Faber.

Luxembourg National Tourist Office. 2008. Hôtels Restaurants et Arrangements. (11/2007 for year 2008), Luxembourg: Imprimerie Saint-Paul.

Luxembourg National Tourist Office. 2008. Sites et Attractions. (12/2007 for year 2008), Luxembourg: Imprimerie Saint-Paul.

Marco Polo. 1995. Luxembourg: Reiseführer mit Insider-Tips. Ostfildern: Mairs Geographischer Verlag.

Mendgen, Eva, Volker Hildisch and Hervé Doucet, eds. 2007. Im Reich der Mitte/ Le berceau de la civilisation européenne. Savoir-faire/savoir-vivre. Constance: Hartung-Gorre.

Merian. 1964. Luxemburg. Merian XVII/7.

Merian. 2007. Luxemburg. Merian 60/03.

Michelin. 2007. Belgium/Luxembourg. Zellik: Le Guide Michelin.

Panorama City Map. Luxembourg: La ville, Luxembourg City Tourist Office. 2008.

Plan de la ville de Luxembourg, Luxembourg City Tourist Office. 2008.

Renwick, George. 1913. Luxembourg. The Grand-Duchy and its People. London: T. Fisher Unwin.

Schisgall, Oscar. 1967. Le Luxembourg, pays de paradoxes. Selection in Reader's Digest 01.1967: 62-69.

Scholz, Ingeborg. 2007. Die Großregion entdecken/Découvrir la Grande Région. Luxembourg: Guy Binsfeld.

Schröder, Dirk. 1995. Merian live! Luxemburg. Munich: Gräfe und Unzer.

Secondary Sources

Adam, Jean-Michel. 1990. La période. De la stylistique à la linguistique textuelle. Stylistique et littérature, Versants, 18, Boudry, La Baconnière: 5-19.
Adam, Jean-Michel. 1997. Le style dans la langue. Pour une reconception de la stylistique. Lausanne/Paris: Delachaux et Niestlé.
Adam, Jean-Michel. 1999. Linguistique textuelle. Des genres de discours aux textes. Paris: Nathan.
Adam, Jean-Michel and Marc Bonhomme. 1997. L'argumentation publicitaire. Rhétorique de l'éloge et de la persuasion. Paris: Nathan-Université.
Alonso, Juan A. 2009. Espace et métalangage. Défense du territoire. Nouveaux Actes Sémiotiques: online.
Amossy, R. and Maingueneau, D., eds. 2003. L'analyse du discours. Toulouse: Presses Universitaires du Mirail.
Austin, John L. 1962. Performatif-Constatif. Cahiers de Royaumont, Philosophie 4: La philosophie analytique: 271-281.
Baudrillard, Jean. 1994. Simulacrum and Simulations. Chicago: University of Michigan Press.
Benveniste, Émile. 1966. Problèmes de linguistique générale 1. Paris: Gallimard.
Berger, Peter L. and Thomas Luckmann. 1966. The Social Construction of Reality. New York: Doubleday.
Blunt, Alison, Pyrs Gruffudd, Jon May, Miles Ogborn and David Pinder, eds. 2003. Cultural Geography in Practice. Oxford: Oxford University Press.
Bonhomme, Marc. 2003. L'éloge de la ville: rhétorique d'une plaquette touristique sur Berne. In Les langages de la ville, ed. P. Marillaud and R. Gauthier. Toulouse: Presses Universitaires du Mirail, CALS/CPST: 13-21.
Bonhomme, Marc. 2005. Pragmatique des figures du discours. Paris: Champion.
Bonhomme, Marc. 2006. Le discours métonymique. Berne: Peter Lang.
Bonhomme, Marc and Jean-Michel Adam. 1997. L'argumentation publicitaire. Rhétorique de l'éloge et de la persuasion. Paris: Nathan-Université.
Brunet, Roger. 1989. Les villes 'européennes'. Paris: La Documentation Française.
Bulot, Thierry and Vincent Veschambre, eds. 2006. Mots, traces et marques. Dimensions spatiale et linguistique de la mémoire urbaine. Paris: L'Harmattan.
Cohen, Erik. 2004. Contemporary Tourism. Diversity and Change. Amsterdam: Elsevier.
Colas-Blaise, Marion (forthcoming). Comment fonctionne le texte de vulgarisation polymédial? Éléments pour une approche sémio-linguistique du rapport texte/image dans le dépliant touristique. In L'image dans le texte scientifique, ed. David Banks. Brest.
European Commission. 2009. Eurobarometer 71.1, QA6a, URL: http://ec.europa.eu/public_opinion/archives/ebs/ebs_308_en.pdf (14.12.2009).

Dominicy, Marc and Nathalie Franken. 2001. Epidictique et discours expressif. In La mise en scène des valeurs, ed. idem, 79-106. Neuchâtel: Delachaux et Niestlé.

Döring, Jörg and Tristan Thielmann, eds. 2009. Spatial Turn. Das Raumparadigma in den Kultur- und Sozialwissenschaften. Bielefeld: Transcript.

Ducrot, Oswald. 1984. Le dire et le dit. Paris: Les Editions de Minuit.

Dumont, Patrick, Fernand Fehlen, Raphaël Kies and Philippe Poirier. 2007. Referendum on the Treaty establishing a Constitution for Europe. Report prepared for the Chamber of Deputies. Luxembourg: STADE/Université du Luxembourg.

Farinelli, Franco. 2009. La crisi della ragione cartografica. Introduzione alla geografia della globalità. Turin: Einaudi.

Farinelli, Franco. 2009. I segno del mondo. Immagine cartografica e discorso geografico in età moderna. Florence: Accademia Universa.

Floch, Jean-Marie. 1990. Sémiotique, marketing et communication. Sous les signes, les stratégies. Paris: PUF.

Floch, Jean-Marie. 1995. Identités visuelles. Paris: PUF.

Fontanille, Jacques. 1998. Sémiotique du discours. Limoges: Pulim.

Fontanille, Jacques. 1999. Sémiotique et littérature. Essais de méthode. Paris: PUF.

Fontanille, Jacques. 2008. Sémiotique des pratiques. Paris: PUF.

Fontanille, Jacques and Claude Zilberberg. 1998. Tension et signification. Hayen: Mardaga.

Freyermuth, Sylvie. 2003. Les marques de l'ordre et de la distinction dans le discours argumentatif de Pascal – Quelques remarques pragmatiques et stylistiques sur un fragment des Pensées. In Actes du Colloque Ordre et distinction dans la langue et dans le discours, ed. C. Schnedecker, M. Charolles and G. Kleiber, 203-216. (Metz), Paris: Champion.

Freyermuth, Sylvie. 2008. Théorie de l'esprit et temporalité subjective chez le personnage flaubertien. In Langages, temps, temporalité. XXVIIIe colloque d'Albi, ed. P. Marillaud and R. Gauthier, 207-214. Toulouse: Presses Universitaires du Mirail, CALS/CPST.

Gebhardt, Hans, Paul Reuber and Günther Wolkersdorfer, eds. 2003. Kulturgeographie. Aktuelle Ansätze und Entwicklungen. Heidelberg: Spektrum.

Genette, Gérard. 1987. Seuils. Paris: Seuil.

Glasze, Georg and Annika Matissek, eds. 2009. Handbuch Diskurs und Raum. Bielefeld: Transcript.

Goodwin, Charles. 2003. Il senso del vedere. Rome: Meltemi.

Greimas, Algirdas J. and Joseph Courtés. 1979. Sémiotique. Dictionnaire raisonné de la théorie du langage. Paris: Hachette.

Grize, Jean-Blaise. 1981. L'argumentation – explication ou séduction. L'Argumentation. Lyon: Presses Universitaires de Lyon: 29-40.

Hajer, Maarten A. 1985. The Politics of Environmental Discourse. Ecological Modernization and the Policy Process. Oxford: Oxford University Press.

Hajer, Maarten A. (2003): Argumentative Diskursanalyse. Auf der Suche nach Koalitionen, Praktiken und Bedeutung. In Handbuch Sozialwissenschaftliche Diskursanalyse, Vol. 2, ed.: Reiner Keller et al., 271-297. Opladen: Leske + Budrich.

Hennig, Christoph. 1997. Reiselust. Touristen, Tourismus und Urlaubskultur. Leipzig: Insel.

Herschberg-Pierrot, Anne. 2003. La question du style. In L'analyse du discours, ed. R. Amossy and D. Maingueneau, 333-339. Toulouse: Presses Universitaires du Mirail.

Kerbrat-Orecchioni, Catherine. 1991. Introduction. In La question, ed.: idem, 5-37. Lyon: Presses Universitaires de Lyon.

Kerbrat-Orecchioni, Catherine. 1991. L'acte de question et l'acte d'assertion – opposition discrète ou continuum?. In La question, ed. idem, 87-111. Lyon: Presses Universitaires de Lyon.

Linden, André and Guy Thewes. 2007. Tourisme et identité nationale. Forum für Politik, Gesellschaft und Kultur in Luxemburg (271): 42-44.

Lossau, Julia and Robert Lippuner. 2004. Geographie und spatial turn. Erdkunde no. 58 (3): 201-211.

Louvel, Liliane. 2002. Texte, image. Images à lire, textes à voir. Rennes: Presses universitaires de Rennes.

MacCannell, Dean. 1976. The Tourist. New Theory of the Leisure Class. New York: Schocken Books.

Majerus, Benoît. 2007. Le petit Européen parfait. L'Europe, le Luxembourg et la construction nationale. In L'Europe de Versailles à Maastricht, ed. N. Beaupre and C. Moine, 225-235. Paris: Seli Arslan.

Marcos, Isabelle, ed. 2007. Dynamiques de la ville. Essais de sémiotique de l'espace. Paris: l'Harmattan.

Marin, Louis. 1983. La ville dans sa carte et son portrait. Cahiers de l'école normale supérieure de Fontenay (30-31): 11-26.

Marin, Louis. 1994. De la représentation. Paris: Seuil/Gallimard.

Mattissek, Annika. 2007. Diskursanalyse in der Humangeographie – 'State of the Art'. Geographische Zeitschrift no. 95 (1-2): 37-55.

Molinié, Georges. 1993. La stylistique. Paris: PUF.

Neve, Mario. 1999. Virtus loci. Lineamenti fondamentali di una teoria dell'informazione spaziale. Urbino: Quattroventi.

Parr, Rolf. 2009. Wie konzipiert die (Inter-)Diskurstheorie individuelle und kollektive Identitäten. Ein theoretischer Zugriff, erläutert am Beispiel Luxemburg. Forum für Politik, Gesellschaft und Kultur in Luxemburg no. 289: 11-16.

Perelman, Chaïm and Lucie Olbrechts-Tyteca. 2000. Traité de l'argumentation. Bruxelles: Éditions de l'Université.

Pinnel, Roland. 1989. Le développement du tourisme luxembourgeois après la Deuxième Guerre mondiale. In Mémorial 1989: la société luxembourgeoise de 1839 à 1989 (941-954). Luxembourg: Les publications mosellanes.

Ricœur, Paul. 1990. Soi-même comme un autre. Paris: Seuil.
Searle, John. 1972. Les actes de langage. Paris: Hermann.
Searle, John. 1982. Sens et expression. Paris: Minuit.
Shapiro, Meyer. 1969. On Some Problems in the Semiotics of Visual Art: Field and Vehicle in Image-Signs. Semiotica 1, III: 223-242.
Shurmer-Smith, Pamela ed. 2002. Doing Cultural Geography. London: Sage.
STATEC. 2007. Annuaire statistique du Luxembourg. Luxembourg: Statec.
Strüver, Anke. 2005. Stories of the 'Boring Border'. The Dutch-German borderscape in people's minds. Forum Politische Geographie no. 2, Munster: LIT-Verlag.
Urry, John. 1990. The Tourist Gaze: Leisure and Travel in Contemporary Societies. London: Sage.
Wahl, François. 1980. Le désir d'espace. In Cartes et figures de la terre, ed. Christian Jacob, 41-46. Paris: Centre Georges Pompidou, Centre de Création Industrielle.
Weichhart, Peter. 1990. Raumbezogene Identität. Bausteine zu einer Theorie räumlich-sozialer Kognition und Identifikation. Stuttgart: Franz Steiner Verlag.
Werlen, Benno. 1995. Sozialgeographie alltäglicher Regionalisierungen. Vol. 1: Zur Ontologie von Gesellschaft und Raum. Stuttgart: Franz Steiner Verlag.
Werlen, Benno. 1997. Sozialgeographie alltäglicher Regionalisierungen. Vol. 2: Globalisierung, Region und Regionalisierung. Stuttgart: Franz Steiner Verlag.
Zilberberg, Claude. 2006. Éléments de grammaire tensive. Limoges: Pulim.

6. Images and Identities

WILHELM AMANN, VIVIANE BOURG, PAUL DELL, FABIENNE LENTZ, PAUL DI FELICE, SEBASTIAN REDDEKER

6.1 IMAGES OF NATIONS AS 'INTERDISCOURSES'. PRELIMINARY THEORETICAL REFLECTIONS ON THE RELATION OF 'IMAGES AND IDENTITIES': THE CASE OF LUXEMBOURG

The common theoretical framework for the analysis of different manifestations of 'images and identities' in the socio-cultural region of Luxembourg is provided by the so-called interdiscourse analysis (Gerhard/Link/Parr 2004: 293-295). It is regarded as an advancement and modification of the discourse analysis developed by Michel Foucault and, as an applied discourse theory, its main aim is to establish a relationship between practice and empiricism. While the discourses analysed by Foucault were, to a great extent, about formations of positive knowledge and institutionalised sciences (law, medicine, human sciences etc.), the interdiscourse analysis is interested in discourse complexes which are precisely not limited by specialisation, but that embrace a more comprehensive field and can therefore be described as 'interdiscursive' (Parr 2009). The significance of such interdiscourses arises from the general tension between the increasing differentiation of modern knowledge and the growing disorientation of modern subjects.

In this sense, 'Luxembourg' can be described as a highly complex entity made up of special forms of organisation, e.g. law, the economy, politics or also the health service. Here, each of these sectors, as a rule, develops very specified styles of discourse restricted to the respective field, with the result that communication about problems and important topics even between these sectors is seriously impeded and, more importantly, that the everyday world and the everyday knowledge of the subjects is hardly ever reached or affected.

The following may serve as a case in point: In Luxembourg, as in all other affected countries, the dangers of the financial crisis can hardly be conveyed by means of the highly specified technical language of the economists. Instead, the subject has to be translated into forceful images, which are often borrowed from other special discourses. Thus an economist warned in the Luxembourg press at the beginning of the crisis about the "tainted financial products" which spread "like a sort of cancer" (image field: medicine). In addition, he drew the comparison to "nuclear energy" that "had been invented without giving any thought to how the new technology should be kept under control" (image field: technology).

Those and similar interdiscursive metaphorical manners of expression have a communicative-integrative effect which, as in the above example, possibly applies for large parts of western European cultures. In addition, the interdiscourses display specific features typical to a culture, so that their analysis is also able to illuminate the cultural specifics of a given society. One can therefore assume that today these interdiscourses make a significant contribution to sustaining a national culture because they provide an identity potential that acts communicatively.

In this chapter then questions on cultural 'identity' do not relate to personal subjects or hardly verifiable psychological structures but rather to (inter)discursively generated identity options of 'We', circulating in the form of images within a given culture and providing the basis for an interplay of symbolically attributed and appropriated identities. These images, in a comprehensive sense of both linguistic and visual, can also be described as collective symbols of a specific culture, as the totality of the collectively anchored, more or less stereotyped 'imagery' of a particular culture. By establishing in a selective and very fragmented way connections between the specific fields of knowledge as well as to the everyday knowledge of the subjects, and, in addition, by being used by different social agencies, collective symbols generate the *idea* of a common, consolidated cultural identity of a society. This can be produced both as perception of self and of others.

The aim of this chapter is the reconstruction of central elements of the system of collective symbols in Luxembourg that is at present culturally identifiable. The question we have posed ourselves is: How are specific notions of a Luxembourg identity generated by linguistic and visual images? In line with the respective fields of research of the contributors, the analysis is distributed across different interdiscursive media: print media, advertisements, comics and art. In terms of interdiscourse theory, this is a 'mix' of elaborated (art photography, art documentation, comics) and elementary interdiscourses (advertisements, print media) – that is to say, a more reflected and intellectual handling of collective symbols on the one hand, and a more everyday one on the other. In addition, the team of authors has agreed on a set of subject areas that serve to analyse in an exemplary manner motifs and applications of Luxembourg's particular collective imagery in the various forms of media. In brief, these subject areas are: 'Europe', 'banking center', 'cultural capital', 'MUDAM'[1], 'migration' and 'Arcelor/Mittal'.

The subject fields consequently cover key areas of the economy, politics and culture. It can be assumed that they are present, albeit in differing degrees, in

---

1 | *Musée d'Art Moderne Grand-Duc Jean*, Luxembourg.

the everyday knowledge of the Luxembourgers and, in equally different forms, reveal attributed as well as appropriated identities. For instance, the subject areas 'Arcelor/Mittal', 'banking center' and to a certain extent also 'Europe' as well as 'migration' are typical for the structural changes that the country has experienced over the last decades when it underwent the transition from a production-oriented society to a service-oriented one. This transition, which was performed within one generation, has undoubtedly led to a huge prosperity in the country and has made Luxembourg one of the richest nations in the world. However, this process also has an effect on collective definitions of identity that, for a long time, have been perceived as continuous. Just how much the balance between appropriated and attributed identities has become unsettled can, for instance, be seen by the fact that the sale of the Arcelor steelworks in 2006 was regarded as a matter of national concern. There is quite obviously still a strong tendency to identify with the industrial past, including the underlying notion of paternalistically operating large-scale enterprises. By contrast, questions concerning the pro-European position of the Luxembourgers and the related notions and problems relating to the opening of society serve to illustrate the crucial importance of attributed identities.

The event 'Luxembourg and Greater Region – European Capital of Culture 2007' is also to be understood in this context as a large-scale attempt to bundle definitions of identity as they drift apart. However, the event also provides enough material to identify their individual components and to question them regarding their past function or also their present one.

In the first part of this chapter (6.2) the origin and functional use of the national imagery relevant for Luxembourg is discussed using a journalistic and literary corpus of text. The double identity movement typical for Luxembourg, of isolation and adaptation is expressed in the central national symbol of the 'fortress'. In the course of the modernisation of society, this national symbol, which plays a central role as a self-image as well as for outsiders' perspective on Luxembourg, increasingly finds itself in a crisis, which then manifests itself openly in the form of journalistic reporting about the 'bank crisis' or the subject of 'Europe'. Finally, we will also examine the imagery assigned in the print media to the projects on the renewal of the national image ('MUDAM', 'cultural capital').

The following part (6.3) analyses the *Superjhemp* comics as a pictorial satire about customary stereotypes of country and people. In his physiognomy, private circumstances, in his occupation and his preferences, the hero, Superjhemp, appears as a projection figure of the Luxembourg national character. In addition, the comic uses the leeway provided by the genre for humorous as well as critical hyperbole about conditions in Luxembourg, where, in particular, the tense relationship between provincialism and wealth is one of the recurring subjects. The comic series owes its success in no small measure to the fact that a sort of fool's mirror is held up to the readers. However, the satirical self-image also clearly presupposes insider knowledge about the conditions in the country and cannot be readily decoded by outsiders.

Section 6.4 is dedicated to the advertising discourse as an interdiscourse that impacts everyday life. Though advertising primarily intends to create positive effects for sales and brand images, it can also contribute to reinforcing specific images with identity-forming potential in Luxembourg or even to generating them. In which way advertising in the Grand Duchy operates with images and symbols and can thereby promote forms of collective identities, is illustrated with examples of advertisements taken from the financial sector and the telecommunications industry as well as from official publications showcasing Luxembourg in the cultural capital year of 2007.

Section 6.5 focuses on one aspect of the strategy of culturalisation of the self-image in the country that has become increasingly visible over the last years. In the context of an ambitious art scene and intensive cultural promotion in Luxembourg, photography has developed into an important medium of the reflexion about identity. To what extent identity-based representations, i.e. appropriated as well as attributed identity patterns, are (de)contextualised and (de)constructed, is shown by the analysis of a selection of works of seven foreign and Luxembourgish photographers. Their commissioned works originated in the context of the cultural capital year Luxembourg 2007 and touch on different subject areas, providing a broad basis for analysis.

The final section, 6.6, centers on an exhibition project realised in the cultural capital year under the title 'Retour de Babel'. The aim here was to confront the established image about immigration in Luxembourg with a more comprehensive one. The contribution inquires into the manner in which the image of Luxembourg as a 'European laboratory', a central one for the concept of this exhibition, is perceived and realised.

6.2 Symbolisms in the Media-Based Perceptions of Self and Others of Luxembourg

Luxembourg in the Context of European National Symbolisms

The following section analyses forms of speech with linguistic imagery in literary and – predominantly – journalistic texts of the last years that evince a particular symbolic discourse about the 'Luxembourgish identity'. The guiding hypothesis here is that even the present media culture cannot do without "mass symbols of the nations" (Canetti 2000). For the established European nations steeped in tradition these have been well known for a long time[2] and continue to be used in the media as elementary literary "semi-finished products" (Link 1983: 9) in the most diverse

---

2 | According to Canetti, the English attribute themselves to the 'sea', the French to the 'revolution', the Germans to the 'forest', the Swiss to the 'mountains' and the Dutch to the 'dyke' (Canetti 2000: 197-208).

variations. For a small country like Luxembourg, however, which even after the Second World War was still struggling to rid itself of the image as an 'operetta state'[3], it was difficult, already for historical reasons, to participate in this long-standing custom of the big European nations of symbolic attributions of self and others, or even to be recognised. This sense of inferiority might also have led to the fact that, for the Luxembourgers, the symbol of the 'fortress', which does not easily blend into the symbolism of other European nations with their references to special heroic achievements or confrontation with nature and history, has assumed a central significance.

Taking this central symbolism as a starting point, we will in the following discuss contexts of its use and attempts to modify it, which result from the rapid social change from which even the spirited Luxembourgers have not been spared. This contribution does not intend any detailed historical reconstruction of the origin of Luxembourg's particular collective symbolism but rather focuses on aspects of its functional use[4].

The 'Fortress' as the Central National Symbol

Luxembourg is one of the few countries that are associated with a building in the perception of their inhabitants, as well as in their public image (Kmec 2007). The 'fortress', as it is called, is the name given to the remaining parts of a huge military fortification enlarged by Vauban after the French conquest of 1684, and expanded over nearly two centuries in rank growth fashion, until, in 1867 France and Prussia agreed, as a specious peacemaking measure, on dismantling it. Today, the key facts are basic tourist knowledge. This knowledge can be enhanced by making mention of the turning points which the history of the fortress has marked in the history of the town as well as of the country itself: the destruction of the medieval town area, alternating periods of so-called 'foreign rule' (Margue 2007) and, finally, the gradual formation of a capital on its remains. The fortifications still visible are, in this sense, material witnesses of an arduous process of national self-assertion.

In the opinion of the former director of the *Service des Sites et Monuments Nationaux*, George Calteux, the fortress history reflects a collective state of mind in

---

3 | An arbitrary, but illustrative example to which degree the national self-image in Luxembourg had for a long time been determined by an adopted image from outside is to be found in the *Escher Tageblatt* of 12.11.1947: There, an article discussing the issue of conscription in Luxembourg ends with the remark that, without an army, the country appeared "... more than ever in our history as an operetta state" (p. 6). Concerning the public image of Luxembourg as an "operetta state", see Romain Kirt: Zu klein, um überhaupt ein richtiger Staat zu sein? *d'Lëtzeburger Land*, 17.08.2001, p. 1.

4 | This contribution is based to a large extent on an evaluation of articles, in particular from the Luxembourg and German daily press of recent years. The articles themselves are referred to in the respective remarks, however, they do not appear in the bibliography.

the country, which has consolidated in the 20th century, owing to the experiences during both World Wars, into a national attitude. He describes the mentality of his compatriots as follows: "*Viele, lange Kriege, der Druck von Herren und Fremdherrschaft haben seit dem frühen Mittelalter in Stadt und Land aus uns zähe und (manchmal) sture Menschen gemacht, die ihre Hände zu Fäusten in der Tasche ballten*"[5] (Calteux 2005: 144).

The remark sums up the Luxembourgers' self-perception which reveals a stoic conservatism, reflected on the one hand by withdrawal imposed by external circumstances and on the other, by a lifestyle which, only reluctantly and only ostensibly conforms to the times. This pattern of self-perception finds its adequate expression in the fortress: 'We are as well-fortified as the fortress in the midst of our capital.' The fact that town and country have identical names facilitates identification with the building that acquires the stature of a representative national symbol and therefore guarantees in a way Luxembourg's attachment to the symbolic discourse of nations that has already been taking place for a long time in Europe.

As self-attribution, the symbol of the fortress of course also operates as an offer to bundle all kinds of ascriptions about the 'Luxembourgers' that are in circulation into one characteristic. The example of the 'fortress' also serves to show, however, how the communication of national symbolisms in the global age is becoming increasingly difficult.

To what degree the self portrait characterised by periods of isolation and adaptation, applies particularly to post-war identity can be gauged from the way the symbolism of the fortress is employed in the work of Roger Manderscheid, the country's most pre-eminent author of that period. Here are some examples: In a volume of sketches, *aufstand der luxemburger alliteraten*[6], Manderscheid describes, in retrospect, the critical function of literature in the country as a Sisyphean task to overcome a mental block: "*in mühseliger kleinarbeit haben die luxemburger literaten über jahrzehnte hinweg probiert, die festungsmauern, die unser geistiges leben gefangen hielten und immer noch halten, stein um stein abzutragen [...]*"[7] (Manderscheid 2003: 16). In a book of poetry published at the turn of the millennium, *summa summarum. gedichte aus einem vergangenen jahrhundert*[8], there is a set of poems about the country under the title *lyrische berichte aus dem innern der festung*[9] (Manderscheid 2000:

---

5 | Personal translation: "Many long wars, the pressure of masters and foreign rule have turned us since the early Middle Ages, in town and country, into tough and (sometimes) headstrong people who, inside their pockets, have clenched their hands into fists".

6 | Personal translation: "Uprising of the Luxembourg Alliterati".

7 | Personal translation: "In laborious and painstakingly detailed work, Luxembourg's literati have attempted over decades to dismantle stone by stone the fortress walls that emprison our mental lives and always have done [...]".

8 | Personal translation: "Summa summarum. Poems from a past century".

9 | Personal translation: "Lyrical reports from inside the fortress".

17). And one passage of a volume entitled *schwarze engel*[10] reads as follows: *"dabei sind die luxemburger die enge gewohnt. Jahrhunderte haben sie hinter festungsmauern gekauert [...] die festungsmauern haben sie durch bankenpaläste ersetzt. Ich meine die grossherzoglichen"*[11] (Manderscheid 2001: 14-15).

The underlying tone of resignation suggests that the concept of an aesthetic education has, up to now, had little effect in changing the widespread fortress mentality. *En passant,* Manderscheid also provides a hint why this is so. In a modern, pluralistic society like Luxembourg, the symbolism of the fortress no longer functions exclusively via the direct reference to an imaginary national character, but is also transferred onto other dominant areas of representation of everyday life: The "fortress walls" have been replaced by "bank palaces", attributes such as "introvert", "secretive", however, continue to persist and can be updated to match present circumstances.

These connections are confirmed if one takes a look at the way the media deal with national symbolism. An article in the *Revue,* for example, about the history of the creation of banks in the country accesses the reservoir of figurative forms of argumentation that has developed over time, with its heading *"Von der Festung zum Finanzplatz"*[12]. While this suggests a certain transformation, the alliteration as such suffices to subtly ensure the continuity of the traditional national symbol.

It hardly comes as a surprise then that the symbolism of the fortress has been used with particular frequency in the recent discussions about banks: *"Risse in der Festung"*[13] was the headline of an article in the *Telecran* about the 'softening' of the banking secrecy, lending a specific national overtone to the, in this context, widespread image of a 'tax haven'[14]. The view from the outside is complementary: the Swiss *TagesAnzeiger* compares the problems in Luxembourg to the "mood in a besieged fortress"[15] thereby almost self-evidently creating a link to supposedly

---

10 | Personal translation: "Black angel".
11 | Personal translation: "Besides, Luxembourgers are used to narrowness. For centuries, they have been cowering behind fortress walls [...] the fortress walls have been replaced by bank palaces. I mean the grand-ducal ones".
12 | Personal translation: "From fortress to financial center". (Wolf, Claude: Von der Festung zum Finanzplatz. *Revue*, 20.09.2006, p. 21. Similar also in the Belgian national media: Le Luxembourg, foreteresse financière. *Le Soir*, 23.01.2002; and in the Luxembourg media: Une foreteresse financière au coeur de l'Europe. *Tageblatt*, 23.01.2002).
13 | Personal translation: "Cracks in the fortress".
14 | Lanners, Maryse: Risse in der Festung. *Telecran*, 18.03.2009, p. 22. One further example will suffice to emphasise the apparently widespread practice to circulate precisely these and similarly illustrative headlines in the Luxembourg media landscape: *"Risse in der Festung, mehr nicht!"* ("Cracks in the fortress, nothing more!") is the *Point 24* headline on the state of the debate on banking secrecy, dated 21.10. 2009.
15 | Israel, Stephan: Die Atmosphäre einer belagerten Festung. *TagesAnzeiger*, 08.05.2009, p. 10.

everyday knowledge about the country. In Luxembourg's media, the image of the besieged city, on the other hand, is taken up again immediately as a element of self-perception:

War es ein Fehler, 1867 die Festung Luxemburg zu schleifen? Liest und hört man die einheimischen Medien, so könnte man den Eindruck gewinnen, es herrsche wieder einmal ein Belagerungszustand. Doch diesmal geht es nicht um militärische, sondern um wirtschaftliche Interessen – um das Bankgeheimnis, genauer gesagt[16].

These examples, of which one could find a great many, suggest that systems of collective symbols have greatly increased in significance in journalism in general and in the mass media in particular, because they have replaced the discussion of complex issues. In the case of national symbolisms, this also assures a coupling with the traditional interpretation patterns typical for a nationality.

In global media culture, the often polemic game with systems of symbolisms can, however, also develop a barely controllable dynamic of its own, plunging national self-images into a crisis. Exactly this seems to have been the case for quite some time for the Luxembourg symbol of the 'fortress' and not only in regard to the subject of 'banks'.

Luxembourg: 'Heart' of the 'Fortress Europe'?

To better understand these problems, it is worth wile to first take a look at the second important component of Luxembourg's image of self which initially evolved independently of the symbolism of the fortress, but was implicitly designed to balance possible deficits of the latter particularly in the way the country was perceived from outside. We are referring here to Luxembourg's European commitment, which began in the 1950s and has gained increasing momentum since the 1980s and which is reflected in the capital's townscape by the establishment of a number of important European institutions on the Plateau de Kirchberg. Besides the establishment of Luxembourg as a 'financial centre', the notion of the nation as the 'heart of Europe' (Stoldt 2008: 19) has acquired a central role in the country's political discourse, not without friction regarding aforementioned image, as public debates have shown. The intensive efforts to present Luxembourg as an "*Akteur der europäischen Integration und 'internationale Plattform'*"[17] (Stoldt 2008: 21) and to gradually harmonise the national interests with the dominant supranational

---

16 | Personal translation: "Was it a mistake to dismantle the fortress of Luxembourg in 1867? If one reads and listens to the local media, one could get the impression that we are once more in a state of siege. However, this time it is not about military, but about economic interests – about the banking secrecy, to be precise". Klein, Raymond: Bankgeheimnis. Deine Rede sei nein, nein. *woxx*, 23.10.2009, No. 1029, p. 4.

17 | Personal translation: "Player of European integration and 'international platform'".

structures of the economy and politics has led to an official self-image of the Luxembourgers as "avant-garde Europeans"[18].

This image, propagated with considerable effort, of a modern, progress-oriented Luxembourg did have, particularly via the rituals of media-produced symbolism policy, a certain amount of positive effects on the image of others. The awarding of the prestigious *Karlspreis* of the city of Aachen is a good case in point: In 1986, the prize was awarded to the entire people of Luxembourg (*"Klein, aber fein"*, *"Das vorgelebte Leitbild eines pluralistischen Staates"*[19]), in 2006 it went to the Prime Minister, Jean-Claude Juncker. Outwardly, it is precisely this personalisation that signals a trans-generational (P. Werner, G. Thorn, J. Santer) continuity of the orientation towards Europe. But also inwardly, Juncker was able to assume the role of a symbolic figure for the politics of modernisation, attributions in the local media like "mediator", "bridge-builder", "arbiter", "motor of Europe" can be interpreted in either direction. At least at this level of politics and media it has been possible to unite the image of self and others.

Under these circumstances, the traditional national symbol of the 'fortress' must be regarded as an exceedingly problematic one. Already for the country's image of self as the 'heartland of Europe', it turns out to be basically counterproductive. The internal symbolism referring to the entity of a nation-state increasingly competes with the new positioning as 'heart', 'core' or 'motor' of Europe that shakes off the mentality of 'fortress' which carries a connotation of confrontation[20] (Parr 2009: 13).

Finally, the problem is compounded by the fact that since the beginning of the 1990s the symbolism of the fortress has had clearly negative connotations in relation to the subject of 'Europe' that has been a particular central one for Luxembourg. During the time of upheaval and a shift from the East-West conflict to a North-South conflict, the image of the 'Fortress Europe'[21] has established itself

---

18 | Werle, Gerd: Luxemburger weiterhin Avantgarde-Europäer. *Luxemburger Wort*, 10.03.2003, p. 3. The metaphor of the 'avant-garde', which has gained renewed currency in the context of the notion of European integration and the 'two-speed Europe', is also evidence for the systematic use of collective symbols. 'Avant-garde' and Luxembourg's traditional symbol of the 'fortress', are both terms originally used in a military context. In contrast to 'fortress', 'avant-garde' refers to the opposition of stasis and motion. Unlike the problematic strategy of 'entrenchment', 'avant-garde' emphasises an offensive 'pioneer' or 'forerunner role' towards inevitable 'progress'.

19 | Personal translation: "Small but excellent. The exemplified model of a pluralistic state". Headline: *Deutsches Allgemeines Sonntagsblatt*, 11.0.1986; *Süddeutsche Zeitung*, 20.05.1986.

20 | For the 'heart' symbolism, see for instance: Schlammes, Marc: Im Herzen Europas. *Luxemburger Wort*, 02.06.2006, p. 2.

21 | From a German perspective, the symbol of the 'Fortress of Europe', has incidentally, a highly problematic history. It was part of the propaganda language of the National Social-as a topos for the criticism of the restrictive migration policy in the EU (Koff 2008). This is a polemic reaction to the official political symbolic language of a "European architecture" (Schäffner 1993). While, within the EU and its most important allies, there is much talk of the 'Common European Home', thus an emphasis on open and communicative structures, critics use the 'Fortress Europe' to point out the downside of rigid borders and entrenchment against other, 'undesirable' third countries. Since the Schengen Agreement, signed in 1985, came into effect in the founding member states of the EU in 1990, it was in principle even possible to equate the national symbol of the fortress with Europe-critical symbolism: Luxembourg could basically be considered as the 'inner fortress' of a 'Fortress Europe'.

The *Mudam* and the Image of Self Controversy

For these reasons, it has, for a long time already, seemed imperative in Luxembourg to modify the discredited national symbolism and to link the national image closer to the European perspective. Certainly the most spectacular attempt to decisively accelerate this protracted process of transformation of national typical attitude patterns was the government's decision in 1990 to contract the 'star architect' Ieoh Ming Pei to build a *'Musée d'Art Moderne'* on the foundations of the Thüngen fortress on the edge of the Plateau de Kirchberg[22].

The many years of vehement debate around the construction of this museum that finally opened to the public in July 2006 are only comprehensible against the background of the tensions generated by the internal and external perspectives of national image of self outlined above, that have been characteristic for Luxembourg after the Second World War. The attempt to steer this dual definition of identity, which had come under pressure, into one particular symbolic political direction, led to the "Battle for Thüngen Fortress"[23] and, temporarily, to distinct rifts in the national collective: on one side, there was an institutionally anchored political elite, placing its hopes on the European-global project, and on the other side, there was a coalition of involved citizens and critical intellectuals, acting within an efficient network of different citizens' groups, which managed to garner significant public support with a signature campaign.

---

ists at the end of the Second World War and is mentioned by Victor Klemperer in his standard work on the language of the Third Reich, see Klemperer, Victor. 2007 [first published 1957]. *LTI – Notizbuch eines Philologen*. Stuttgart 2007, p. 73.

22 | I would like to thank André Bruns for the opportunity to review the material he has collected on this subject.

23 | Pauly, Michel. 1991. Schlacht um Fort Thüngen. *Forum für Politik, Gesellschaft und Kultur in Luxemburg* 128-129, p. 3-7.

The advocates welcomed the planned art museum as a signal of *"der geistigen Öffnung des bislang eher weltverschlossenen Festungsgeistes der Luxemburger"*[24]. The avantgardistic building, conceived as a work of art itself and erected on a long neglected location rich in symbolism, was designed to build a "bridge between history and modernity"[25] not only within the urban landscape. With the increasing competition between European cities the *Musée d'Art Moderne* (MUDAM) was to become a point of attraction and a distinctive 'icon' and redirect the image of the 'bank fortress' to a cultural one. As a self-representation with positive external effects, it would contribute to the metropolisation of the town and move it closer to "the vicinity of the so-called 'Stararchitecture Cities'" (Schulz 2008: 93).

The opponents, by contrast, feared the thoughtless and irreversible destruction of parts of the Thüngen fortress and with it the disposal of historical testimony of the past national identity through the construction of what in the initial concepts still appeared to be an edifice of monumental proportions. Major points of criticism were the financial risks, the lack of an acquisition strategy, but above all, the facelessness of a global architectural language that flouts local and historical particularities.

'Arcelor/Mittal' in the National Identity Discourse

While the MUDAM symbolises the connection of town and country to globalisation as well as a culturalisation of the until then dominant notion of globalisation as a purely economic process, this strategy of the modernisation of the self-image suffered a setback even before the museum opened. In a controversy conducted in the media at the beginning of 2006, over the sale of the *Arcelor*[26] steel group to the Indian entrepreneur Mittal, issues of national identity were raised similar to those that marked the quarrel over the Thüngen fortress, issues that only reveal themselves as such when they touch on conspicuous landmarks – in this case the administrative building of the enterprise as well as the industrial zones in the south of the country perceived as monuments of a grand, industrial past. "We are

---

24 | Personal translation: "Of an opening-up of the fortress mentality of the Luxembourgers that had hitherto displayed a penchant towards withdrawal".
25 | Ina Helweg-Nottrot: Eine Brücke zwischen Geschichte und Modernität. *Luxemburger Wort*. 1.7.2006, p. 8.
26 | An enterprise that was already multinational at the time and listed on the stock exchange, with representative group headquarters in Luxembourg. An essential component of the *Arcelor* group, which had been founded in 2001 by fusion, was the *Arbed* (Aciéries Réunies de Burbach-Eich-Dudelange; Vereinigte Stahlhütten Burbach-Eich-Düdelingen), a Luxembourg steel group founded in 1911 that, for a long time, had been among the biggest in the world and was of great significance for the industrial history and the national identity of the country.

Arcelor"[27] – read the remarkable headline in the *Luxemburger Wort*, with an explicit allusion to the transformations of 'we' sentiments, which were tested in Germany in the course of the peaceful revolution of 1989 and later at the German pope's election in 2005, into forms of a national consciousness seeking acceptance. After the debate over the MUDAM project that had revealed extremely divergent attitudes towards the national image of self, the Arcelor/Mittal debate now offered the opportunity to rhetorically strengthen the 'social cohesion' and, in turn, to jointly take a stance against an all too extensive, misguided modernisation. Headlines like "Juncker: This is about Luxembourg"[28] or another one taking up a remark by the Prime Minister that the Luxembourgers were already "happily globalised" even without Mittal[29], does not merely indicate a call on the 'mediator' to advocate a reversal and limitation of the hitherto strongly promoted policy of progressive opening. In this period of "war", of "defensive struggle"[30], which is perceived from the outside also as a "battle over steel" and is even likened to a "duel from the age of chivalry"[31], the symbolism of the 'fortress' reasserts itself unawares. In addition, the 'front' against the Indian group leads, at least temporarily, to a positive re-coding of the 'Fortress Europe'. The implication here is: the "regular global order" (Link 2006: 431) must under no circumstances be invalidated in the course of global competition. According to this order, the Western world, and specifically the 'core of Europe', continues to occupy the upper 'class of normality', while economically emergent 'threshold countries', like India need to content themselves with positions on the lower rungs, due to their unequal standards of living fluctuating between immensely 'rich' and extremely 'poor' There is an allusion to these contexts as subtle innuendo when referring to the Indian entrepreneur as a "steel maharaja"[32] (see. 6.3). Moreover, the 'Arcelor/Mittal complex' is described as a battle between "two cultures"[33] thereby establishing a link to the essentialist thesis of the "Clash of Civilizations" propagated and popularised by Samuel Huntington in the 1990s, and to the fears, kindled by it, of losing cultural supremacy (Huntington 1996).

Altogether, the MUDAM as well as the Arcelor/Mittal debate supply the articulatory framework for an otherwise vague sense of national identity, which however – and this is substantially different from the identity constructions in the

---

27 | Glesener, Marc. Wir sind Arcelor. *Luxemburger Wort*, 04.02.2006, p. 5.
28 | Zeimet, Laurent. Juncker: Es geht um Luxemburg. *Luxemburger Wort*, 01.02.2006, p. 3.
29 | Langner, Arne. Glücklich globalisiert. *Luxemburger Wort*, 16.02.2006, p. 14.
30 | G. S.: Arcelor rechnet mit monatelangem Kampf gegen drohende Übernahme. *Zeitung vum Lëtzebuerger Vollek*, 28.01.2006, p. 3.
31 | Braunberger, Gerald. Die Ritter der Stahlschlacht führen ein hartes Duell. *Frankfurter Allgemeine Sonntagszeitung*, 12.02. 2006, p. 39.
32 | Chaton, Cordelia. Wo Berater versagen, kommt der Stahl-Maharadscha zum Erfolg. *Luxemburger Wort*, 01.02.2006, p. 4.
33 | Hirsch, Mario. Zwei Kulturen. *d'Lëtzebuerger Land*, 03.02.2006, p. 1.

period of unqualified nationalism – is no longer primarily expressed through direct demarcation from other nations, nor even from the two big neighbours. Rather, the counterpole here is formed by the image of 'Europe' as a meanwhile all-powerful supranational institution, which appears as a 'gateway' to an uncontrollable and ruthless globalisation. One prospect of curbing this development is offered by the media, when differentiating between 'good' and 'bad' globalisation. These opposing poles are personified by the 'honest' mediator Juncker on one side and by the architect Ieoh Ming Pei and the entrepreneur Lakshmi Mittal on the other, portrayed as 'devious' global players[34].

National Symbolisms in the Cultural Capital Year 2007

The *MUDAM* controversy in particular can be seen as exemplary for the conflict between attributed and appropriated identities within an image of self seeking to acquire more distinctive contours. Even though the Arcelor/Mittal debate has had a negative impact on the modernisation of the national image encouraged by the political institutions ('top down'), it nevertheless has had an integrative effect in the run-up to the cultural capital year 2007. Against this background, it is then possible to further develop the intentions associated with this event: Expressed in advertising terms, the cultural capital year 2007 was to provide new impulses for the 'branding' of the 'brand' of Luxembourg.

The 'social cohesion', which was shown to be a problematic factor in the media coverage of the two controversies over Luxembourg's self-image, is taken into account here in so far as an identification potential suited for daily use is provided by the central topic of the 'Greater Region'. For the creation of a regional perspective neutralises the still very characteristic awareness of a contrast between 'global' urban space and 'local' periphery and Luxembourg is presented as one integral and comprehensive space in the 'center of the Greater Region'. In keeping with the collective symbolism of 'core of Europe', Luxembourg becomes, for its inhabitants, the "Middle Kingdom", requiring a new "gauging of the border"[35] (see 4.7).

At the same time, the project of repositioning, initiated in connection with the *MUDAM*, is also being pursued. Architectural images of transition, among others, have been inserting themselves between the old image of self as 'fortress' and

---

34 | In the *MUDAM* as well as the *Arcelor/Mittal* reporting approach, this aspect of an identifiable physiognomic character plays a rather essential part. Just like the entrepreneur Mittal was portrayed as "the smiling man" (Meyer, Roman. Der Mann des Lächelns. *Revue*, 08.02.2006, p. 30), there was not one portrait of the architect Pei – who is also considered the "Architect of the Mighty" – without a mention of the "typical broad smile of the Asians" (e. g.: Morbach, Fern. Der große alte Mann der Architektur. *Télécran*, No. 40, 30.09.1995, p. 29).

35 | Langenbrink, Christophe. Im Reich der Mitte. *Luxemburger Wort*, 10.05.2007, p. 13; Wahl, Susanne. Eine Auslotung der Grenze. *Luxemburger Wort*, 31.05. 2007, p. 13.

the envisioned new cosmopolitan self-representation that apparently as yet has generated no concise collective symbolism. The preferred symbol here is that of the 'bridge', which seeks a sense of continuity similar to that of the 'fortress': 'Building bridges' between the regions, between the 'old' and the 'new', between past and future, etc. (see 6.3). In ever new variations Luxembourg is assertively presented as 'intermediate space', as the 'European laboratory' or as an 'experimental region' which in turn enables to establish links to the symbolism of 'heart', 'centre' and 'core'.

Beyond Luxembourg's borders, the attempt to secure connections for national symbolism as well as to search for new orientations, has by no means gone unnoticed. The country is seen as "Europe's multicoloured bridge"[36], and one is well aware that the country is not only home to "bankers and bureaucrats"[37], although the alliteration again emphasises the reversion to traditional stereotypes, to the exclusion of any positive definition. The image of the "treasury of the fortress Europe"[38] is obviously a similarly equivocal one resonating with ambivalencies regarding the intended culturalisation of the economic sector, which still dominates public perception. The German travel magazine *Merian* processes this symbolism on the cover of its 'Luxembourg' issue on the cultural capital year 2007 in an ideal-typical way in the form of an emblem: The curved gallery of the Luxembourg Philharmonic acts as *pictura*, as *subscriptio*, Luxembourg is characterised twice as an "intermediate" region, and in the third statement Prime Minister Juncker is identified as the conciliatory mediator figure and guarantor for this transitional state (see 5.5).

The Media as Agent of Attributed and Appropriated Identities

The question which national symbolism will be able to establish itself or will be established in the near future for Luxembourg remains an open one. This differentiation is important. Even though the media discourses outlined here have failed to lead to a consensus about national symbolism, they do constitute an area where attributed and appropriated collective identities are put into mutual context through a negotiation process, with the effect that they are often no longer easily distinguishable. The application of national symbolisms in the media in particular presumes a close correlation and as an interface makes clear just how much both identity patterns are mutually dependent. However, this also means that collective identities cannot simply be reinvented, even, or especially, in post-national times of image campaigns, nor can the traditional ones simply be perpetuated.

---

36 | Schiemann, Hans. Europas bunte Brücke. *Merkur*, 23.02.2007, p. 29.
37 | Meyer, Ulf. Nicht nur Banker und Bürokraten. *Die Welt*, 20.07.2006, p. 26.
38 | Schümer, Dirk. Die Schatzkammer der Festung Europa. *Frankfurter Allgemeine Zeitung*, 11.06.2007, p. 42.

6.3 The Superjhemp Saga – an Ideal Projection Screen

In 'superhero comics' with national overtones, one frequently finds discourses which are constructs on the identities of the respective population. As such the Luxembourg comic series *Superjhemp* provides a particularly interesting case example for exploring the questions which appropriated and attributed identities are regularly chosen as a central theme and how the satirical representation compares with the actual identity constructs. The hero's identity features play a crucial role in the targeted readers' practice of appropriation. Luxembourg's superhero, Superjhemp, for instance, seems to combine various qualities of foreign comic superheroes. Among others, the figure seems to borrow some of his features from *Superman, Batman, Spiderman, Popeye, Asterix, Tintin*, etc. However, for their primary source of inspiration the *Superjhemp* authors – Lucien Czuga und Roger Leiner – must have drawn on the French figure of *Superdupont* from the comic series of the same name, which reveals very conspicuous similarities in terms of intentions, humour and general character. Even though *Superjhemp* – as the numerous borrowings from other characters show – is the product of a globalisation of popular culture and therefore belongs, like basically all comics, to the interdiscourses, it nevertheless displays numerous identity-related character traits which have their origin in Luxembourg regionalism.

The anthology *Comics in, aus und über Luxembourg*[39] (Haas 2007) shows that the comic landscape in the small nation of Luxembourg, which has the population of a medium-size town (about 490,000 inhabitants) is a rather lively one. Though the *Superjhemp* stories of the last 20 years have been unmatched as far as success, national visibility and popularity are concerned, there had already before this time been attempts to establish some long-term comic series with the Luxembourg reading public. Most of these products, however, were not published in book form but serially in weekly papers or daily newspapers. The comic compilation mentioned above includes the Luxembourg cartoonists. At the level of signifiers, the comic uses a symbolic language that hyperbolically distorts figures and objects, exaggerates some details while leaving out others. This creates an intended feedback to the character of the depicted signifier. This is particularly true for *Superjhemp* when iconically visual resemblances to famous Luxembourg personalities and objects are established. Formally, the series belongs to the type of comic which consistently employs the means of caricature of that genre. The cartoonising stylistic elements produce, just like in *Asterix*, a certain distortion of reality, which is quite different to the purely external, realistic representations of figures and environment in leading US superhero sagas (see *Superman, Spiderman*, and 'graphic novels' in general). On the internationally level, there is a considerable diversity of comic genres. The samples we will presently analyse show that *Superjhemp* defies being

---

39 | Personal translation: "Comics in, from and about Luxembourg".

uniquely labelled as a 'comic book superhero epic' and indicate that it fits into several categories at once, as we will elaborate below.

In view of *Superjhemp*'s success story of more than 20 years, we have to ask ourselves what it is exactly the authors use to cater to the Luxembourg readers. The *Superjhemp* comic contains many references to the social and political life of Luxembourg. The authors of the series erect a sort of parallel world to the model Luxembourg. Many a state of affairs in Luxembourg has been made the target of penetrating and witty caricature by lampooning well-known politicians and institutions; the authors hold up a fool's mirror to the locals. And they seem to like what it shows them. The series' consistently high sales – some volumes are out of print, others were reissued as compilations – attest to the degree of enthusiasm the satirically distorted staging of Luxembourg conditions provokes among the readers. Like the court jester for his king, so do Czuga and Leiner formulate caricature-like stories on the identities of the Luxembourgers. And at times, these are uncomfortable truths too; however, the sarcastic projections are often defused by linguistic and visual humour, making them easier to accept or they are depicted in such an exaggerated fashion that it raises palliative doubts as to their credibility.

Figure 1: Cover examples of Superjhemp *comic books (© Editions Revue, Luxembourg).*

In the almost homonymous construct "*Luxusbuerg*", the authors turn the perceptions of self and others of Luxembourg into a subject of discussion: Identities which are partially attributed and those which have been appropriated to a higher or lesser degree by parts of the population. *Superjhemp* therefore belongs to the genre of comic 'superhero epic' that functions as a "reflection of societal conditions" (Umberto Eco quoted after Ditschke/Anhut 2009: 148) "*Sie [die Comicheldgeschichten] referieren zwar unterschiedlich stark auf tatsächliche soziokulturelle Ereignisse und Strukturen, trotzdem kommen die "in den Comic Books dargestellten 'Wirklichkeiten' [...] der Realität* *doch sehr nahe" (Th. Sieck) – einerseits hinsichtlich zugrunde liegender gesellschaftlicher, ökonomischer und kultureller Strukturen, andrerseits hinsichtlich spezifischer Ereignisse [...]"*⁴⁰ (Ditschke/Anhut 2009: 149), which have significant socio-political relevance. Because the authors of *Superjhemp* are very close observers of 'the man in street' and a lot of what they see and hear from the gossip factory is transposed by caricature, one can suppose that the Luxembourgers are quite aware of numerous perceptions of self and others and sometimes even – like in the comic series – play with them.

With its more than 20 volumes, the *Superjhemp* saga represents an almost inexhaustible repertoire of possible samples regarding Luxembourg identities. Due to lack of space, the following qualitative analyses will have to limit themselves to a few particularly characteristic identity discourses. Because comics are eminently semiotic events, we have taken the triadic model of Peirce (see Peirce 1907, German new edition, 2000) as a theoretical basis for the discourse-analytical method, extended with the causal character concept of symbolisation and referencing developed by Ogden and Richards (see Ogden/Richards 1923). Socially specific codes and symbols play a causal role, not only for the selection and representation but also for the receptance and pragmatism of the signs used in *Superjhemp*. The intermeshed sequence that Jakobson outlines in his communication model (see Jakobson 1960) serves to reveal the interrelationships between comic production, social contexts and discourses (e.g., financial centre, steel industry) and the reception of *Superjhemp*. The approach is necessarily an interpretational one. The quantitative data are, wherever possible, put in context to the interpreting results.

In order to discover further details about *Superjhemp*'s relative intensity of perception and the social structure of the readership, the following question was asked when gathering quantitative data: "Have you ever read *Superjhemp*, either as a comic book or in the media?" The latter is relevant because the advance publication of the books occurs in a weekly rhythm of respectively two pages in the *Revue*, a quite widely read weekly magazine. The results indicate that the majority (63 %) of Luxembourg's residential population is familiar with the megahero. The comparison of the different milieus shows high levels of name recognition throughout with little variation: from 69 % in the privileged conservative milieu up to 81 % in the alternative as well as in the privileged liberal milieu.

Appropriated Eating Culture

By highlighting food predilections, which are considered at least by parts of Luxembourg's population as specific to their identity, the *Superjhemp* authors

---

40 | Personal translation: "Though they [the comic hero's stories] refer in varying degrees to actual sociocultural events and structures, nevertheless, the 'realities' depicted in the comic books [...] are not very far removed from actual reality (Th. Sieck) – on the one hand in regard to underlying social, economic and cultural structures, on the other regarding specific events [...]".

emphasise appropriations that have evolved over a longer period of time. What spinach is to Popeye and the magic potion to *Asterix*, *Kachkéis*[41] is to our Superjhemp. This is the substance that gives him his supernatural powers and enables him to embark on his reckless aerial exploits. Many Luxembourgers regard *Kachkéis* as a national gastronomic speciality, but it is by no means a product exclusive to Luxembourg. In other European regions, too, it belongs to the traditional types of cheese. This partial appropriation mirrors a certain local eating habit[42] since even today the supermarket shelves continue to be well stocked with *Kachkéis*. This gastronomic preference is also reflected in the Luxembourgers' popular song culture. In his *"Lidd vum Kachkéis"*[43], the well-known cabaret writer Pier Kremer describes the virtues of the sticky cheese. *"Kachkéis, Bouneschlupp, Quetschekraut a Mouselsbéier"*[44], goes a sung advertisement for a Luxembourg beer brand. The lyrics were written by Marc Schreiner. The popular refrain, which inspired listeners to sing along, was later taken up by the local music band *Cool Feet* and presented as a full-fledged song. While the miraculous powers of *Superman* and *Asterix* are more of a cosmic and magic origin, Czuga and Leiner equip their hero deliberately with a folksy and witty character: he derives his extraordinary abilities from the consumption of a banal and mass-produced cheese which has, however, special significance for identity in the national context. In one episode, *"Luxusbuerg"* is renamed *"Kachkéisien"* already in the title (see Czuga/Leiner 2005). *Kachkéis* also becomes the saviour in times of crisis to ensure full employment: Superjhemp suggests to the Prime Minister that he compensate impending job losses in the financial sector due to the demise of bank secrecy, by building additional job-creating *"Kachkéis"* factories (Czuga/Leiner 2009: 6; 48). In the burlesque world of the comic, the proposal, which politicians in the 'real' Luxembourg would dismiss outright as absurd, becomes a plausible possibility to create jobs because the identity-forming food *"Kachkéis"* transforms in *"Luxusbuerg"* into a veritable miracle substance and can be used like a *deus ex machina*, depending on the predicament in question, as a multiple defensive weapon, as superglue, as a *Spiderman* net and as a foil to entrap US stealth bombers (Czuga/Leiner 2003: 40).

The authors also demonstrate in other stories that they have a special weakness for the traditional eating culture of the Luxembourgers. For instance, *"Judd mat Gardebounen"*[45] is mentioned in several stories. This dish is frequently indicated in Luxembourg cookbooks and tourist pamphlets as a sort of national dish. The ingredient, beans, plays a crucial role in the volume entitled *Superjhemp an déi grouss Gefor* (see Czuga/Leiner 2007a). The *"Luxusbuerg"* hero even hoards large stocks of

---

41 | Personal translation: "Cooked cheese", a runny cheese called *Cancoillotte* in French.
42 | See also section 7.4.
43 | Personal translation: "The Song of the Cooked Cheese".
44 | Personal translation: "Cooked Cheese, bean stew, prune marmalade and *Mousel* beer".
45 | Personal translation: "Pork neck and sow beans".

cans of the aforementioned *"Bouneschlupp"* in his cellar. And finally, his real name is Charel Kuddel and he is married to Felicie Fleck, which combines to *Kuddelfleck*, a dish containing beef stomach, probably more popular with the older generations. When *Superjhemp* swears, he says *"Poznennö"*, the reverse of *Önnenzop*, a type of onion soup that, once again, is not found exclusively in Luxembourg. This expletive is not part of the spontaneous vocabulary of the Luxembourgers but is an invention of the authors, probably a phonetic allusion to the common but vulgar *Nondidjö*, the Luxembourgish form of *nom de Dieu*[46]. *"Poznennö"* is one of the special expressions inherent to *Superjhemp* that Czuga and Leiner define in their *Luxusbuerger Lexikon* (Czuga/Leiner 2008a). In the parallel world of *"Luxusbuerg"*, virtually all names referring directly to Luxembourg are either spoofed or slightly distorted. By contrast, the already mentioned dishes have curiously retained their original names. In the comic series, Luxembourgish is the predominant, 'uncorrupted' identity which is common to both *"Luxusbuergers"* and Luxembourgers. Even linguistic regionalism – in the form of dialect variants – is given a place.

The traditional national dishes appropriated by parts of the population and nowadays only prepared on special occasions are simple and hearty and made from rather cheap ingredients. They refer back to a time during the 19th century when Luxembourg still used to be a nation of peasants and grinding poverty forced many into emigration. These appropriations therefore originated from circumstances that reflected a state of need at the time. It was only with the industrialisation during the first half of the 20th century and later with the development of the banking centre during its second half that relative wealth arrived. Consequently, prosperity and luxury are another central subject matter of *Superjhemp*, whose textual and iconic representation aims at contexts of collective symbolism.

Wealth and Globalisation Fears

The pun is an obvious one; the comic country is called *"Luxusbuerg"* and the inhabitants are the *"Luxusbuerger"*. For the French speaking cross-border workers who commute to Luxembourg every day for work, the term 'Luxo' not only constitutes an abbreviation for the name 'Luxembourger', but it is also carries a connotative meaning. In *Superjhemp*, this abbreviation is used by the authors several times. For instance, they have a sign indicate *"Luxoland"* (Czuga/Leiner 2007: 19) in the nearby French border region or, another example, French and Belgian workers on strike are shown during a demonstration outside the headquarters of the former Arcelor company holding up a banner that says *"A bas les Luxos"*[47] (Czuga/Leiner 2003: 3).

The representative symbol for luxury and prosperity in *Superjhemp* is the *"Luxonit"*, a cosmic element that had landed back in the 19th century in *"Luxusbuerg"* in the form of a meteorite. Its substance, allegedly, unites all the characteristics

---

46 | Personal translation: "Name of God".
47 | Personal translation: "Down with the Luxos".

and features of the *"Luxusbürgertum"*[48] (Czuga/Leiner 1998b: 9). The absence of *"Luxonit"* has effects on the consumer behaviour of the *"Luxusbuerger"*; no one buys *"Luxusbuerg"* products or any other consumer items anymore (Czuga/Leiner 1998b: 37). This means that the seemingly most important thing taken for granted in *"Luxusbuerg"* society is being called into question. With the *"Luxonit"*, the authors create a specific collective icon for *"Luxusbuerg"* and, at the same time, once again borrow from the American hero, *Superman*. Although the cosmic material seems to act in a similar way, its effects are exactly the opposite: while the presence of green "cryptonite" robs *Superman* of his powers, the absence of *"Luxonit"* stops the *"Luxusbuergers"* from continuing to engage in blind consumerism. By employing deconstructive images and texts the authors sarcastically point to the 'dramatic' effects caused by the loss of consumer routines that justify the frequently attributed identity of 'intensive consumer': the *"Luxusbuerger"* seem to become disoriented, slightly confused and begin to question a number of their consumption habits. (Czuga/Leiner 1998b: 37). They leave their cars at home and walk instead, take their televisions to the recycling depot or, when in a bar, order water instead of beer.

The first two syllables of *"Luxonit"*, bring the notion of luxury to mind as well as the already mentioned French name for the Luxembourgers. The suffix customary for minerals, '-it', could refer to an imaginary ore and hence to the partial origin of prosperity in Luxembourg – the establishment of the iron and steel industry at the beginning of the 20th century. In the corresponding episode *"Luxonit"* looks like a brown stone, pointing to an imaginary type of ore. The mysterious matter is a sort of catalyst and cannot generate wealth by itself. The rare *"Luxonit"* is kept, durably and well protected, in the building of the State Bank – the *"Luxusbuerger"* Savings Bank – like a national shrine and serves as a symbol for the money reserves deposited at banks by residents and foreigners. Should the *"Luxonit"* disappear, the country too would come under foreign rule. (Czuga/Leiner 2008: 52).

In the volume *Den Dossier Hexemeeschter*, Czuga and Leiner quite specifically show the connection between the relative wealth of the Luxembourgers and the circumstance of their position as an international financial centre. The subject provides the authors with the opportunity to deal with several attributed and appropriated identities. The banks at the "King's Boulevard" (the actual Boulevard Royal) are iconically depicted as washing machines that serve for laundering foreign money (Czuga/Leiner 1991: 15). The association of washing machine (image) and laundering (connotation) shows, in an exemplary fashion, the manner in which the authors' team operates with collective symbolism.

And yet it is not only by means of visual wit that Czuga and Leiner, in a provocative way, advertise the image of a banking centre, consistently officially repudiated but frequently attributed to Luxembourg by the foreign press: for instance, one *"Luxusbuerg"* financial institution is called "Bank for Cocaine and Crime International". There is a clear connection between the origin of the money and organised

---

48 | Personal translation: "Bourgeoisie of Luxury".

Figure 2: The banks at the 'King's Boulevard' (Czuga/Leiner 1991: 15) © Editions Revue, Luxembourg.

crime. The acronym BCCI, furthermore, establishes the connection with the real finance scandal of the Bank of Credit and Commerce International (BCCI), which caused a stir across the nation in 1991, because the Luxembourg branch of the BCCI was also implicated in criminal activities. The silhouette of financial institutions on Kirchberg in the volume *Alarm am Öro Zuch* shows that precisely those nations that derogate Luxembourg as a 'tax haven' are present there with their national banks in order to turn a profit from the 'haven' with tax refugees from their own countries: the usual puns and spoofs that can be found here, like "Deutsche Dash Bank", "Whyte and Wash Bank" or "Blanchibas", leave no doubt as to which institutions they stand for. The connotative reference to laundry is plain. Quite specifically, examples are also provided for the private clientele which the international press likes to make out as the essential tax evaders: dentists from Germany, Belgian notaries and cattle dealers as well as French politicians (Czuga/Leiner 2001: 9).

Symbolisms like 'tax haven' and 'money laundering' have, of course, a damaging effect on the desired serious image of the financial centre. Ever since the BCCI scandal, the Luxembourg banking authority, on order of the respective governments, has been trying to keep out dubious financial institutions. The authorities are continuously working on trying to rid Luxembourg of the negative image of money laundering. At the height of the financial crisis, in autumn 2008, Prime Minister Juncker reacted very annoyed on French television when, prior to being interviewed, he was unexpectedly shown some satirical footage confronting him with the image of money laundering: a black suitcase is put into a washing machine and a white suitcase is taken out again[49]. At the same time Luxembourg diplomats protested violently against the country being included on the OECD tax haven 'grey list'. Fittingly, a 'grey veil' descends on "*Luxusbuerg*" (Czuga/Leiner 2009: 5). The image, borrowed from detergent ads, again directly refers to laundry. While Luxembourg managed to get itself removed from the grey list relatively quickly, the question remains whether

---

49 | 21.10.2008: Le journal télévisé de 20 heures, France 2. http://www.youtube.com/watch?v=YwFhCdznVwM&feature=related

the country, once it had agreed, as a concession, to an exchange of tax information with some key states, will continue to remain as interesting to foreign customers in spite of the softened banking confidentiality. Massive job cuts and shrinking tax revenues at the banks would have a strong negative effect on the prosperity of the Luxembourg resident population. In the second year of the global financial crisis, the *Superjhemp* volume of 2009 highlights these possible developments as a central theme. The ironic title *Cräsh am Paradäis* refers not only to the image of 'tax haven' (more evident in the German *Steuerparadies*) but also to the seemingly heavenly living conditions in Luxembourg attributed in some press articles.

The topic of 'danger to the banking centre' is a recurring one in the individual stories. For instance, already in the first volume, *De Superjhemp géint de Bommeléer* (Czuga/Leiner 1988), the background to the series of bomb explosions in Luxembourg, still unclear at the time, was explained with the competing financial centre of the principality of *"Monastein"*, wanting to instill an air of insecurity in *"Luxusbuerg"*, inducing the banks to migrate, together with their customers, to *"Monastein"*. With the make-up of the name, from the first two syllables of Monaco and last one of Liechtenstein, the authors have created a deliberately cryptic construct. In *D'Patte wech vum Luxonit*, the contracted criminals confess to stealing the *"Luxonit"* on the instructions of the principality of *"Monastein"* in order to destroy the identity of *"Luxusbuerg"* together with the banking centre (Czuga/Leiner 1998b: 47).

The menacing loss of income from the financial centre was also a central subject in 1991, in *Dossier Hexemeeschter*: The foreign money in the resident banks disappears suddenly and inexplicably. The savings bank director of *"Luxusbuerg"* sums the matter up when he says: *"Wann ons auslännesch Clienten dat gewuer gin, dann as et Pilo mat eiser Finanzplaz"*[50] (Czuga Leiner 1991: 17). The authors here highlight the fact that the country's precarious prosperity depends on the existence of the international banking centre. The constant flow of high tax revenues from petrol, spirits and tobacco products is prone to the same insecurity. And since this is also a frequent issue in Luxembourg's media, one can assume that many Luxembourgers are well aware of the uncertain duration of this source of revenue as well as of what it would mean for the country if these sources dried up. With the statement of the savings bank director, the authors voice a subliminal but latent fear of many Luxembourgers.

Fears of loss relating to the local steel industry were also triggered among large parts of Luxembourg's population when, in 2006, the Indian steel magnate Lakshmi Mittal virtually enforced the merger of Arcelor with his own company Mittal Steel[51]. In their iconic depiction, Czuga and Leiner use the means of caricature to show that, in the age of globalisation, traditional identity is lost in

---

50 | Personal translation: "If our foreign customers find out about this, it's over with our financial centre".

51 | See also section 6.2.

"*Luxusbuerg*" and substituted by a new 'foreign' one: for instance, the neoclassical historicising architecture of the former Arcelor respectively Arbed headquarters is suddenly complemented by a monumental gate in Indian architectural style, reminiscent of the Taj Mahal.

Figure 3: The former Arcelor building turns into the "Taj Mittal" *(Czuga/Leiner 2006: 20)* © *Editions Revue, Luxembourg.*

The building, which for many Luxembourgers has the character of a collective symbol owing to its obvious reference to the emergence of the country's steel industry, is sarcastically re-christened into "*Taj Mittal*" (Czuga/Leiner 2006: 20). As what appears to be a visionary anticipation of the aforementioned merger, in the *Superjhemp* episode of 2005, a dictator from Central Asia buys up all of "*Luxusbuerg*" on the world market and renames the country – as a protected trademark – "*Kachkéisien*" Czuga/Leiner 2005: 23). The *Superjhemp* saga metaphorically points to the sources of the Luxembourgers' wealth while at the same time also showing the types of dangers that could wipe it out almost instantly.

In a work commissioned for the cultural year 2007[52], the British photographer Martin Parr has documented the relative luxury of the inhabitants of Luxembourg in an ostensibly ethnographic manner. Just like the authors of *Superjhemp*, he holds up a kind of mirror to the Luxembourgers. High income levels and ostentatious consumer behaviour are often considered as being 'typically Luxembourgish'. The first feature at least is a statistical fact. According to a study conducted in 2009 by

---

52 | See also section 6.5.

Eurostat, the inhabitants of Luxembourg are the richest within the EU (Weltonline 2009).

A Nation of Civil Servants?

Another stereotype is that of civil service: Czuga and Leiner quite obviously play on existing prejudices in the population when they attribute to civil servants certain identities which would actually have to keep them from reading *Superjhemp*: Civil servants, allegedly, are lazy and corrupt – they sort their private stamp collections at work and sleep through their working hours. The stereotyped negative representation of civil servants in texts and images is a satirical practice frequently encountered in Western democracies.

Quantitative surveys have shown that, among all the professions, *Superjhemp*'s widest readership is to be found among the civil servants, equalling 78 % of its total readership. A further recent study (Pigeron-Piroth 2009: 3) determined that the number of Luxembourgers working in the civil service sector is disproportionally high at 42.3 % (as of March 2008) when compared to all available jobs in the country. If one considers the occupation of most protagonists in *Superjhemp*, the equation fits almost perfectly: "*Luxusbuerger*" equals civil servant.

Charel Kuddel works in the "*Ministry of Unsolved Matters*" in the "*Department for Hopeless Cases*". He is a civil servant who can easily afford to be conspicuous by his frequent absences from work because he constantly has to save the country and its people in the course of his undercover activity as a megahero. *Superjhemp*, therefore, has a secret identity and in this respect he is no different from the general identity pattern of traditional American comic superheroes. (see *Superman, Spiderman, Batman*). The third syllable of *Superjhemp* is derived from the Luxembourg nickname '*Jhempi*' for gendarme. He is, therefore, a kind of undercover super cop for special cases.

A kind of cronyism has been established among high-ranking civil servants in "*Luxusbuerg*": In this context, different scandals which were taken up by Luxembourg's media are caricatured with caustic sarcasm. However, there are some detectives – friends of *Superjhemp* – who surpass themselves in perilous situations and therefore save the honour of their guild; the message here is that they are, despite everything, somehow indispensable for the country. These actions mostly involve protecting certain interests of the nation and the dynasty or even of safeguarding "*Luxusbuerg*" against perdition. *Superjhemp* is a fighter against a good many looming identity losses and material circumstances related to them.

In terms of content, the series reinforces the genre of 'comic superhero epic', which is all about preserving moral, political, economic or social constructs and of reinforcing these through the superhero's actions (Ditschke/Anhut 2009: 156). Nevertheless, the authors of *Superjhemp* follow a path quite distinct from US models (e.g. *Superman, Spiderman*) by using caricatures and parodies to take a critical stance on social conditions. The discourse is in a way paradoxical in the sense that the central figure *Superjhemp* stands for the same constructs and does not question them. He is the quintessential loyal civil servant who serves and does not question authority. Here, an image of the average Luxembourger is established: In his daily life, he is a petty bourgeois (Charel Kuddel) who only takes visionary flights in his dreams.

A Trenchant Depiction of the Locals

The only rebellious aspect of *Superjhemp* is his relished habit of not coming flying in through the door but through the window, which, to the great annoyance of his superiors, gets shattered each time. Also physically, *Superjhemp* displays certain features of the antihero. His build is certainly not an athletic but a rather chubby one. Since he lacks *Superman*'s aerodynamic Adonis-like figure, the obligatory tights look rather ridiculous when worn by this particular superhero. His funny lumpy nose and cute shape are derived from the "baby schema" ("*Kindchenschema*", described by Konrad Lorenz) – designed to induce sympathy among the readers. His hat and sometimes also the cape has a checkered pattern in the national colours (red/white/blue). Similar hats, albeit in neutral colours, are frequently worn by elderly male Luxembourgers. The checkered cape brings a kitchen table cloth to mind. Charel Kuddel likes wearing checkered vests – as do some of his civil servant colleagues – sometimes he also dons a pair of checkered trousers. Since superheroes act as a role model and function as a surrogate, one may wonder whether the authors are employing visual wit to attribute to the "*Luxusbuergers*" a certain kind of petty-mindedness. The fact that *Superjhemp*, when he is at home, likes having things comfortable and orderly might support this view. In the evenings, he enjoys watching TV nursing a glass of cool "*Uelzechtbéier*".⁵³ The bedsheets that he sleeps in at night have the pattern of the national flag on them. Since superheroes belong to the public domain as it were, the most they can ever expect to have is an unrequited, platonic love to a girlfriend (like Superman, Obelix) or they are totally asexual beings (like Asterix, Tintin). Never do they have, as Charel Kuddel, a wife as well as several children. "*Luxusbuerger*" megaheroes just happen to be different: in their spare time, they like to enjoy the discreet charm that only a bourgeois, idyllic family life can offer.

The attribution of the petty bourgeois idyll can also be found in Martin Parr's photo documentation mentioned earlier. The objects representing this, for instance residential houses in what only appears to be a differentiating uniform style, he calls the "vanities" of the middle class. The petty bourgeois mentality which the *Superjhemp* authors, as well as Martin Parr, attribute to the so-called average Luxembourger, is of course based on their subjective view and is not free of stereotypes. One might think that Martin Parr's photographs are objective

---

53 | Beer named after the river Alzette *(Uelzecht)*. Here, the authors establish an analogy to Mousel beer, the name of which makes tonal reference to the Luxembourgish name for the river Moselle, which is *Musel*.

ethnographic pieces of evidence. However, this is not the case because Parr selects his motifs according to the criterion of the 'petty bourgeois mentality', partially stages them and subjectively influences them with the artistic and formal means of photography – like framing, focus range and emphasising particulars.

In literature, the petty bourgeois is, among other things, described as a conformist who is narrow-minded, closed to the outside world and anxious for social security. The character of the petty bourgeois pervades the entire European literature and is in many countries a favourite target for comedians. In their research on the European petty bourgeoisie, Haupt and Crossik ask the question whether, considering the empiric heterogeneity, one can actually speak of a uniform class or social group (see Haupt/Crossik 1998). They show that one can also extract positive qualities from the negatively connoted petty bourgeoisie. The features of the petty bourgeois as stereotyped in fiction, can in fact be found throughout all social groups. In *Superjhemp*, entrepreneurs, artists and even intellectuals from academia are attributed petty bourgeois features. Basically, no social milieu is spared the authors' ridicule. Means of distinction used by the different groups to differentiate themselves culturally and economically from each other are satirised with a sarcastic approach. Like a narrative metalepsis, the authors even include themselves in the sarcasm by interrupting the flow of the story in some episodes and self-mockingly presenting themselves in words and images.

On account of existing perceptions of self and others, Czuga and Leiner attribute identities to the Luxembourgers which are partly based on their own projections: as they subjectively perceive the locals or would sometimes also like to see them, for the caricature to take full effect. The persiflage feeds on attributed stereotypes – and/or clichés – as well as on appropriations that are considered odd. The deliberately subtle reinterpretation creates a partial re-contextualisation of perceptions of self and others in the construct "*Luxusbuerg*" and, accordingly, a critical appraisal of identities regarding Luxembourg. Here, the grotesque serves as an instrument of deconstruction. Finally, the concentrated accumulation of all kinds of appropriated and attributed identities generates a discourse which reflects itself, as it were, into infinity and thus refers to the mirror in the reflecting character of the *Superjhemp* saga. The fact that the reflecting surface turns into a distorting mirror which grotesquely deforms the so-called 'Luxembourg Identities' is, to be sure, one of the deconstructive intentions of the two comic book authors.

6.4 Collective Symbols and (New) Identity Options in Luxembourg's Advertising

Images and collective symbols also play an important role in advertising, an interdiscourse which has become a fixture in our everyday lives. Advertising is employed by various societal players in order to achieve specific sales objectives and to generate images in the public perception. To this end, linguistic and visual images are accessed, reinterpreted or re-assigned. Since people use the information presented to them in part consciously in order to close knowledge gaps, orientate themselves and position themselves in the (consumer) world, this chapter will investigate to which extent the 'advertising' interdiscourse holds a communicatively active identity potential. We will focus our attention in particular on advertising or product communication produced specifically with a view to Luxembourg, since the images employed can impact the generation of a peculiar notion of 'Luxembourg identity'. Advertisements as a form of media content provide *"Attribute für die Konstitution von Identität"*[54] (Krotz 2003: 41). They are reflected in the sense of a process of attribution and are purposefully elaborated. When advertisements reach the consumers, there is the possibility that the latter absorb their content, understand and accept it and appropriate the discourse positions. In a further step, this can contribute to constructions of identity.

First, however, advertising has to be produced and it is necessary to create a communicatively active identity potential. With the progressive destandardisation of lifestyles the creative heads of the advertising sector are presented with a formidable challenge. Mass marketing as a basic strategy is proving to be increasingly inappropriate. There are more and more doubts whether traditional advertising patterns still work. In addition, the issues of communication in advertising in a diversified society are, in Luxembourg, shaped by an extremely multicultural and multilingual environment. Already quite small target groups are even more difficult to reach if one is dealing with a number of different cultural codes and a variety of possibilities for the choice of languages to be used in advertising messages. The question to be investigated here is whether and how advertising in Luxembourg works with a specific Luxembourgish imagery that can be identified as collective symbolism. By discursive processing of collective symbols advertising attempts to overcome the border between product and consumers. Ideally, the symbolism unites the product with the consumers in the sense of an 'associative crosspoint'[55]. In certain cases the national space is imagined as something uniform, for example, by exploiting over and over again the same familiar sceneries and skylines, or also traditions like folk festivals and religious holidays for advertising purposes. In Luxembourg, in particular, the homogeneous representation of national space has proven to be a difficult task because the targeted consumers are very heterogeneous, which is, among other things, due to the distinctive border-crosser mentality[56] and the high proportion of persons with a migration background[57]. The heterogeneity also becomes evident in the acting out of consumer patterns which permit appropriated identities to partly manifest themselves. With the aid of examples

---

54 | Personal translation: "Attributes for the constitution of identity".
55 | The symbol acts as an 'associative crosspoint' if the promoted product can be connected to the symbol and, at the same time, the targeted consumers can identify with the symbol.
56 | See the remarks on cross-border workers in section 7.5.
57 | See section 6.6.

taken from the finance and telecommunications sector as well as from the cultural capital year *Luxembourg 2007*, we will in the following illustrate how advertising in Luxembourg can serve as an interdiscourse with identity-forming potential.

Examples of Advertising from the Finance and Telecommunications Sector

In terms of enterprises respectively clients, the advertising discourse in Luxembourg is marked by a mixture of state institutions and ministries, major international corporations, national enterprises and local companies. They distinguish themselves primarily by the budgets set aside for advertising measures, by the nationality structure of the employees which shows itself in preferences for certain styles of communication and in the choice of language, as well as by the competitive situation, because, depending on their size, enterprises either operate only on the domestic market or also internationally. Luxembourg's market as such is a very small one and accordingly highly competitive in some sectors. The qualitative survey conducted among Luxembourg's resident population has shown that a number of enterprises (mainly Luxembourgish companies) and their brands constitute symbols for Luxembourg as well as Luxembourg's economy, and are also absorbed collectively in the process. The enterprises, respectively the brands and their advertisements, are described as 'typical' for Luxembourg and for Luxembourgish advertising. This can be interpreted as an identity-based appropriation. The reasons given frequently state personal preferences, traditional and national embeddedness as well as efficiency and prominence of advertising. Interviewees mentioned, for instance, the National Savings Bank, *Banque et Caisse d'Epargne de l'Etat* (BCEE). It has been present in Luxembourg for over 150 years and by now embodies the Luxembourgish bank *par excellence*. With its policy of proximity to the people, it was able to establish an image of trust from which it profited particularly during the financial crisis of 2008. Not infrequently tourists confuse its headquarters in Luxembourg City with the grand-ducal Palace on account of its imposing appearance and its tall tower. By integrating the building into its company logo the bank has, since decades, emphasised its *"Verankerung und Geschichte in der Gesellschaft Luxemburgs"*[58] (Jungblut 2007: 290). This makes it one of the few financial institutions which in their message unambiguously highlight the financial centre Luxembourg. *"Seule la BCEE perdure et laisse une trace visible, tant architecturale (par son bâtiment plateau Bourbon) qu'à travers son logo (le même bâtiment avec le pont Adolphe)"*[59] (Auxenfants 2007: 230).

---

58 | Personal translation: "Anchoredness in the history and society of Luxembourg".
59 | Personal translation: "Only the BCEE survives and leaves a visible trace, architecturally (by its building on the Plateau Bourbon) as well as by its logo (the same building with the Adolphe Bridge)".

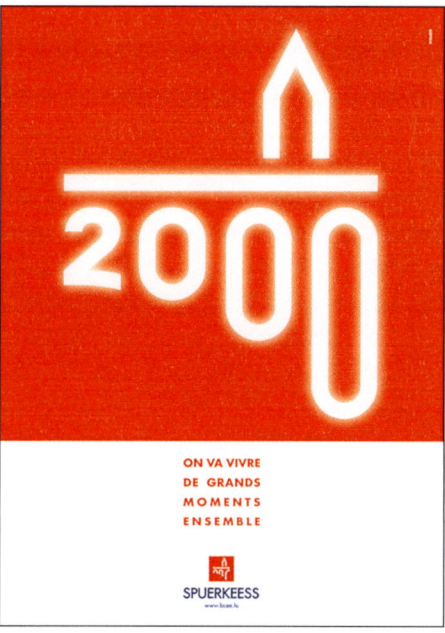

Figure 4: BCEE ad (Mikado, Luxembourg). Modified BCEE logo commemorating the turn of the century 1999/2000.

Figure 5: BGL ad (Mikado, Luxembourg).

However, besides local savers and investors, the cross-border workers are also important customers for the banks. They are courted with special cross-border worker offers, tailor-made to personal requirements and specific legal frameworks. Comparable to the slogan "*Wir machen den Weg frei*"[60] of the German *Volks- und Raiffeisenbanken*, Luxembourgish institutes advertise their ability to remove border-related obstacles and to offer cross-border banking services. The ad of the *Banque Générale du Luxembourg* (BGL), which has meanwhile merged with the *BNP Paribas*, integrates several symbols simultaneously: the national colours, with red providing a red carpet, the typical businessman and the archway which is open to both sides. Here, too, the path is cleared, boundaries are lifted which here not only involves financial but also of physical boundaries. The new *BGL BNP Parisbas* (since 21.9.2009), according to its own press release, unites in its name "*die tiefe nationale Verwurzelung von BGL als auch [...] die Solidität und das internationale Renommee von BNP Parisbas*"[61] while emphasising its position in today's society with the slogan "*Die Bank für eine Welt im Wandel*".[62]

Other service sectors, too, work with collective symbols with reference to Luxembourgish peculiarities. The mobile phone provider *LuxGSM* promoted its roaming offer by means of the collective symbol of the 'bridge'. The Pont Adolphe is shown as a national counterpart to the bridge of the 25th of April (Ponte 25 de Abril) in Portugal[63] and, at the same time, is its linear complement.

The bridge as a symbol of connection establishes the link to the product as well as the link to the consumers, in this case the Portuguese residents of Luxembourg. The image of the bridge is used on the assumption that the consumers are familiar with it, thus creating a disposition for a positive perception. Both the bridge and the mobile telecommunication establishes a connection between two places. Even without being familiar with the specific bridges, the ad can be understood, which underlines the bridge's function as a collective symbole.

---

60 | Personal translation: "We clear the path".
61 | Personal translation: "The profound national embeddedness of BGL as well as [...] the soundness and international reputation of BNP Parisbas".
62 | Personal translation: "The bank for a changing world".
63 | The bridge connects Almada with Lisbon. A landmark, although hardly discernible, is the Christo-Rei-statue in the background. At first glance, the bridge could easily be mistaken for the Golden Gate Bridge. This produces a sort of twofold meaning: If the specific national coding (Luxembourg/Portugal) is recognised, the ad, beyond the general symbolic meaning of the bridge, develops a potential added value in terms of national identification. If, however, it acts 'only' as Golden Gate Bridge or any nameless bridge, it serves as a general symbol for connections.

Figure 6: Ad for LuxGSM/Vodafone (Advantage, Luxembourg).

Communication and Identification in *Luxembourg and Greater Region – European Capital of Culture 2007*

A further example will serve to illustrate how Luxembourg is being represented graphically and textually. The cultural capital year *Luxemburg and Greater Region – European Capital of Culture 2007* was organised in the Grand Duchy and the surrounding Greater Region. As far as marketing communication and, in particular, advertising for this event were concerned, the goal was to identify Luxembourg in the context of the Greater Region by a process of attribution. "The Greater Region, laboratory of Europe" was the unifying leitmotif of Luxemburg 2007 and, at the same time, also an indication of the problems involved in its development and realisation (see Luxembourg 2007: 4-8). The image of the European laboratory could therefore also be utilised in a metaphorical sense in many areas of the cultural capital year and became the connecting collective symbol for the Greater Region. In addition to the usual difficulties which such big events can pose, the organisers saw themselves faced with the major challenge of integrating four countries, five regions and three languages into a coherent whole. "In these circumstances, the normal process of creating a coherent and accepted corporate identity became a major issue" (Luxembourg 2007: 53). One major goal of the marketing and communication operations was to construct a new (greater) regional 'identity' and the 'cultural identity' of the region. They were part of a superordinate strategy which, however, did not exist independently of specific contents, meaning the individual events and actions. In the eyes of the organisers the project was "*[dennoch] nicht nur ein Kulturfestival, sondern auch eine Standortpositionierung für die Großregion im europäischen Wettbewerb*"[64] (Garcia 2004: 5). The aim here was to emphasise Luxembourg's position as the 'motor' of Luxemburg 2007

---

64 | Personal translation: "*[The project]* was not merely a cultural festival; it also allowed the Greater Region to position itself in the context of European competition".

(see Luxembourg 2007: 53). For Luxembourg in particular, communication had the purpose to extend the image of how the Grand Duchy was perceived abroad beyond the clichés of 'financial centre', 'banks', 'Juncker' and 'petrol'. "Like the citizens of every capital, Luxembourgers sometimes tend to think they are the hub of the universe. Luxembourg may be strong on the financial and political map, but a fairly improbable cultural epicenter" (Luxembourg 2007: 100). From the outset it was clear that an image change is a protracted process that cannot be achieved by one event alone – even if it is a major one like the cultural capital year. Even if a comprehensive image change has not been achieved, it was at least possible to indicate the direction for future developments and Luxembourg was at least able to record a slight improvement in terms of the connection between cultural tourism and Luxembourg. The press campaign was summed up in the following words: "For once, Luxembourg had international media coverage unrelated to banks or Mr. [sic!] Juncker" (Luxembourg 2007: 77).

As a logo and therefore as a visual identity of the cultural capital year 2007, the 'Blue Deer' was chosen, suggested by the Luxembourg agency Bizart as their entry for the logo competition. The deer, it was said, would be able to connect the different parts of the Greater Region, based on the following considerations:

During the creation process, we tried to represent the impressive woods and large landscapes of the Greater Region, the nature which doesn't change from one country to the other. Of course there was this ironic touch in our graphical approach. Luxembourg is not London, Paris or New York. The blue deer represents in a very humble way the energy and the ambition of Luxembourg and the Greater Region to develop cultural life without ignoring the past of the 'terroir'[65].

The Blue Deer surprises with its unusual colour and, as an animal, it transcends the borders of the countries. Therefore, surprise and border-crossing – two central elements of the cultural capital concept – were united in one logo[66]. The varied discussions[67] surrounding the choice of the logo led to increased attention being paid to the event itself but also to its visual object of identification, the deer. Thanks to a multitude of banners, posters and blue steel sculptures, it established itself in Luxembourg as *the* symbol of *Luxembourg and Greater Region – European Capital of Culture 2007*[68].

---

65 | http://www.bizart.lu (13.10.2009)
66 | See http://www.granderegion.net/de/news/2005/03/20050311-2/index.html (16.12.2009)
67 | "The whole local press was scandalised and the audience just felt ridiculous to be identified by a primitive animal" (http://www.bizart.lu, 13.10.2009).
68 | "And then... after a few months, people discovered the humour and the fun of the logo, shame turned into pride... the blue deer which allowed 1000 and 1 interpretations

Figure 7: The Blue Deer, logo of the cultural capital year Luxembourg and Greater Region – European Capital of Culture 2007.

Beyond Luxembourg's borders, awareness of the cultural capital year was rather low, which, according to the concluding report, was due to several factors: the geographic expansion, the large number of involved partners, the three languages which loaded the already full programme even more, the programmatic marketing approach of equal treatment[69], and the comparatively late emphasis on beacon projects (Luxembourg 2007: 65). The communication strategy was very specific regarding the choice of the media being primarily geared towards the domestic audience. The media schedule which was also developed by a Luxembourg agency, had a budget of two million euros, yet scheduled only 10 % for international advertising (see Luxembourg 2007: 54). One of the principal reasons for this was the cost factor 'multilingualism' since the great majority of publications were published in three languages, German, French and English. This also explains why roughly 70 % of the media investments were allocated to the print sector (see Luxembourg 2007: 56-7). In Luxembourg, integrating newspapers, radio and television into the project was particularly successful. All in all, a large variety of media and means of communication were utilised.

In the field of PR, two main campaigns were launched, one for business customers and one for the general public. For the Luxembourg retail trade, the campaign "We support 2007" was initiated, aimed in particular at the tourism sector. 345 companies participated. For the visible identification with *Luxembourg and Greater Region – European Capital of Culture 2007*, they received a sticker with the slogan of the campaign and the Blue Deer logo, as well as a package with decoration material featuring the corporate design of the cultural

became one of the strongest brands Luxembourg had ever seen" (http://www.bizart.lu, 20.02.2010).

69 | Such an equal treatment was complicated particularly by the fact that the events and venues differed greatly in type and nature making it difficult to incorporate them under a common conceptual roof. The superordinate concept aside, the events primarily stood for themselves with each one requiring its own specific marketing.

capital year. The Blue Deer was frequently used by commercial sponsors during marketing campaigns, in this way visualising their identification with the event. Some domestic companies developed special products or altered them with a view to *Luxembourg and Greater Region – European Capital of Culture 2007*. The mineral water company *Rosport* identified its *Rosport Blue* with the Blue Deer, the winemaking cooperative *Domaines de Vinsmoselle* launched a new product, the *Blu-Blu-Deer* sparkling wine and the porcelain maker *Villeroy & Boch* produced cups bearing the deer logo (see Luxembourg 2007: 75). In this way, the purchase and consumption of these products and many other merchandising articles provided people with a multidimensional identification with the event.

In addition to the simple marking of this major event with the aid of the uniform design featuring the striking blue colour coding and the deer, we will now seek to examine some other ways how interdiscursive, respectively metaphorical forms of expression were established within the framework of *Luxembourg and Greater Region – European Capital of Culture 2007*, providing further possibilities for association. An analysis of selected advertising and information material[70] serves to reveal the degree of characteristic representation of Luxembourg in images and words. Here, too, it is primarily a matter of attribution processes. What, according to this information and advertising material, constitutes Luxembourg's 'identity'? Which main focuses are established? Can we see a departure from the stereotype and progress towards new aspects, including culture as a translocal medium? In the symbolism of the imagery or graphic representation of the Grand Duchy, two larger complexes seem to emerge which can, in turn, be arranged into smaller, thematically distinguishable sub-complexes: 'Tradition' and 'Modernism'.

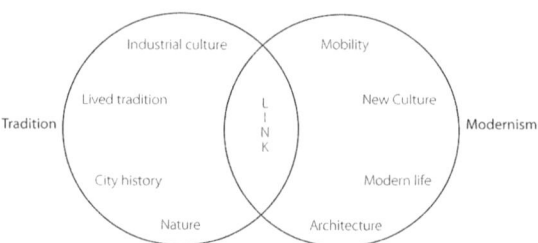

Figure 8: Complexes of Luxembourg representations.

The complex 'tradition' incorporates the following areas (in brackets examples of the images which can be assigned to the corresponding areas): Industrial culture

---

70 | The following leaflets were taken into account: *"Tourisme Tourismus"*, *"Mobil(e) 2007"*, *"Panorama 2007"*, *"Luxembourg et Grande Région, Capitale européenne de la culture"*, *"LuxembourgCard 2007"*, *"Luxembourg and Greater Region, European Capital of Culture 2007"*, *"Trans(ident)city"*, *"explorator"*, *"Avant-Programme. Nouveaux espaces – Lieux insolites"*, *"Luxemburg und Großregion Kulturhauptstadt Europas 2007"*.

(industrial facilities in Belval), history of the town and the fortress[71] (*Bockfiels/ Kasematten*), nature (waterway), practiced traditions (Schober fair, large funfair of Luxembourg City). These areas are visualised in the examples mentioned above and others. 'Modernism' constitutes a second complex. It can be divided into the following subareas: Mobility (TGV connection to Paris), new culture concepts (long night of the museums), architecture (red bridge[72]), modern living/leisure activities (Cocque sports and event centre). Some images cannot be clearly assigned to either category and can therefore be seen as a representation of the connection between tradition and modernity, respectively transition. This includes, for example, an image with the perspective '*Bockfiels, Dräi Eechelen, Mudam, Kirchberg*'[73], which visualises the chronology of development, of the joining of the old with the new.

Several brochures also include maps of the Greater Region[74]. They exist in two different versions. One features solely the Greater Region intersected by the various regional and national borders, while the other displays the Greater Region on the European map, where it is shown as one coherent unit without borders.

Figure 9: The Greater Region – without borders and in the heart of 'the core of Europe', as this map seems to suggest.

---

71 | See also section 6.2.
72 | Important bridge connection between Luxembourg city and the commercial and EU quarter of Kirchberg.
73 | While the *Bockfiels* is thought to have been the first location of a fortification dating fom the year 963, the Kirchberg with its bank and EU buildings represents modern Luxembourg. Here, we can also find the *Mudam*, the *Musée d'Art Moderne Grand-Duc Jean*. Between the two stands the rebuilt fort called *Dräi Eechelen*.
74 | "*Tourisme Tourismus*", "*Mobil(e) 2007*", "*Luxembourg et Grande Région, Capitale européenne de la culture*", "*Luxembourg and Greater Region, European Capital of Culture 2007*", "*explorator*", "*Luxemburg und Großregion Kulturhauptstadt Europas 2007*".

The pretension to being a region that offers employment across borders or opportunities for creative (cultural) work uninhibited by boundaries is expressed here symbolically in cartographic terms. To the beholder, the following is suggested: the Greater Region is well and truly a really large region in the centre of Europe and has uniform features. The operationalisation of the space takes place by means of iconic or symbolic coding in the sense of an attribution process (see Dünne 2008: 50). Here, it is not only a matter of the illustration of social contexts within a given space and/or the depiction of existing territories, but the cartography fulfills both functions. Therefore, the map is a sort of medium for "*Welterzeugung*"[75] (Dünne 2008: 52). And, in the age of globalisation, it is also an aid for providing individuals as well as groups with an overview in the midst of processes that are far from clear. From this could follow the preservation of individual and collective capacity to act in the political sense of the term (see Dünne 2008: 53). The Greater Region as a sphere of action, at least at a socio-economical level, is to a large extent a reality, albeit partly only on a small scale and not comprehensively. At a cultural level, *Luxembourg 2007* should contribute important stimuli.

Let us now turn our attention to the texts of the brochures. These relate to the illustrations, but also point to other images and symbols which can meanwhile be identified as collective symbols, not only for Luxembourg but presumably also for the Greater Region. We will take a closer look at two larger discursive units: 'border' and 'Europe'. The cultural capital tour 2007 is described as a 'cross-border experience'. The "*Blick über den Tellerrand*"[76] implies this crossing of borders which already looks back on a certain tradition in the region, in fact on "*2000 Jahre wechselvolle, geteilte Geschichte(n)*"[77]. Consequently, the crossing of borders is also described as a 'communal' action. Besides the notion of the crossing, we can also find the aspect of boundlessness which, conversely, would make a crossing of borders impossible because borders no longer exist. It is in this context that one should see the claim to "place the 'unified' Greater Region on the European map" (which cartographically has already been done). The transborder cultural programme is introduced as a unifying project in which borders are to be seen "*nicht als Hindernisse, sondern (als) Beitrag zur Dynamik*".[78]

There are many commonalities between the transborder discourse and the European discourse, which is dealt with in a very specific manner regarding Luxembourg and the Greater Region. Linguistic-symbolic representations of Luxembourg play a central role: "*Europa kompakt*"[79], "*(im) Herz(en) Europas*"[80], "mix of communities, cultural identities and emotions", "European Laboratory",

---

75 | Personal translation: "Creating the world".
76 | Personal translation: "Looking over the rim of the (proverbial) teacup".
77 | Personal translation: "2000 years of eventful and shared history and stories".
78 | Personal translation: "Not as obstacles but as contributing to dynamism".
79 | Personal translation: "Compact version of Europe".
80 | Personal translation: "(In) the heart of Europe".

"*eine Hauptstadt Europas*".[81] The significance of the space is underlined by using the symbolism of the heart which not only clarifies the geographical position, but also implies that the heart is the central element of a body[82]. The symbolism of the laboratory relates to the mixture of cultures as well as to the "compact version of Europe", because these are the two attributes that define the laboratory setting in Luxembourg and its surroundings. In this context, allusions to the traditional attributes 'international banks' and 'European quarter' seem unavoidable.

In addition and in analogy to the analysis of the visual symbolism, it is worth giving some attention to textual representations that mark a sort of transition or are located at interfaces. For instance, there is mention of the old and new as being "in harmony" or the *MUDAM* art museum is described as a connection between the old and the new. In the comments dealing with the Dudelange steel factory, the following quote is a good example: "*Stahlschmelze als 'Schmelztiegel' für Mentalitäten und Kulturen*".[83]

This, in its effects, positive representation of a situation that appears to be exemplary in every way is the result of a rigorous and consistent implementation of the conceptual objectives for *Luxembourg 2007*. The outcome is a reduced use of customary symbols and clichés which cannot be entirely abandoned since without them an effective characterisation of Luxembourg presumably would not work beyond the region. They are joined to new, and different, surfaces of identification and connection at whose argumentational key points culture can become an effective medium of identification.

New Options for 'We' Identity in Luxembourg's Advertising Discourse?

Marketing communication in Luxembourg, typical examples of which were discussed above relating to advertising in the (financial) service sector and communication in the framework of *Luxembourg and Greater Region – European Capital of Culture 2007*, employs, in certain cases, concepts which characterise the Grand Duchy in terms of an attribution process by means of a specific iconographic and written language. Here, symbolisms are brought into play which can be identified as collective symbols because they are also evident in other interdiscourses, such as in the journalistic discourse[84]. Their utilisation permits the construction of a uniform discursive space. In terms of an appropriation process, this facilitates the association of individuals or groups with the images and the symbolisms conveyed by them. Whereas examples from the private sector tend to rely on classical semantics (tradition, trust etc.), communication relating to *Luxembourg and Greater Region – European Capital of Culture 2007*, by contrast, attempts to induce an image

---

81 | Personal translation: "A European capital".
82 | See section 6.2 and 5.6.
83 | Personal translation: "Steel melt as a 'crucible' for mentalities and cultures."
84 | See section 6.2.

change by combining familiar/classical images with new ones (tradition/modernism, border/Europe). It would be a worthwhile task for future investigations to examine the question to what extent Luxembourg's advertising discourse has been and is absorbing new images and symbolisms that distinguish themselves from the traditional ones. If this amounted to an image change, it could indeed indicate a re-orientation in the notion of a 'Luxembourg identity'.

6.5 Decontextualising and Deconstructing Representations of Identity: an Analysis of the Works of Seven Photographers

The emergence of an inter-/national artistic milieu, which has coincided with the opening of new spaces for contemporary art, and the creation of European art events in Luxembourg offer ample opportunities for studying questions on the (de)construction and decontextualisation of attributed and appropriated identities in the framework of visual and linguistic representations. A number of major cultural events, such as 'Luxembourg and Greater Region – European Capital of Culture 2007', as well as specific commissions linked to questions of Luxembourg's cultural identity, such as the project in the MUDAM[85] (*Portraits du Luxembourg*), or initiatives by some cities (*Portraits d'une Région, Moins de la Photo*, etc.), have influenced the choice of works that illustrate the artists' positions.

The current situation, a result of artistic and photographic education based on mobility, interdisciplinarity and the decompartmentalisation of artistic expression, shows the importance of photography's role in scrutinising representations within contemporary art.

The works by the seven photographers from Luxembourg and other countries, who were chosen on the merit of their artistic competence and standing, are set in the context of the loss of artistic, cultural, political, social and identity-related reference points. The dissolution of borders and the increasing importance of the circulation of ideas, that have proven conducive for the flourishing of multiculturality and even transculturality, have had a disruptive effect on the representations connected with this discourse. Rather than bringing a specific locality into focus, the analysed images show both a contextual approach and an international openness that take into account issues relating to the medium of photography and its equivocal relationship to reality.

Today's photographic practice no longer restricts itself to recording reality, thereby going beyond the stage of faithful representation. Concerning this process of metamorphosis, we concur with Philippe Dubois, who noted that, "*la photographie*

---

85 | *Musée d'Art moderne Grand-Duc Jean.*

est moins un contact (un indice) qu'un mouvement vers le contact (fiction)"[86] (Dubois 1983, as quoted by Labelle and Bonaccorsi 2005).

With the photographers whose work we analysed, their relation to the real lies in the sphere between indexicality and iconicity, the *print* only being the point of departure from which the photographic idea develops. This idea is also linked to the contexts of production and circulation; it determines the photograph's auratic dimension and requires a process of creative interpretation, which involves the viewers' significant participation in the sphere between physical image and mental projection.

Drawing on specific examples of photography produced within institutional contexts, this study seeks to identify the particularities and singularities that are possible in the interrelationship between attributed and appropriated identities. For the purposes of this study we chose seven photographers of international standing whose commissioned works have been presented in recent exhibitions and publications, notably in connection with the cultural year 2007.

In terms of methodology, we chose four strands of analysis relating to the images' production, description/analysis, reception/diffusion as well as the correspondence and comparison between them. By using *interdiscursive* references and borrowings, this interaction between the authors and their works, encourages the debate with the viewer in a hermeneutic approach. We identified the following themes from the corpus of selected images:

1. Middle-class *vanitas*[87], consumer society, clichés, stereotypes;
2. Anachronisms, resistance to progress, timelessness;
3. Decontextualisation of symbols, questioning of identity-forming referents.

We have arranged the themes and the authors based on their differences and complementarities, with a particular emphasis on the comparison between photographers of different nationalities.

Enacting Clichés and Stereotypes

Our first thematic category shows how an English artist and a Luxembourgish artist interpret, in entirely different visual languages, clichés and stereotypes by means of locations and enactments of consumption.

Invited for *Luxembourg and Greater Region – European Capital of Culture 2007*, Martin Parr (born 1952) contributed the series *Luxembourg 2006/Assorted Cocktail*

---

86 | Personal translation: "Photography is less a contact (an indication) than a movement towards contact (fiction)".

87 | We use the term *vanitas* here in the sense of an expression of superficial vanity and transitoriness, as well as of triviality and complacency, particularly in connection with a consumer-oriented way of life.

(commissioned by Coordination 2007, in collaboration with *Magnum Photos*) which depicts scenes from everyday life. As he has done in other countries and cities before, he searched for significant situations in Luxembourg's 'typical' places: vernissages, restaurants, confectioneries, shop windows, single-family homes, and small gardens. At first glance, these photographs taken during his travels appear to be random snapshots, but a closer look reveals that Parr has mastered what Cartier-Bresson calls the "*instant décisif*"[88] in the composition of these images. This can be observed in the entire series, which is characterised by a mixture of shots shaped by the immediacy of the situation and personal projections inherent in the artist's photographic language.

Figure 10: Martin Parr, Luxembourg 2006/Assorted Cocktail © *Martin Parr/Magnum Photos.*

In the photograph of the hands (fig. 10), we can see how Parr, choosing an impromptu situation, deconstructs the image, opening it up to multiple visual and iconic interpretations. Compared to the peasant women's coarse and work-worn hands in Russell Lee's "*photographie humaniste*" (*Family of Man*)[89], which unequivocally subscribes to a monosemantic iconography, Parr's composition underscores the dualities of natural/artificial, true/false, strong/fragile. Details such as the gold jewellery or the sleeves' fur hem contrast ironically with the black-and-white zigzag pattern of the artificial fingernails and the bandaid on the right hand's index finger. The shallow depth of field, the close-up format and the downward angle allow the

---

88 | Personal translation: "Decisive moment".
89 | Even though Martin Parr stated his interest for the *Family of Man* exhibition, his own artistic stance is quite distinctive in that he emphasises, through the framing, the colours and the lighting, the ironic and caustic side of his approach.

photographer to focus on the somewhat stereotypical gesture of hands holding a wallet, as a metonymous substitution of consumer society.

Figure 11: Martin Parr, Luxembourg 2006/Assorted Cocktail
© *Martin Parr/Magnum Photos.*

In associating this photograph with the photograph LUX (fig. 11), on which we see a detail of a sign post[90]. Parr illustrates the triviality of luxury, by reinforcing the cliché of Luxembourg as a country of artificial and superficial values. The chosen detail from an object referring to the word Luxembourg, is significant to Parr's approach. With his partial views and his focus on suggestive details, he seeks to give the viewers food for thought.

This stance of contemplating and observing is stimulated by enhancing the symbolic elements that echo iconographic references, and by establishing formal and thematic links within the series *Luxembourg 2006/Assorted Cocktail*.

In this series, the human presence is often limited to the specific active or inactive parts of the body in banal contexts that acquire their significance in the overall picture. The hands in Parr's photographs have different, sometimes ambiguous meanings. This contrast of contents and forms is all the more important as it constantly creates associations with real situations and attributed identities: one photo shows work-worn hands that have been given an exaggerated significance by the conspicuous artificial nails, while on another wee see truncated hands whereby the steep angle emphasises the lack of communication. On this last picture (fig. 12), the fur hat in the foreground appears to metaphorically fill the void between the fork and knife.

---

90 | The two photographs were featured on the same page of a leaflet released for the exhibition *Luxembourg 2006/Assorted Cocktail* as part of *Luxembourg and Greater Region – European Capital of Culture.*

Figure 12: Martin Parr, Luxembourg 2006/Assorted Cocktail © *Martin Parr/ Magnum Photos.*

Rather than observe the stereotypes in real situations, the Luxembourgish artist Jeanine Unsen creates depictions that are the result of a long process of searching, during which she gathers countless accessories that become a theatre of artificial situations, where Luxembourgish tourist knick-knacks and human subjects are assembled to form the elements of photographic paintings.

In her series *Odd, small and beautiful,* commissioned in 2009 by Luxembourg City, Unsen speaks of Luxembourgish identities in an expressive, vivid language that permits, due to the exaggeration of the depiction, a certain detachment and, at the same time, a feeling of appropriation, due to the accumulation of mementos, suggesting potential personification. The artist integrates identity-forming representations in scenographic contexts and portraits that complement the scene with their stereotypical dimension.

With kitschy consumer objects representing collective national symbols (images of the Palace, the Grand Ducal couple, the coat of arms, Adolph Bridge, plates imprinted with *Banque et Caisse d'Epargne de l'Etat*[91], glasses, wallpaper, etc.) she develops what she calls a *"nostalgie critique"*[92], i.e. a vision that is both caustic and nostalgic.

Il y a quelque chose des traditions villageoises en moi qui perdure et que je ne ridiculise aucunement, mais que je relève à travers mes mises en scène photographiques. Chaque

---

91 | Luxembourg's State Savings Bank.
92 | Personal translation: "Critical nostalgia".

accessoire me rappelle en quelque sorte mon enfance alors que paradoxalement ces objets sont fabriqués en tant que souvenirs pour les touristes[93] (di Felice 2009).

Figures 13-16: Jeanine Unsen, Odd, small and beautiful, *2009 © Jeanine Unsen. Courtesy MHVL.*

---

93 | Personal translation: "There is something of a village tradition in me that prevails and that I don't ridicule at all, but that I reveal through my photography. Each accessory reminds me somehow of my childhood, although paradoxically these objects are made as souvenirs for tourists."

The figures represented in the four photographs by Unsen (a heterosexual couple, a homosexual couple, and two portraits of women, fig. 13-16) belong to the scenery of this artificial universe. By adopting a fictional character, the photographs question the clichés through mementos representing symbols that are intended to be moved (e.g. postcards and knick-knacks with images of the Grand Duke, the Adolphe Bridge, etc. generally acquired in remembrance of the place), but re-integrating them into an artificial everyday context.

Whereas Parr draws his inspiration from Luxembourg's reality when taking his photographs in his own particular style (geared more towards the alienation of behaviour and the universality of contexts than national differentiations of identity – images of Madonnas in Luxembourg and in Mexico, images of consumption in Mexico, Luxembourg, Ireland, etc.), Unsen reconstructs situations in artificial Luxembourgish contexts that directly refer to symbolic representations.

In presenting his photographs as *vanitas* that express middle-class archetypes found in different countries, Parr allows us to interpret scenes that contain both particularities and universalities regarding the Luxembourgish context. Thus the photographs *Luxembourg 2006/Assorted Cocktail* show the vision a 'foreign' artist has of Luxembourg – with characteristics shared within the same middle class everywhere as the central theme running through his work – but also allows Luxembourgers to discover in these stereotypical images a reflection of their own notions of identity.

Current Representations of a Bygone Era

The second thematic category is concerned with the representation of past and present in today's Luxembourg in the black-and-white works of Luxembourgish photographer Yvon Lambert ("*photographie humaniste*") and French photographer Valérie Belin ("*photographie plasticienne*").

With the series *Derniers feux*[94], commissioned by the city of Esch-sur-Alzette, Yvon Lambert retraces the final days of operation of blast furnace B at Esch-Belval, thereby paying tribute to the Minette region as a place of remembrance that shows the energy of work in a poetic and sacral ambience (fig. 17 and 18).

We only ever get to see partial views of the blast furnace, while innumerable details (pipes, gloves, bolts, funnels, casting samples, chutes, etc.) contrast with the dark backgrounds and the blurred sections of the black-and-white photographs. The dramatic lighting underscores the sublimation of the worker's movement (*flou-bougée*) (see Lorgé 1998) and establishes the metaphysical relationship between man and his work environment, which is aesthetised by the photographer.

---

94 | These photographs were taken in August 1997 at the latest. Blast Furnace B at the Joint Steelworks of Burbach, Eich and Dommeldange (ARBED), the last blast furnace of the Grand Duchy of Luxembourg, was shut down on 28 August 1997 at 19:00 hours.

Figure 17: Yvon Lambert, Coulée et granulation de laitier[95] *1997 © Yvon Lambert.*

Figure 18: Yvon Lambert, Nettoyage des bleeders[96] *1997 © Yvon Lambert.*

Lambert chooses a photographic language (composed framing, saturation of black, lighting contrasts, etc.) that reflects *"la force plastique d'un environnement à priori plus soucieux de productivité que d'esthétique"*[97] (Lambert, 1998: 3), that an entire region identifies with. In choosing this type of black-and-white photography, he attempts to confer timelessness to a bygone era.

In the series *Differdange – à la rencontre d'un lieu*, commissioned by the city of Differdange and created between 2003 and 2005, we again encounter this anachronistic attitude and Lambert's way of neutralising temporality with his work techniques (slowness, reconnaissance, documentation, etc.) and his photographic style that marks all of his projects (fig. 20-22).

In an interview with journalist Thierry Hick, Lambert says: *"... J'ai aussi voulu montrer que cette industrie reste toujours d'actualité dans la région. Mes photos sont un trait d'union entre le passé et le présent"*.[98] Hick continues: *"Dans son travail, le photographe, un 'Minettsdapp'*[99]*, part à la recherche de son identité, mais aussi de ses racines. Une recherche valable tant pour l'artiste que pour le visiteur"*[100] (Hick 2003: 9).

---

95 | Personal translation: "Wetting and granulating the slag".
96 | Personal translation: "Cleaning the bleeders".
97 | Personal translation: "The palpable power of an environment inherently more concerned with productivity than with aesthetics".
98 | Personal translation: "...I've also wanted to show how this industry is still relevant in the region. My photos are a link between past and present".
99 | *Minettsdapp* refers to a resident of the Minette region
100 | Personal translation: "In his work, the photographer, a *Minettsdapp*, goes in search of his identity, but also his roots. A worthwhile search both for the artist and for the visitor".

Figure 19: Yvon Lambert, Differdange, Arcelor-aciérie[101], *2003* © *Yvon Lambert*.

The image of Differdange that Lambert suggests shows little, apparently insignificant things and unspectacular situations, rather than 'postcard' representations of the town.

The play between past and present in the photographs (fig. 20 and 21) *Differdange, Grand-Rue 2003* and *Differdange, rue Michel Rodange 2004* is remarkable. Despite the contrasts illustrating the changes in this region, these images show the artist's nostalgic affection for his origins.

Figure 20: Yvon Lambert, Differdange, Grand-Rue, *2003* © *Yvon Lambert.*

Figure 21: Yvon Lambert, Differdange, rue Michel Rodange, *2004* © *Yvon Lambert.*

Figure 22: Yvon Lambert, Differdange, Café Chez Quim, *2004* © *Yvon Lambert.*

While we can observe a certain symbiosis between the photographer and his environment in the photographs described here, the series *Vitrines du Luxembourg*

---

101 | Differdange, Arcelor steelworks.

(2003, fig. 23 and 24) by French artist Valérie Belin reveals, by contrast, a significant degree of conceptual detachment. This series, commissioned by the MUDAM in 2002 as part of a project entitled *Portraits du Luxembourg*, is composed of seven large contemporary prints in black and white, representing seven antiquated looking shop windows in Luxembourg City exhibiting old-fashioned clothing and accessories in window displays reminiscent of the 1960s.

Figures 23-24: Valérie Belin, Vitrines du Luxembourg, 2003 © *Valerie Belin. Courtesy* MUDAM.

Belin has gone in search of places where the past is still present. She achieves this by avoiding the common and stereotype motifs that would normally be used for a portrait of Luxembourg. The photographs of objects representing the Luxembourg of old, mirror the city of today and explore the hidden identity aspects of a city in transition.

Despite the apparent similarities of Lambert's and Belin's shop windows, they are diametrically opposed in that the photographer of *Differdange – à la rencontre d'un lieu* creates a space of projection where his personal biography (*Minettsdapp*) mix with the appropriated identities of the viewer, while the photographer of *Vitrines du Luxembourg* seems to erect a screen on which the dualities of past/ present, old/new and interior/exterior are projected.

By placing the residents of the Minette region at the centre of his work, Lambert creates images that facilitate the viewer's identification and complicity with the place – in contrast to Belin, who substitutes mannequins and clothing for people, creating an image of detachment that leaves little room for identity-forming notions.

Decontextualisations

Coming to our third theme, the decontextualisation of emblems, we will attempt to explore the symbolic places represented in the photographs of Andrés Lejona, Marco Godinho and Joël Tettamanti.

To mark the occasion of the national holiday on 23 June, when the Grand Duke's birthday is celebrated, a series by the Spanish photographer Andrés Lejona, a resident of Luxembourg since the mid 1960s, was published in the magazine *Rendez-Vous*[102], entitled *F(en)êt(r)es Nationales* (fig. 25-27). The series presents ten colour photographs of shop windows in the capital that show the Grand Ducal couple in official or family photos, partly in window displays especially arranged for the national holiday.

Like Martin Parr, Lejona draws his inspiration from Luxembourgish reality, in this particular instance the national holiday, isolating the national symbols with tight framings and, by combining them with other details, making them appear grotesque. The photo of the Grand Ducal couple, sometimes set in a conventional window display (clothing, toys, etc.), sometimes integrated into a sophisticated staging (flag of Luxembourg, the red lion from the national coat of arms – fig. 27) is the *leitmotif* that dominates the centre of these images.

Figures 25-27: Andrés Lejona, F(en)êt(r)es Nationales, *2009 © Andrés Lejona. Courtesy Rendez-Vous.*

Positioned between critical thinking and sympathy, the photographer has shown a fine sense of humour in creating this series, which is a tribute to the Luxembourgers while at the same time questioning the cult around the Grand Duke. One of the images shows the Grand Ducal couple as if they were part of a fairy-tale world (Snow White, Tintin, the Smurfs, etc.), ridiculing the depiction of monarchist veneration (fig. 25), whereas in another, the photograph of the couple finds itself

---

102 | Lejona, Andrés. 2009. F(en)êt(r)es nationales. Rendez-Vous. City Magazine Luxembourg 6: 46-57.

trapped between the shop window and the metal security gate (fig. 26), suggesting the ambiguity between protection and imprisonment.

Through the interplay of the picture in the picture, successive image planes and reflections, Lejona creates a subtle detachment in relation to the 'representations of national identity'. Even if these photographs were taken within the framework of a national holiday, they are characteristic of Lejona's search for the unusual, which permits an alienation of real situations and aims to decontextualise the representations.

With the work *Le guide mental du Luxembourg* (2007) (fig. 28-31), commissioned by the Luxembourg City Historical Museum for 'Luxembourg and Greater Region – European Capital of Culture 2007', Portuguese-born Luxembourg artist Marco Godinho presents a photographic installation composed of horizontal photo strips on the topic of migration and population movements in Luxembourg.

Figure 28: Marco Godinho, Le guide mental du Luxembourg, *2007 © Marco Godinho Courtesy MHVL.*

From digital photographs, Godhino created a panoramic collage (fig. 29-31) in which he transfers, repeats and shifts symbols, emblems and signals in order to blur the lines of identification. He explores identity referents in order to deconstruct them and compare them to different processes of transculturality, examining among other things the notions of territory, borders and geographic belonging.

L'œuvre se lit comme une carte d'un monde où les trajectoires reflètent les flux migratoires, pose la question du multiculturalisme, de l'immigration au Luxembourg et reflète l'essence même de la mobilité et des échanges interculturels, entre passé, présent et avenir[103] (Damiani n.d.).

---

103 | Personal translation: "The work can be read like a map of the world, where the trajectories reflect migration flows, posing the question of multiculturality, of migration to Luxembourg, and reflects the very essence of mobility and intercultural exchanges, between past, present and future".

Figure 29-31: Details.

If Godhino's work of fiction illustrates the notion of topographical displacement, the series *LUX 2005* (fig. 32 and 33), created as part of the commission *Portraits du Luxembourg*, by Joël Tettamanti shows how decontextualisation is produced by means of post-industrial landscapes in the Minette region, which connect the traces of past and present.

Chosen by the Swiss photographer of Italian origin because of his identification with an area where immigration has played a big role, the Minette region reflects, for him, a specific regional identity that he has sought to capture in its process of change.

Figures 32-33: Joël Tettamanti, LUX 2005, 2005 © Joël Tettamanti Courtesy MUDAM.

These large photographic tableaus with their almost abstract forms and colours symbolising the region (red earth) tell of sites fallen into decline and reveal the footprints of an era.

As in a palimpsest, these photographs show the traces of destruction and reconstruction of these sites that are witnesses to an industrial past associated with the cultural identity of a region in transition.

In this third thematic series then, we can distinguish the humorous and ironic alienation of symbols in Lejona's compositions and Godhino's collages on the one hand, and the temporal and spatial shift in the photographic tableaus of Tettamanti on the other.

Conclusions

To summarise, we have seen that the Spanish photographer Lejona's occasionally caustic usage of national identity representations corresponds with the accumulation of symbols in the living pictures of Luxembourg artist Unsen, even if the works differ in their poietic perspectives. In his take on the representations of the Grand Ducal couple as the symbol of the nation, Lejona creates detachment, but also in his search for the unusual and the shift of emphasis within real situations. By contrast, Unsen distances herself from these representative images, constructing interiors where emblems are reduced to decorative elements.

There are also correspondences between Tettamanti's post-industrial landscapes and Belin's 'anachronistic' windows, created by the decontextualisation and spatio-temporal shifts leading to the loss of appropriated identity referents. The urban reflections symbolising a past that is still present are juxtaposed with the palimpsests signifying the marks of transition in post-industrial landscapes.

Whereas Godhino, in deconstructing Luxembourg's significant landscapes, does not take an outright stand but creates a space of questioning obliging the viewers to adopt a reflexive stance towards their own identities, Parr, in his familiar photographic style, lays the emphasis on the behaviour patterns of the Luxembourgers, by comparing vulgarity, superficiality and lux(ury). Closer to reality, the series *Luxembourg 2006/Assorted Cocktail* by Parr appears to mirror the image of Luxembourgish society as it is often perceived in the form of collective clichés and analysed in subsections 6.2, 6.3 and 6.4. However, Parr's particular photographic language, with its fragmented views and its focus on suggestive details, allows us to go beyond this stereotypical perspective and encourages us to take a closer look, provoking a rupture with the identification process inherent in these images.

Without discounting the effect they might have on the construction of identities in Luxembourg, more importantly, the photographs discussed here reveal the significance of each artist's notions about identity attributions. By drawing their inspiration from similar situations and contexts, the artists recreate a personalised universe where different types of reproduced, constructed, re-appropriated or attributed images come together, questioning the representations as much through the image within an image technique (*mise en abyme*) as through the deconstructions of identity discourses. Instead of submitting the different representations to objective scrutiny, the artists *avoid* the national context and express their dissenting views in visual constructions, which they transpose into a personal formal language.

There is no doubt that all these examples of photographs that were created in a specific contemporary artistic context *sketch*, in various degrees and manners, the question of appropriated and attributed identities, but rather than assign a significant role to the construction of identities, they offer a space for questioning and reflection in relation to our own identities, which find themselves increasingly deconstructed from one image to the next.

6.6 The Representation of Italian Immigrants in the Exhibition Catalogue *Retour de Babel*

As already outlined in section 6.2, the major event *Luxembourg and Greater Region – European Capital of Culture 2007* as an interdiscursive event provided the opportunity to renegotiate different collective symbols. In this context, the term 'European laboratory' assigned to this cross-border region is of fundamental significance. It refers, among other things, to the 'multicultural' composition of Luxembourg society in which the foreign population exceeds 40 %. In the light of this, it is no surprise that the coordinating body of the event, in 2007, decided to make 'migration' the central theme. Both in the historiographic and in the political discourse of the last decades Luxembourg society has been defined as 'open' and 'integration-friendly'. Frequent reference is made to historic 'phases' of immigration and emigration movements in order to emphazise Luxembourg's international and traditionally multicultural character. The exhibition *Retour de Babel* was, according to the organisers, the main event of the 'European Capital of Culture 2007' on the subject of 'migration' and was on display over several months in the former ironworks of the city of Dudelange. In offering a comprehensive picture as possible of the immigration and emigration movements in Luxembourg, the aim was not only to erect a memorial to the migrants, but also to sensitise the audience to the various forms of migration. In the following we will inquire how and whether collective identity is attributed to Italian immigrants in the catalogue *Retour de Babel*.

Migration in Luxembourg

Historical overview

The image, still widespread among the population, of Luxembourg as a poor emigration country up to the time of industrialisation and since then as a rich immigration country, has long been called into questioned by the findings of historical studies, but also by various articles in the catalogue *Retour de Babel* (see Pauly 1986; Reuter/Ruiz 2008). According to the prevailing public discourse[104], the history of Luxembourg as a country of immigration does not begin until the 1890s in connection with the (so-called) 'first immigration wave' of Italians looking for work during the industrialisation. Historians have however proven that the first Italian industrial workers already came to Luxembourg via Lorraine from the 1870s onwards, in search of employment mainly in the steel industry. Evidence has also shown that there was work migration in Luxembourg already in medieval times (Reuter 1995). Sedentariness is declared a myth and migration the norm (Hahn 2008: 16). It was only the demarcations of the nation states that turned people into 'indigenous and foreigners'. Bilateral agreements between Portugal and Yugoslavia (1972) as well as familial and local networks explain the conspicuous presence of Italian and Portuguese migrants in Luxembourg.

The Italian immigration wave continued into the early 1960s, after which Portuguese immigration increased. Male immigrants mainly included steel workers and construction workers, but also freelancers, above all craftsmen and grocers (Gallo 1992). The major part of the female immigrants were wives who

---

104 | E.g. in *Histoire du Luxembourg. Le destin européen d'un 'petit pays'*, one can read the following: "En s'industrialisant, le Luxembourg, de pays rural pauvre et donc d'émigration, se transforme en terre d'immigration" (Trausch 2003: 268). Personal translation: "At the outset a poor rural country typified by emigration, Luxembourg transformed itself, in the course of its industrialisation, into a territory for immigration".

followed their husbands after some years; many of them were employed as shop assistants, cleaners and partly also as blue-collar workers in industry. Today, Italian immigration is low and comprises, above all, highly skilled employees who work in the banks and EU institutions (Langers 1999).

Political Discourses on Immigration in Luxembourg

In Luxembourg it was recognised considerably earlier, at least at the political level, than in the two big neighbouring countries France and Germany that the country is a 'country of immigration' and consequently that immigrants were not 'guest workers' but people who had come to Luxembourg to stay and now belonged to its society. This perception is revealed in many different political discourses, particularly on the occasion of international state visits, or in general on the subject of 'Europe', which time and time again emphasise the multiculturalism and traditional openness of the Luxembourgers. Nevertheless, this representation has but little effect on, firstly, concrete measures for a better co-existence or for a conscious integration policy and secondly on a broader recognition within society of Luxembourg as a 'country of immigration'.

However, at least since end of the 1970s, parts of the civil society have been concerning themselves with the issue of immigration in Luxembourg. For instance, in 1978, the *Association de soutien aux travailleurs immigrés* (ASTI) was founded, followed by the *Comité de liaison des associations étrangères* (CLAE) (1985) and *Centre de documentation sur les migrations humaines* (CDMH) (1996), to name but the largest organisations. While these may have different aims and political motivations, they have one thing in common in that they are committed to the recognition of migrants in Luxembourg.

It was indeed the two last-named organisations, which, together with the municipality of Dudelange, also prepared the exhibition *Retour de Babel* which aimed at showing the different phases and forms of migration in Luxembourg.

We will deal here mainly with the representation of Italian immigrants in the exhibition catalogue *Retour de Babel* because there is a 'master narrative'[105] about Italian immigration, related to history and recollections, to which one can compare these representations. The image of Italian immigrants outlined in the 'master narrative' attributes to them a collective identity which is based on the image of the steel worker and the notion of successful integration.

Discourses on Italian Immigration in Luxembourg

In order to examine discourses on Italian immigration, political speeches, publications as well as the activities and contents of the websites[106] of different

---

105 | Also known as 'Meta' or 'Grand Narrative'. One can define the 'Master Narrative' as the main image conveyed by public historical experience (see Lyotard 1979).
106 | www.italiani.lu, www.passaparola.info

organisations were reviewed. The catalogue *Retour de Babel* is also to be understood as a generator of these discourses.

Consensus discourse or 'Master Narrative': Italian immigrants are perceived primarily as steel workers[107] whose labour has contributed to industrialisation and with it to the wealth of Luxembourg. This image appears in the introductory text of the catalogue; however, it is also being conveyed at a political level. Until recently, reference to this was made in speeches of the head of state, the head of government as well as the President of the Italian Republic during his official state visit to Luxembourg. A publication entitled *Il Centenario* (Gallo 1992), which celebrated the centenary of Italian immigration in Luxembourg, is a further important generator and carrier of the consensus discourse. The 'master narrative' is capable of consent because a majority of the population can identify with the image of wealth generated by industrialisation – and therefore also by the labour of the Italian immigrants. Besides this 'Master Narrative', we were able to identify two further discourses in references on Italian immigration in Luxembourg.

The marginal left-wing discourse or anti-fascist discourse is based on episodes from the interwar period that have only partly been scientifically analysed. The catalogue *Retour de Babel* makes it visible, not only by the representation of the Italians it portrays but also by its scientific articles which examine events within the anti-fascist movements or the Resistance. This discourse is supported by some historians and politically left-wing public figures: Denis Scuto, Henry Wehenkel, Marcel Lorenzini and others. Since the image of the politically committed (Italian) antifascist does not, for political and ideological reasons due to the connection between Italian antifascism and the Communist party, have an identity-creating potential for the majority of society this discourse remains marginal.

The cultural discourse ignores the image of the worker in favour of that of Italian culture (Roman Empire, republics, artists, composers, etc.). This discourse originated in the 1970s, at a time when the immigration of Italian labourers was replaced by the influx of highly-qualified Italian employees. Generally, the supporters of this discourse are the following organisations: *Amitiés italo-luxembourgeoises* and *italiani.lu*, which organises an annual *Miss-Italia-Luxemburg-Wettbewerb*[108], and the *Istituto italiano di cultura*, which has close ties with the Italian embassy. Another generator of the cultural discourse is the organisation *Convivium* which places special emphasis on a Luxembourgish-Italian culture. Even though the discourses of the different organisations diverge regarding contents, the focus with all of them is on culture and less on historical events, as is the case with the discourses mentioned above.

---

107 | In a speech delivered by HRH The Grand Duke during a banquet in honour of His Excellency the President of the Republic of Italy and Madame Giorgio Napolitano (2 February 2009). Grand-Ducal court of Luxembourg, 28 Decembre 2009. http://www.monarchie.lu/fr/Presse/Discours/2009/02/VisiteEtat_Italie/index.html.

108 | Personal translation: "Miss Italia – Luxembourg Contest".

The *Retour de Babel* Exhibition

The exhibition titled *Retour de Babel* offered a historical overview of the various phenomena of immigration and emigration of Luxembourg within the framework of the 'cultural capital 2007'. The objective here was to show the diversity of migration, which is largely ignored by society.

The exhibition catalogue

The breakdown of the catalogue by topics reflects those of the exhibition: *Partir*[109] (Volume 1), *Arriver*[110] (Volume 2), *Rester, être*[111] (Volume 3). These verbs refer to migration *per se*: the reasons why one leaves one's country, how one copes in a new environment and, finally makes the decision to stay. Only the last verb is 'out of line' as it were, because '*être*' (being) describes a state and therefore does not necessarily fit into the processual representation of migration.

Besides portraits of immigrants from the various countries which were on show in the exhibition, the catalogue contains a great number of scientific articles which deal with a diversity topics concerning migration. Furthermore, the catalogue includes portraits of deceased historic celebrities like Victor Hugo who had found political asylum in Luxembourg, but also of lesser known people who immigrated to Luxembourg for political or economic reasons.

The Portraits

The total of 57 portraits includes eight Italians, all of them either immigrants or members of the so-called second generation[112]. These eight people were interviewed in Italian or in French. After the transcription the interviews, these

---

109 | Personal translation: "Leaving".
110 | Personal translation: "Arriving".
111 | Personal translation: "Staying, being".
112 | Miserini, Renato and Claudine Scherrer. 2007. Un choix de vie. In *Retour de Babel. Itinéraires, Mémoires et Citoyenneté*, ed. Antoinette Reuter and Jean-Philippe Ruiz. Gasperich: Retour de Babel a.s.b.l., vol. 1: 108-116. Malvetti, Mario and Claudine Scherrer. 2007. Plus on grandissait, plus on s'intégrait. In *Retour de Babel. Itinéraires, Mémoires et Citoyenneté*, ed. Antoinette Reuter and Jean-Philippe Ruiz. Gasperich: Retour de Babel a.s.b.l., vol. 2: 58-63. Plebani, Emidio and Kristel Pairoux. 2007. Pour qu'un pont résiste, il faut deux piliers. In *Retour de Babel. Itinéraires, Mémoires et Citoyenneté*, ed. Antoinette Reuter and Jean-Philippe Ruiz. Gasperich: Retour de Babel a.s.b.l., vol. 2: 154-161. Boggiani, Rosina and Claudine Scherrer. 2007. Je ne me suis jamais vraiment sentie étrangère. In *Retour de Babel. Itinéraires, Mémoires et Citoyenneté*, ed. Antoinette Reuter and Jean-Philippe Ruiz. Gasperich: Retour de Babel a.s.b.l., vol. 2: 190-196. Peruzzi, Raymond and Maria Louisa Caldognetto. 2007. A la maison des Romagnoli... In *Retour de Babel. Itinéraires, Mémoires et Citoyenneté*, ed. Antoinette Reuter and Jean-Philippe Ruiz. Gasperich: Retour de Babel a.s.b.l., vol. 2: 209-215. Piticco, Flora and Dominique Sander-Emram.

were partly translated, summarised and finally edited for the catalogue. However, this process, which is not unusual, also has as a consequence the insertion of several levels of interpretation, producing specific images of those portrayed. In other words: while it would go too far to say that this created stereotypes, certain features were more strongly emphasised than others. In this way, a shift took place from the representation of appropriated identities intended by the publishers of the catalogue to a representation of attributed identities, which can indeed sometimes be identical. The attribution takes place by the selection of interview headings and the subheadings which structure the respective texts and which, already in terms of layout, guide the reader's eye. However, the identity-creating image that is produced in this manner can also correspond to the self-image of the person interviewed.

In addition to the text, every portrait comprises one photograph taken especially for the exhibition, as well as several private photos and a personal object which is significant for the biography of the person portrayed. Finally, the migration paths with their respective stages are graphically illustrated.

The staged photographs

On those photographs that Andrés Lejona[113] took especially for the exhibition, we can see the following: the portrayed individuals, each standing in one corner of their living room that is orientated in the cardinal direction of their homeland. The photographer sees this corner as an 'arrow' pointing to the direction of origin of the portrayed (*"la direction de leur pays, de leurs origines"*).

Thus, this corner establishes a context which is, however, not clearly recognizable for the beholder. In terms of space it is located behind the immigrated person, suggesting a symbolism that may be interpreted in the sense that the immigration is completed and the attachment to the native country and/or origin has been overcome. But this interpretation is called into question by the explanation of the photographer who intended this to mean an indication of a direction, which points more to nostalgia, ties with the native country, the inability to find closure on the past, dividedness of affiliation, multiculturality and return.

2007. J'ai la double âme. In *Retour de Babel. Itinéraires, Mémoires et Citoyenneté*, ed. Antoinette Reuter and Jean-Philippe Ruiz. Gasperich: Retour de Babel a.s.b.l., vol. 3: 67-73. Rech, Louis and Claudine Scherrer. 2007. Celui qui nie ses origines et son passé ne mérite pas l'avenir. In *Retour de Babel. Itinéraires, Mémoires et Citoyenneté*, ed. Antoinette Reuter and Jean-Philippe Ruiz. Gasperich: Retour de Babel a.s.b.l., vol. 3: 82-89. Rinaldis, Marinella and Kristel Pairoux. 2007. Quand on regarde les gens dans leur individualité, on ne regarde pas leur nationalité. In *Retour de Babel. Itinéraires, Mémoires et Citoyenneté*, ed. Antoinette Reuter and Jean-Philippe Ruiz. Gasperich: Retour de Babel a.s.b.l., vol. 3: 334-343.

113 | Also see section 6.5.

Italian Immigration in Luxembourg: New Perspectives

The representation of Italian immigration in the exhibition catalogue *Retour de Babel* reproduces a whole series of stereotypes. The most frequently mentioned ones are the extended family, Italian cuisine, football, Italian regional associations, multilingualism, the Catholic faith and Luxembourg as an 'American Dream' in terms of the opportunities immigrants are offered in Luxembourg. It will suffice to examine here only a few of these in more detail. These familiar *topoi* aside, one element stands out, namely the social and politically left-wing commitment of some of the portrayed or that of their relatives.

The aspects of the 'extended family' and in a more broad sense of 'Italians as a community' (*"Ils étaient nombreux, les Italiens!"*), linked with the idea of solidarity, are stressed, among other things, by one of the portrayed women, Rosina Boggiani, during her interview, when she describes the building of her house as a collective undertaking. The *Casa Grande* or *Casa dei Romagnoli*, a house in the working class neighbourhood of the city of Esch/Alzette, where several Italian families had lived over decades, is a symbol of the extended family and of the Italian community as a whole. Raymond Peruzzi, whose interview carries the title *A la casa dei Romagnoli...*, grew up there and regrets being virtually isolated from this community after moving to a small village. Mario Malvetti tells a similar story. Further examples of solidarity linked to places of residence can be found in Flora Piticco's testimony who mentions the solidarity in Brill street, and that of Louis Rech who grew up in the Italian quarter of Dudelange and refers to it as an "Italian island". These descriptions create the image of a close-knit immigrant community which keeps to itself. In addition to nostalgic recollections of Italy, another nostalgia becomes visible that is projected towards a community which has ceased to exist, and the kind of solidarity which has disappeared with it.

The image of the Italian community's co-existence in Luxembourg's society is closely associated with the notion of multilingualism, depicted here either as a positive dynamism or as a problem. Italians raised in Luxembourg generally take a positive view on multilingualism, regardless of potential difficulties at school, and see it as an integrating factor. Marinella Rinaldis is an exception here. She has complaints about, among other things, the educational system where children are taught literacy in German.

The Italian cuisine is often mentioned as one of the cultural contributions of the Italians in Luxembourg. To former mayor Louis Rech, the Italian cuisine is the last surviving "tradition", and the last connection to the Italian origins. For Mario Malvetti, one of the portrayed already mentioned above, the Italian cuisine is a fundamental link not only to his own origins, but also to Italy as a whole and, above all, to the grandfather who, in 1924, brought with him from Italy the rolling pin that is used to make the dough for pasta.

What we have called here the 'American Dream' is the representation of Luxembourg as an open country which offered the immigrants incomparable opportunities and quality of life. Rosina Boggiani, for instance, points out that those who had returned to Italy now wish they had stayed in Luxembourg. Renato Miserini relates that he decided to emigrate to Luxembourg once he had seen immigrants who had managed to build a house for themselves in Italy after having spent some years in Luxembourg. Despite her less favourable experiences, Marinella Rinaldis is also convinced that growing up in Luxembourg has spared her a "different fate" (Rinaldis/Pairoux 2007: 341).

The chapter *Rester, c'est s'engager*[114] contains the portraits of Louis Rech and Flora Piticco, his because of his activities as a trade unionist and politician, hers because of her involvement in various associations dealing with migration issues. Among the remaining eight portraitees, a total of six are either politically active, involved in charity organisations or related to people who are. In the light of such a high percentage, one might wonder by which criteria the interviewed Italian immigrants in the exhibition catalogue were chosen. For with this particular selection of portraitees the marginal left-wing discourse acquires a higher profile than it commonly has. For instance, Renato Miserini was also active as a trade unionist and in politics and helped establish the Luxembourg City section of the Italian Communist Party. Raymond Peruzzi, son of the resistance fighter Luigi Peruzzi, emphasises that he has not emulated his father in every single way, however, antifascism is still a major feature of his portrait. And father Emidio Plebani is, within the Catholic Church, a promoter of interculturalism and bringing together all communities.

In general, the eight portraits convey the impression of a progressive, successful 'integration'. In the majority of instances, this notion is linked to associations and clubs, a football club for example, or a singing association. However, in parallel with this representation, most portraits also raise the question of 'identity'. The connections between 'integration' and 'identity' have for each of the portrayed their own specific meaning. Flora Piticco, for instance, believes that the Italians are "integrated" but not "completely" so – they had assumed a Luxembourg mentality, she says, but their roots were still in Italy. Referring to herself, she calls this state *"double âme"*, a "double soul". With the subheading *Nous étions des étrangers*[115], she continues to describe how, following the war, Italians became less and less the targets of xenophobic remarks. Favourable holiday memories of Luxembourgers visiting Italy, but also the influx of Italian employees working in European institutions, she feels, have contributed to a positive change in the way Luxembourgers perceive Italians. The title of the interview with Rosina Boggiani, *Je ne me suis jamais vraiment sentie étrangère*[116] is slightly misleading here. It suggests 'integration' but her remark about not feeling herself as a stranger does not refer to Luxembourg society but rather to her immediate environment, which was almost

---

114 | Personal translation: "Staying means committing oneself".
115 | Personal translation: "We were strangers".
116 | Personal translation: "I've never really felt a stranger".

exclusively Italian. This, in turn, raises the question what is actually meant when the integration of the Italian immigrant population is described as successful or 'good' in public statements.

Finally, let us turn our attention to three female portraits. The first impression, when merely looking at the photographs and the portrait titles, is that of a certain degree of stereotype. Rosina Boggiani, for instance, represents the typical image of the 'mother' which, however, is primarily generated by photographs that are exclusively family portraits. Besides this rather traditional image of the family-oriented 'Mamma', there is the emancipated, politically active woman, Flora Piticco, public information officer of the Organisation *Unione Donne Italiane*. The photographs show her at big rallies, with a microphone in her hand. This picture is complimented by the text which dwells on the hard life of blue-collar workers and on the experience of being a foreigner. The chapter *être*, finally, introduces Marinella Rinaldis. In contrast to the other women portrayed, who often make historical references, she does not present her biography in a larger framework. Except for a short reference to her grandparents, no element of the Italian immigration history comes into play. Precisely because she clearly positions herself in the present, remarks about experienced discrimination take on a particular importance. The portrayal of this young woman does not coincide with the public representation of 'good integration', and therefore her portrait on the subject *être*, which is presented schematically as goal and outcome of the successful migration process *partir, arriver, rester, être*, casts certain doubts on the positive model of Italian migration and integration in Luxembourg.

Conclusion

Besides the usual depiction of Italian immigration in Luxembourg, the exhibition catalogue *Retour de Babel* places special emphasis on political, social and union committedness. Accordingly, a greater emphasis than usual is being placed on the left-wing discourse, which is not due to the manner of representation so much as to the selection of the Italian immigrants interviewed.

The collective identity of Italians as successfully integrated workers attributed by the consensus discourse is, on the one hand, confirmed by details, on the other, however, it is also questioned by the important role assigned to the anti-fascist organisations and to social and political committedness.

The 'good integration' of the Italians as a part of their attributed collective identity is also being questioned by the fact that those portrayed differentiate their statements about their own integration and do not associate them directly with the question of their own identity. However, origins as well as social environment play an important part in the self-image of the migrants and are often described, for instance, with the term "double identity", or *"double âme"*.[117]

However, one must also bear in mind that it was a major concern of the exhibition organisers to provide a broader – and partly divergent – image than the traditional one of immigration in Luxembourg. In the remaining portraits, for instance, one encounters nationalities which as yet have gone unmentioned in the public discourse. The overall image of immigration in Luxembourg presented here therefore overcomes the established one that the country has of its immigrants: well-integrated Italians, a comparatively more difficult Portuguese immigration process, and immigrants from former Yugoslavia or in general from non-EU countries who, in parallel to a European illegalisation discourse, are increasingly being portrayed as criminals. The portraits in the exhibition catalogue counteract this discriminating discourse, among them the story of a woman who immigrated from Niš (Serbia) to Luxembourg via France long before the outbreak of the war; or that of a dancer from Brazil; of a mother with her child who both hide their heads in a box so as not to be recognised because they are living in Luxembourg without papers and hence, illegally. Moreover, with its generally large proportion of female portraits the exhibition catalogue breaks with the traditional representation of migration as male.

Furthermore, the variety shown in the catalogue reflects the collective symbol of 'European laboratory', even if the epithet is not explicitly mentioned. The presentation's structure itself suggests the image of an open nation, which manages to accommodate (almost) without discomfort its more than 40 % of foreign population.

6.7 Conclusions: National Identities in a Post-national Age?

Nations are "imagined communities" (Anderson 1991). To ensure a binding feeling of belonging, they depend on the imagery of the old and new media. Verbal and visual images have accumulated over a long period of time to form an extensive repository of collective symbols that nations draw on for reasons of recognition, profiling, for reasons of dissociation or polemics, but also motivated by the need for self-understanding and self-critical examination.

In the post-national, global age, major symbolic confrontations such as "profound Germans" versus "frivolous French" (see Florack) that were frequently a prelude to or a concomitant of actual power struggles, have fortunately lost their significance. Nevertheless, political-cultural acting, which continues to express itself on a national or regional scale, still depends on symbolic representations of identities. While it is true to say that increasing social differentiation, interconnectedness and

---

117 | Personal translation: "Double soul".

specialisation of society is pushing these identity discourses out of the the principal functional domains, the issue of cultural cohesion of a society organised in a clearly definable space like Luxembourg becomes all the more pressing.

Using examples from different fields of communication, from the print media, advertising, comics, art and art documentation and their respective addressees, the contributions on the subject 'Images and Identities' in Luxembourg have shown that the search for and the discussion of forms of clear and distinct collective identity patterns are part of everyday discourses in Luxembourg. However, this does not signify that these collective identity images are an everyday occurrence. They are capable of attracting a large amount of attention without being continuously present. In order to be generated and perceived at all, they require external mediatic impulses (the cultural capital year, the Arcelor/Mittal debate, the bank discussion, advertising campaigns etc.) which are sometimes hard to anticipate. This makes positive identity attribution difficult and identity appropriations, which often are only present in negative form, unclear. One can suspect here an underlying basic uneasiness in dealing with schematisations, which are particularly dependent on images and symbols, and assignation of identities to a national whole. In the 20th century, notions of collective identities have been thoroughly discredited.

Nowadays, with an accelerated shift of media attention, interest in identity images generated by a particular event seems to fade away as rapidly as the event itself. The mechanism of mediatic application of national identity symbols determines the dynamic relationship between appropriated and attributed identities in Luxembourg. Even in the post-national age of image campaigns, it is as difficult to reinvent collective identity symbols as it is to simply perpetuate the traditional ones.

6.8 References

Primary Sources

Czuga, Lucien and Roger Leiner. 1988. De Superjhemp géint de Bommeléer. Luxembourg: Ed. Revue (New edition 2001 in Anthology 1).
Czuga, Lucien and Roger Leiner. 1989. Dynamit fir d'Dynastie. Luxembourg: Ed. Revue.
Czuga, Lucien and Roger Leiner. 1990. D'Affair vum Jorhonnert. Luxembourg: Ed. Revue.
Czuga, Lucien and Roger Leiner. 1991. Den Dossier Hexemeeschter. Luxembourg: Ed. Revue (New edition 2006 in Anthology 2).
Czuga, Lucien and Roger Leiner. 1992. Panik am Studio 2. Luxembourg: Ed. Revue.
Czuga, Lucien and Roger Leiner. 1993. Superjhemp contra Superjhemp. Luxembourg: Ed. Revue.

Czuga, Lucien and Roger Leiner. 1994. D'Geheimnis vun der Waliss. Luxembourg: Ed. Revue.
Czuga, Lucien and Roger Leiner. 1995. Requiem fir de Superjhemp. Luxembourg: Ed. Revue.
Czuga, Lucien and Roger Leiner. 1996. Operatioun grouss Botz. Luxembourg: Ed. Revue.
Czuga, Lucien and Roger Leiner. 1997. Geheimcode bloe Stär. Luxembourg: Ed. Revue.
Czuga, Lucien and Roger Leiner. 1998a. Aktioun Réiserbunny. Luxembourg: Ed. Revue.
Czuga, Lucien and Roger Leiner. 1998b. D'Patte wech vun Luxonit. Luxembourg: Ed. Revue.
Czuga, Lucien and Roger Leiner. 1999. Terror em den Troun. Luxembourg: Ed. Revue.
Czuga, Lucien and Roger Leiner. 2000. Lescht Chance fir Luxusbuerg. Luxembourg: Ed. Revue.
Czuga, Lucien and Roger Leiner. 2001. Alarm am Öro Zuch. Luxembourg: Ed. Revue.
Czuga, Lucien and Roger Leiner. 2002. S.O.S. Cosa Mia. Luxembourg: Ed. Revue.
Czuga, Lucien and Roger Leiner. 2003. D'Aaxt vum Béisen hat. Luxembourg: Ed. Revue.
Czuga, Lucien and Roger Leiner. 2004. De Fluch vun der 23. Luxembourg: Ed. Revue.
Czuga, Lucien and Roger Leiner. 2005. Countdown fir Kachkéisien. Luxembourg: Ed. Revue.
Czuga, Lucien and Roger Leiner. 2006. Déck Mënz fir de Prënz. Luxembourg: Ed. Revue.
Czuga, Lucien and Roger Leiner. 2007a Superjhemp an déi grouss Gefor. Luxembourg: Ed. Revue.
Czuga, Lucien and Roger Leiner. 2007b Kids, Kachkéis a Kuddelmuddel. Luxembourg: Ed. Revue.
Czuga, Lucien and Roger Leiner. 2008a. Luxusbuerger Lexikon. Luxembourg: Ed. Revue.
Czuga, Lucien and Roger Leiner. 2008b. De Kinnek vun Öropa. Luxembourg: Ed. Revue.
Czuga, Lucien and Roger Leiner. 2009. Cräsh am Paradäis. Luxembourg: Ed. Revue.

Secondary Sources

Speech delivered by HRH The Grand Duke during a banquet in honour of His Excellency the President of the Republic of Italy and Madame Giorgio Napolitano (2 February 2009). Grand-Ducal court of Luxembourg, 28 Decembre 2009.

http://www.monarchie.lu/fr/Presse/Discours/2009/02/VisiteEtat_Italie/index.html.

Auxenfants, Marc. 2007. D'Finanzplaz. La place financière. In Lieux de mémoire au Luxembourg. Erinnerungsorte in Luxemburg, ed. Sonja Kmec, Benoît Majerus, Michel Margue and Pit Péporté. Luxembourg: Saint Paul.

Bernas, Steven. 2009. La photographie et le sensible. Paris: L'Harmattan.

Calteux, Georges. 2005. Mir wëlle bleiwe wat mir sinn, mä wat sin mir? In Actes du cycle de conférences Lëtzebuergesch: Quo Vadis? ed. Projet Moien! Sproochenhaus Wëlwerwolz. Mamer: Wilwerwiltz, 143-154.

Canetti, Elias. 2000. Masse und Macht. Frankfurt/M.: Fischer Verlag [first: 1960].

Centre de documentation sur les migrations humaines. 1999. Luxembourg-Italie: Hommage au père Benito Gallo, ed. Centre de documentation sur les migrations humaines, Dudelange.

Cicotti, Claudio. 2007. D'Italiener. In Lieux de mémoire au Luxembourg, ed. Sonja Kmec, Benoît Majerus, Michel Margue and Pit Peporte, 109-114. Luxembourg: Imprimerie St. Paul.

Damiani, Didier (n.d.) Marco Godinho, Passeur de temps. Accessed on 08 October 2009: http://www.galeriesdudelange.lu/artistes.php?artiste=00121.

di Felice, Paul. 2009. Jeanine Unsen, Odd, small and beautiful. In Café Crème, Mois Européen de la Photo 2009, Luxembourg: Café Crème Edition: 28.

di Felice, Paul. 2006. Regards distanciés sur le Luxembourg. Les expériences photographiques de Valérie Belin, de Charles Fréger et de Joël Tettamanti. In MUDAM Luxembourg, Eldorado, Luxembourg. Musée d'Art Moderne Grand-Duc Jean: 60-67.

Ditschke, Stephan and Anjin Anhut. 2009. Menschliches, Übermenschliches. Zur narrativen Struktur von Superheldencomics. In Comics. Zur Geschichte und Theorie eines populärkulturellen Mediums, ed. Stephan Ditschke, Katerina Kroucheva and Daniel Stein, 148, 149, 156. Bielefeld: transcript.

Dubois, Philippe. 1983. L'acte photographique. Paris/Bruxelles: Nathan/Labor.

Dünne, Jörg. 2008. Die Karte als Operations- und Imaginationsmix. Zur Geschichte eines Raummediums. In Spatial Turn. Das Raumparadigma in den Kultur- und Sozialwissenschaften, ed. Jörg Döring and Tristan Thielmann. Bielefeld: transcript.

Florack, Ruth. 2001. Tiefsinnige Deutsche, frivole Franzosen. Nationale Stereotype in deutscher und französischer Literatur. Stuttgart: Metzler.

Gallo, Benito. 1992. Centenaire. Les Italiens au Luxembourg. 1892-1992. Luxembourg: Imprimerie St. Paul.

Garcia, Robert and Jürgen Stoldt. 2004. Kulturhauptstadt: die Zweite. Forum für Politik, Gesellschaft und Kultur in Luxemburg 241: 4-7.

Gerhard, Ute, Jürgen Link and Rolf Parr. 2004. Interdiskurs. In Metzler Lexikon Literatur- und Kulturtheorie. (3rd revised and expanded edition), ed. Ansgar Nünning, 293-4. Stuttgart/Weimar: Metzler.

Haas, Luke. 2007. Comics in aus und über Luxemburg. Luxembourg: Ed. Schortgen.
Hahn, Sylvia. 2008. Migration – Arbeit – Geschlecht. Arbeitsmigration in Mitteleuropa vom 17. bis zum Beginn des 20. Jahrhunderts. Göttingen: V&R.
Haupt, Heinz-Gerhard and Geoffrey Crossick. 1998. Das Kleinbürgertum. Eine europäische Sozialgeschichte des 19. Jhd. Munich: C.H. Beck.
Hick, Thierry. 2003. A la découverte d'un lieu. Exposition de photographies d'Yvon Lambert à Lasauvage. Une ville passée au crible. La Voix du Luxembourg, 06.09.2003.
Huntington, Samuel. 1996. The Clash of Civilizations and the Remaking of World Order. New York: Simon & Schuster.
Jakobson, Roman Osipovich. 1960. Linguistics and Poetics. In Style in Language, ed. Thomas A. Sebeok. Cambridge Massachusetts: MIT Press.
Jungblut, Marie-Paule. 2007. D'Spuerkess. In Lieux de mémoire au Luxembourg. Erinnerungsorte in Luxemburg, ed. Sonja Kmec, Benoît Majerus, Michel Margue and Pit Péporté. Luxembourg: Saint Paul.
Klemperer, Victor. 2007. LTI – Notizbuch eines Philologen. Stuttgart: Reclam [first pulished 1957].
Kmec, Sonja. 2007. Gibraltar des Nordens. In Lieux de mémoire au Luxemburg. Usages du passé et construction nationale, ed Sonja Kmec, Benoît Majerus, Michel Margue and Pit Péporté, 267-72. Luxembourg: Saint-Paul.
Koff, Harlan. 2008. Fortress Europe or a Europe of Fortress? The Integration of Migrants in Western Europe. Brussels: Peter Lang Verlag.
Krieps, Rosch. 1991. Parallelen zum Fort Thüngen. Forum für Politik, Gesellschaft und Kultur in Luxemburg 130: 22.
Krotz, Friedrich. 2003. Medien als Ressource der Konstitution von Identität. Eine konzeptionelle Klärung auf der Basis des Symbolischen Interaktionismus. In Carsten Medienidentitäten. Identität im Kontext von Globalisierung und Medienkultur, ed. Carsten Winter, Tanja Thomas and Andreas Hepp. Cologne: Halem.
Labelle Sarah and Julia Bonaccorsi. La contribution de la photographie d'écrivain à la médiation littéraire sur le web. Le cas de Raymond Queneau. *Accessed on 01 October 2009:* http://www.archimuse.com/publishing/ichim05/labelleSELECT05.pdf.
Lambert, Yvon. 1998. Derniers feux. Photographies, Esch-sur Alzette: Ville d'Esch-sur-Alzette.
Lambert, Yvon and Nico Helminger 2005. Brennweiten der Begegnung, Differdange: Ville de Differdange.
Langers, Jean. 1999. L'hétérogénéité de la main-d'œuvre étrangère au Luxembourg, Differdange: STATEC, CEPS/Instead, IGSS, Population et emploi 3, série bleue: 1-4.
Lejona, Andrés. 2009. F(en)ê(r)es nationales. Rendez-Vous. City Magazine Luxembourg 6: 46-57.

Link, Jürgen. 1983. Elementare Literatur und generative Diskursanalyse. Munich: Fink.
Link, Jürgen. 2006. Versuch über den Normalismus. Wie Normalität reproduziert wird. 3rd supplemented, revised and newly designed edition, Göttingen: Vandenhoek & Ruprecht.
Lorgé, Marie-Anne. 1998. La Habana. Luxemburger Wort (5 May 1998).
Luxembourg and Greater Region – European Capital of Culture 2007. Final Report, Luxembourg. 2007.
Manderscheid, Roger. 2000. summa summarum. gedichte aus einem vergangenen Jahrhundert. mit zeichnungen vom autor. Echternach: Phi-Verlag.
Manderscheid, Roger. 2001. schwarze engel. Geschichten mit 23 Zeichnungen des Autors. Nospelt: Ed. ultimomondo.
Manderscheid, Roger. 2003. Der aufstand der luxemburger alliteraten. notizen zur entwicklung der luxemburger literatur in der zweiten jahrhunderthälfte. Esch: Phi-Verlag.
Margue, Michel. 2007. Les dominations étrangères. In Lieux de mémoire au Luxemburg. Usages du passé et construction nationale, ed. Sonja Kmec, Benoît Majerus, Michel Margue and Pit Péporté, 29-34. Luxembourg: Saint-Paul.
Ndiaye, Pap. 2008. La condition noire. Essai sur une minorité française. Paris: Calmann-Lévy.
Merian Magazin: Luxemburg, 60th edition, No. 03, 2007.
Noiriel, Gérard. 1992. Le Creuset français. Histoire de l'immigration (XIXe-XXe siècle). Paris: Seuil, coll. "Points-histoire".
Ogden, Charles Kay and Ivor Amstrong Richards. 1923. The Meaning of Meaning. 8th ed. New York: Harcourt, Brace & World, Inc.
Parr, Rolf. 2009. Wie konzipiert die (Inter-)Diskurstheorie individuelle und kollektive Identitäten? Ein theoretischer Zugriff, erläutert am Beispiel Luxemburgs. Forum für Politik, Gesellschaft und Kultur in Luxemburg 289: 11-16.
Parr, Martin. 2007. Luxembourg 2006/Assorted Cocktail. Luxembourg: Luxembourg et Grande Région, Capitale européenne de la Culture 2007.
Parr, Rolf. 2009. Diskursanalyse. In Methodengeschichte der Germanistik, ed. Jost Schneider, 89-107. Berlin: De Gruyter.
Parr, Martin. 2006. Mexico. London: Chris Boot Ltd.
Pauly, Michel. 1991. Schlacht um Fort Thüngen. Forum für Politik, Gesellschaft und Kultur in Luxemburg 128-129: 3-7.
Pauly, Michel. 2000. Eglise et immigration. Un entretien avec le père Benito Gallo. Forum für Politik, Gesellschaft und Kultur in Luxemburg 197: 59-62.
Pauly, Michel. 1984. L'immigration dans la longue durée. In Lëtzebuerg de Lëtzebuerger? Le Luxembourg face à l'immigration, 7-21. Luxembourg: Guy Binsfeld.
Peirce, Sanders Charles. 2000. Semiotische Schriften. 3 volumes, Frankfurt/Main: Suhrkamp.
Pigeron-Piroth, Isabelle. 2009. Le secteur public. Economie et statistiques, Working Papers du Statec 34:3.

Poivert, Michel. 2002. La photographie contemporaine. Paris: Flammarion.
Reuter, Antoinette. 1995. Cinq siècles de présence italienne au Luxembourg – XIIIe-XVIIIe siècles. In Itinéraires croisés. Luxembourgeois à l'étranger, étrangers au Luxembourg/Luxemburger im Ausland, Fremde in Luxemburg. Menschen in Bewegung, ed. Antoinette Reuter and Denis Scuto, 46-57. Esch/Alzette: Ed. Le Phare.
Reuter, Antoinette and Jean-Philippe Ruiz. 2007. Retour de Babel. Itinéraires, Mémoires et Citoyenneté, 3 volumes. Gasperich: Retour de Babel a.s.b.l.
Sayad, Abdelmalek. 1999. La double absence. Des illusions de l'émigré aux souffrances de l'immigré. Paris: Seuil.
Schaeffer, Jean-Marie. 1987. L'image précaire. Du dispositif photographique. Paris: Seuil.
Schäffner, Christina. 1993. Die europäische Architektur – Metaphern der Einigung Europas in der deutschen, britischen und amerikanischen Presse. In Inszenierte Informationen. Politik und strategische Information in den Medien, ed. Adi Grewenig, 13-30. Wiesbaden: Verlag für Sozialwissenschaften.
Schulz, Christian. 2008. Die 'Metropolisierung' Luxemburgs. In Periphere Zentren oder zentrale Peripherien? Kulturen und Regionen Europas zwischen Globalisierung und Regionalität, ed. Wilhelm Amann, Georg Mein and Rolf Parr, 89-98. Heidelberg: Synchron.
Scuto, Denis. 2008. Historiographie de l'immigration au Luxembourg. Hémecht 60: 391-413.
Stoldt, Jürgen. 2008. Luxemburg – Kern Europas. In Aus Politik und Zeitgeschichte 8: 19-25.
Weltonline – Wirtschaft (25.06.2009): dpa news item, http://www.welt.de/die-welt/article4001464/Luxemburger-sind-die-reichsten-Buerger-in-der-EU.html.
Wey, Claude. 2005. Discours et politiques d'immigration et d'intégration au Luxembourg. In 20 ans de discours sur l'intégration, ed. Vincent Ferry, Piero-D. Galloro and Gérard Noiriel, 151-62. Paris: L'Harmattan.
Williams, Val. 2004. Martin Parr. London: Phaidon Press Ltd.

7. Everyday Cultures and Identities

CHRISTEL BALTES-LÖHR, AGNES PRÜM, RACHEL RECKINGER, CHRISTIAN WILLE

7.1 INTRODUCTION: ON THE RECIPROCAL RELEVANCE OF EVERYDAY CULTURES AND IDENTITY CONSTRUCTIONS

The main focus of this contribution is on the empiric analysis of interactions in everyday social life. For the purpose of our common research we will investigate the following questions: How are everyday-cultural identities negotiated in the conflicting areas of attributed and appropriated identities? How and why does this identity-based interdependency express itself in everyday life? How are actions and attitudes explained, legitimised and interpreted? These questions are examined by researchers from the viewpoint of their respective disciplines in terms of gender perceptions, 'banal' forms of consumption and social orders.

The everyday practice that we will analyse with the aid of discursive practises (see below) is compounded of collectively shared values, attitudes and standards (Conceptas), as well as modes of perception, belief, evaluation and action as they appear in the course of social interaction (Perceptas) (Bolten 2007). In the results presented below, the collective always resonates in the individual and the individual in the collective, which lends a certain variability and complexity to the examined identities. The defining feature of this interpretation of the identity concept is its pluridimensionality, which does not conflate individuals to rigid categories (e.g., man/woman) but also takes contextual and intersectional affiliations into account (e.g., sociocultural milieus, age groups, affinity groups etc.).

Everyday Cultures Seen from a Praxeological Perspective

In the following analyses the focus therefore does not lie on ready-made structures of cognitive meaning and sense of 'everyday culture' but on its practical application, which is not to mean what people do every day but rather which self-evidencies and irritations in attitudes and activities are shared by the subjects. This is based on the assumption that culture finds its expression in the concrete confrontation with the material and social environment: *"Kultur lässt sich [...] erst im Umgang mit Dingen und Körpern wirklich 'dingfest', d.h. sichtbar, aufzeigbar, nachweisbar, nachvollziehbar machen"*[1] (Hörning/Reuter 2004: 12). This refers to practical contexts in which the cultural aspect expresses itself. In particular, intermediate category forms are significant here, such as "third Spaces" (Bhabha 2000), which are explained under the keyword of ambivalence. The specific conception of culture outlined above will be subsumed under the key term, of 'everyday cultures' with the plural form chosen here, aiming at drawing attention to the parallel and different processes of social interaction and their effects.

The first aspect of this twin term emphasises how close to real life our approach is, which centres on unquestioned *"vertraute Selbstverständlichkeiten, eingelebtes Alltagswissen und routinisiertes Alltagshandeln"*[2] (Hillmann, 2007: 19). Routines, rituals and personalisations should, in this context, not be understood as mechanical, rigid repetitions of everyday attitudes and sequences of events but rather as permanent, minor shifts in the sense of a transformation (Butler 1993; Deleuze 1968) which Derrida denotes with the term *"différance"* (Derrida 1968). While the shifts referred to here permit individual latitude, they do not dispute the intersubjectivity in action situations. Collective stocks of knowledge can be unsystematic, judgemental and partly contradictory (Schütz 1972), i.e. they may constitute a pragmatic simplification of everyday actions – whereby they combine a certain openness of interpretation with a normative regularity. Despite the capability for intersubjective consensus of everyday knowledge *"machen sich infolge soziokultureller, gruppenspezifischer und biogaphischer Einflüsse individuelle Differenzierungen [...] bemerkbar"*[3] (Hillmann 2007: 20), which, in turn, have an impact on everyday knowledge.

The second aspect contained in the concept of 'everyday cultures' connects to the cultural-theoretical debate. As suggested above, what is pertinent here is not a normative or holistic understanding of the concept of culture, but rather one that is meaning- and knowledge-oriented (Reckwitz 2001; Reckwitz 2004). This is based on the assumption that different complexes of behaviour emanate, are reproduced and altered against the background of symbolic structures of the social environment, forming the level of the cultural. This notion of culture is continually modified and developed in the social and cultural sciences, which raises the question whether culture is to be understood as a configuration of supra-subjective symbolic structures or as a result of subjective-interpretative performances. This question

---

1 | Personal translation: "Culture can only be rendered tangible [...] by dealing with things and objects, i.e. it becomes visible, traceable and understandable".

2 | Personal translation: "Familiar self-evidencies, ingrained common knowledge and routine everyday actions".

3 | Personal translation: "Individual differentiations [...] manifest themselves as a result of socio-structural, group-specific and biographical influences".

can be addressed with a praxeological synthesis of both perspectives. While useful in revealing culture as a supra-subjective attribution, the structuralistic view does not give sufficient consideration to phenomena of cultural change or subjective appropriation. Here, the conceptualisation of culture as a result of a performance of subjective interpretation proves more effective, for instance when examining the subject's everyday-cultural and innovative appropriations. However, these do not occur disconnected from the socio-cultural circumstances and resources available to the acting subjects due to their different, yet circumscribed positions in the social space, as praxeology implies (Bourdieu 2000 [1972]; Bourdieu 1980).

This contribution adopts the above praxeological synthetic model and views processes of identity-based attribution in the structuralistic sense explained above and appropriation processes and methods as interpretative performances of the subjects. By conflating both perspectives, the dualism of culture as a structure on the one hand, and culture as a subjective performance on the other, can be overcome – as phenomenologically and structurally oriented approaches are married theoretically and empirically. This means that the socio-structural embeddings in the social environment are envisaged simultaneously with the subjective attitudes and actions of the actors. In this sense, a given practice – be it as attribution or appropriation of gender concepts, forms of consumption or societal categories – represents a complex of behavioural routines that carry meaning and are subject to change, performed via discursive practices (see below) whose cohesion is ensured by an implicit 'logic of everyday life'. The contributions attempt to reveal these kinds of logic of everyday cultures by tying them up to the practices of the sociocultural milieus of Luxembourg's resident population.

Constructions of Identities as a Social Practice

A particular feature of identity work performed in everyday cultures in the analysed areas is a certain 'invisibility' since, as a rule, it is not queried in the practice of everyday life and is subject to the pragmatism of concrete action. It is only the interview situation that elicits a reflected verbalisation with regard to the topic in question[4]. It allows insights into subjective worlds of meaning articulated in interactions during the interview. This discursive act as well as its contents of meaning are understood as discursive practices, as defined by Foucault:

Il s'agit de faire apparaître les pratiques discursives dans leur complexité et dans leur épaisseur; montrer que *parler, c'est faire quelque chose* – autre chose qu'exprimer ce qu'on pense, traduire ce qu'on sait, autre chose aussi que faire jouer les structures d'une langue; montrer qu'ajouter un énoncé à une série préexistante d'énoncés, c'est *faire un geste compliqué et coûteux, qui implique des conditions* (et pas seulement une situation,

---

4 | This does not mean that there is no reflection in everyday life but, rather, that everyday-cultural decisions are barely questioned during their implementation.

un contexte, des motifs) *et qui comporte des règles* (différentes des règles logiques et linguistiques de construction); montrer qu'un changement, dans l'ordre du discours, ne suppose pas des 'idées neuves', un peu d'invention et de créativité, une mentalité autre, *mais des transformations d'une pratique* [...][5] (Foucault 1969: 272; authors' emphasis).

This means on the one hand that different discourses mutually influence each other and, on the other, that their interactions are performative, so that the individuals – in our case the interviewees – "do something with the words" (Austin 1970). However, the words also 'do' something with them. This interaction is a defining feature of "discursive practice" and makes clear that discourses structure the practices (discursivity of the practices) and, at the same time, practices structure the discourses (performativity of the discourses) (Reckinger 2008). This approach serves to see discourses and practices not as autonomous, sociocultural elements suspended in space, but to draw attention to their constructed relationship.

This raises the question, in terms of methodology, to what extent social practices can be captured with empirical techniques of data gathering. A fundamental distinction has to be made between the various procedures by which social practices become accessible either indirectly or directly. The latter, for instance, includes participatory observations or experimental procedures which imply a controlled framework and, for the interviewees, a certain removal from everyday life. By contrast, surveys, interviews or content analyses permit an indirect access, which favours a verbal approach, making it more suitable for our purposes. In this way it was possible, for instance, during qualitative interviews and quantitative surveys, to enter into contact with subjects that are acting or participating in social practices and to obtain, via their statements, specific information about social practices, their regularity and frequency as well as about their subjective significance. Furthermore, the discourse-practical content analysis enables a reconstruction of different aspects of an action, with the focus being not on the actions themselves but on their performativities. For the purposes of our investigation we have analysed legal texts, information material and statistical data with the aim to reveal evidence of social practices and to draw conclusions regarding the varieties of 'logic of everyday life'.

Aside from the outlined methodological aspect, the identities under investigation and the differentiations made by the subjects require further scrutiny (Reuter/

---

5 | "It is an attempt to reveal discursive practices in their complexity and density; to show that to speak is to do something – something other than to express what one thinks; to translate what one knows, and something other than to play with the structures of a language (langue); to show that to add a statement to a pre-existing series of statements is to perform a complicated and costly gesture, which involves conditions (and not only a situation, a context, and motives), and rules (not the logical and linguistic rules of construction); to show that a change in the order of discourse does not presuppose ‚new ideas', a little invention and creativity, a different mentality, but transformations in a practice [...]" (Routledge translation).

Wiesner 2008). Dealing with these categories has become more complex in the course of globalisation and liberalisation. Forms of hybridisation or hyphenated constructions put classical theories to the test and undermine binary categories and notions of difference. For instance, the theoretical figures of inter-categorical structures (Reuter/Wiesner 2008) are increasingly being (re)discovered within the framework of poststructuralistic and postmodern approaches as ambivalent contemporary phenomena. What they have in common is the breakdown of binary logic of female/male, good/bad, familiar/strange etc. which are generally used as explanatory categories. Inter-categorical concepts (Bhabha 2000; Welsch 2005; Breinig/Lösch 2006) attempt to register the penetration of pre-established differences and draw attention to *"prozesshafte, dynamische, flüssige Vermischungen, die sich nicht ohne weiteres feststellen lassen"*[6] (Reuter/Wiesner 2008: 132). This state of ambivalence, of 'in between', which defies clear classifications permanently re-invents itself.

The research interest of the present chapter is directed, among other things, at such fleeting moments of ambivalence at the level of everyday cultures. It assumes that the binarity of differences can be broken up within social practices and innovatively reconfigures itself by following an 'everyday logic'. This approach therefore is not about the dissolution of differences but about the transgression of binary categories in everyday culture. The focus thus shifts from the binary-coded logic of "either-or" to the ambivalent logic of "as well as"[7], hitherto a largely neglected aspect of the practices of everyday cultures. This shift should not be seen as a substitution but as an expansion, because at the phenomenological level both the reconstruction of binarities and their transgression and reconfiguration can be observed.

It is against this background that the present chapter will look at examples of instances where ambivalence and the related dynamics of identity constructions manifest themselves in the areas of everyday cultures in terms of gender perception, forms of consumption and appropriation of social structures. First, we will attempt to establish the degree of power exercised by gender images and subsequently take a look at the relevance of gender among women and men living in Luxembourg. We will investigate hegemonically effective attribution processes in the context of gender identity constructions as well as individual appropriation processes in their different forms of expression. For this purpose we will examine homogenising or differentiating notions of gender identities against the background of an intersectional foil and explore the relevance of the dichotomy between constructivist and essentialist gender notions. In addition to the question of the relevance of gender in interhuman contact, preferences for different models for reconciling professional and private life will be presented both in relation to each other and

---

6 | Personal translation: "Processual, dynamic, fluid comminglings that are not easily identified".
7 | See Baltes-Löhr 2006: 70.

to the respective milieus. Additionally, we will assess the categorial discriminatory power of gender as an analytical category in respect of gender topics of everyday cultures, with their interlacing between attribution and appropriation processes.

A further subject we will address is the standard and the understanding of 'good' food between political model and individual everyday practice. In an initial step, the analysis will focus on an attributive concept of political action which, in its recommendations, attempts to provide a certain health orientation – in a creative, but object-related way. The attention will subsequently move to everyday dietary routines whose forms of appropriation revolve around self-responsibility, action potential and hedonistic pragmatism in a more person-centered perspective. The dynamic interactions between these two types of interpretation of 'good' food create contextual margins for identity constructions.

Finally, the example of cross-border workers in Luxembourg will serve to draw some conclusions about processes of identity construction, in particular concerning the way how cross-border workers are perceived by the Luxembourg resident population, which evinces different forms of construction of this phenomenon. The aim here is to retrace identity appropriations or positions of the Luxembourg resident population in relation to cross-border workers. For this purpose, we will examine inclusion and exclusion strategies used in everyday cultures and determine on this basis the status of the cross-border workers in the Grand Duchy. In a second step, we will assess which conclusions we may infer about processes of identity formation from the partly ambivalent appropriations revealed here.

7.2 Permanent Performances: Gender in Motion

This part of the study will investigate the impact of gender representations. Which are the prevalent gender representations among women and men living in Luxembourg? Assuming the construction processes of attributed gender identities via hegemonic gender discourses, the investigation primarily seeks to explore processes of appropriation of gender identities and gender representations in the context of intersectionality. Here, two questions come into play that have guided our research: first, to what extent are dualistically connoted differentiations between essentialistic and constructivist gender representations mirrored in the empirical material, and second, can gender still be considered as an analytical category with a selective discriminatory power? In other words, to what extent does the category of 'gender' play an important role in the analysis process of the interviewees' responses?

Based on the data supplied by a representative study and 27 semi-structured interviews, we analysed performances of femininity, masculinity, homo- and transsexuality. The analysis also included the importance of the category of 'gender' in processes of social interaction, as well as assessments regarding gender equality and gender discrimination in Luxembourg. In addition, we examined the gender models favoured by interviewees in terms of the assumed potential of these models for a better work-life balance, and finally the extent of the respondents' awareness and knowledge of gender-related national legislation and campaigns[8]. The following paper is based on the evaluation of four statistical item sets comprising a total of 22 items as well as 290 interview sequences from 27 female and male interviewees.

Theoretical Framework

Identities, including gender identities, are understood as results of pluridimensional, intersectional and performative construction processes (see McCall 2005; Hirschauer 2001; Klinger/Knapp 2005; Baltes-Löhr 2006: 66). Besides the category of 'gender' – for many years considered as the social structural category *par excellence* – and the body-related biological category 'sex', also ethnic and socio-economic aspects as well as age become more and more important for such identity construction processes[9]. Regardless of the number of 'sections', the significance of the category 'gender' is put into perspective by its intersectional contextualisation and could be considered as dedramatised.

Besides their intersectional constitution, identities can be regarded as snapshots of constantly shifting and changing performative construction processes. Notwithstanding all fluidity and changeability, certain aspects of identity seem to evaporate, while others deposit themselves either in the hegemonic discourse or in everyday individual practice. Performative construction processes as well as performative actions (Butler 1993: 123) generate their subject, thus also identities, through naming, enactment and repeated presentations in time and space. Such recurring performative actions have the potential to consolidate that what is repeated. They may also lead to the discursive deconstruction of prevailing notions creating a diversification of binary patterns, by for instance producing different facets of gender identities.

If the potential to reveal multiple aspects of a given subject is inherent to repetitions and thereby enables dualistic hierarchies to change, shift and dissolve, then one can assume that repetitions have dehomogenising and heterogenising effects. Differences are given space. At the same time, similarities can become

---

8 | For this purpose we examined and analysed, concurrently with this research project, legislation passed in Luxembourg since the end of the 1960s on the subject of gender equality and equal rights. The findings of this document analysis have been published in a publication dedicated to this subject and receive only cursory treatment here. Baltes-Löhr, Christel and Susanne Stricker. *Eine Untersuchung der luxemburgischen Gesetzgebung in Bezug zur Konvention CEDAW und dem ihr implizierten Gleichstellungsprinzip*. Luxemburg 2009.

9 | There are different opinions about which 'other' categories are significant in terms of identity constructions. Knapp (2005) adds "race" and "class". Lutz/Wenning (2001) identify thirteen categories of difference, while at the same time pointing out that this list is not exhaustive. McCall (2005) mentions "gender", "race" and "class" and adds the category of "region"; Baltes-Löhr (2009) adds the category of "physical constitution".

visible and be reinforced. Novelty or 'the new' therefore always originates in relation to something else, usually to 'the old', 'the established' and 'the familiar'. Novelty emerges out of processes of slowly shifting changes.

Just as cultural pluralism and cultural differences can be identified not only between cultures but also within cultures (Kumoll 2006: 86) the same can also be assumed for identity constructions. It is important to understand the process of "becoming minor" (Deleuze following Rölli 2006: 39) as a rule of differentiation. This means understanding actually existing features, which are used to identify cultural attributions, as effects of a prior attribution of meaning. Such conceptions of "becoming minor" distinguish themselves from the idea of otherness and of not being identical, which carries an essentialist connotation. Hegemonic identity attributions can therefore be dismantled or deconstructed if the processes of 'becoming minor' are emphasised, so that established, self-evident or even seemingly natural structures of the majority and by extension frequently also of power, as understood by Foucault, can appear to be contingent and as such changeable (Rölli 2006: 40).

As with the different cultural representations, "in-between" spaces or "third spaces" (Rutherford 1990: 207-221; Chambers 1996: 78; Gregory 1997: 228) are of particular significance for articulations of identitary minorities or minority positions. If we can say, with Bhabha, that "*Kulturen [sind] zwar durch das Begehren nach Stabilität und Determination, beispielsweise im Sinne einer Nation, gekennzeichnet [...], müssen aber gerade in der Instabilität, der Gleichzeitigkeit von inkommensurablen Geschichten (Narrativen und Historizitäten) und Orten gedacht werden*"[10] (Bhabha following Bonz/Struve 2006: 141), then this applies equally to identity construction processes. A typical feature of identity constructions is their differentiatedness. Identities become an arena for negotiations and expressions. However, identities and identitary subjects do not necessarily merge but can be different. Thus apparently homogenous identities can contain identitary differences. Just as Bhabha argues against a multiculturally-oriented cultural diversity and in favour of cultural difference, which takes account of the cultural antagonisms, contradictions and incommensurabilities (Bonz/Struve 2006: 149), so can accepting identitary differences (constructivist approach) better accommodate contradictions and contrasts actually lived and perceived than can searching and striving for homogeneous, identitary identities (essentialist approach).

---

10 | Personal translation: "While cultures are typified by a desire for stability and determination, for example in the sense of a nation, it is [...] precisely in terms of instability and the concurrence of incommensurate stories (narratives and historicisms) and places that we have to conceive of them".

Our analysis will therefore address the following questions:

- Which homogenising or differentiating ideas of gender identities are recognisable alongside other intersectional components?
- How relevant is the constructivist versus essentialist dichotomy?
- How significant is gender in processes of social interaction and what reactions are there to otherness and others?
- Which models are favoured in terms of a work-life balance?
- What specific knowledge is there about provisions and legislation relating to the equality of women and men?

Resistant Remnants. To which Extent are Essentialist Gender-related Performances still Operating Today?

The representative study shows that 90 % of the interviewees agree with the assumption that there is a natural difference between women and men. *At the same time*, 77 % assume that female and male behaviour is learnt during the course of life. 96 % of all interviewees emphasise that women are just as capable as men of taking on leadership functions in society. This indicates that the frequently invoked and elaborated divergence between essentialism and constructivism does *not* exist as the presumed binary dichotomy, but that both attitudes can coexist.

The markedly high approval rating for the assumption of gender-independent capabilities in terms of taking on leadership positions comes along with the finding that only 56 % of the interviewees believe that the supposed equal professional opportunities for women and men in Luxembourg are also actually exploited in the same degree. This indicates that a factual gender disparity within Luxembourg's labour market is still considered to be a significant discriminatory factor between women and men. This is also confirmed by the interviewees' statements: gender discrimination is primarily perceived in the under-representation of women in leadership positions and in salary inequalities.

The findings are interesting in terms of women's and men's response patterns. Men assume a natural difference between the genders significantly more often, which is more indicative of an essentialist position. This correlation was first seen for Luxembourg in the study: *"Bedeutung des Geschlechteraspektes für die berufliche und persönliche Entwicklung/Biographie von zukünftigen Erziehenden und Lehrenden"*[11] (Baltes-Löhr et al. 2005: 87).

---

11 | Personal translation: "Significance of the Gender Aspect for Professional and Personal Development/Biography of Future Educators and Teachers". A complete census carried out in March/April 2003 among students and/or pupils of the former ISERP (*Institut Supérieur d'Etudes et de Recherches Pédagogiques*) and of the secondary level teacher education at the CUNLUX (*Centre Universitaire de Luxembourg*) and at the former IEES (*Institut d'Etudes*

In the present study, significantly more women than men agree with the assumption that both genders are equally suited to taking on leading functions in society. On the other hand, significantly fewer women hold the view that both genders exploit professional promotion prospects to the same extent. This is supported by the fact that considerably more women are prepared to hold back their careers so as to be able to reconcile work and family better. Here too, it is worth reviewing the results of the above-mentioned study, namely that *"bei tatsächlich stattgefundenen Einstellungsveränderungen scheinbare Resistenzen bei Frauen und Männern 'übrig bleiben'"*[12] (Baltes-Löhr et al. 2005: 85).

In the current study we see such 'resistant remnants' in the fact that significantly fewer men believe women to be equally suited for leadership positions, i.e. that, from a male perspective, men are still more likely to be better suited for professional life and for executive positions in particular. These findings are reflected in men's perceptions of existing discrimination at the work place as well as in male attitudes towards their own private lives. In contrast to women, men are more likely to assume that female colleagues today are not subject to discrimination in the professional field and, on the other hand however, are significantly less often prepared to curtail their own professional activities to achieve a better balance between work and family life. A glance at the figures indicating the percentage of fathers taking up the option of paternity leave in Luxembourg shows that these attitudes and preferences still reflect lived realities. Whilst the proportion of men taking paternity leave in 2002 was 13 %, it increased to 22 % in 2006. Just as it was summarised in "Bedeutung des Geschlechtsaspektes für die berufliche und persönliche Entwicklung/Biographie von zukünftigen Erziehenden und Lehrenden" that *"Frauen kritischere Haltungen gegenüber Traditionalismen einnehmen"*[13] (Baltes-Löhr et al. 2005: 86), in the current case too, it appears that it is again the women who, more so than men, have cast off traditional notions of gender roles. Women exhibit 'resistant remnants' of so-called traditional notions primarily in matters concerning the responsibility for reconciling work and family life while for men they appear in the form of more naturalistic concepts of an essential difference between the genders and men's greater aptitude for professional life.

The interview responses cover the whole range of opinions on socially perceived gender relations, from: *"Es ist gut so, we es ist, und es soll sich nicht ändern"*[14] to *"Wir sind im Wandel und auf einem guten Weg"*[15] all the way to *"Es geschieht zwar etwas,*

Educatives et Sociales) including educator and social education worker training and studies (*Educatrice graduée/Educateur gradué*).

12 | Personal translation: "Notwithstanding actual changes in attitude, an apparent resistance among women and men still remains".

13 | Personal translation: "Women adopt a more critical attitude toward traditionalisms".

14 | Personal translation: "Things are fine as they are and nothing should change".

15 | Personal translation: "We are in a period of transition and are heading into the right direction".

aber Gleichberechtigung oder Gleichstellung der Geschlechter bleiben unerreichbare Utopien"[16]. Both women and men of various ages emphasise that there are changes within the labour market, that more and more women are obtaining good educational qualifications and are working, and that increasing numbers of men are taking paternity leave.

Competence, Performance and Remuneration Discourse

What clearly emerged in the survey is a 'discourse of competence'. During the interviews it was repeatedly stressed that whether someone is suited for a given profession is more a matter of competence and performance quality than of gender. Competence matters, irrespective of gender, skin colour, nationality and age. Performance matters. The following point was emphasised during the interviews: just as men earn respect based on their commitment and achievements, so too should women. This discourse reflects two notions: first the image of the "*defizitäre Frau*"[17] (see Baltes-Löhr 2006; 2009) who needs to adapt herself to male standards if she wishes to attain the same recognition as a man, and second the assumption that housework is something intrinsically unattractive. According to many interviewees, a lot of men would find it "uncool" to say that one is a househusband who hoovers the house and this, allegedly, is why a lot of men do not actually do any housework. Interviewees repeatedly point to *wage inequality* as a clear case of discrimination. While competence, quality of work and performance all tend to be regarded as a basis for social recognition and status applicable to both sexes, unequal payment remains an indicator of the fact that discrimination against women persists. The interviewees often interpret the economic independence of women as a sign of emancipation.

Essentialist concepts of femininity and masculinity can be found in statements on the supposedly fundamentally different kinds of work performed by women and men. A drastic example: women, it is argued, cannot not perform certain tasks involving physical exertion as well as men and therefore unequal payment is justified. If, the argument continues, women "are as strong as men", they would still remain less efficient than their male colleagues. This quasi essentialist gender difference is then related to the hierarchical structure of the workplace: after all, it is argued, labourers, bricklayers and foremen on the building site are also paid differently.

Otherness and Resistant Remnants

The interview statements reveal further types of 'otherness': while for men image cultivation, stressing their own importance and relevance, takes precedence over actual activity, women are experienced and represented as being more subject-

---

16 | Personal translation: "Something is happening but equal rights or gender equality remain unattainable utopias".
17 | Personal translation: "Deficient woman".

focused and object-oriented. Women in leading positions are often perceived as being specifically female, meaning soft, empathetic etc., and therefore different to male bosses, or else it is assumed that they would have to adapt to the male style. The latter is linked to the concept that gender behaviour can be situation dependent, can be learnt and can therefore also be changed. However, the assumption that there is something such as a "specifically feminine (female) boss" points to the existence of a deeply-rooted essentialist concept of gender: women are still thought of as being stereotypically feminine even within so-called masculine domains. This particular mind set continues to be in full operation where the perception of working women is dominated by the notion of stereotypical intrinsic femininity. Here, once again, there is evidence of 'resistant remnants' whenever essentialist ideas of gender are *not* broken down by emancipatory changes like increasing female employment rates. Essentialist discourses therefore appear to be more powerful than factual changes in professional life and politics. To discover exactly how these effects are constructed i.e., how they are produced performatively through repetition, alterations, shifts as well as consistencies and resemblances, requires further research.

What is evident, based on the current data, is that to some extent women also remain fixed in their traditional attitudes. For instance, some interviewees stress that women have prevented an equal interaction between the genders by not trusting men to be able to "manage the housework". Employment is often, but not always, seen as a token or even the symbol of emancipation. According to some interviewees, women wishing to adhere to traditional roles want to be respected nevertheless. We can, however, say that the majority of interviewees assume that there are more women working in a job than there are men who are actively involved in the household, and in the care and education of children. Therefore, it can be assumed that the permeability between the traditional 'gender domains', the porosity of gender boundaries[18] from the so-called female into the so-called male domains seems to be more pronounced than boundary crossings by men into so-called female domains like household, care and education.

Handling Otherness and Others

The Relevance of Gender in Social Interaction

Based on the concepts of intersectionally and pluridimensionally constituted identities which change across time and space through ongoing construction processes and can be described as the results of permanent performances, our analysis examined the significance of cultural background, professional position, age, gender, religion as well as sexual orientation in the framework of social interaction.

---

18 | Albeit the image of porosity would, at first sight, seem to suggest a uniform fluidity and permeability from A to B, this image is modified here inasmuch as the respective openings of the permeable pores should be viewed as being variously sized and pronounced.

It was shown that gender comes in second last position, followed only by religion, which seems to be even less important in social interaction. Age and cultural background are most important, followed by professional position and sexual orientation. Gender is particularly important to men when interacting with others. For Italians living in Luxembourg, as well as for those with only a lower school education, gender is also significantly important in social interaction. Sexual orientation is mainly of importance to men, interviewees of Portuguese origin, those with lower school education, the unemployed as well as to pensioners. In terms of age, occupation, marital and civil status, there are no significant findings in the response behaviour of the interviewees. The relevance of gender (27 % approval) and sexual orientation (34 % approval) plays the greatest role within the underprivileged milieu. Within the alternative milieu, gender (9 %) is considered the least significant. In interaction with others, sexual orientation matters to a mere 5 % of the interviewees within the status-oriented milieu.

Homosexuality

65 % of all interviewees consider homosexuality and heterosexuality equivalent. The significantly highest approval rates are found among the women (74 %) in comparison to the men (57 %), among the 21 to 29-year-old interviewees of German nationality, among students and people living in de facto marriage/civil union partnerships[19]. Acceptance of the equivalence of homosexuality and heterosexuality is highest (78 %) within the status-oriented milieu, and lowest within the privileged conservative milieu (54 %).

During the interviews, some of the respondents stated that they had never before thought about this topic. One interview partner preferred not to make a statement because he said of himself that he had a "racist" attitude towards this issue, which he nonetheless subsequently elaborated upon. To his mind, homosexual people were not normal and homosexuality threatened the further existence of mankind: "*Wenn alle so wären, dann würde es keine Kinder mehr geben*".[20] This statement shows how the minority status of homosexuals is constructed through homogenisation – "if everybody was like that" – in conjunction with generativity. The same goes for statements to the effect that a homosexual person always feels that he/she does not conform to the default paradigm that women and men were made for each other. In the majority of interviews, however, respondents confirmed that in terms of approaching homosexuality and homosexuals in Luxembourg, something had changed and that the 'other' is met with greater tolerance. However, the increasing official acceptance did not always correspond to unofficial opinions and attitudes.

---

19 | The legislation pertaining to registered partnerships also enabled marriage-like partnerships between same-sex couples (Legislation from 09.07.2004). Those who have registered such a partnership (*Pacte Civil de Solidarité* – PACS for short) will in the following be referred to as de facto marriage/civil union partners.

20 | Personal translation: "If everybody was like that then there would be no more children".

The establishment of a de facto marriage/civil union partnership model for same-sex couples (PACS) had not fundamentally changed this: *"Die Bevölkerung schaut aber immer noch schief"*.[21] Homosexuals are still regarded as 'others', as different and therefore queer. The term 'gay' is still a serviceable swearword. This reflects a hegemonic, heteronormative discourse of normality, in which the focal object is considered as *"das Nicht-Normale"*[22] (Knapp 2010: unpublished speech delivered during the inaugural meeting of the *Fachgesellschaft Geschlechterstudien*[23] in Berlin, 29/30th January 2010; Jakobson 1971). It is often emphasised that knowing homosexual people helps to break down existing prejudices. Some interviewees consider homosexuality to be a form of discrimination "from the outside". They assume that it takes a great deal of self-confidence to "come out": *"Wenn der Homosexuelle die Homosexualität als Normalität betrachtet, dann kann er sich outen, wenn er sich nach der Familie oder den Freunden richtet, dann nicht"*[24]. However, an understanding for the fear of coming out is also justified quantitatively: *"Weil das eine Ausnahme ist"*[25]. This conflates the fear of coming out with a supposed minority status while it is also stressed that homosexuals do not necessarily consider themselves a minority. Quantitativity as a self-evident fact of majority-oriented democracies, often seems to coincide with a rather poorly developed understanding of or weakly developed tolerance for minorities (protection of minorities): the majority counts and is therefore also right. In the final analysis, the 'others' are required to fit in or remain marginal. Differentiation-competent tolerance and acceptance are often lacking, as is sensitivity for the fact that both the owness and the collective subject in the majority position is the non-owness for the marginalised others. Gay men are described as more sensitive people, not only in comparison to other men, but also – and this is noteworthy – to women. This transcends the traditional, essentialist notion of the duality of gender in that sensitivity is not, as it were, attributed automatically to women per se as an essential behavioural disposition. Although none of those interviewed called him/herself homosexual or lesbian, some interviewees explicitly called the notion of gender normality itself into question; uncertainties are admitted and some concede: *"Wer weiß schon, was normal ist?"*[26].

The extent to which liberal attitudes can go hand in hand with ethnically connoted discrimination is shown by the statement of one interviewee who believes that today's society is much more liberal in its approach to homosexuality and

---

21 | Personal translation: "But the populace still looks askance at it".
22 | Personal translation: "The non-normal".
23 | Personal translation: "Gender Studies Association".
24 | Personal translation: "If the homosexual person herself regards homosexuality as the norm, she/he can come out; if he/she orients him/herself on family or friends, then he/she can't".
25 | Personal translation: "Because that [meaning homosexuality] is the exception".
26 | Personal translation: "Who can say what is normal, anyway?".

homosexuals: *"Heute ist alles liberaler, außer vielleicht bei den Portugiesen, die noch Angst haben, mit ihren Eltern darüber zu sprechen"*[27]. Here too it can be seen how easily even democratically motivated majority discourses construct minorities and assign them a marginalised status and how closely tolerance and discriminatory attitudes can be aligned.

Transsexuality

75 % of those questioned do understand that there are people who do not feel comfortable in their gender role and 52 % can understand people who wish to change their sex. Among the status-oriented milieu, an understanding for people who do not feel comfortable in their gender roles is very marked, at 80 %, as is that for transsexuals, at 73 %. This value is lowest in the petty bourgeois milieu. However, even within this group 70 % still show understanding for not feeling comfortable in the gender role. At 43 %, sympathy for transsexuals is significantly lower.

The following table shows the significantly highest and/or lowest values:

Categories	Highest Approval Rating	Item	Lowest Approval Rating
Gender	Women	Understanding for discomfort with the gender role	Men
Nationality	n.a.		n.a.
Age	45-59		60 plus
Education	n.a.		n.a.
Occupation	n.a.		n.a.
Type of employment	Housewife/househusband		Other work
Family situation			n.a.
Civil status	n.a. de facto marriage/civil union partnership		Widowed
Gender	Women	Understanding for transsexuals	Men
Nationality	German		Portuguese
Age	30-59		60 plus
Education	University		Lower school
Occupation	Housewife/househusband		Pensioner
Type of employment			Unemployed
Family situation	Housewife/househusband		n.a.
Civil status	n.a. de facto marriage/civil union partnership		Widowed

Table 1: Views on/attitudes towards transsexuality (n.a. = not applicable).

---

27 | Personal translation: "Today everything is more liberal, except maybe among the Portuguese, who are still afraid to discuss it with their parents".

Here, two things emerge: the responses regarding understanding for discomfort with the gender role show no significant results in respect to nationality, education, occupation and family situation, pointing to the fact that responses are equally distributed across these categories. It is women, those aged between 45 and 49, those who are homemakers and those living in de facto marriage/civil union partnerships, who show the highest significant approval rating.

We can observe a stronger polarisation in the response behaviour when interviewees were asked about showing understanding for transsexuals. Only with regard to the family situation are there no significant answers. Again, it is women, 30 to 59-year-olds, German nationals, university graduates, homemakers, as well as those living in de facto marriage/civil union partnerships, who approve strongly. The lowest approval rating to these questions, above all concerning the attitude towards transsexuals, can be found among men, over 60, lower school graduates, the widowed, pensioners and the unemployed.

In the interviews nobody referred to themselves as transsexual. Only three of the interviewees reported knowing transsexuals. Some stated having acquaintances who know transsexuals, others had vaguely heard of them and some reported having seen something about them on television documentaries. One interviewee remembered a female classmate in secondary school who looked like a boy and thought this could be somebody who later became a boy. She mentioned how deeply uncertain everyone at school was at the time, approximately 15 years ago, about how to approach the girl. Generally, in the interviews, transsexuality was closely associated with homosexuality or was associated with, for instance, breast enlargement. It was often mentioned that, due to the uncertainty about how to approach transsexuals, these are frequently subjected to ridicule. Interviewees repeatedly emphasised the importance to immediately consult a psychologist or doctor at the first signs of transsexual behaviour. Alongside this tendency to pathologize, there were also calls for tolerance while underlining the fact that this is easier in theory than in practice.

During the interviews, we also asked how the interviewees would approach a child who did not feel comfortable in his/her own gendered body. The answers indicate a lack of knowledge, helplessness as well as insecurity in approaching such a child. Some of those interviewed said that this would perhaps/hopefully only be a passing phase: "*Wenn es sich wieder einrenkt, ist es eben gut*"[28]. With regard to adults, however, other interviewees believe that it would be absolutely necessary for those who would like to change their sex to do so, because remaining in a state of such discontent can also make you ill.

The subject of transsexuality, like homosexuality, is still associated with fear and is regarded as a blow of fate. The further the subject penetrates into people's private lives, the more of a threat it appears to become. A line of demarcation is set up between the genders when interviewees repeatedly stress that men have more

---

28 | Personal translation: "If it straightens itself out again, that would be just great".

issues with this subject than women. But it is also stated that it might be a challenge for mothers should their boy prefer to be a girl or vice versa. The latter would be more difficult for the mother to understand: after all, she herself is content to be female. This reveals the relevance of identification with one's own gender. If this is called into question, irritations arise. For instance, one interviewee stressed that a father would have a greater issue with the outing of a homosexual son than would a mother, because he is a man.

Gender Models

Favoured Gender Models: Egalitarian Role Distribution – As Long as There Are No Children

Attitudes towards different gender models were determined using the following questions:

Which work distribution model within a life partnership do you consider best?

A. The man works full-time, the woman is not employed and she takes care of the household and family
B. The man works full-time, the woman part-time and she takes care of the household and family
C. Both partners share work, household and family chores equitably
D. The woman works full-time, the man part-time and he takes care of the household and family
E. The woman works full-time, the man is not employed and takes care of the household and family

The individual models received the following approval ratings:

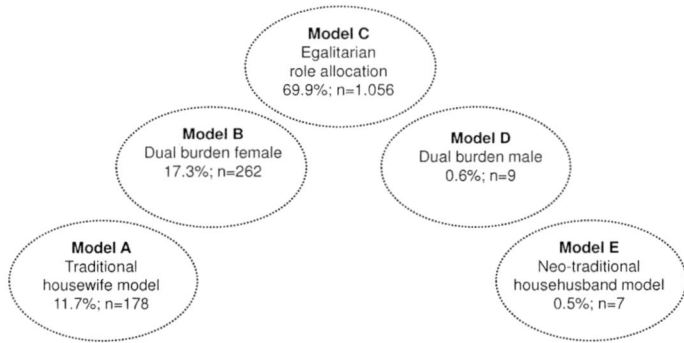

Figure 1: Approval ratings for the models A-E in % and absolute numbers of respondents.

Because it is not possible to calculate the statistical significances for models D and E due to the low number of answers (n < 30), we shall, in the following paragraphs, briefly outline which groups of people responded to these most often: model D is primarily endorsed by young, single students or those living in partnerships with or without children, in households of 3-5 people, possibly in shared accommodation close to town or in the parental home and of French origin. Those who endorse this model come from all income groups except that of € 5,000-7,000 and are most strongly represented in the alternative milieu. Astonishingly, model E is primarily endorsed by the over 45-year-olds, by people without children, people who are widowed or those living in 1- or 2-person households in rented or owned accommodation. People with a household income of € 4,000-5,000 are most likely to endorse this model, as are members of the hedonistic milieu.

The frequency with which model C is named is quite surprising, since it unambiguously advocates an egalitarian division of tasks between the genders. The response behaviour of women and men *does not differ* significantly in relation to models A, B and C. We can therefore say that differing gender models are represented in distinct profile whereby it is, however, not possible to demonstrate that the gender of the interviewee is a discriminating category. This indicates that concepts relating to different gender models are not (re)produced through gender affiliation itself but that there may be other categorisations that have a greater bearing on gender models. Among other things this means that, when it comes to explaining existing representations of questions of gender, it may seem appropriate to follow an intersectional approach.

Childlessness seems to raise the approval rating for the egalitarian model amongst both those living in partnerships and those living alone. Put differently, as soon as children appear within a relationship, the approval rating for egalitarian partnership and occupational models decreases. It is easier to endorse gender equality when not confronted with the actual reality of bringing up children. Parenthood/childlessness, therefore, play no insignificant role in the context of identity attribution and appropriation processes, and should be included in the intersectional canon.

While there are clear differences in response behaviour with regard to models A and C, the percentage spread of response behaviour for model B is small. From this one can conclude that this model of a dual burden for the woman is most readily accepted by a broad segment of the population across all categories such as age, school education etc.

Although model C – the egalitarian distribution of tasks – meets with the highest approval rating, only 51 % of all interviewees state that they themselves would be willing to curtail their professional activities, for instance to better be able to balance their family and work commitments. Even though gender was not revealed to be a significant factor in response behaviour in terms of endorsing model C, it is nevertheless the case that significantly more women are prepared to curtail their own professional ambitions to achieve a better balance between work and family life. The following table provides an insight into the highest and lowest approval ratings for models A, B and C:

Highest Approval Rating	Models	Lowest Approval Rating
Over 60-year-olds Luxembourg nationality Partnership with children Widowed Helping members of the family Lower school graduates	Model A: Traditional housewife model	20-29-year-olds French nationality Single without children Separated, single, living in de facto marriage/civil union partnership Students, freelancers Public officials Etudes Supérieures
All age groups except 20-29-year-olds Italian nationality Partnership with children Living in de facto marriage/civil union partnership Employees Other educational levels	Model B: Dual burden for the woman	20-29-year-olds British nationality Single without children Single Students University
20-29-year-olds British nationality Single without children Single Students University	Model C: Egalitarian role distribution	Over 60-year-olds Italian nationality Partnership with children Widowed Helping members of the family Lower school graduates

Table 2: Gender model preferences.

Model A, the traditional housewife model, is most favoured within the petty bourgeois milieu. Members of several milieus favour model B, a dual burden for the woman, at 20 % each: the petty bourgeois, the underprivileged, the status-oriented and the meritocratic-oriented milieus. Model C, an egalitarian distribution of roles, is most favoured by members of the privileged liberal milieu. As stated above, model D, a dual burden for the man, finds the highest approval rating among members of the alternative milieu, and model E, the neo-traditional househusband model, among members of the hedonistic milieu.

Lived Gender Models

The interviews clearly showed that all gender models are represented. Interviewees repeatedly stressed that women and men should be able to decide freely how to arrange their private lives. Some however also stated that a lack of childcare facilities, the low quality of these facilities and financial constraints, influenced the decision about who stays at home. Many female interviewees affirmed they enjoyed staying home as a mother. However, in individual cases, they then also elaborated on how much they missed external contact and intellectual activity. A further subject broached concerned the 'competition among mothers', for instance, when organising the perfect children's party becomes a yardstick for determining the 'quality' of mothers. It was frequently emphasised that bringing up children requires an "all-out commitment" and that men often do not consider themselves capable of meeting the demands of household and child education. They do not feel capable of performing educational tasks, it was said, above all with babies or toddlers, even if they are their own children. It is also evident that collectively organised households change once a child is born: as a rule it is the women who stay at home. Raising children is still not a matter of course for men. This confirms the results in the Favoured Gender Models Section presented earlier that role allocation based on partnership is closely linked to childlessness and parenthood. If, however, men do become active in the household or in bringing up slightly older children (mostly upwards of four years of age), then they, as well as their female partners, mentioned that this was often done with pleasure and enjoyment.

Another factor that contributes to a non-traditional distribution of housework and child care is professional independence, which facilitates the life-work balance because flexible working hours also enable fathers to spend more time looking after the children. The aspect of effectiveness is also mentioned: who can do what best and fastest? Ranked on a par with this are physical size, professional workload and the time factor. In terms of cooking, a lot also depends on what needs to be cooked and for whom, i.e. the degree of sociability. In one case, the woman cooks whenever there are English-speaking visitors so that she does not have to converse in English, which is left to the husband. Gender, culture, ethnic origin, linguistic competence and cooking all intersect in this instance: a clear example of how the concept of intersectionalty manifests itself in everyday life. Yet, Goffman-type front and back stages (Goffman 1969) also emerge in the interviews. For instance, when it is reported that in one relationship described as a partnership, the woman is responsible for doing the laundry in the basement and he for what happens "upstairs": she does the laundry and hangs it up; he irons and folds the clothes. Interestingly, this picture recurs in the spatial division of cleaning: "*Sie putzt den hinteren Teil der Wohnung und ich den vorderen*"[29].

Concerning the question what prompted the decision to adopt a changed gender model, some of the interviewees cited their parents as a role model.

---

29 | Personal translation: "She cleans the rear side of the flat and I do the front".

Others emphasised that they had conceived and applied their own gender model in pronounced contrast to what they had experienced at home with their parents. However, considerably more research is needed to gain a more precise understanding of these routes to change.

In the interviews, traditional gender models were often referred to as something completely normal and natural. The traditional aspect was generally never called in question. Also, it was often emphasised that there was even no need to discuss it. Here we can clearly observe both the non-explicitness of discourses of normality and the related 'discussion-free' adoption of role attributions. This could be seen as evidence for the assumption that in the hegemonic, discourse of normality only the non-normal is highlighted. For instance, the interviews often showed that the 'still' normal seems to be frequently sneered at by those who have freed themselves of it. Which, in turn, can provoke annoyance among the 'traditionalists' about the so-called arrogance of the 'others'.

Knowledge of Laws and Provisions Relating to Male and Female Equality

The over 60-year-olds, in particular, are familiar with laws or Luxembourgish regulations relating to the equality of women and men. On the other hand, it is clearly the 16 to 20 year-olds who are aware of the *Girls' and Boys' Day* (GBD), an event meant to sensitise girls and boys to so-called atypical professions and which has been in existence in Luxembourg for girls since 2002 and for boys since 2005. Whereas the *Girl's Day* is equally familiar to women and men, it is unequivocally clear that men are more likely to be familiar with legislation while women are more likely also to have heard about the *Boy's Day*. The laws and regulations are most familiar to Germans living in Luxembourg, while it is without doubt the GBD that is most widely known among Luxembourgers. On the whole, familiarity with laws, regulations and the GBD increases in proportion to the level of education.

A remarkable lack of awareness and knowledge of existing laws and regulations is evident from the interviews. More or less known are the following: pregnancy protection regulations, the "*Wegweisungsgesetz*"[30], laws concerning equality of pay, marital status laws, divorce legislation, registered partnerships. Despite all ignorance, it is still frequently and emphatically claimed that legislation tends to favour women. The relevance of the laws and regulations for everyday life is negated in proportion to the level of ignorance. Interviewees are barely aware of the fact that they live in a society regulated by contracts. Laws and regulations are considered to be necessary only for special circumstances, for example, in the case of domestic violence. It is also stressed that one has to stand up personally for one's rights, even in the case of gender equality. The quota debate is often dismissed as nonsense.

---

30 | A law with provisions to combat domestic violence. It allows for an abusive member of a household to be expelled from that household by court order.

Here we see an interesting cross-link to the discourse of competence, when it is stated that it is competence and not gender that matters. Gender disparities, it is argued, cannot be diminished by legislation, instead, it is a question of education, upbringing and a change of attitudes, and this takes time.

Gender Category within the Polyphonic Choir of Intersectionality

While, until the late 1990s, gender was considered to be *the* structural category within scientific feminist discourse, the present findings show that gender has lost some of its discriminatory power as a category of analysis. Having become just *one* aspect within the polyphonic choir of intersectionality, gender has been put into perspective. Individual sections emerge more or less strongly within the overall mesh of identities, depending upon the situation. At times it is age, sometimes professional standing, sometimes sexual orientation that is more significant and becomes the aspect that identifies the subject. According to the present findings therefore, gender assumes a rather inferior role in social interaction. When it comes to assumptions concerning femininity and masculinity, essentialist and constructivist notions of identities and genders are discursively tightly intertwined. This possibly points to an astonishing proximity and overlapping of these discourse figures, which are often treated as a dichotomy within the prevailing paradigm. Something similar obtains in the case of tolerance and discriminatory attitudes. In terms of preferences for gender models, hegemonic discourses of normality seem to have become as shaky as traditional notions of homosexuality and transsexuality, although they have not yet lost their effectiveness as an instrument of inclusion and exclusion and can still contribute to the marginalisation of minorities. Nevertheless – according to the findings – a lot has happened within Luxembourgish society in terms of increasing gender equality. Gender barriers have become more porous although the porosity does not yet seem to be in balance: it seems to be easier to transit from the so-called female side to the so-called male side than vice versa. And yet it is clearly evident that traditional gender representations have by no means completely lost their power, in particular in relation to parenthood. Parenthood still seems to impede the implementation of egalitarian partnership and professional practice. Women are still more likely than men to be willing to prioritise the family *at the expense of* their own professional activity. Actual structural changes such as rising employment rates for women, increasingly improved levels of education as well as a growing presence of women in politics and in the public eye (Allegrezza et al. 2007; *Ministère de l'Egalité des Chances* 2006; *Ministère de l'Education Nationale et de la Formation Professionnelle* 2007) have been proven to have had no direct influence on people's attitudes to the subject of gender. We can, therefore, speak of the persistence of 'resistant remnants' that, in the case of women, are likely to emerge in the areas of motherliness and responsibility for reconciling professional and family life and, in the case of men, in naturalistically based assumptions of essentially different genders as well as men's superior aptitude for professional life.

Clearly, however, such gender-polarising attribution processes are undertaken by all genders in a gender-crossing manner. Notwithstanding these 'resistant remnants', (gender) identities are increasingly appearing as permanent performances within the intersectional canon. They form a space within which subjects can position themselves interactively and in which time and again the gender affiliations of the protagonists can play a role – and do so. The effectiveness of the categories is in a state of flux. The gender category has been set in motion: gender in motion.

7.3 'Good' Food. Oscillation between Political Concept and Individual Everyday Practice

Researching Identity-Relevant Food Standards and Practice

The following identity construction case study is about normative ideas about 'good' food and how 'good' eating takes place in practice. The qualitatively as well as quantitatively oriented analysis body simultaneously covers institutional as well as individual dynamics: on the one hand, it is based on a group interview with experts as well as on political publications on the topic and, on the other hand, on a representative survey as well as qualitative interviews among Luxembourg's resident population.

This research topic offers the possibility of investigating the intermeshing of normative influences with largely routine and unquestioned discursive practices, by way of the subjects' banal and recurring need to eat. Because of human omnivorism[31] (Fischler 1990), these discursive practices give rise to questions concerning the resource-driven food selection (what to eat?), its preparation and compilation (how to eat?) and communal eating with selected companions (with whom to eat?). The everyday, individual handling of these questions (*Perceptas*) permits an analytic look into their underlying and collectively available values, attitudes and standards (*Conceptas*)[32] – which in turn, enables one to draw conclusions about meaningful processes of "identity work", articulated through everyday actions (see Keupp et al. 2006). In this context, the concept of identity work is understood to be a form of autonomous self-construction as well as collective co-creation at the level of community and/or society. For it is precisely through bodily actions like eating that the individual consciously constructs itself as 'I' with idiosyncratic preferences and habits. At the same time, it is being both physiologically and symbolically constituted by the food ingested. It forms collective concepts of 'good' food by interpreting them, albeit individually, but without breaking out of the traditional framework. At the same time, the individual repertoire of actions, which includes

---

31 | The physiological fact that humans can eat nearly everything – however, within a framework of the culturally acceptable.
32 | See Section 7.1.

recipes, menu composition, taste preferences, table manners, meal creation, values and attitudes to food, food conversations etc. – is framed by the prevailing, collective (cultural, socio-economic and milieu-specific) attitudes, thought and knowledge bases (Bourdieu 2000; 1994; 1980). This suggests that everyday eating behaviour is closely interwoven with individual or collective identities; however, the relationship between them is neither unequivocal nor constant (Scholliers et al. 2001).

A certain lack of visibility, non-mentionability and intimacy are inherent in the apparently self-evident aspects of identity-relevant discursive practices. This has practical consequences for research, as interviewees in a qualitative partially-guided conversation are not easily able to verbalise those contexts and value concepts, which are of interest to us, due to the, for many, unusual subject area and the frequently unincisive self-reflection in relation to one's own eating habits. One consequence in terms of conducting the interviews was the need to steer the conversation towards the subject of collective identifications. Thus, the interviewees articulated the topics of food and identity in relation to ethnic, national or family affiliations through ostentatious or festive, often stereotyped, consumption of certain dishes or ingredients on specific occasions[33]. For instance, they made statements like: "We Portuguese eat a lot of fish" or "*Quand on va boire un café dans un bistrot en Italie, dans n'importe quelle ville, on papote avec tout le monde sans problème*"[34]. Such verbalisations at the collective level seem unproblematic, since they merely involve invoking existing collective attributions, the construction of which has already been completed and which are available as cultural identity choices. By contrast, it seems to be a far more complex task for interviewees to verbalise food and identity at an individual level. This is the area of self-construction, i.e. implicit, ongoing subjectivisation, which is often perceived to be problematic. It is characterised by potential selections between varying normative options (Corbeau/Poulain 2002)[35] and accordingly generates insecurity on account of insufficient univocity. The latter can be experienced as a questioning of the self and therefore as a general feeling of vulnerability in the course of the autonomous modelling of *identity in progress*.

In order to lessen the effect of the described problem areas, research interest was directed towards an external and contrastive point of reference. This consisted of the interviewees' positioning their food-related discursive practices in relation

---

33 | The aim of this investigation was not to analyse the role of *produits du terroir* and regional cuisine in Luxembourgish identity constructions; this will be done elsewhere.

34 | Personal translation: "When you drink a coffee in a bar in Italy, no matter where, you can chat with anybody without a problem".

35 | According to the food manufacturers and distributers, the variety of the possible menu plans is meant to simplify personal decisions by avoiding repetitive boredom; in fact, however, the orientation according to different standards, behind the various products, causes confusion. For instance, industrial, mass-produced ready-to-serve meals coexist alongside non genetically manipulated biological canned food. Both simplify food preparation, but they correspond to diametrically opposite production chains and consumption positionings.

to a specific concept of 'good' food: a national action plan coordinated[36] by four Luxembourgish ministries and launched in July 2007 under the programmatic title *"Gesond iessen, méi bewegen"*[37]. In the current context, this national action plan (hereinafter referred to as GIMB) is deemed to be the institutional attribution of an identity option, which is represented as being politically and socially desirable. This impression is reinforced when the substructure for the action plan – international comparisons of scientific findings as well as moral governing efforts in the field of public health (see below) – is taken into account. The converging as well as the divergent interactions between these morally loaded, collective attributions on the one hand and the ethically coined, individual appropriations on the other hand[38] provide an insight into the subjects' dynamic identity work in the Luxembourgish context.

Health Orientation at a Political Level

Political Concept of Action

To find out which performative attribution, in the sense of a moral identification ideal, is being conveyed, via GIMB, one must begin by explaining the self-image of those responsible at a political level. The initial assumptions for political (prophylactic and, if necessary, corrective) intervention in the field of public health, concerning nutrition and exercise, are based on comparative scientific studies from the *World Health Organisation* (among others WHO 1999; WHO 2008) and the *European Commission* (among others CE 2007; CE 2005). In particular, recurring reference is made to the definition of obesity as an epidemic, which, it is assumed, accompanies increasing purchasing power and leads to a series of secondary illnesses[39]. At the national level, a study by the Luxembourgish

---

36 | In detail, this concerns the relevant ministries in the areas of health, education, family and sport.

37 | Personal translation: "Eat healthily, get more exercise."

38 | We are following Foucault in his differentiation between morals and ethics. Morals stand for "a collection of values and action guidelines, which are foisted upon the individual and groups by various dictating instances – family, educational institutions, churches etc. It can be the case that these rules and values are emphatically formulated as part of a coherent doctrine and comprehensive system of instruction. But it can also be the case that they are transmitted in an unstructured manner and that, rather than forming a systematic whole, they constitute a complex interplay of mutually compensating, correcting, partially mutually exclusive elements, which therefore allow for excuses and compromises" (Foucault 1984a: 36). This "moral code" goes hand in hand with the ethical "way and manner in which one acts and behaves – how one constructs oneself as a moral subject, who acts in relation to the regulations constituting the code" (*ibid.*, 36).

39 | Cardiovascular diseases, cancer, Type 2 diabetes, osteoporosis, etc.

Ministry of Health and *Ministry of Education*[40] produced similar results to those in neighbouring countries, which legitimised similar action strategies by the political decision makers within the scope of GIMB – from the integration into European and international networks up to exchanging information about the respective strategies.

In light of this background, any peculiarities of the Grand Duchy are not to be sought in the initial problem but rather in the political intervention's implementation[41]. Institutional courses of action at a national level are based on a panel of experts[42], an inter-ministerial committee[43] and on texts from the public domain[44]. The conceptual approach is based on the principles of *Health in All Policies*[45], the policy of *Santé 21*[46] and the *European Charter on Counteracting Obesity*[47]. Based on a "multi-factorial"[48] understanding of health, these initiatives result in an interdisciplinary and intersectional political approach. Specifically the

---

40 | *Ministère de l'Education Nationale et de la Formation Professionnelle/Ministère de la Santé*/University of Karlsruhe 2006.

41 | Even though the current two to four language communication system (German and French, at times extended to include Portuguese and English) represents a considerable additional effort, it also constitutes a considerable value-add by catering to different cultural patterns and points of references.

42 | Primarily, this involved discussions between medical practitioners of various disciplines about a scientific-technical consensus on nationally defined nutritional guidelines. In particular, the focus was on a sustainable and active implementation in the creation of a public health policy, i.e. of "uniting partners and enthusing them".

43 | This has a coordination and evaluation role for the projects submitted by partner institutions, which are to be run under the label and the logo of GIMB.

44 | In particular the policy signed on 05.07.2006 by four ministries (health, education, sport and family) known as *"Politique commune favorisant l'alimentation saine et l'activité physique"*, in the form of the *"Programme national pour la promotion de l'alimentation saine et de l'activité physique 'Gesond iessen méi bewegen'"*, but also the criteria to be met by submitted projects to obtain the right to use the GIMB label and logo.

45 | Flagship initiative of the Finnish Ministry for Social Matters and Health (in international political cooperation), during the Finnish EU presidency in 2006, for promoting "healthy decisions" and "health education" (Ståhl *et al.* 2006: 15).

46 | The World Health Organisation's framework policy concerning health in the European zone (51 nations).

47 | European ministerial conference, Istanbul, 15.-17.11.2006.

48 | The interview quotes from the section "Health Orientation at a Political Level" are taken from the expert discussion on 16.12.2008 with the responsible team in the Ministry of Health (which, as is not unusual in Luxembourg, was held in various languages, but has been reproduced in English for reasons of legibility), whereas the quotes from the section "Personal Responsibility in Everyday Nutritional Management" come from interviews with members of the resident population of Luxembourg.

health ministry draws together thematically and temporally circumscribed "actions" or "projects" initiated by partner institutions like schools, *Maisons Relais pour Enfants*[49], local authorities, but also by associations and the like, and implemented under the GIMB motto. In addition, the ministry provides these "actors in the field" with a platform for the exchange of experiences and networking, but without systematised feedback of the results of their initiatives. Much less is there any formal communication between the ministry and the population as a whole, except via school children. These are supposed to come into contact with state-funded educational materials[50] distributed throughout all schools and to then sensitise their parents. This process – if it happens at all – is designed for the long term and geared towards social and cultural change. This "profound change of habits" is exactly what those responsible for GIMB are striving for, i.e., for "awareness creation that leads to mobilisation, interest and commitment". GIMB projects, therefore, are not about a "one-to-one implementation of the ministerial guidelines, but are based upon a creative interpretation of what is practically achievable".

Information Campaign for the Resident Population

So those responsible for GIMB see themselves primarily as impulse providers for a sustainable and long-term process, which they support from the top down through different institutions and would ultimately like to see embedded in society. As a counterpart to the core activity of the ministerial assignment of the GIMB logo and label for specific actions, a bilingual information pamphlet containing guidelines on health-promoting exercise and nutrition in daily life was distributed to the entire resident population.

The resident population's engagement with GIMB detected during our interviews shows that only the above-named public relations work has been perceived. The "green pamphlet"[51] – as the pamphlet "*Freude am gesunden Essen. Spaß an der Bewegung/Le plaisir de bien manger et d'être actif!*"[52] (2007 edition) was often called by those interviewed – is divided into a two-page introduction, nutritional recommendations, advice on physical exercise (one and a half pages) as well as an address list of central institutions (half a page). The main emphasis, at a total of seven pages, is on nutrition, which can presumably be traced back to the

---

49 | A form of day-care centres for children, founded as part of the grand-ducal Règlement of 20.07.2005.

50 | Various topical folders were developed in collaboration with the publisher aid (Bonn, Germany), which are designed to be attractive, practically oriented and playful. Teachers are free to use these in everyday school life at their own discretion.

51 | The bright green colour chosen as a background for the entire pamphlet makes a statement because it connotes vegetables on the one hand (representing the aspect *"gesond iessen"*, see also our interview analysis) and nature on the other (as backdrop for outdoor leisure activities as a young family related to the aspect of *"méi bewegen"*).

52 | Personal translation: "Enjoying healthy food, enjoying exercise!".

numerous options available in this area, in contrast to the catchy maxim "exercise at least 30 minutes a day" (page 9).

Notwithstanding the pamphlet's serious contextual foil – which points out the statistical correlation between poor nutrition and insufficient exercise with the diseases of civilisation, health insurance costs and death rates, making "urgent action necessary" (page 1) – the authors have endeavoured to keep the tone playfully positive and encouraging. The pamphlet's summery-fresh colours and amusing illustrations emphasise this additionally. On the whole, the recommendations are formulated in a positive manner, e.g., "consume milk and dairy products every day" (page 5), etc. Wherever it is not possible to rephrase the negative aspects of a message, an alternative is offered, e.g. "limit the consumption of fatty food. Use vegetable fats in preference to animal fats" (page 4). Thus rather than some foods being "forbidden", value is placed on variety and food intake based on the nutrition pyramid, i.e., based ultimately on the assumptions of dietetics[53].

Figure 2: Cover page of the pamphlet "Freude am gesunden Essen. Spaß an der Bewegung!/Le plaisir de bien manger et d'être actif!" *(2007 edition) (Enjoying healthy food, enjoying exercise).*

---

53 | Significantly, the *Association Nationale des Diététicien(ne)s du Luxembourg* is the only national level non-state partner organisation mentioned in the pamphlet.

In the Health Minister's introduction to the pamphlet, the legitimacy of the euphemistically described effort, which the intended change of eating habits entails ("*I* wish *you* stamina"), is reinforced by greater self-esteem arising from "joy" and "feeling comfortable in your skin" among other things. For instance, "I wish you stamina" goes hand in hand with the "fun of discovering new eating and exercise habits and incorporating them into *your* daily life" (page 1). This distance-creating grammatical form conceals a judgement: a specific 'I' appears in a position of superiority, which provides benevolent advice to the readership. An inclusive formulation would have been more able to articulate solidarity as expressed, for instance, by the authors of the collaborating institutions: "Let's discover the benefit and fun *together* [...]; they are an important component of *our* well-being" (page 2). But even in this text passage, the 'bad' habits – which make action by the state necessary – are attributed to the readership constructed as an alterity: "By no means is it necessary to abstain completely from *your* favourite foods for good health". The apparent complicity at this point creates the impression, through the affectively felt experience of eating, that there is a natural relationship between what is unhealthy and what is preferred. The basic concept behind the pamphlet can ultimately be summed up in a result derived from "various studies"[54]: "*every fourth* adolescent and *every second adult* suffers from obesity" (page 2). On the one hand, this statement refers to obesity in terms of an 'ailment'[55], the existence or impact of which is not or is only to a small extent considered by those affected[56]. Thus the people we interviewed, for example, did not primarily refer to their body weight as a motivation for healthy eating. Rather, they raised the issue of an ethical endeavour to handle their own general health-capital responsibly – however, not in terms of preventing specific pathologies. From a formal point of view, the radical attribution of 'ailment' represents a break with the reformist-constructive change of habits, which the pamphlet endeavours to convey through the use of a respectful and considerate vocabulary. On the other hand, the statement cited above focuses on the individual and, in this regard, comes close to the everyday experience of eating. Our interviews confirm the feeling of the interviewees that for the most part, food choice and food preparation is an individual and complex decision, which concerns the person and his/her immediate environment (e.g. when he/she cooks for family, roommates, guests, etc.). According to the survey results, the demand for a well-balanced meal has a tendency to increase when children are present at the family dining table. The pamphlet acknowledges this circumstance in as much as the illustrations exclusively depict young families, which implicitly represent the

---

54 | Remarkably, these scientific statements are translated in the French version of the pamphlet as *"faits"* (personal translation: "Facts") (p. 2).
55 | A more value-free description could have been "[...] overweight" (although this too smacks of a reference to a standardised ideal value).
56 | The HBSC studies on this topic carried out at an international and national level are only available in relation to adolescents.

most important target group. In terms of content, the focus on the individual food components[57] assumes an analytical knowledge of cooking ingredients, food and meal combinations – although the ministerial recommendations view themselves in general as more pragmatically oriented and provide specific guidance[58]. Thus, the recommendations can also appeal to other population groups, as will be shown on the following pages.

Personal Responsibility in Everyday Eating Practice

Selective Internalisation of General Dietary Recommendations

The authors of the institutional identity option GIMB consider 'good' food to be 'healthy' food, which is varied and balanced and the consumption of which should provide pleasure. The interviewees' understanding deviates partly from this health-oriented concept, due to the selective acceptance of different aspects of this approach while disregarding others, as well as extending the category of 'good' food by differently oriented, individual or intersubjective criteria.

Part of these relative divergences can be traced back to the level of familiarity with GIMB: 70 % of the interviewees state that they have heard of GIMB. However less than half of these (43 %) have actively engaged with it (above all from the privileged liberal and the alternative milieus, i.e. mainly people with university degrees and a high income (€ 5,000-7,000), mostly with children). Apart from that, not much attention is paid to the nationwide ministerial information campaign: "I didn't give it much thought", *"Also schon eng Kéier duerchgekuckt, jo mä net méi"*[59], *"do war mol sou e Flyer"*[60] or *"ech kennen nëmmen d'Iwwerschrëft"*[61].

Remarkably, the information provided by the interviewees about their daily and weekly menus indicates – at least at a discursive level – a selective internalisation of general dietary recommendations, even if these are not specifically associated with GIMB. This result is only partially associated with the socio-cultural milieus considered; in particular for the categories sweets and pastries, fruit and vegetables, as well as cereal products, there is a consensus in all milieus (no deviation from the average of greater or less than 5 %), and for alcoholic beverages and meat in nearly all milieus (one deviation of greater or less than 5 %). The food categories least influenced by socio-demographic variables[62] – the consumption of which is thus the most stable for society as a whole – are milk and dairy products, cereal

---

57 | Fruit and vegetables, fats, liquid, pastries, dairy products, salt and sugar.
58 | For instance, the fact that one can estimate the approximate fat content of pastry by the "grease spots on the packaging" (p. 4).
59 | Personal translation: "Well, I have leafed through it once, yes, but not any more".
60 | Personal translation: "There was one of those flyers once".
61 | Personal translation: "I only know the title".
62 | Age, gender, education, occupation, family situation and occupational state of the interviewees.

products as well as fruit and vegetables[63]. Accordingly, 81 % of the interviewees stated the following as the most widespread dietary ideal: "light and briefly cooked meals constitute good food".

Food category	Total percentage (a + b)	Most frequent answer (a)	Second-most frequent answer (b)
Information on how often consumed per day			
Milk and dairy products	85 %	Two to three times per day (43 %)	Once per day (42 %)
Fruit and vegetables	83 %	Two to three times per day (44 %)	Once per day (38 %)
Alcoholic beverages	78 %	Never (43 %)	Once per day (35 %)
Sausages and cold cuts	77 %	Once per day (48 %)	Never (29 %)
Salty snacks	77 %	Never (52 %)	Once per day (25 %)
Sweets and pastries	71 %	Once per day (56 %)	Less than once per day (15 %)
Soft Drinks	65 %	Never (39 %)	Once per day (26 %)
Information on how often consumed per week			
Cereal products	95 %	More than three times per week (78 %)	Two to three times per week (17 %)
Meat	90 %	More than three times per week (50 %)	Two to three times per week (40 %)
Fish	87 %	Once per week (57 %)	Two to three times per week (30 %)
Potatoes	80 %	Two to three times per week (44 %)	More than three times per week (36 %)

Table 3: The Luxembourg resident population's daily and weekly food consumption frequencies.

In response to the interview question about what is important in relation to nutrition, "balance" is stated as a central concern, and also the moderate consumption of any type of food. This also corresponds to a central concern that is communicated in the GIMB brochure (see above), and it is certainly the most innovative aspect of contemporary international dietary campaigns (Coveney 2006), because it approaches the interviewees' eating habits. They often stated that "more fruit and vegetables" is desirable; only now and then, however, was this mentioned in one breath with the "five a day" slogan. Finally, the interviewees stated that the diet should not be "too fatty" – but here, the health aspect overlaps with the powerful ideal of slimness. The more specific recommendations relating

---

63 | A more detailed depiction of the results is not possible here.

to water and alcohol, pastries, dairy products, salt and sugar, on the other hand, are never or rarely mentioned spontaneously. To some extent, this bracketing out can be traced back to the extremely high everyday value of food, which entails a certain resistance to self-reflection.

'Doing Identity' between Personal Responsibility, Potential to Take Action and Pragmatism

This everyday experience concerning 'good' food comprises several identity-relevant dimensions, which extend beyond the boundaries of the technical preparation of meals (as conveyed by GIMB and other nutritional approaches). These can be collected into three discourse-practical strands of *Doing Identity*:

1) The most common discourse is that of *personal responsibility*, which can be divided into three variants (positive, flexible, negative) and fulfills different demands (subjectivation, responsibility for children and a consumption that is oriented on ethical ideals).

In the positive variant, the daily concern for 'good' food constitutes a challenging field of action, within which self-determined subjectivations can be tried out (through one's own cooking) and developed (by way of the resulting preferences). This is about *"einfach ze probéieren"*[64] and enjoying without feeling guilty (*"ët soll schmaachen"*, *"Schëllegkeet erof"*[65]). *"Aimer ce qu'on mange"*[66] is understood in the double sense of good taste and a positive fundamental attitude towards food, and the options available on the market are seen as an opportunity instead of being taken for granted (*"mir kënnen eis kafen wat mir wëllen"*[67]).

Ich bin grundsätzlich mit meiner Ernährungsweise im Alltag zufrieden. Ja. *Die hängt ja von mir ab.* Wenn ich was Falsches koche, dann kann ich nicht sagen, ich bin beim Kochen nicht zufrieden[68] (Male, 50 years old, Luxembourger, Junglinster).

Ech passen zimlech op datt et ë bëssen gesond ass, jo vill Uebst. Ech denke mer, et kann een jo awer vill maachen fir seng Gesondheet, dat kann een nët alles den Genen iwwerloossen, ech mengen et kann een och sälwer maachen[69] (Female, 74 years old, Luxembourger, Dudelange).

---

64 | Personal translation: "Simply to try things out".
65 | Personal translation: "It has to taste good"; "without feeling guilty".
66 | Personal translation: "Love what you eat".
67 | Personal translation: "We can buy what we want".
68 | Personal translation: "I am basically happy with my daily eating habits. Yes. It depends on me, after all. If I cook something wrong, I can't say, I am not happy with the cooking".
69 | Personal translation: "I do take care that it is healthy, yes, plenty of fruit. I think that you can do a lot for your own health, you can't leave it all up to the genes, I mean, you can make a contribution of your own".

Ech sin zefridden mat menger Ernährungsweis am Alldag, wëll ech éischtens mol doheem sälwer kachen, dat heescht ech sichen sälwer eraus wat ech iesse wëll. [...] Firdrun hun ech alles giess wat mir an d'Aën geflunn ass, ewourobber ech Loscht hat, an elo kucken ech vill méi drop wat ech genau iessen, zum Beispill méi Friichten, manner Schokela, nët zevill naschelen [...]. Am wichtegsten ass esou équilibréiert wéi méiglech, elo nët all Dag Nuddelen, mee esou vill wéi méiglech an verschidden ewéi méiglech an och... jo nët ze vill Naschereien dertëschent, dat heescht datt ech wirklech ee fixe Plang hunn[70] (Female, 18 years old, Portuguese, Stadtbredimus).

However, more widely spread than such decidedly voluntaristic positions, we find flexible arrangements where individual deviations are tolerated if the overall balance seems subjectively adequate:

Ech denke mëttlerweil datt ech also net sou schlecht..., awer bon, 't sinn mol Saachen derbäi, déi net onbedéngt misste sinn. Mee bon, se sinn derbäi[71] (Female, 27 years old, Luxembourger, Vianden).

By contrast, the negative variation of the discourse of personal responsibility is often associated with the argument of "lack of time" but also with culinary conservatism. However, this justification seems rather like a passive avoidance of the complexity of self-technologies in the culinary area[72], which means having to plan as well as to take *ad hoc* decisions, positioning oneself in a field of nearly boundless options, coming up with a wealth of ideas, technical skill and scheduling.

J'aimerais manger plus équilibré, plus... disons que je n'ai pas trop le temps donc euh... Et puis quand on mange au travail, on est toujours obligé de manger des choses qui vont vite euh... – Et vous pensez que vous pouvez un jour changer ça? – Non, je pense pas, mais pourquoi pas? Enfin, il faut se prendre peut-être le soir pour cuisiner quelque chose en avance et ramener au travail, euh je ne sais pas, j'ai pas encore trouvé la solution mais euh... – Qu'est-ce qui l'empêche en fait? – Ben le temps, le temps. C'est que quand on rentre du travail le soir, on est fatigué... Si, je pourrais, je pourrais... mais il y a des jours où ça va, mais c'est pas régulier, ça peut être un jour où je vais manger très bien, vraiment,

---

70 | Personal translation: "I am happy with my daily eating habits because, first of all, I cook for myself at home, which means that I choose what I want to eat. [...] I used to eat everything I saw, whatever I felt like and now I pay much more attention to what exactly I am eating. For example more fruit, less chocolate, not too much snacking [...] The most important thing is balance, so not pasta every day but as much as possible and as varied as possible and also... yes, not too many snacks in between, which means, that I really do have a definite concept".
71 | Personal translation: "These days I reckon I'm not doing all that badly... but, yes, sometimes there are things that are not absolutely necessary. But okay, they are there".
72 | It remains to be clarified to what extent this concerns a self-assessment (lack of confidence) or being overwhelmed (lack of competence).

salade, légumes, tout ça, poisson, et l'autre jour ça va être catastrophe[73] (Female, 28 years old, French, Luxembourg City).

Ausgewogen na ja ... aber wir essen jeden Tag etwas anderes, unterschiedliche Speisen, aber ... Ich könnte vielleicht schon noch einiges ändern, aber es müsste alles so in der gleichen Geschmacksrichtung liegen, die wir gewohnt sind[74] (Male, 38 years old, Portuguese, Consdorf).

One person, however, realises that the aforesaid lack of time has to do with a subjective priority allocation in other areas (in particular the professional field):

Ech sinn eigentlech net zefridden mat menger Ernährungsart a -weis, wëll ech u sech wéisst, wéi ee sech gesond ze ernähren hätt a probéiere menge Kanner dat ze vermëttelen, mä mech selwer awer meeschtens sou ënner Drock setzen, datt ech mech net drun halen[75] (Female, 30 years old, Luxembourger, Dippach).

The ideal of responsible self-government – whether it is being implemented with a certain openness or with doubts and displeasure – gains significance if, in addition to the 'I', it also concerns one's own children. This feeding role seems to be internalised to the extent that it is still considered meaningful even in connection with adult offspring. The discourse of the necessary model role of the parents for their children includes in particular a normative upgrading of the category 'fruit and vegetables'.

Ech sinn zefridden mat der Art a Weis méi ech mech ernähren wëll dat bestëmmen ech jo selwer. An ech kucken wëll ech zwee Kanner hei am Stot hunn, bon deen een ass 18, dat

---

73 | Personal translation: "I would like to eat better-balanced meals, more... let's say that I don't have a lot of time, so, eh... And if one eats at work, one is forced to eat stuff which can be prepared quickly, eh... – And do you think that you will be able to change that one day? – No, I don't believe it, but then again, why not? Oh well, maybe one should take the time to cook something in advance in the evening and take it to work, eh ... I don't know, I haven't yet found the solution, but eh... – What stops you from doing it? – Oh, the time, the time. When you get back from the work in the evening, you are tired... However, I could, I would be able to... but there are also days when it would be possible but not regularly so, there can be a day where I eat very well, salad, vegetables, all that stuff, fish, and then there are other days where it is catastrophic".

74 | Personal translation: "Balanced ah, well... but we are eating something different every day, different meals but... I could probably still change a few things here or there but it would have to be along the same taste as what we are used to".

75 | Personal translation: "Actually I am not happy about my eating habits because, basically, I do know what I should be eating and I also try to get this across to my children, but I usually put myself under so much pressure that I don't keep it up".

anert ass 24... kucken ech awer datt bëssen Uebst a Geméis... a variabel, datt d'Iessen net langweileg ass an datt se gär iessen, jo[76] (Female, 53 years old, different nationality, Lenningen).

Ich finde Suppe sehr wichtig für die Ernährung. [...] Und es ist eine gute Art, die Kinder dazu zu bringen, Gemüse zu essen[77] (Female, 47 years old, Portuguese, Putscheid).

The care for one's own children is, to some extent, associated with an ethical kind of consumerism. From a statistical point of view, this attitude is found among a section of the population that tends to include the older generation, with a slightly greater proportion of women, likely to be either not employed (housewife/househusband, retired) or to be self employed, with children and university degrees. Essentially this profile corresponds to that of those people, who know and have engaged with the GIMB, which means that GIMB is primarily reaching people, whose dietary habits are already orientated in the "desired" direction. In this context, action taken that is explicitly expressed as being of a responsible nature is either directed at the food itself (for instance, traceability or quality of the product) or at the production chain as a whole (for instance, seasonality, regionality, organic farming, fair trade or species-appropriate animal husbandry). Because efforts towards sustainability are motivated by a perceived added value for one's own health or also by the perceived affectivity during the production – i.e. by identity-relevant criteria – this attitude must be regarded as being ambivalent (Lamine 2008):

Ech ginn haaptsächlech an Bio Rayonen akafen. [...] Haaptsächlech Geméis muss wierklech... do muss nach eppes dra sinn. [...] Ech sinn iwwerzeegt, datt déi industriell Nahrungsmëttel, datt do, alles wat sou ouni Léift gemaach ass, datt do wierklech just nach minimal eppes Guddes fir eis dran ass[78] (Female, 41 years old, Luxembourger, Bous).

2) Another thread within the discursive practice under review is that of the *hypothetical potential to take action*; in particular in the case of unexpected health problems or acute weight gain *"wéisst een, wat een ze maachen hätt"*[79]. However, as

---

76 | Personal translation: "I am happy with my eating because it is me who decides. And I see to it, because I have two children at home, well, one of them is 18, the other one is 24... however, I see to it that a bit of fruit and vegetables... and alternately, that the food isn't boring and that they enjoy eating".
77 | Personal translation: "I consider soup to be very important for a healthy diet. [...] And it is a good way of getting children to eat vegetables".
78 | Personal translation: "I mainly buy organic food. [...] Primarily vegetables really have to... there still has to be something in it. [...] I am convinced that these industrial foodstuffs, that everything produced without love, only has a minimal amount of goodness left in it for us".
79 | Personal translation: "Would one know what to do".

long as no significant changes are detectable, indulgence prevails with regard to the occasional 'lapse' – however these may be defined in daily life.

Fir déi Leit déi sech selwer iergendwéi iwwergewiichteg fannen oder déi selwer fannen datt se net gesond iessen ass dat vläicht ee flotten... een Input, sou ze soen an si gesinn, okay wann jiddereen dat mécht, dann kann ech och dozou bäidroen, mee ech perséinlech, also nee[80] (Male, 18 years old, Italian, Strassen).

This attitude can extend to a consciously stressed alternative attitude:

Da kuckt een dat [*above-named pamphlet*], et stellt een awer keng Gedanken drop, da leet een et rëm op d'Säit. Wëll mir beweegen eis net sou gär![81] (Female, 66 years old, Luxembourger, Ettelbruck).

A contradiction is often detectable between general and personal discourse levels. Initiatives like the GIMB (but also information about 'good' food in the media and in specialist literature) are considered to be generally desirable, however, the individual does not feel that it applies to them; thus for instance: "ech fannen et gutt datt de Ministère eppes mécht. Ob et eppes déngt, dat ass eng aner Fro".[82] This is a typical everyday-cultural paradox, which is often circumnavigated by using humour. The ambivalence of the 'solution' is thereby defused for everyday use, but it is not nullified:

– Wie sind Sie auf das Programm *Gesond iessen méi bewegen* aufmerksam geworden? – Durch die Medien. – Und was halten Sie davon? – In unserer Gemeinde gibt's auch so ein Slogan ein Mal pro Jahr. Da werden die Straßen hier für den Verkehr abgesperrt und ich glaube das geht in dieselbe Richtung[83]. – Haben denn diese ...? [*Interrupts*] – Die bewegen aber leider bei mir nicht sehr viel [*laughs*]![84] (Male, 37 years old, Luxembourger, Bertrange).

---

80 | Personal translation: "For people who themselves somehow think they are overweight or who feel that they aren't eating healthily, that might be a nice... input, so to speak, and they can see, okay if everybody is doing this, I can also contribute to it, but for me personally, not really".
81 | Personal translation: "Then you look at it [the above-named pamphlet], but you don't waste a thought on it and then you put it away again. Because we don't really like exercising all that much!".
82 | Personal translation: "I think it is good that the ministry is doing something. Whether it will help, that is another question".
83 | In the sense of a thematic action day, e.g. car-free Sunday.
84 | Personal translation: "– How did you become aware of the Gesond iessen méi bewegen campaign? – Through the media. – And what do you think of it? – Once a year there's a slogan like that in our local community as well. The streets are closed to traffic and I reckon that is

3) Finally, one can detect *pragmatism in the face of contradictory circulating standards* against the background of the preceding discourse-practical threads. Effectively this pragmatism constitutes the most 'banal' and widespread pattern of behaviour in relation to the daily diet – precisely because of its inherent ambivalence, which does recognise the contradictions but is able to come to some arrangement with them. "Personal responsibility" and "hypothetical potential to take action" by contrast, function more as consciously adopted positions. The contradictory nature of the eating standards is perceived with differing degrees of intensity (from bewildering to indifferent to demanding). It can also be structured in a temporal manner – for instance, if the moral concepts of earlier food socialisation do not match those of the current habits. Furthermore, the ambivalence revealed by our research can have an ethical orientation, in particular at the structural development level of the food offer – for instance, if the industrialisation of food production gives rise to doubt about its quality. It also emerges depending upon the situation, mainly at the level of individual confrontation with specific constraints – for instance when there is a discrepancy between dietary recommendations and food supply. The following quote sums up these dimensions:

On n'arrive jamais à vraiment... Parce qu'en plus, la télé, les médecins, ils vous disent: "il faut manger comme ça", en plus maintenant la nourriture n'est plus aussi saine qu'avant alors... [...] On vous dit tout le temps, on vous dit plus quoi manger que dans le temps. Je veux dire, nos parents, on leur disait toujours: "mange, finis ton assiette, mange bien", et nous on nous dit: "attention, ne mange pas trop"! [...] Il faut faire plus attention. [...] Y a beaucoup plus de choix et puis d'un autre côté, on vous dit: "attention, n'en fais pas trop", alors on est un peu frustré[85] (Female, 28 years old, French, Luxembourg-city).

However, no matter how much cognitive effort is put into nutritional composition in everyday experience, it is compensated by a pragmatic focus on the communicative value and community formation through eating. Thus communal eating "*am Familljekrees*"[86] or "*all zesummen*"[87] is very important to many interviewees;

---

along the same lines. - Have these...? - [Interrupts] Unfortunately, they aren't achieving a lot in my case [laughs]!".

85 | Personal translation: "You never really manage... Because, in addition, television and doctors are telling you: 'You have to eat this and that'. Furthermore, food today is not as healthy as it used to be, therefore... You are constantly being told, they tell you much more than before, what you should be eating. What I mean to say is that our parents used to be told: 'Eat! Eat everything on your plate, eat well', and to us, they are saying: 'Be careful, don't eat too much!' [...] You have to be a lot more careful. [...] You have a far greater choice and on the other hand, you are told: 'Careful, don't overdo it', and then you get a bit frustrated".
86 | Personal translation: "With the family".
87 | Personal translation: "All together".

accordingly, the statement "on working days, eating is a good chance for me to get together with others" was endorsed by 74 % of those interviewed[88]:

't ass einfach fir zesummen ze sinn an bëssen, jo, ze schwätzen. [...] Et schafft een, also déi eng ginn schaffen, déi aner ginn an d'Schoul, d.h. et ass ee bal ni zesummen a wéinstens ass een dann, wann een ësst, dann ass een zesummen. Et soll een och e bësse Kommunikatioun hunn[89] (Male, 18 years old, Italian, Strassen).

Oscillations of Identity

The case example cited has highlighted convergences and discrepancies between moral attribution and ethical appropriation within the field of 'good' food, as an example of the crystallisation of identitary concepts at a political-institutional and everyday-cultural level. The process-oriented and creatively set up approach to health at the political level is practice-driven. While it focuses exclusively on food itself – its balanced composition and the resulting sensory wellbeing – it nevertheless deals with only the analytic-cognitive part in respect of the 'good' eating habits of the resident population. Therefore, it appeals in particular to those people who take a positive or flexible view of the challenge of personal responsibility and subjectivation in relation to eating and who possess the necessary capital to do so. In these cases, identity work, in the above-mentioned sense, in the field of nutrition becomes to some extent a matter of self-realisation – for instance, when a deliberately chosen, health-oriented dietary ideology (e.g., whole foods, organic or organic-dynamic production, regional products, vegetarianism, or similar) acts as a specific, distinctive identity symbol. By contrast, the majority of the interviewees have a pragmatic, less purist and less health-oriented attitude towards nutrition, which is lived out in a less object-centered and more person-centered manner. Here, the focus is on subjective experience – more spontaneous, less thought through and, from a health perspective, possibly short-sighted – as well as on the intersubjective and cultural dimensions of communitarisation (Reckinger 2008). The latter manifests itself in particular in terms of concern for the children and communicative solidarity between meaningful others, i.e. as affective and social identity work in a more comprehensive sense than a focus on health alone. It is precisely this pragmatic-hedonistic and person-focussed orientation at the

---

88 | Primarily there are two statistically significant variables in terms of this attitude: age and employment. In particular those who are not yet or no longer working, as well as the unemployed, place a high value on this kind of everyday sociability – which confirms, once more, that the emotional availability is decisive for eating.

89 | Personal translation: "It's just for the sake of being together and, yeah, to talk. [...] You go to work, well, some go to work, others go to school, that means you are almost never together and at least you are together whenever you're eating. You have to have a bit of communication as well".

individual and collective level, which is being disregarded within the political identity option in question[90]. Accordingly, a permanent oscillation can be discerned in the interaction between the attributions and appropriations considered, because the institutional government aspiration in the sense of Foucault (here: GIMB) and the everyday-cultural aspiration for self-government (here: the members of the resident population we interviewed) partially overlap, thus allowing the existence of a permanent and fundamentally ambivalent variation. The ethical appropriation of the 'good' food ideal can be in harmony with the moral, intentional and correcting logic of the political attributions (*identitary adaptation*), deviate from them (*identitary opposition*) or follow completely different patterns (*identitary independence*). It is precisely this dynamism that constitutes the significance of the selected case example in terms of governmentality[91] research and for investigating identity-related construction processes.

7.4 Cross-Border Workers as Familiar Strangers

Given its development and significance for Luxembourg society, the cross-border worker phenomenon suggested itself as a further illustrative example of processes of identity formation. With a total of 147,400 men and women (2009) commuting daily from Saarland and Rhineland-Palatinate (Germany), from Lorraine (France) or Wallonia (Belgium) to Luxembourg to work, the Grand Duchy has the highest number of cross-border workers in the EU 27 (European Commission 2009: 18-20)[92]. Half of them are French, while Belgians and Germans each account for one quarter. Their total number has multiplied six-fold since the end of the 1980s and in 1995 there were for the first time more cross-border workers than resident foreigners working in the Grand Duchy while in 2001 the number of cross-border workers was greater than that of employees holding Luxembourgish citizenship. Today (2009), Luxembourgers make up 29 % of the workforce, resident foreigners 27 % and cross-border workers 44 %. Aside from soft factors (adequate jobs, career

---

90 | However because the GIMB was designed as a long-term and social "process" and not as a "project" with immediate tangible effects (Wagener 2008: 25), this kind of synergy would not be impossible in future.

91 | Following Foucault (1993; 1984b; 1983; 1982b; 1978; see also Bröckling/Krasmann/Lemke [2001] this neologism is made up of *"gouverner"* (to govern) and *"mentalité"* (mentality) and permits a simultaneous and relational reading in collective and individual forms of identity governance in the form of moral and political rationalities as well as of ethical and individual approaches to the self. Thus state control converges with control of the self. However, this convergence is fundamentally dynamic and vriable as demonstrated by the case example presented here.

92 | Only in Switzerland are there more cross-border workers from the neighbouring countries.

paths etc.), the strong attraction of the Grand Duchy can be primarily traced back to an attractive net income and the range of jobs on offer. For in contrast to the neighbouring regions, even during the economic recession more jobs are created in Luxembourg than can be filled with resident manpower, as shall be explained later.

Theoretical Approach to the Status of the Cross-border Workers

In view of the exceptionally high quantitative importance of and dependence on manpower from the neighbouring regions in evidence since decades, the question arises which status is assigned to cross-border workers in Luxembourg, that of the stranger or that of the one who is familiar. This study therefore focuses primarily on the Luxembourg resident population's perceptions of the cross-border worker phenomenon which represent different forms of appropriation or construction of the latter. On a theoretical level, preoccupation with the strange first of all leads us to that direction of sociology which Stichweh calls the "classical sociology of the strange" (Stichweh 2005). This refers to Georg Simmel's essay "The Stranger" in which the author establishes a relationship between the stranger as a traveller and a given social community. He draws a distinction between the consequences for the absorbing community and their observation from the perspective of the stranger (Simmel 1908). These positionings are expanded by Robert Park in his concept of the *marginal man* who inhabits the borderline between two cultures and must develop resources in order to solve a cultural conflict (Park 1974). Finally, from an action-theoretical perspective, Alfred Schütz poses the question of the psychological processes that the stranger has to deal with once he enters a field of unfamiliar civilisation patterns (Schütz 1971). Just like Park, Schütz measures the status of the stranger by whether he/she manages to accept the rules prevailing in the absorbing community or whether, as a stranger, he/she ends up neither fully belonging to his/her old nor to the new environment. The common characteristic of these approaches lies in the fact that they both consider the stranger an 'intruder' into a given society which is described as a normatively integrated collective. This notion of homogeneous ingroups which are only barely accessible to outsiders presumably goes back to the experience of uni-directional and permanent migration in the 19th and 20th centuries and can be best associated with the dichotomic figure of thought of *familiar/strange*. With respect to the cross-border worker phenomenon as a circulatory form of mobility, this would mean that the status question could be solved via norm-related affiliation. Therefore, cross-border workers could either be defined as *familiar insiders* – who have mastered the normative set of rules of Luxembourg society – or as *alien outsiders*.

However, with transnational lives becoming an evermore widespread phenomenon (Pries 2008; Kreutzer/Roth 2006) that also includes cross-border workers, the figure of thought based on norm-related affiliation has become too limiting. Rather, we need to question *"um welche Modalitäten es sich eigentlich handelt, in denen jemand als Fremder erfahren werden kann*"⁹³ (Stichweh 2005: 141). From a transnational perspective, therefore, the question of the stranger or the alien can no longer point to national supercollectives and 'intruders' required to adopt given norms or standards, but needs to focus on the constructions of the strange and the familiar performed by resident nationals. For if the perspective of the normatively integrated societies is to be broken up and the strange is to assert itself as a theoretical category also in post-modern everyday life, one needs to inquire into the processes that construct social phenomena as alien and/or familiar. With respect to the cross-border workers, it is therefore, necessary to determine their status on the basis of the appropriations and perceptions of the Luxembourg residential population. Armin Nassehi's approach, which introduces the dichotomy of positive and negative appropriation (+/-) of social phenomena, provides some conceptual clues for addressing this task (Nassehi 1995). According to this approach the familiar – as the reverse of the strange – can carry a binary connotation: a positive and a negative one. This theoretical approach, which can be expressed in the thought model of *familiar (+/-)/strange*, makes forms of internal social differentiation tangible. On the other hand, the thought model retains the category of the strange, which absorbs certain social phenomena that resist positive or negative appropriation by the subjects and therefore remain beyond the limits of the familiar. With respect to the status of the cross-border worker phenomenon, this means that the cross-border worker can be identified as being familiar if the appropriations performed by the residential population are either positive *or* negative. He/she would need to be defined as a stranger if the respective appropriations have to be considered ambivalent, i.e. if the residential population adopts a positive *as well as* a negative attitude towards the cross-border worker phenomenon. Such appropriation processes of the strange/alien or familiar are practiced in all societies, since they depend on the identity-constituting differentiations that are performed in everyday life by inclusion (positive appropriation) and exclusion (negative appropriation). This refers to inclusive and exclusive practice strategies that, as forms of everyday-discursive appropriation, construct collective identities through specific semantics. It is against this background that we will take a closer look at the appropriation processes of the resident population in relation to the cross-border worker phenomenon.

Everyday-discursive Appropriations between 'Indispensability' and 'Threat'

Owing to the development of the Luxembourg employment market outlined above, there has been a growing awareness of cross-border workers within the resident population. The interviewees are convinced that the cross-border worker

---

93 | Personal translation: "Which are the actual modalities, under which somebody can be experienced as a stranger".

phenomenon has become a much more prominent theme in everyday discourses than was the case during the 1980s. This in particular is due to the fact that commuters have become more conspicuously present and that, as a consequence, matters such as job competition or language contact have become substantial issues. It is also remarked that cross-border workers increasingly serve as a projection surface for social discontent, or, as an interviewee puts it: *"Et gëtt ee gesicht, dee schold ass"*[94]. The following insights into appropriation strategies concerning the cross-border phenomenon touch on aspects of the economy and the labour market as well as language and culture in Luxembourg. In the surveys, positive and negative implications of cross-border worker employment were addressed in order to create links to the thought model described above.

First of all, we will attempt to identify which appropriations of the cross-border worker phenomenon relate to socio-economic factors. To ascertain this we asked whether cross-border workers were necessary for Luxembourg's economy, which was confirmed by 87 % of the interviewees, clearly reflecting a positive-inclusive attitude towards the commuters. This is based on two inclusion strategies: on the one hand, it has to do with the usefulness of labour provided by cross-border workers which is brought up as an issue under the aspect of the insufficient resident manpower and the demand for specific qualifications that can only be partially met by Luxembourg's residents. This is a consequence of Luxembourg's rate of economic growth, which would not have been (and be) possible without the contribution of cross-border workers. For instance, already for several years about two thirds of new jobs created annually have been filled with cross-border workers, not only bringing the necessary manpower into the country, but also the required qualifications.

Dat fannen ech ganz richteg, well mir hu jo eendeiteg net genuch Leit, déi schaffe ginn; an menger Usiicht no, wa mir keng Grenzgänger hätten, hätte mir vill méi Problemer hei zu Lëtzebuerg. Da giff eis Economie och guer net fonctionnéieren; an vu que datt mir awer déi Grenzgänger hunn, hu mer eng Chance fir ze fonctionnéieren, respektiv, wat elo mat der Finanzkrise kënnt, weess ee jo awer net; also, mä et sinn och vill Lëtzebuerger, déi einfach... bon, et wäert sécher alt, gesot: ze liddereg si fir schaffen ze goen; respektiv, si hunn einfach näischt geléiert, dat heescht si hunn op der 9ième opgehal, an... 'Oh mir kréie jo eng Plaz'. Mee haut kriss Du keng Plaz méi ouni, a mëttlerweil hunn d'Grenzgänger zimlech vill Chancen, well si awer vill méi Ausbildung hunn, wéi esou munnechen Lëtzebuerger[95] (Female, 18 years old, Luxembourger, Heinerscheid).

---

94 | Personal translation: "They are looking for somebody to take the blame".
95 | Personal translation: "I think this is perfectly fine because we clearly don't have enough people here who are working; in my opinion, if we had no cross-border workers, we'd have a lot more problems here in Luxembourg. The economy certainly wouldn't run properly; but because we have the cross-border workers, it does; but then again, we don't know what's going to happen after the financial crisis ...; well, there are also many Luxembourgers who ..., yes,

The second inclusion strategy also aims at the indispensability of cross-border workers without however, any direct social valorisation. According to the interviewees, their indispensability is derived from work activities which Luxembourgers are reluctant to perform. They sum it up by saying that "Luxembourgers think such work is beneath them" or "don't want to get their hands dirty", which is why cross-border workers are employed for "the dirty work". It is also remarked that cross-border workers are especially indispensable for badly-paid jobs which Luxembourgers refuse to take on.

An et sinn der och vill, wou verschidde Lëtzebuerger sech ze gutt sinn, fir déi ze maachen. … Also, di Drecksaarbechten. Wann dat net bei der Gemeng ass oder esou, da si vill Lëtzebuerger, déi soen: 'Oh nee dofir ginn ech awer net schaffen'. Also do kennen ech der awer och, déi dat gesot hunn. Oder: 'Fir déi Paie ginn ech net'[96] (Female, 31 years old, Luxembourger, Rambrouch).

When the qualifications of cross-border workers and their labour for low-paid jobs are emphasised, the interviewees also see in this a competitive advantage over Luxembourgers. This means, in everyday discourse, exclusive strategies are also practiced which can be subsumed under the keyword of 'job competition'. For instance, one third (34 %) of the resident population are of the opinion that cross-border workers take away jobs from the Luxembourgers and in this context the latter activate various exclusion strategies. They argue with the growing number of jobless who should be employed instead of cross-border workers, as well as with the low wages of cross-border workers, which allegedly push the Luxembourgers with their salary expectations out of the job market. Reference is also made to the image of the cross-border workers as "motivated employees", which is described as being the decisive factor for many employers and as being to the detriment of the Luxembourgers. In addition, there are a number of references to the "cross-border workerisation" of enterprises, accompanied by calls for the introduction of "quotas for Luxembourgers". Resident foreigners in particular emphasise the competitive relationship with cross-border workers and deplore that these speak just as little Luxembourgish as themselves, but still get a far better access to the job market. Two main reasons for this is the specific structure of selection mechanisms in

---

I suppose one can say who are simply too lazy to work;... or they just never had any training, they left school after the 9th grade and..., 'Yeah, we'll get a job somehow'. But nowadays you can't get a job anymore without, and meanwhile, the cross-border workers have quite a lot of opportunities because they've had better training than many Luxembourgers".

96 | Personal translation: "There are also many Luxembourgers who think certain kinds work are beneath them... in other words the dirty work. If they can't work for the municipality... there are many Luxembourgers who say: 'Na, I wouldn't work for that kind of money'. Well, I know some people who've actually said that. Or: 'I'm not budging for that kind of dosh'".

Luxembourg's education system and the rising unemployment rates since 2001, which particularly affect foreigners, adolescents and women (Statec 2009: 108).

Sie könnten ja auch die Zahl der Grenzgänger irgendwie begrenzen, statt 130.000 hereinzulassen ..., wenn das so weitergeht und immer mehr Leute hereingelassen werden, dann sieht es in Luxemburg bald nicht mehr so gut aus, so ist die Lage. ... Ein Portugiese kann praktisch nicht mehr hierher kommen, wenn er kein Luxemburgisch kann, und die anderen können doch erst recht kein Luxemburgisch; warum sollen die also herkommen dürfen und wir nicht?[97] (Male, 38 years old, Portuguese, Consdorf).

Already since the 1990s one can identify also on a practical level an exclusion strategy which has led to a segmentation of the job market. This involves the tendency of employees with Luxembourgish citizenship to increasingly withdraw from the private sector in favour of jobs in the public and semi-public sector (see Statec 2009). These are not only attractive in terms of job protection and social security but they also offer a 'safeguard' against the competition of foreign manpower. This development, called "withdrawal strategy" by Fehlen and Pigeron-Piroth (2009) becomes possible due to a "national entrenchment capital", which includes, aside from Luxembourgish citizenship, the respective language skills, socio-cultural knowledge and social networks within the country, something that, as a rule, is only to a limited extent available to cross-border workers.

[Le secteur public] constitue une sorte de refuge, dans lequel les salariés luxembourgeois peuvent faire valoir leurs compétences particulières (notamment linguistiques) qui sont raréfiées sur le marché. Il se trouve ainsi à l'abri de la concurrence des travailleurs étrangers, de plus en plus nombreux et qualifiés[98] (Fehlen/Pigeron-Piroth 2009: 11).

Next, we will examine the appropriations regarding the cross-border worker phenomenon in the socio-cultural context of Luxembourg's culture and language. For this, members of the resident population were asked whether they considered

---

97 | Personal translation: "They could also somehow limit the number of cross-border workers, instead of letting 130,000 of them in ... if this goes on and more and more people are allowed in, then soon it won't look that rosy in Luxembourg anymore, that's the situation.... A Portuguese practically can't come here anymore if he can't speak Luxembourgish and the others really don't know a word of Luxembourgish; why should they be allowed to come here then, and not us? The Germans can't speak Luxembourgish either and yet they come here and work for the municipalities. In these cases, I don't think that's right. Why should they be allowed to come here ...?".

98 | Personal translation: "[The public sector] constitutes a refuge of sorts, where the Luxembourgish employees can exploit their particular (primarily linguistic) competences which have become rare on the market. It is thus protected from the competition of foreign workers who are becoming more and more numerous and qualified".

cross-border workers an enrichment to Luxembourg's culture. More than half of the interviewees (55 %) said they did, although we have to assume that the social desirability effect influenced the responses to a certain degree. For the inclusion of cross-border workers in the sphere of the familiar, as expressed here, corresponds first of all to a public discourse[99] which unfolded particularly in the context of the cross-border worker festival in 2008. For instance, a press release of the *Ministry of Culture, Higher Education and Research* reads as follows:

Unter dem Motto 'Zusammen arbeiten, zusammen feiern, zusammen leben' hat das Fest zum Ziel, über die Arbeitsbeziehungen hinaus und außerhalb der Bürozeiten, einen echten interkulturellen Dialog und einen gemeinschaftlichen Geist zwischen Grenzgängern und Anwohnern, sowie unter den Grenzbewohnern selbst zu fördern. Das Fest der Grenzgänger hofft so ebenfalls zur Entwicklung einer gemeinsamen regionalen Identität beizutragen. [...] Für Luxemburg als 'Land der 100 Nationalitäten' ist die Vielfalt kein leeres Wort, und das Fest der Grenzgänger ist dazu berufen, keine einmalige Initiative zu bleiben[100] (*Ministry for Culture, Higher Education and Research* 2008: 1).

In contrast to this inclusive strategy of identity attribution, the interviews also brought negative appropriations of the cross-border worker phenomenon to light. In these instances, the familiar is constructed by identity-constitutive differentiations when cross-border workers are expected to adapt themselves to Luxembourg's culture and show greater interest in and respect for Luxembourgers.

Et ass och fir mech een wichtegen Aspekt datt Frontalieren, wann se an Lëtzebuerg kommen, datt se net nëmmen heihinner kommen fir ze schaffen, mä datt se sech wéinstens e bëssen fir eis Kultur souzesoen interesséieren an och vläicht iergendwéi een Austausch oder kommunizéieren mat den Lëtzebuerger. Et sinn wierklech vill Frontalieren, déi gesinn Lëtzebuerg nëmmen als Staat, wou een Suen verdéngt; d.h. si kommen heihinner, si schaffen dann ginn si nees zeréck an si interesséieren sech guer net. Dat fannen ech ëmmer e bëssen blöd. Leit, déi awer dann heihinner kommen an vläicht dann eben sech integréieren an eis Gesellschaft dat fannen ech dann besser an wann si dann och no

---

99 | See also section 5.5.

100 | Personal translation: "With the theme 'working together, celebrating together, living together' the festival aims at promoting – beyond work relations and office hours – a true intercultural dialogue and a spirit of community between cross-border workers and local residents, as well as among the cross-border workers themselves. The cross-border worker festival hereby hopes to also contribute to the development of a common regional identity. [...] For Luxembourg, as the 'country of 100 nationalities', diversity is not an empty phrase and the cross-border worker festival is predestined to become more than a mere one-off initiative".

versichen e bëssen Lëtzebuergesch ze schwätzen an dann fannen ech dat och gutt[101] (Male, 18 years old, Italian, Strassen).

As the quote suggests, there is also an exclusive appropriation practice with respect to the Luxembourgish language. This is exhibited in the opinion that cross-border workers are a threat to the Luxembourgish language (57 %) as well as in the statement that cross-border workers should be able to at least understand Luxembourgish (86 %)[102]. The interviewees report that they are not able to communicate in Luxemburgish in the public space, in particular in the retail and catering trade and the health sector[103], and state that anyone working abroad should, as a matter of course, also speak the local language, by which, in this case, they exclusively mean Luxembourgish. While cross-border workers are not expected to have advanced language skills, say the interviewees, they should however display at least elementary linguistic competences which would also be sufficient to "show their goodwill".

Ech fannen et ganz schlëmm, datt een am Cactus, op lëtzebuergesch keng Wirschtecher méi bestelle kann, well si een net verstinn. Also, ech fannen ee Minimum vu Sprooch missten si awer kënnen, well wa mir an d'Ausland ginn, do këne mer och net soen 'Hei, mir si Lëtzebuerger, mir kommen, hei schwätzt emol lëtzebuergesch mat eis'[104] (Female, 31 years old, Luxembourger, Rambrouch).

The differentiation made above between people who speak Luxembourgish and those who have no knowledge of the language, as well as the fact that interviewees were prepared to qualify the linguistic competences expected from cross-border workers reveal that the Luxembourgish language, in the context of the cross-border worker phenomenon, functions primarily as an identity marker (Lüdi 2008: 187,

---

101 | Personal translation: "This is also an important aspect for me, that the cross-border workers, when they come to Luxembourg, don't only come here for the work but that they also take at least a little interest in our culture, or that they maybe somehow mingle with Luxembourgers or communicate with them. There are really many cross-border workers who see Luxembourg as a state where they can earn money; that is, they come here, they work and then they go home again and have no interest whatsoever [in the country]. I always find that a bit stupid. But if people come here and then maybe integrate into our society, then that's a lot better. And if they even try to speak a little Luxembourgish, then that's good too".
102 | See also section 4.2.
103 | See also section 4.3.
104 | Personal translation: "I think it's absolutely disgraceful that one can't order sausages in Luxembourgish anymore at the *Cactus* [a Luxembourg supermarket chain] because they don't understand you there. Well, I think they should at least know the basics of the language; because if we go abroad, we can't very well go and say to someone 'We're Luxembourgers, here we are, talk to us in Luxembourgish'".

190) rather than as an effective means of communication. This is partially also reflected by the strategies of language usage employed by the interviewees, who, in terms of language contact with cross-border workers, can be subdivided into four different types:

- The *confrontational* ones strategically try to exclusively speak Luxembourgish with cross-border workers and will, for example, leave a store if someone tells them "*En français, s'il vous plaît*" or "*Comment?*"[105].
- The *constructive* ones, on the other hand, concede that cross-border workers cannot learn Luxembourgish if the resident population actively speaks the languages of the cross-border workers. Therefore they act inclusively and even speak Luxembourgish in difficult conversational situations if they notice that shop assistants or waiters "are making an effort".
- The *pragmatic* ones remain exclusive in their approach and speak apriori French, because experience has taught them that they will achieve their communicative objective by using this *lingua franca*.
- Finally, there are the *mediating* ones who absorb linguistic information in the context of greeting, or in conversation with another customer/guest/patient, and then act in a strategically inclusive manner by linguistically adapting to the shop assistant/waiter/care assistant.

The overall analysis of the findings shows that the Luxembourg resident population practises positive-inclusive as well as negative-exclusive strategies in respect to the cross-border worker phenomenon. On the basis of the quantitative data, one can take the investigation a step further and ask which strategies are activated in which social field. This requires a comprehensive examination of socio-cultural and socio-economic aspects, for which the positive and negative statements about the cross-border worker phenomenon need to be collated (table 4).

Positive Appropriation (+)		Negative Appropriation (-)	
Socio-cultural field	Socio-economic field	Socio-cultural field	Socio-economic field
Cross-border workers are an enrichment for Luxembourg culture.	Cross-border workers are needed for the Luxembourg economy.	Cross-border workers are a threat to the Luxembourgish language.	Cross-border workers take jobs away from the Luxembourgers.
55 % (approval)	87 % (approval)	57 % (approval)	34 % (approval)

Table 4: Positive and negative appropriation strategies of the Luxembourg resident population.

---

105 | Personal translation: "In French, please" or "What?".

Approval in %	Socio-cultural field		Socio-economic field		
	Cross-border workers are a threat to the Luxembourgish language.	Cross-border workers are an enrichment for Luxembourg culture.	Cross-border workers take jobs away from Luxembourgers.	Cross-border workers are needed for the Luxembourg economy.	Appropriation overall
	Negative appropriation (-)	Positive appropriation (+)	Negative appropriation (-)	Positive appropriation (+)	
Luxembourg resident population	57	55	34	87	/
Status of cross-border workers	Strangers		Familiar +		Familiar strangers
Privileged conservative milieu	37	62	15	93	/
Status of cross-border workers	Familiar +		Familiar +		Familiar +
Petty bourgeois milieu	64	48	38	87	/
Status of cross-border workers	Familiar -		Familiar +		Strangers
Tradition-oriented milieu	74	45	54	86	/
Status of the cross-border workers	Familiar -		Strangers		Familiar strangers
Underprivileged milieu	64	53	56	75	/
Status of the cross-border workers	Familiar -		Familiar -		Familiar -
Meritocratic-oriented milieu	59	58	30	91	/
Status of the cross-border workers	Strangers		Familiar +		Familiar strangers
Privileged liberal milieu	46	62	16	89	/
Status of the cross-border workers	Familiar +		Familiar +		Familiar +
Hedonistic milieu	59	50	49	82	/
Status of the cross-border workers	Strangers		Familiar -		Familiar strangers
Alternative milieu	45	68	28	88	/
Status of the cross-border workers	Familiar +		Familiar +		Familiar +
Status-oriented milieu	53	48	26	93	/
Status of the cross-border workers	Familiar -		Familiar +		Strangers

Table 5: Status of cross-border workers in socio-cultural milieus.

As far as the positive-inclusive appropriation strategy is concerned, one can note that the Luxembourg resident population tends to apply it in particular in the socio-economic field, for instance in the case of the indispensability of cross-border workers for the national economic growth (87 %) compared to the cultural enrichment of Luxembourg (55 %). Negative-exclusive appropriation strategies, on the other hand, take effect particularly in the socio-cultural field, for instance in the answers to the question concerning the threat to the interviewees' own language posed by cross-border workers (57 %) compared to job competition (34 %). However, this overview merely provides initial indications concerning the applied appropriations by social sectors and allows no statements about possible ambivalent appropriation strategies or about the status of the cross-border workers in socio-cultural milieus.

On the Status of the Cross-border Workers in Socio-cultural Milieus

Following on from the figure of thought outlined above of *familiar (+/-)/stranger*, the table 5 presents a systematised representation of the status of cross-border workers, based on the appropriation strategies of the Luxembourg resident population and on socio-cultural milieus. The observations are based on quantitative survey results and point to three essential types of status of cross-border workers in Luxembourg.

Cross-border workers as familiar individuals: The appropriation of the cross-border workers as familiar individuals is based on an unequivocally positive *or* negative construction of the phenomenon. In the case of cross-border workers being appropriated as *negative familiar individuals* – as they are in the underprivileged milieu – we tend to find mostly negative and exclusive appropriation strategies in both socio-cultural and socio-economic fields. In the latter these strategies are reflected by an emphasis on job market competition and the downplaying of the need for cross-border workers. With respect to the appropriation of cross-border workers as *positive familiar individuals* – predominant in the privileged conservative, privileged liberal and alternative milieus – positive and inclusive strategies prevail in the examined fields, expressed in the emphasis on the positive implications of cross-border worker employment and in the relativisation of the negative ones.

Cross-border workers as strangers: The appropriation of cross-border workers as strangers is based on an ambivalent construction of the phenomenon. This means that the interviewees applied positive as well as negative appropriation strategies in respect of the cross-border worker phenomenon. This form of appropriation is a feature of the petty bourgeois and status-oriented milieus which, on the socio-cultural level, tend to display an exclusive attitude towards the cross-border worker phenomenon and, on the socio-economical level, an inclusive one. The factor of cultural enrichment is qualified in favour of a supposed linguistic threat by cross-border workers, which is particularly marked in the petty bourgeois milieu. Nevertheless, the need for cross-border workers is confirmed, and the alleged job market competition is seen as a relatively insignificant issue, particularly in the status-oriented milieu.

Cross-border workers as familiar strangers: The appropriation of cross-border workers as familiar strangers reflects a circumstance not foreseen by Nassehi, in the sense that in the social fields under review the cross-border worker is constructed in an ambivalent as well as in an unambiguous manner. This status is reflected in the appropriations of the Luxembourg resident population as a whole and the members of the hedonistic milieu in particular, who, from the socio-cultural aspect, construct the cross-border worker phenomenon both positively *and* negatively. An illustration of this is the simultaneous assumption that cross-border workers provide cultural enrichment on the one hand and present a threat to the local language on the other. However, when it comes to their constructions in the socio-economic field, the groups mentioned above show marked differences: while the Luxembourg resident population in general stresses the indispensability of cross-border workers for the economy in an inclusive manner, the hedonists emphasise the job competition aspect, thereby assuming a rather exclusive stance. The status of cross-border workers as familiar strangers is also evident in the appropriation strategies of the tradition-oriented milieu. Here, however, we find an ambivalent construction on the socio-economic level with an emphasis on job market competition and the concurrently expressed need for cross-border workers, contrasting with a predominantly negative and exclusive strategy on the socio-cultural level.

On the Figure of the (Familiar) Stranger

The analysis carried out here shows that the applied inclusion and exclusion strategies of the Luxembourg resident population represent different appropriation forms in respect of the cross-border worker phenomenon. In the socio-economic field, the predominant strategy tends to be the inclusion of cross-border workers by emphasising their economic indispensability. On the socio-cultural level, however, there is a marked tendency towards exclusion strategies based primarily on the perceived threat to the Luxembourgish language. These appropriation processes, which vary by socio-cultural milieus, were further examined for coherence, as a result of which partly contradictory constructions were revealed. These differ depending on the examined socio-cultural milieu and point to a largely ambivalent status of cross-border workers in Luxembourg, which has been represented by the figures of the *stranger* and the *familiar stranger*.

In view of the introductory remarks, these findings may at first seem to present an identitary dilemma. However, by interpreting them a potential logic in the strategic interplay of everyday-cultural inclusions and exclusions can be brought to light. For while, during the second half of the 20th century, the presence of immigrants and cross-border workers *"in den Köpfen zu einer Selbstverständlichkeit wurde"*[106] (Fehlen 2008: 82) due to local enterprises' demand for them, and xenophobic discourses thus barely evolved in Luxembourg, protectionist strategies against competition by foreign manpower have established themselves particularly since the periods of economic downturn in the new millennium. In the research findings these are reflected not so much by an open and consistent rejection of cross-border workers in the sense of the *negative familiar* but are conceded, for the reasons mentioned above, their economic indispensability. However, from the point of view of many Luxembourgers, this ends at the threshold to the public and semi-public sector, something which is regulated by the already mentioned entrenchment competence. Against this background, the logic of the strategic interplay of socio-economically motivated inclusion strategies on the one hand, and socio-culturally motivated exclusion strategies on the other, which aims at securing growth and prosperity at home and at protecting the job market, becomes clear. According to the findings, cross-border workers are considered important for the economy by the resident population, however, if they knew Luxembourgish, they might gain broad access to those sectors currently 'protected' from competition by 'foreign labour'. The socio-cultural argument of the linguistic threat – in particular in the tradition-oriented, underprivileged and petty bourgeois milieus – is applied in an exclusive manner in order to secure the competitive advantage over cross-border workers in the socio-economic field.

Therefore, appropriation processes concerning the cross-border worker phenomenon that at first glance may seem contradictory can indeed follow an 'everyday logic' that submits to the desire for security by imagining a community by demarcation. This suggests a further investigation of everyday-cultural appropriations of the cross-border worker phenomenon, which cannot be categorised along the lines of *familiar* or *stranger*, in terms of their nature as intermediate categories. This means explicitly focusing on the appropriations of the resident population with their inherent contradictions and thereby reconstructing the cross-border worker as an ambivalent yet independent category. At a conceptual level this implies a broadening of Nassehi's approach by the figure of thought of the *familiar stranger [familiar (+/-)/ stranger]*; at the empirical level, the task involves further clarifying the positions of the subjects between inclusive and exclusive appropriation processes and thereby elucidating the ambivalent logic of everyday culture.

7.5 Conclusions: Identities and Ambivalences of Everyday Cultures

In the present chapter we investigated examples of different areas of everyday cultures and showed the (political) attributions and (individual as well as milieu-specific) appropriations in respect to identity-constitutive forms of action in circulation. It

---

106 | Personal translation: "Came to be taken for granted in people's minds".

involved issues of gender-related performances and gender experiences, of attitudes concerning food and of the perception of cross-border workers in Luxembourg. In addition to their everyday relevance and identity-constitutive potential, it was possible to establish a further common characteristic of these topics: a distinctive ambivalence. This was clearly evident in the social practice under examination, where the binarities male/female, good/bad and familiar/strange are broken up in a productive and partly arbitrary manner, revealing different patterns of 'everyday logic'.

A remarkable result in the area of gender is the fact that the interviewees showed a tendency to embrace the ideal of sexual equality in their actions while *at the same time* still remaining mentally rooted in their traditional patterns. Conversely, they advocated gender equality while acting, for instance in the case of parenthood, according to traditional patterns.

This contradiction is also reflected in attitudes concerning food: findings on forms of attribution show that 'good' food tends to be treated in an object-centered manner (for instance in the form of nutritional guidelines), while, in terms of appropriation, there is a tendency to experience it in a person-centered way (for instance in the form of subjectification and communitisation). Here we see forms of practice that *simultaneously* integrate the attributed identification characteristics in a selective, context-related and constantly varying manner (e.g. in the form of adaptation, opposition or autonomy concerning nutritional guidelines).

Finally, while conceding that cross-border workers are important for Luxembourg's economy, interviewees critisise their Luxembourgish language competence, which is perceived as inadequate in everyday situations. *At the same time*, more importance seems to be attached to an appreciation of what is regarded as one's 'own' – to be performed by linguistic means – rather than to linguistic competence itself, in particular when it comes to those areas of the job market that are largely dominated and 'protected' by Luxembourgers and that very often can only be accessed by those who have a command of Luxembourgish.

In the case examples of everyday cultures examined here, we can identify discursive practices which pragmatically transcend a binary 'either-or logic' and follow a flexible 'as-well-as logic' – for instance, when, in the experience of gender, essentialisms as well as constructivisms are practised in parallel, when contradictory standards and habits of 'healthy' as well as 'indulgence' food mutually penetrate each other, or when cross-border workers are perceived both positively as well as negatively – and thus as 'familiar strangers'. In the context of our Luxembourg investigation, the various latent forms of 'everyday logic', by which dynamic identity constructions can be identified, therefore appear to be to a large degree pragmatic and self-related: a self-concept of the subjects, which experiences gender as only one aspect of everyday practice among many others and, depending on the context, argues either naturalistically or culturally; which favours pragmatic-hedonistic food habits in everyday life, or a self-image which gives in to the desire for that which is considered own's 'own' by ambivalent constructions of the 'strange'.

In view of the above, it should be noted that this chapter deals primarily with appropriated identities and examines, in addition, to what extent attributed identities are (not) adopted, in the course of which strategies of adaptation, opposition and autonomy are activated in regard to models for identification. Therefore, identities are neither predetermined nor unalterable, but can only be traced as a snapshot and in a specific context of everyday practice.

7.6 References

Primary Sources

Ministère de la Santé/Ministère de l'Education Nationale et de la Formation Professionnelle/Ministère de la Famille et de l'Intégration/Département Ministériel des Sports. 2007. Freude am gesunden Essen Spaß an der Bewegung!/Le plaisir de bien manger et d'être actif! Luxembourg.

Secondary Sources

Allegrezza, Serge, Armande Frising, Antoine Haag, Jean Langers, Liliane Reichmann and Marco Schockmel. 2007. Egalité Hommes-Femmes. Mythe ou Réalité? Cahier Economique. No 105 du Statec, Luxembourg.
Antoni-Komar, Irene, Reinhard Pfriem Thorsten Raabe and AchimSpiller, ed. 2008. Ernährung, Kultur, Lebensqualität. Wege regionaler Nachhaltigkeit. Marburg: Metropolis.
Austin, John. 1962. How To Do Things with Words. Oxford: University Press.
Baltes-Löhr, Christel. 2006. Migration und Identität. Portugiesische Frauen in Luxemburg. Frankfurt/M./London: IKO-Verlag für Interkulturelle Kommunikation.
Baltes-Löhr, Christel. 2009. Umgang mit Differenzen. In Maison Relais pour Enfants. Le Manuel – Das Handbuch, ed. Manuel Achten, Christel Baltes-Löhr et al., 88-117. Luxembourg: Edition le Phare.
Barlösius, Eva. 2008. Weibliches und männliches rund ums Essen. In Kulinaristik. Forschung, Lehre, Praxis, ed. Alois Wierlacher and Regina Bendix, 35-44. Berlin: Lit.
Bhabha, Homi K. 2000. Die Verortung der Kultur. Stauffenburg Verlag: Tübingen.
Bolten, Jürgen. 2007. Einführung in die Interkulturelle Wirtschaftskommunikation. Stuttgart: UTB.
Bonz, Jochen and Karen Struve. Homi K. Bhabha: Auf der Innenseite kultureller Differenz: "in the middle of differences". In Kultur. Theorien der Gegenwart, ed. Stephan Moebius and Dirk Quadflieg, 140-153. Wiesbaden: VS-Verlag.
Bourdieu, Pierre. 2000 [1972]. Esquisse d'une théorie de la pratique. Précédé de trois études d'ethnologie kabyle. Paris: Le Seuil.

Bourdieu, Pierre. 1994. Raisons pratiques. Sur la théorie de l'action. Paris: Le Seuil.
Bourdieu, Pierre. 1980. Le sens pratique. Paris: Editions de Minuit.
Breinig, Helmbrecht and Klaus Lösch. 2006. Transdifference. Journal for the Study of British Culture 13/2: 105-122.
Bröckling, Ulrich, Susanne Krasmann and Thomas Lemke, ed. 2000. Gouvernementalität der Gegenwart. Studien zur Ökonomisierung des Sozialen. Frankfurt/M.: Suhrkamp.
Brunner, Karl Michael, Sonja Geyer, Marie Jelenko, Walpurga Weiss and Florentina Astleithner. 2007. Ernährungsalltag im Wandel. Chancen für Nachhaltigkeit. Vienna, New York: Springer.
Brunnett, Regina. 2009. Die Hegemonie symbolischer Gesundheit. Eine Studie zum Mehrwert von Gesundheit im Postfordismus. Bielefeld: transcript.
Butler, Judith. 1993. Für ein sorgfältiges Lesen. In Der Streit um Differenz, ed. Seyla Benhabib et al., 123-132. Frankfurt/Main: Fischer.
Chambers, Iain. 1996. Migration, Kultur, Identität. Tübingen: Stauffenburg.
Commission des Communautés Européennes (CE). 30 mai 2007. Livre blanc. Une stratégie européenne pour les problèmes de santé liés à la nutrition, la surcharge pondérale et l'obésit. Bruxelles: COM (2007) 279 final, non publié au Journal Officiel, http://europa.eu/legislation_summaries/public_health/health_determinants_lifestyle/c11542c_fr.htm.
Commission des Communautés Européennes (CE). 8 décembre 2005. Livre vert. Promouvoir une alimentation saine et l'activité physique. Une dimension européenne pour la prévention des surcharges pondérales, de l'obésité et des maladies chroniques. Bruxelles: COM (2005) 637 final, non publié au Journal Officiel, http://europa.eu/legislation_summaries/public_health/health_determinants_lifestyle/c11542b_fr.htm.
Corbeau, Jean-Pierre and Jean-Pierre Poulain. 2002. Penser l'alimentation. Entre imaginaire et rationalité. Paris: Private.
Coveney, John. 2006 [2000]. Food, Morals and Meaning. The Pleasure and Anxiety of Eating. London: Routledge.
Csergo, Julia. 2009. Trop gros? L'obésité et ses représentations. Paris: Autrement.
Fischler, Claude. 1990. L'homnivore. Le goût, la cuisine et le corps. Paris: Poches Odile Jacob.
Deleuze, Gilles. 1968. Différence et Répétition. Paris: PUF.
Derrida, Jacques. 1968. La différance. Bulletin de la Société Française de Philosophie 62.3. Paris: 73-120.
European Commission. 2009. Scientific Report of the Mobility of Cross-Border Workers within the EU-27/EEA/EFTA Countries. (Directorate General for Employment, Social Affairs and Equal Opportunities), Luxembourg.
Fehlen, Fernand. 2008. Streit um den roten Löwen. Diskurse über das nationale Selbstbild Luxemburgs im Spannungsfeld von Modernisierung und Rückwärtsgewandtheit. In Periphere Zentren oder zentrale Peripherien? Kulturen

und Regionen Europas zwischen Globalisierung und Regionalität, ed. Wilhelm Amann, Georg Mein et al., 61-87. Heidelberg: Synchron Verlag.

Fehlen, Fernand and Isabelle Pigeron-Piroth. 2009. Mondialisation du travail et pluralité des marchés du travail: L'exemple du Luxembourg. Discussion contribution of the 12e Journées de Sociologie du Travail, 25 and 26 June 2009, GREE, Université de Nancy. (http://gree.univ-nancy2.fr/digitalAssets/53345_JIST_Fehlen_Pigeron.pdf).

Foucault, Michel. 1993. About the Beginnings of the Hermeneutics of the Self. Two Lectures at Dartmouth. Political Theory, n° 21/2: 198-227.

Foucault, Michel. 1984. Histoire de la sexualité, Tome 2: L'usage des plaisirs. Paris: Gallimard.

Foucault, Michel. 1984. L'éthique du souci de soi comme pratique de la liberté. In Michel Foucault. 1994. Dits et écrits. Tome 4: 1980-1988. Paris: Gallimard, pp. 708-729.

Foucault, Michel. 1983. On the Genealogy of Ethics. An Overview of Work in Progress. In The Essential Foucault. Selections from the Essential Works of Foucault 1954-1984, ed. Paul Rabinow and Nicolas Rose (2003 [1994]). New York & London: The New Press, pp. 102-125.

Foucault, Michel. 1982a. The Subject and Power. In The Essential Foucault. Selections from the Essential Works of Foucault 1954-1984, ed. Paul Rabinow and Nicolas Rose (2003 [1994]). New York & London: The New Press, pp. 126-144.

Foucault, Michel. 1982. Technologies of the Self. In The Essential Foucault. Selections from the Essential Works of Foucault 1954-1984, ed. Paul Rabinow and Nicolas Rose (2003 [1994]). New York & London: The New Press, pp. 145-169.

Foucault, Michel. 1978. La gouvernementalité. Séminaire au Collège de France en 1977 et 1978: Sécurité, territoire et population. Aut-Aut, n° 167-168, Paris: Gallimard: 12-29.

Foucault, Michel. 1969. L'archéologie du savoir. Paris: Gallimard.

Goffman, Erving. 1969. Wir alle spielen Theater. Munich: Piper.

Gregory, Derek. 1997. Lacan and Geography. The Production of Space Revisted. In Space and social theory. Interpreting modernity and postmodernity, ed. Georges Benko and Ulf Strohmayer, 203-234. Oxford: Blackwell Publishers.

Hillmann, Karl-Heinz. 2007. Wörterbuch der Soziologie. Stuttgart: Alfred Kröner.

Hörning, Karl H. and Julia Reuter. 2004. Doing Culture. Kultur als Praxis. In: Doing Culture. Neue Positionen zum Verhältnis von Kultur und sozialer Praxis, ed. Karl Hörning and Julia Reuter, 9-15. Bielefeld: transcript.

Hirschauer, Stefan. 2001. Das Vergessen des Geschlechts. Zur Praxeologie einer Kategorie sozialer Ordnung. In Geschlechtersoziologie. Ed. Bettina Heinz, 208-235. Westdeutscher Verlag: Opladen. Sonderheft der Kölner Zeitschrift für Soziologie und Sozialpsychologie.

Jakobson, Roman. 1971. Signe zéro. In Selected Writtings, II: Word and Language, ed. Roman Jakobson, 211-222. Den Haag: Parin.

Klinger, Cornelia and Gudrun Axeli-Knapp. 2005. Achsen der Ungleichheit – Achsen der Differenz – Verhältnisbestimmung von Klasse, Geschlecht, "Rasse"/ Ethnizität. Transit 5/2005.

Kreutzer, Florian and Silke Roth. 2006. Transnationale Karrieren. Biographien, Lebensführung und Mobilität. Wiesbaden: VS Verlag.

Kumoll, Karsten. 2006. Clifford Geertz: Die Ambivalenz kultureller Formen. In Kultur. Theorien der Gegenwart, ed. Stephan Moebius and Dirk Quadflieg, 81-90. Wiesbaden: VS-Verlag.

Lamine, Claire. 2008. Les intermittents du bio. Pour une sociologie pragmatique des choix alimentaires émergents. Paris: Editions de la Maison des Sciences de l'Homme & Editions Quae.

Lüdi, Georges. 2008. Der Schweizer Sprachencocktail neu gemixt. Sprache als Brücke und Barriere. In Die neue Zuwanderung. Die Schweiz zwischen Brain-Gain und Überfremdungsangst, ed. Daniel Jentsch-Müller, 185-203. Zürich: Avenir Suisse.

McCall, Leslie. 2005. Managing the Complexity of Intersectionality. Signs (2005), 30(3): 1771-1800.

Ministère de l'Education Nationale et de la Formation Professionnelle/Ministère de la Santé/Universität Karlsruhe. 2006. Gesundheit, motorische Leistungsfähigkeit und körperlich-sportliche Aktivität von Kindern und Jugendlichen in Luxemburg. Untersuchung für die Altersgruppen 9, 14 und 18 Jahre. Abschlussbericht zum Forschungsprojekt. Luxemburg.

Ministère de l'Education Nationale et de la Formation Professionnelle. 2007. Les chiffres clés de l'éducation nationale 2005/2006. Statistiques et indicateurs, année scolaire 2005/2006. Luxembourg.

Ministère de l'Egalité des Chances. 2006. Gleiche Rechte für Mädchen und Jungen, Frauen und Männer. Luxembourg.

Ministère de la Santé/Ministère de l'Education Nationale et de la Formation Professionnelle. 2005. Das Wohlbefinden der Jugendlichen in Luxemburg im internationalen Vergleich. Luxemburg.

Ministère de la Santé/Ministère de l'Education Nationale et de la Formation Professionnelle. 2005. Das Wohlbefinden der Jugendlichen in Luxemburg, 5. und 6. Klasse, Grundschule. Luxemburg.

Ministère de la Santé/Ministère de l'Education Nationale et de la Formation Professionnelle. 2002. Das Wohlbefinden der Jugendlichen in Luxemburg. Luxemburg.

Nassehi, Armin. 1995. Der Fremde als Vertrauter. Soziologische Beobachtungen zur Konstruktion von Identitäten und Differenzen. Kölner Zeitschrift für Soziologie und Sozialpsychologie 47: 443-463.

N.N. 2008. 1. Fest der Grenzgänger – Grenzenlos feiern im Namen des interkulturellen Dialogs. Press release of the Luxembourg Ministry for Culture, Tertiary Education and Research of 26.09.2008.

Park, Robert. 1974. Human Migration and the Marginal Man. In Collected Papers of Robert Ezra Park, vol. 1, 345-356. New York: Arno Press.
Pries, Ludger. 2008. Die Transnationalisierung der sozialen Welt. Frankfurt/M.: Suhrkamp.
Poulain, Jean-Pierre. 2002. Manger aujourd'hui. Attitudes, normes et pratiques. Paris: Private.
Reckinger, Rachel. 2008. Les pratiques discursives oenophiles entre normativité et appropriation. Contribution à une sociologie des cultures alimentaires: 2 volumes, PhD dissertation in Sociology. Marseille: Ecole des Hautes Etudes en Sciences Sociales.
Rose, Nicolas. 1999 [1989]. Governing the Soul. The Shaping of the Private Self. London: Free Association Books.
Reckwitz, Andreas. 2004. Die Kontingenzperspektive von Kultur. Kulturbegriffe, Kulturtheorien und das kulturwissenschaftliche Forschungsprogramm. In Handbuch der Kulturwissenschaften. Themen und Tendenzen, ed. Friedrich Jaeger and Jörn Rüsen, 1-20 Stuttgart: Metzler.
Reckwitz, Andreas. 2001. Multikulturalismustheorien und der Kulturbegriff: Vom Homogenitätsmodell zum Modell kultureller Interferenzen. Berliner Journal für Soziologie, volume 2, edition 11: 179-200.
Reuter, Julia and Matthias Wiesner. 2008. Soziologie im Zwischenraum: Grenzen einer transdifferenten Perspektive. In Kulturelle Differenzen begreifen. Das Konzept der Transdifferenz aus interdisziplinärer Sicht, ed. Lars Allolio-Näcke and Britta Kalscheuer, 129-143. Frankfurt/M.: Campus.
Reuter, Julia. 2002. Ordnungen des Anderen. Zum Problem des Eigenen in der Soziologie des Fremden. Bielefeld: transcript.
Rölli, Marc. 2006. Gilles Deleuze: Kultur und Gegenkultur. In Kultur. Theorien der Gegenwart, ed. Stephan Moebius, Dirk Quadflieg, 30-41. Wiesbaden: VS-Verlag.
Rutherford, Jonathan. 1990. The Third Space. Interview with Homi Bhabha. In Identity: Community, Culture, Difference, ed. Jonathan Rutherford, 207-221. London: Lawrence and Wishart.
Scholliers, Peter, ed. 2001. Food, Drink and Identity. Cooking, Eating and Drinking in Europe since the Middle Ages. Oxford & New York: Berg.
Schütz, Alfred. 1972. Gesammelte Aufsätze. Band 2: Studien zur soziologischen Theorie, ed. Arvid Brodersen. Den Haag: Nijhoff.
Schütz, Alfred. 1971. Der Fremde. Ein sozialpsychologischer Versuch. In Gesammelte Aufsätze. Band 2, 53-69. Den Haag: Martinus Nijhof.
Simmel, Georg. 1908. Soziologie. Untersuchungen über die Formen der Vergesellschaftung. Duncker & Humblot: Berlin.
Ståhl, Timo, Matthias Wismar, Eeva Ollila, Eero Lahtinen and Kimmo Leppo, ed. 2006. Health in All Policies. Prospects and Potentials. Ministry of Social Affairs and Health, Finland & European Observatory on Health Systems and Policies (http://www.euro.who.int/document/E89260.pdf).

STATEC. 2009. L'économie luxembourgeoise. Un kaléidoscope 2008. Luxembourg.
STATEC. 2009. Le secteur public. Economie et Statistiques, Working papers du STATEC 34.
Stichweh, Rudolf. 2005. Inklusion und Exklusion. Studien zur Gesellschaftstheorie. Bielefeld: transcript.
Wagener, Yolande. 2008. Promotion de la santé au Luxembourg. Promotion & Education, Hors-Série Promotion de la santé: Besoin de recherche francophone et perspectives, n° 1: 22-25.
Weischer, Christoph. 2007. Sozialforschung. Weinheim: Beltz.
Welsch, Wolfgang. 2005. Auf dem Weg zu transkulturellen Gesellschaften. In Differenzen anders denken. Bausteine zu einer Kulturtheorie der Transdifferenz, ed. Lars Allolio-Näcke, Britta Kalscheuer and Arne Manzeschke, 314-341. Frankfurt/M.: Campus.
World Health Organisation Europe (WHO). 1999. Santé 21. La politique-cadre de la Santé pour tous dans la Région européenne de l'OMS. Série européenne de la Santé pour tous, n° 6.
World Health Organisation Europe (WHO). 2008. Inequalities in Young People's Health. Health Behaviour in School-Aged Children (HBSC). International Report from the 2005/2006 Survey. Health policy for children and adolescents, n° 5.

8. Identity Constructions in Luxembourg

RACHEL RECKINGER, CHRISTIAN SCHULZ, CHRISTIAN WILLE

The focus of this book was on constructions of identities in Luxembourg. This deliberately 'comprehensive' wording indicates that it was not national identity(ies) or cultural identity(ies) that we were primarily concerned with but rather processes of the subject-related and actor-related everyday *"Identitätsarbeit"*[1] (Keupp et al. 2006)[2] – something we have conceptualised with the term *Doing Identity*. Against this background, four particularly relevant subject areas were examined in more detail: the linguistic and everyday-cultural practices, which occur more on the negotiational level, on the one hand, as well as the space-related constructions and confrontations between images of self and others, which are to be found more at the representational level, on the other. These four subject areas, which respectively focus on languages, everyday cultures, spaces and images, were systematically linked to the cross-cutting theme of social structure analysis by milieus (Vester et al. 2001). It was our particular concern to document the dynamic and dialogical character of identity options and constitutions. With varying degrees of emphasis, the respective chapters consequently take politically and medially desired or projected *attributions* of identities (*top-down identifications of*) into account as well as *appropriations* of identities (*bottom-up identifications with*).

This conceptual approach from the perspective of *Doing Identity* always refers to the dimension of the development and changeability of identities. Taking linguistic identities as an example, it becomes abundantly clear that equating language usage and identities would produce a foreshortened view. In fact, the study we conducted on the practised linguistic consensus and the publicly negotiated positions on language provides insights into identity constructions which cannot be defined by a simple formula. They partly reflect divergent relationships between appropriated and attributed identities, different practices of multilingualism and a wide range

---

1 | Personal translation: "Identity work".
2 | See section 2.1.

of ideas concerning 'good' and 'bad' multilingualism. The authors finally arrive at the conclusion that an increased awareness and social acceptance of the various linguistic standards and multilingual constellations that were identified in the course of this study can make an essential contribution to social cohesion in Luxembourg. Furthermore, using linguistic and visual images, we explored the symbolic representations of identities. The areas of communication investigated for this purpose, functioned, in the context of selected media events, as vectors for 'imagined communities' and for various constructions of Luxembourg, which are based on a rich repository of collective symbols. Social change and plurality have produced both continuities and discontinuities in their constitutional mechanisms and functionalities, which express themselves medially. The relationship between attributed and appropriated identities, which can be described as multi-faceted, is determined in Luxembourg by this medially-based application. Furthermore, under the keyword 'geographies', the authors established various space-related constructions of Luxembourg and, at different scale levels, scrutinised the identity characteristics that revealed themselves in the process. First of all, we examined, as crystallisation points of spatial identities, the representations and semiotic strategies articulated in the tourist discourses. It appeared that the identity constructions within the spatial levels we examined are partially very heterogenic, yet that they always indicate – also from a diachronic perspective – a certain uniqueness, exceptionality and in particular a diversity, which mesh with the notion of a 'Luxembourg entity' in a contrasting and ambivalent manner. In view of the idealising character of the public tourist discourse on the one hand and the representations and social practices of Luxembourg's resident population on the other, the relationship between appropriated and attributed identities, as elucidated in this study, can only be described as divergent. Such divergences as well as ambivalences of identity constructions were also found in different areas of everyday culture. With respect to the relationship between appropriated and attributed identities in the context of different notions of 'good' food, we were able to establish an idealising typology (adaptation, opposition, autonomy). This reflects contradictory forms of 'everyday logic' as well as the living and experiencing of gender roles or the perception of cross-border workers, which each pragmatically break open the binary 'either-or logic' and only become accessible from a perspective of 'as well as'.

The research findings, whose main points we have highlighted above, clearly indicate the nature of identities: the identifications and identities empirically investigated in Luxembourg are as varied as they are complex. This means that concise and therefore homogenising, static and foreshortened equations – in particular concerning collective identity(ies) – can never be anything but normative and ideological. Therefore, we will forego generalising summaries and refer to the *constitutive ambivalences* of identity constructions discovered in the course of our survey. Appropriated and attributed identity patterns generally exhibit more or less distinctive discrepancies, which emanate from the interaction between these categories, respectively from their communicative relationship. Furthermore, the respective identification options or identification practices as such are alterable, plural and polysemic (and therefore potentially contradictory). In this respect, identities – as permanent but always temporary resultants of the aforementioned communicative processes – always comprise challenges and potential for change. On account of the socio-cultural milieu affiliations and the respective resources of the subjects, this can however 'only' mean a *"Veränderung in Grenzen"*[3] (Straub 2004: 284).

These dynamics can be *sympathetic* (e.g. in the case of tourism discourses or advertising), *critical* (e.g. in the case of gender constructions, food standards and eating habits, artistic or journalistic critique) or *conflictual* (e.g. in the case of the cross-border worker issue or multilingualism). The most significant potential for conflict can be found in those aspects of social life, which are metonymically abstracted and can be used for political-social purposes as collective symbols, capable of consensus because they unite polysemic, i.e. different, perspectives. For this reason, the issue of language became particularly topical. It seems to condense the social change in Luxembourg and the fears coupled to it, although Luxembourgish is currently spoken by more people than ever before. Therefore, in particular for those areas with a high potential for conflict, the following statement applies: *"Identität wird nur in ihrer Krise zum Problem"*[4] (Eickelpasch/Rademacher 2004: 5), since in these instances it is always more a matter of subjective perceptions, feelings of belonging, self-assessments, and less one of objective 'facts'. Still, the 'working out' of identities on the part of the subjects should be seen as a performance of continuity and on no account as something substantially adherent to their selves. This self-relationship is evident in synchronous as well as in diachronic ways of experiencing society and the world and is narratively processed, communicated and passed on. This process of *Doing Identity* aims at a *"flexible Kontinuität und Sinnhaftigkeit des Selbst"*[5] and serves less for the depiction or definition of objective 'facts' (Straub 2004: 284-286).

The results of the three-year long interdisciplinary research work[6] presented in this volume reflect the wide range of identity options in Luxembourg and also the pluralism and changeability of identification practices. Since categories that

---

3 | Personal translation: "Change within limits".
4 | Personal translation: "Only when in a crisis does identity become a problem".
5 | Personal translation: "Flexible continuity and meaningfulness of the self".
6 | The project benefited to a very high degree from the comprehensive sharing of information among researchers and scientists of different disciplines as well as from the interactively structured scientific culture within the IPSE research unit (*Identités, Politiques, Sociétés, Espaces*) at the Faculty of Language and Literature, Humanities, Arts and Education (FLSHASE) of the University of Luxembourg. A subsequent project, currently in preparation, will also be embedded in this context. It will deal with the transnational dimension of identity constructions.

are perceived as traditional and providing orientation are increasingly losing their meaning, issues of social cohesion in Luxembourg and beyond can no longer align themselves with a notion of societies as normatively integrated and homogeneous groups. Rather, it is a matter of opening up to and acknowledging social pluralism and internal differentiation.

From the perspective of a critical accompanying research of current social developments, questions of social cohesion must therefore aim at the make-up and dynamism of social interactions and on the meshing of different identity concepts in cultural practice. With the findings of the research project "IDENT – Socio-Cultural Identities and Identity Policies in Luxembourg" presented here, the authors hope to have contributed in some degree to injecting the current intensive political, social and medial debate around identity questions in Luxembourg and elsewhere with a heightened awareness for more differentiating considerations and less reductionist argumentation patterns that regard social diversity and multiple identity patterns as a 'standard scenario' rather than as a 'problem'.

Authors

Wilhelm Amann (PhD German studies) is a researcher at the University of Luxembourg. His research focuses on cultural globalisation/regionalisation and discourse analysis. Together with Georg Mein and Rolf Parr he is co-editor of *Gegenwartsliteratur und Globalisierung. Konstellationen – Konzepte – Perspektiven* (Synchron, 2010).

Christel Baltes-Löhr is the University of Luxembourg's Gender Representative and, as Associate Professor of Gender Studies, head of the Gender Studies Department. She is also coordinator of the "European Migration Network – National Contact Point – Luxembourg" at the University of Luxembourg. She represents Luxembourg at the European Commission as a gender expert in the EU Helsinki Group "Women and Science".

Viviane Bourg is a head lecturer in art and its didactics for the Bachelor Course of Studies in Educational Sciences at the University of Luxembourg. The main focus of her work is on art education at school and aesthetic-biographical research for teacher training.

Marion Colas-Blaise is Professor of French Linguistics and Semiotics at the University of Luxembourg. She is the author of numerous publications on literary and visual semiotics, stylistics and discourse analysis. As a co-editor, she has recently published *Le sens de la métamorphose* (Pulim, 2009).

Paul Dell is a lecturer and researcher for visual arts at the University of Luxembourg. The focus of his research activity within the Department of Visual Arts and IPSE is on contemporary art. In his research he also explores media and mediation techniques in the art field.

Fernand Fehlen is a lecturer at the University of Luxembourg, focusing on empiric social research. His main research interests and activities concern sociolinguistics, electoral research and social structural analysis. His most recent publication is a sociolinguistic study entitled *Luxemburgs Sprachenmarkt im Wandel* (Sesopi, 2009).

Paul di Felice (PhD Fine Arts) is a head lecturer of art history and art didactics at the University of Luxembourg where he is also head of the Department of Visual Arts. As an art critic (member of the AICA) he regularly publishes articles primarily on the development of contemporary photography on *lacritique.org*.

Sylvie Freyermuth is Professor for French Language and Literature at the University of Luxembourg. Her research projects and publications are at the interface between literature and linguistics. She is a specialist on the works of the French novelist Jean Rouaud.

Peter Gilles is Professor of Linguistics at the University of Luxembourg. His main areas of research are Luxembourgish phonetics/phonology, variation linguistics and sociolinguistics.

Sonja Kmec is Associate Professor of History and teaches history and cultural science at the University of Luxembourg. In the field of memory research, she has co-authored and edited, together with Michel Margue, Pit Péporté and Benoît Majerus, *Lieux de mémoire au Luxembourg* (Saint-Paul, 2007) and *Inventing Luxembourg* (Brill Publishers, 2010).

Fabienne Lentz is currently completing her dissertation at the University of Luxembourg, on the subject of "Italian immigration in Luxembourg: between private recollection and public representation". She is also involved in research on the history of European integration in the context of national identity questions.

Georg Mein is Professor of Modern German Literature at the University of Luxembourg. His research focuses on the literature of the 18th century to the present, media and cultural theories, sociology of literature, literality research.

Agnès Prüm is a lecturer in English Literature at the University of Luxembourg. Her research interests concern utopian and dystopian writing, gender and the interaction between narratives and identity constructions. Her publications on popular culture include articles on *CSI* and *Frankenstein* as motifs in Western cultures.

Rachel Reckinger (PhD Sociology) works as scientific project coordinator at the University of Luxembourg. She conducts research and publishes in the fields of identity constructions, food (food production, consumerism, experts' assessment and politics), ethics and morality, sustainability as well as governmentality.

Sebastian Reddeker is a PhD candidate at the University of Luxembourg. His research focuses is on the Luxembourg advertising discourse, identity and advertising, as well as normalism and inter-discourse theory.

Christian Schulz heads the IPSE research unit at the University of Luxembourg. The main focus of his work as Professor of Geography is in the field of international regional development and environmentally-oriented economic geography. He is a co-editor of the *Atlas du Luxembourg* (Emons Verlag, 2009).

Sebastian Seela is an assistant at the Department for Geman Studies at the University of Luxembourg. He teaches Middle High German and linguistics and is currently preparing his dissertation on the diaries of Victor Klemperer as an interface between linguistics and social sciences.

Heinz Sieburg is Associate Professor of German Linguistics and Medieval Studies. His research and publications include historical word formation in the Central Franconian-Luxembourgish region. His most recent publication is *Literatur des Mittelalters* (Akademie Verlag, 2010).

Gian Maria Tore (PhD Semiotics) conducts research in the fields of media semiotics, film semiotics and art semiotics at the University of Luxembourg. He also teaches at the university of Metz and regularly works together with the Cinémathèque de Luxembourg. He is co-editor of *L'expérience. En sciences de l'homme et de la société* (Pulim, 2006).

Melanie Wagner (PhD Socio-Linguistics) is a postdoctoral candidate at the Department of Luxembourgish Linguistics and Literatures at the University of Luxembourg. She conducts research primarily in the field of sociolinguistics and publishes on sociolinguistic topics such as language variation, standards consciousness, language attitudes and language ideologies.

Christian Wille is a scientific project coordinator at the University of Luxembourg. His research focuses on space constructions and identity constructions in European border regions and publishes in areas such as intercultural communication, international cooperation and labour mobility in the Greater Region SaarLorLux.